"Amid all the controversy about the benefits of single-sex versus coeducation for women (and men), this historically grounded and theoretically sophisticated study of four comparable institutions finally brings some illumination to the issues involved. Dr. Miller-Bernal combines extensive archival work, longitudinal surveys and wide-ranging interviews at Wells, William Smith, Hamilton and Middlebury colleges to bring to life the experiences of their students, faculty, and alumnae over time. She offers powerful proof of the benefits of chosen separatism for social groups, such as women, denied a full share of society's resources, and shows the lessons coeducation might draw from single-sex models. A masterful and exhaustive study that should be the new benchmark for all future discussions of this issue."

Frances A. Maher, Professor of Education, Wheaton College, and co-author, The Feminist Classroom

"Leslie Miller-Bernal has written a wonderful and valuable book on women's colleges. There are several unique strengths to this book: first, it focuses on four non-elite colleges, which responds to those critics who have argued that women's colleges are only successful because they are elite; second, it provides an unparalleled set of comparisons by including a women's college, a long-time coeducational college, a coordinate men's and women's college, and a former men's college that recently became coeducational; and third, it provides a remarkably detailed historical description of how each of these schools has changed over the past century. Miller-Bernal skillfully analyzes the stories of these schools and concludes with a practical set of suggestions for achieving greater gender equity in coeducational colleges."

Cornelius Riordan, Professor of Sociology, Providence College

Separate by Degree

History of Schools and Schooling

Alan R. Sadovnik and Susan F. Semel
General Editors

Vol. 9

PETER LANG

New York • Washington, D.C./Baltimore • Boston • Bern
Frankfurt am Main • Berlin • Brussels • Vienna • Oxford

Leslie Miller-Bernal

Separate by Degree

Women Students' Experiences in Single-Sex and Coeducational Colleges

PETER LANG
New York • Washington, D.C./Baltimore • Boston • Bern
Frankfurt am Main • Berlin • Brussels • Vienna • Oxford

40510503

Library of Congress Cataloging-in-Publication Data

Miller-Bernal, Leslie.
Separate by degree: women students' experiences in single-sex
and coeducational colleges / Leslie Miller-Bernal.
p. cm. — (History of schools and schooling; v. 9)
Includes bibliographical references and index.
1. Women college students—Northeastern States—Longitudinal studies.
2. Coeducation—United States—Longitudinal studies. 3. Small colleges—
Northeastern States—History—Case studies. I. Title. II. Series.
LC1601.M55   378.1'9822—dc21   98-54164
ISBN 0-8204-4412-X
ISSN 1089-0678

Die Deutsche Bibliothek-CIP-Einheitsaufnahme

Miller-Bernal, Leslie:
Separate by degree: women students' experiences in single-sex
and coeducational colleges / Leslie Miller-Bernal.
–New York; Washington, D.C./Baltimore; Boston; Bern;
Frankfurt am Main; Berlin; Brussels; Vienna; Oxford: Lang.
(History of schools and schooling; Vol. 9)
ISBN 0-8204-4412-X

Cover art from top: *photos one, three, and four:* courtesy of Wells College Archives, Louis
Jefferson Long Library, Wells College, Aurora, New York;
photo two: courtesy of Archives, Warren Smith Library, Hobart and
William Smith Colleges, Geneva, New York, 14456

Cover design by Lisa Dillon

The paper in this book meets the guidelines for permanence and durability
of the Committee on Production Guidelines for Book Longevity
of the Council of Library Resources.

Printed in the United States of America

To the memory of my mother

Mary Frances Reilly Dunkel

Table of Contents

PART ONE
The Historical Background of Women's Education
in Four Liberal Arts Colleges

PART TWO
The Single-Sex versus Coeducation Debate:
Experiences of Women Students at Wells, Middlebury,
William Smith, and Hamilton Colleges

Illustrations

Tables

Figures

Preface

Women's colleges have always lived under a banner of controversy. At their founding they were regarded in many circles as dangerous institutions, shaping women in ways thought to be unseemly. Recipients of curious speculation as well as harsh criticism, their very presence questioned an old world order. While their early history can be characterized as steeped in a fair amount of paternalism, the mere fact of their existence opened wide the path to higher education for women.

As they developed and became an important part of American higher education, stereotypes have often been used to describe them. Nunneries, places for wallflowers, schools for rich girls, hotbeds of feminism or radical lesbianism, institutions of loose women or man haters—all these epithets, in a self-contradictory way, fill the annals of discourse about women's colleges. These characterizations border on amusing, but they have also been damaging in their ability to obscure the educational value of women's colleges and to confuse, if not terrify, potential applicants.

In this book Leslie Miller-Bernal seeks to move beyond stereotypes by offering us a comparative study of four liberal arts colleges: Wells, a stand-alone women's college; William Smith, a coordinate women's college; Hamilton, which absorbed its women's college; and Middlebury, which added women to its male population to become coeducational. By examining the history of each, she helps us understand more clearly the issues and arguments affecting higher education for women. By offering a longitudinal survey of the women who enrolled in the class of 1988 at each institution, she provides us with significant insight into how these women viewed themselves and how the educational environments they chose affected them. This survey, which contrasts the perspectives and experiences of a sample of women at all four institutions, allows the author to conclude that women's colleges benefit women students in the support they give to them, the faculty role models they provide for women, and the opportunities they offer to develop leadership skills. While these conclusions are not new thoughts about the contributions of women's colleges to their students, the comparative methodology and substantive research which underlie them are very valuable additions to our understanding of women's colleges. Moving beyond women's institutions, the author offers a series of very welcome recommendations about how to make coeducational colleges and universities more supportive of their women students.

In some respects this book has an unhappy ending in the author's observation that she fears now more than when she began her study that women's colleges that do not have a close association with a coeducational college may disappear, except perhaps for well-known and wealthy institutions. Indeed, except for a small group of well-endowed institutions among them, the majority have had to struggle for existence, often existing in fragile financial conditions. During the last several decades, beginning in the 1970s when most of the formerly men's institutions were turning to coeducation, the circumstances of enrollment decline and fiscal difficulties prompted many of the women's colleges to focus on strategies for survival. These strategies have included programs for nontraditional women students, stronger marketing efforts, and generally more entrepreneurial activity. These efforts notwithstanding, some have not survived. A number of the colleges also moved from traditional liberal arts curricula to more vocational offerings. It is accurate to say that the majority of women's colleges have been deeply engaged in adapting to their challenges.

Like the author, I fear for the future of the less well-known women's colleges and even worry a bit about some of the better known. Having had the privilege of serving as president of Wells College, one of the "little sisters," I have seen firsthand what a supportive environment a women's college can provide for its students. And it is not only its students who are accorded this kind of support. Women on the faculty and in the administration benefit as well. My own points of comparison are my presidencies in both a women's college and a coeducational institution. Not having attended a women's institution, I entered the environment of Wells College with few preconceptions, but I quickly became a strong advocate for the benefits that Leslie Miller-Bernal describes in her study. I hope that women's colleges of all shapes, sizes, and endowments can continue to survive not simply for their own sake, but also for the sake of American higher education, which is better for their presence and for future generations of women students whose lives will be enriched in immeasurable ways by them.

Patti McGill Peterson
Executive Director
Council for International Exchange of Scholars
and Vice President
Institute of International Education

Acknowledgments

The social nature of scholarship is never more apparent than when one thinks about all the people who have contributed to a project. Not only would this book not have been possible without the help of the people I mention below—and others whom I may have unintentionally overlooked —but they have made working on it much more enjoyable than a solitary enterprise would have been.

Archivists and library staff have been wonderful in helping me to locate information and photographs, often going out of their way to accommodate my schedule. I would particularly like to thank Helen Bergamo at Wells College; Charlotte Hegyi at Hobart and William Smith Colleges; Robert Buckeye at Middlebury College; and Frank Lorenz and Waltraut Wuensch at Hamilton College. Other people in the libraries have also been generous with their assistance: Danielle Rougeau, Michael Knapp, Will LeBlanc, and Kay Lauster at Middlebury College; Jeri Vargo at Wells College; and Ilana Feitlovitz at Hamilton College.

My book would have been less complete without the assistance of people who shared information about the colleges in the past or present. Rudolph Haerle, my first sociology professor when I was a student at Middlebury College, gave me the results of survey research done by some of his classes. Linda LeFauve, a former student of mine at Wells College worked for a time as the Director of Institutional Research at Middlebury College and alerted me to recent reports on gender relations. I also want to thank the following people for their helpful input: Samuel Babbitt, former President of Kirkland College; Catherine Frazer, former Dean of Kirkland College; Robin Krasny, who wrote her Princeton undergraduate thesis on Kirkland College; Valerie Tomaselli, a Kirkland alumna, who shepherded me around a reunion and provided me with useful contacts then and later; Mary Duffy, administrator of May Belle Chellis Women's

Resource Center at Middlebury; Nancy Rabinowitz, Professor at Hamilton College, who has played a key role in developing the Kirkland Project; David Stameshkin, author of a two-volume history of Middlebury College; Michael Groth, a history professor at Wells College, who provided me with a useful reference; and Jane Dieckmann, neighbor, Wells alumna, and author of a recent history of Wells College.

I am grateful to key administrators at each college who gave me permission to carry out portions of this research, and when I requested, consented to be interviewed: Lisa Marsh Ryerson at Wells; Erica Wonnacott, Robert Schine, and Ann Hanson at Middlebury; Richard Hersh, Rebecca Fox, Debra DeMeis, and Clarence Butler at Hobart and William Smith; and Eugene Tobin, Bobby Fong, and Janis Coates at Hamilton.

For assistance in obtaining contacts and in carrying out surveys at the four colleges, I wish to thank Peter Marcy and Sue Pollard Jones at Wells College; Rudolph Haerle and Hugh Marlow at Middlebury College; Betsy Ahrnsbrak, Gordon Brown, Elizabeth Gura, and Laura Brophy at Hobart and William Smith Colleges; and Mary Detweiler, Nancy Thompson, John Mavrogenis, and Tom Brush at Hamilton College.

The students who helped me with data coding deserve a special note of thanks. Helen White did a wonderfully accurate job with the alumnae surveys in the same semester she was writing her senior thesis. Earlier, Ruth Boyer, Monya Freudenheim, Connie Manwell, Deirdre McDonald, Karen Mirsky, Deidre Pope, and Carol Sawicki helped me code data from the three waves of the longitudinal surveys of the class of 1988. In addition, Nancy Taylor, a former staff member at Wells College, interviewed juniors at Wells College.

This project could not have been completed without the willingness of members of the class of 1988 to answer my surveys. I hope they find their accomplishments and concerns adequately reflected in this book.

Wells College has provided me with extra time and some financial support for my research. Both have been critical to the completion of this project.

For advice and technical help with the photographs, I want to thank Erik Borg, David Barreda, Susan Ceballos, DeVillo Sloan, Janet Mapstone, and Clayton Adams, as well as the archivists and library staff at all four colleges.

I have benefited enormously from the encouragement and advice of colleagues and friends. Particularly important in this regard were Laura Kramer, Anne Russ, Laura Purdy, Kate Perry, Carol Naughton, Ann

Stanton, Bob Buckeye, Alan Sadovnik, Susan Semel, Arnold (Sandy) Shilepsky, Spencer Hildahl, Susan Sandman, Ellen Hall, Lisa Ryerson, Robert Plane, Cornelius Riordan, and David Riesman.

It is difficult to express the gratitude I feel for the diffuse, yet crucial, support of my family. Without their love and concern, writing this book would not have been worthwhile. My mother did not live to see me finish this book, but she did read earlier drafts of some of the chapters. Her positive response to them typified the confidence with which she has always inspired me. My sons, Adam and Patrick, provided needed balance in my life and occasionally asked probing questions. My step-children and their partners—Sophie, Mark, William, Vanessa, Paul, and Sarah—have tolerated my distracted state at family gatherings and provided me with happy distractions. Undoubtedly my biggest debt is to my husband, Martin Bernal, whose brilliance and renown do not prevent him from being interested in and supportive of my research, nor from shouldering an impressive amount of domestic work. He has shown, once again, that behind every reasonably successful woman there usually is a helpful partner.

PART ONE

THE HISTORICAL BACKGROUND OF WOMEN'S EDUCATION IN FOUR LIBERAL ARTS COLLEGES

Chapter 1

Introduction

Single-sex higher education in the United States is increasingly rare. Up until the mid-1960s, men's and women's colleges, while not common, were a prestigious option, particularly in the Northeast. The social movements of the later 1960s—civil rights, anti-war, student and women's movements—as well as demographic changes, led such previously all-male elite schools as Yale, Princeton, Amherst, and Williams to admit women. The number of women's colleges declined too, as some, including Vassar, Connecticut, and Skidmore, opened their doors to men and others shut down. Thus single-sex education came to be viewed as anachronistic, coeducation as progressive. Despite some recent publicity about the success of graduates of women's colleges, including Hillary Clinton, many people still assume that coeducation is superior. *Separate by Degree* challenges this notion.

My basic thesis is that single-sex education for women can promote gender equity.[1] Many people would probably accept this claim for the past when access to education was a key issue for women's rights, but not for today when women are admitted to virtually all colleges.[2] I argue that single-sex education still has advantages for women. Despite their statistical rarity (fewer than 80 out of over 2,000 institutions of higher education) and despite the fact that these institutions were not established for this purpose, they are one of the best educational means of addressing deep-rooted, relatively intractable aspects of sexism.

Many of the arguments in the United States in favor of women's colleges are made on pragmatic grounds: they produce better results. Research has found that women who have graduated from women's colleges are proportionately more likely than women who have graduated from coeducational colleges to receive advanced degrees, particularly in the sciences, and to become leaders in their fields. To understand why this is so, people have pointed to the research in coeducational institutions that indicates that women students are not taken as seriously nor given as much support, financially and otherwise, as men students. Women's colleges redress this gender inequity by being solely about and for women students. More specifically, women's colleges benefit their students in three major ways: by having a high proportion of women faculty who can serve as role models for students; by giving young women more opportunities to develop their leadership skills; and by providing a supportive atmosphere for women students in a "room of their own," where they do not have to defer to men in the way ordinarily demanded by our larger, male-dominated society.

By focusing on four similar private liberal arts colleges that vary in the manner in which they admitted and educated their women students, and by studying these same institutions over time, I will show that neither women's colleges nor coeducational colleges are the same today as they were one hundred or so years ago. In the past, coeducational colleges focused almost exclusively on their men students, marginalizing their women students by limiting their numbers or establishing a separate curriculum for them. Today formal separation in coeducational institutions has ended, but male dominance among students, faculty, administration, and trustees is still the norm. Women's colleges have likewise changed. In the nineteenth and early twentieth century, many women's colleges were modeled on the family, with men in control as trustees and presidents, and women in the lower positions of teachers and deans. Today women's colleges are a model of coeducation in the composition of their boards of trustees, administrations, and faculties; the only way they remain single-sex is in students' academic and co-curricular programs. I intend to do more than simply chronicle the changing meaning of single-sex and co-education, however. My real interest is in determining which institutional structure has best met women's needs for education, enabling them to develop their mental, physical, and social natures to the fullest extent possible.

The colleges that I compare—Wells, Middlebury, William Smith, and Hamilton—are neither the most elite nor the most famous colleges in the United States. Rather than this being seen as a drawback of my study, however, I would argue that it is an advantage. We already have some excellent studies of women in the famous "seven sisters colleges" (cf. Horowitz 1984, Palmieri 1995) and in such illustrious universities as Stanford and Chicago (Gordon 1990), Yale (Lever and Schwartz 1971), and Cornell (Conable 1977). It would be a mistake to treat elite institutions as representative; to understand women's experiences of higher education better, we need to look at a full array of institutions. This book contributes to our knowledge by focusing on women students in a particular type of institution: small, private liberal arts colleges in the northeastern United States. The multiple case study approach that I am using is ideal for elucidating dual themes of commonality and diversity, as Leslie (1977) has argued. While the four colleges I have studied are similar to each other in many respects, they differ dramatically in the ways in which they have handled the education of their women students.

Wells College, where I have been on the faculty for twenty-three years, is one of the oldest women's colleges in the country. It was founded in 1868, early in the "reform era" (Palmieri 1987), by Henry Wells, of Wells, Fargo fame, in an area in central New York State that remains isolated to this day. Wells opened as a seminary, an important transitional type of educational institution somewhere between a high school and a college. Although legally Wells became a college in 1870, it retained seminary-like characteristics much longer. Middlebury College, located in rural Vermont, was a men's college from when it was founded in 1800 until it admitted women students in 1883, toward the end of the reform era. I began my own college career at Middlebury in 1964 and so, like other students of the time, "knew" that it had been coeducational for a long time, but I did not know about the efforts that had been made to return Middlebury to an all-men's college or at least to contain women students in another, affiliated college. Less than fifty miles from Wells is William Smith College, founded in 1908 during a period of backlash against women's higher education (Palmieri 1987). William Smith is neither a pure women's college nor a coeducational institution, but rather a coordinate of Hobart, an older men's college. Hobart and William Smith have always shared faculty, curriculum, and most facilities, but women and men students have been admitted separately and have had their own government and athletic programs. The fourth college, Hamilton, also located in central New York State, was a men's college from its opening in 1812 until it established a coordinate college for women, Kirkland, in 1968, an expansionary period for higher education. Ten years after Kirkland opened, Hamilton took it over, becoming a regular coeducational college. Thus the four colleges in my study represent a women's college, a long-time coeducational college, a coordinate college, and a men's college that has recently become coeducational.

To understand how women students have negotiated these different educational environments, I have used a variety of methods. From extensive work in each college's archives, I have learned not only about the reasons these institutions opened up to women students, but also about the nature of the colleges women encountered—the curriculum the women students studied, the activities they organized, the faculty they studied under—and sometimes, their reactions to their experiences and their attempts to modify them, when recorded in letters to family members or in articles written for student newspapers. In 1984 I began a longitudinal study of women students, class of 1988, in the four colleges. Using questionnaires, I surveyed the same 260 women three times during their college years on their family backgrounds; educational and career goals; attitudes toward women's and men's roles, the women's movement, and feminism; and their college experiences (relations with faculty, college activities, and how supportive they found their colleges). During students' junior year, I interviewed a small sample of the women at each college who had answered the questionnaires to get a more in-depth understanding of their concerns and how they viewed college life. The final phase of this longitudinal study occurred in the autumn of 1994, when some of the women who had been studied as undergraduates were surveyed as alumnae to determine what had happened to them after college, whether they had achieved what they had hoped when they were freshwomen, and whether their attitudes toward a variety of issues, but particularly feminism, had changed since they left college.

   Separate by Degree is divided into two parts. Part One gives a brief history of each college, focusing on the circumstances under which it admitted women and relating these events to the larger context of the educational opportunities for women at that period of time. The colleges are presented chronologically in terms of when they admitted women students, with comparisons among the colleges discussed at the end of each chapter. Chapter 2 describes the founding of Wells College; since it was the first of these four colleges to admit women, for comparative purposes I use information about Vassar College, the most famous women's college, which had opened just three years earlier than Wells. In Chapter 3, I discuss the entrance of women students into Middlebury College and compare their situation to that of Wells students at the end of the nineteenth century. Chapter 4 adds information about the coordinate college, William Smith, and presents comparisons among all three colleges (Wells, Middlebury, and William Smith) in the pre-World War I era. In Chapter 5, I discuss major changes in the education of women students at Wells, Middlebury, and William Smith, from the period around World War I to the 1960s. This period was critical for establishing the current direction of these colleges, and also a time of many tensions; for example, Middlebury vacillated between accepting women as permanent members of a coeducational institution and separating them out to enable the college to have the prestige of an all-men's college. The last chapter in Part One deals with the tumultuous late 1960s and 1970s, when colleges across the country had to come to terms with student activism. Kirkland, a progressive women's college established as a coordinate of a men's college (Hamilton), serves as an archetype for an educational institution of that time period. With its students, president, and faculty chosen for their unconventionality, and with no traditions of their own to constrain them, this new college embodied some of the major concerns of the day, particularly students' rights and women's liberation. The end of Chapter 6 describes all four colleges from the 1960s to the mid-1980s as they admitted more diverse student populations and institutionalized new governance structures.

Part Two of *Separate by Degree* relates the contemporary debate over the merits of single-sex education for women to the experiences of women at these four colleges since 1984. Chapter 7 summarizes the arguments for and against single-sex education, historically as well as today. In Chapter 8, I introduce my own longitudinal survey of women students, class of 1988, at Wells, Middlebury, William Smith, and Hamilton Colleges. The students who entered these colleges in 1984 are compared in terms of their family and educational backgrounds, their career and educational goals, and their attitudes toward gender roles, the women's movement, and feminism. Chapter 9 briefly describes major developments at each college during the time the class of 1988 was in attendance and then discusses differences in the students' college experiences—their relations with faculty, their participation in college activities, and how supportive they found their college—according to whether they attended a single-sex institution (Wells, or less completely, William Smith) or a coeducational college (Middlebury or Hamilton). I focus particularly on the question of whether the experiences these women students had at college related to changes in their attitudes and aspirations. In Chapter 10, I describe what these same women were doing six years after they left college, how they then evaluated their college experiences, and the degree to which their attitudes remained the same or changed from when they were in college. This chapter also discusses developments at the colleges in the 1990s in order to assess the degree to which they have changed in the direction of greater gender equity. In the concluding chapter I speculate about the future of single-sex education as we enter the twenty-first century. Is it destined to disappear given its unpopularity and consequent survival problems for colleges like Wells? If so, can coeducational institutions preserve the benefits of separatism for women, as some formerly women's colleges such as Wheaton are trying to do? To answer such questions I will summarize some of the major advantages of single-sex education for women and analyze the degree to which it would be possible to establish programs in mixed-sex institutions to obtain these benefits.

I approach my work as a person committed to reducing social inequalities based on such factors as gender, race, social class, and sexual preference. The irony of my studying relatively elite, private liberal arts colleges, established as Protestant institutions that did not welcome Catholics, never mind Jews or African-Americans, for most of their histories, does not escape me. I have tried throughout my work to be sensitive to the issue of the reproduction of privilege and to be aware of which groups of women were being included, which excluded, at various historical periods.

Some people have charged that the single-sex versus coeducation debate is a "liberal feminist" issue that seeks to change women to make them fit better into a (white, middle-class) men's world. I do not entirely accept this claim, however, since I hope to show that single-sex environments, at least under certain conditions, have a greater potential to challenge male hegemony than do mixed-sex environments. My goal in *Separate by Degree* is to provoke readers to think differently about the meaning and possible uses of single-sex groups in the struggle for a more just world.

Notes

1   By gender equity I mean equality between women and men in all spheres of life, including educational, occupational, domestic, and social arenas. It is the antithesis of sexism, in which men—their activities and concerns—are taken to be the norm and thereby more important than women and their activities.

2   There are still about ten private, all-men's colleges, with Wabash, Morehouse, Hampden-Sydney, and two-year Deep Springs probably being the best known.

Chapter 2

"Consecrated" to the "Ideal of True Womanhood": Wells College's Beginnings

When Wells Seminary opened in 1868, few young people of either sex were enrolled in institutions of higher education in the United States. Estimates are that in 1870 only about 2 percent of the college-aged population received education beyond the secondary level (Sicherman 1988). Virtually all the prestigious colleges and universities that today are coeducational, were then for men exclusively; for example, in the Northeast, Harvard, Yale, Princeton, Columbia, Williams, Dartmouth, and Amherst Colleges admitted only men. Women's educational options were much more limited than men's. Those women who wanted advanced education usually studied in seminaries.

Over the course of the nineteenth century, seminaries for women gradually replaced academies for women. Today the term seminary is associated with religious education, but in the nineteenth century the word mainly implied serious education in an institution with many regulations[1] (Horowitz 1984). Seminaries were probably not much more religious than other educational institutions, which were almost all Christian, even if not denominationally specific. The best seminaries, such as Wheaton Female Seminary, Troy Female Seminary, Hartford Female Seminary, and Mount Holyoke Seminary, offered a mixture of high school and collegiate work. A careful study of the curriculum of Wheaton, for example, shows that its first two years were approximately equivalent to that of the best high schools, and its last two or two and one-half years, equivalent to Vassar College's first two years (Helmreich 1985, 42–43).

Colleges came to be considered more prestigious than seminaries, so some institutions for women, particularly those founded before the Civil

War, called themselves colleges even though their curriculum did not warrant it. Historians today debate which was the first women's college. Mary Sharp College in Winchester, Tennessee, which issued its first diplomas in 1855, is one candidate for this honor as its four-year curriculum included Greek and higher mathematics (Woody 1929 II, 171; Solomon 1985, 24). Elmira Female College in Elmira, New York, which opened in 1855, had admissions requirements similar to Amherst's and also required the study of Latin and some Greek (Woody 1929 II, 178). But the opening of Vassar College after the Civil War in 1865, just three years before Wells Seminary admitted its first students, was undoubtedly the major landmark for women's colleges. Vassar was the first four-year collegiate institution for women with high standards and a large endowment (Horowitz 1984).

Although coeducation was uncommon for institutions of higher education in the mid-nineteenth century, it had existed since 1837, when several women entered the collegiate course at Oberlin College. By the time Wells Seminary opened, there were a few more coeducational colleges, notably Antioch, Swarthmore, and several religiously inspired small colleges, located mostly in the Midwest (Rury and Harper 1986; Solomon 1985, 50). Cornell University, the first prestigious coeducational university in the East, opened in 1868, the same year that Wells did, but no women attended until several years later. Women who were enrolled in these coeducational institutions did not necessarily study the same curriculum as the men students, however, but rather often had a separate program deemed more suitable to women's abilities and proclivities.

Why Not Educate Women?

One reason there were so few options for the higher education of women is that education was believed to be inappropriate or even harmful for them. Arguments against women's higher education stemmed from a belief in separate spheres for women and men. The ideal (white, middle-class) woman was expected to conform to four precepts of True Womanhood: domesticity, piety, purity, and submissiveness. Woman's true place was held to be by her fireside, from where she could perform her great task: bringing men back to God. She was expected to dispense "comfort and cheer," promote others' happiness, and be a "spring of joy" (Welter 1973, 234).[2] Religiously based education for women in separate institutions that were mindful of woman's sphere was acceptable, but education for self-fulfillment or for training for professional work other than teaching was not.

Many people in the nineteenth century doubted women could do the same intellectual work as men. These arguments extended to the physical realm, too, as women were considered physically weaker than men and liable to put their reproductive organs at risk by too much mental strain. Dire consequences were predicted for women who stepped beyond their sphere by studying inappropriate subjects for too many hours. Five years after Wells Seminary opened, retired Harvard professor and doctor Edward H. Clarke wrote an influential book, *Sex in Education; or a Fair Chance for the Girls*, that promoted these arguments forcefully. Clarke claimed he was using physiology to find an "appropriate method of education for girls," since the current system was the cause of the "rapidly fading beauty" of American women, as well as their "pallor and weakness." Without changes in education that recognized the needs of women's reproductive systems, Clarke warned, we will become a "feeble race."

Clarke argued that women needed to rest every fourth week; if they did not obey this "law of periodicity," they were likely to experience such pathological conditions as amenorrhea, dysmenorrhea, hysteria, anemia, chorea—even insanity.[3] A large section of *Sex in Education* described seven women, some of whom were students or graduates of colleges. A Vassar College student who fainted in gym (at a time in the month when she should have been "comparatively quiet") was found to have an "arrest of the development of the reproductive apparatus . . . in examining her breast . . . [he observed that] the milliner had supplied the organs Nature should have grown." Associated with such arrested development, Clarke noted, are "character" changes—less fat, more muscular tissue, coarser skin, decline in "maternal instincts"—all of which he compared to a "sexless class of termites or eunuchs of Oriental civilization" (Clarke 1873, 92–93).[4]

Clarke's book is important for several reasons. Not only does it spell out in dramatic form some of the objections to women's higher education common in the mid-nineteenth century, but it also shows the new cultural legitimacy of biological arguments as applied to social issues (Zschoche 1989). Clarke's book resonated with and enhanced many people's fears about educating women, evident from how often it was reprinted (seventeen times within a few years). Even a stalwart feminist like M. Carey Thomas, who became the second president of Bryn Mawr, admitted many years later that she and other college-aged women in the 1870s had been "haunted" by the "clanging chains of that gloomy little specter, Dr. Edward

H. Clarke's *Sex in Education*" (Thomas 1908: 69). But Clarke's book also had a positive effect in that it galvanized proponents of women's higher education, leading them to demonstrate that women could be both educated and healthy.

In 1874, one year after Dr. Clarke's book was published, famous educators including Mary Peabody Mann, John Bascom, Thomas Wentworth Higginson, Julia Ward Howe, and Elizabeth Phelps, responded with *Sex and Education, a Reply to Dr. E. H. Clarke's "Sex in Education."* This book included statements by people who had attended or presided over coeducational institutions, testifying that women in colleges were seldom ill and, in fact, were generally stronger than women who had not pursued higher education and therefore lacked aims and discipline (Woody 1929 II: 129). A woman doctor, Mary Putnam Jacobi, won Harvard's prestigious Boylston Prize in 1876 for her study that set out to test Dr. Clarke's ideas systematically. In *The Question of Rest for Women During Menstruation* (1878), Dr. Jacobi used questionnaire as well as experimental data to prove that women did not need to rest during their menstrual periods. Jacobi's study did not do as much to alter public perceptions about the dangers of higher education for women as a later study did, however (Zschoche 1989). The Association of Collegiate Alumnae (ACA) surveyed its members in 1885 and found that nearly 80 percent of the 705 women graduates who returned the questionnaires reported themselves in good health (Rosenberg 1982, 20).

Despite many currents of opinion against higher education for women, several ideas common in the nineteenth century favored their obtaining at least some education. In order to raise informed and disciplined sons who could lead the Republic, it was commonly argued, women could not themselves be too ignorant. The stability of the nation was held to depend on virtuous citizens who in turn needed mothers who were "well informed, 'properly methodical,' and free of 'invidious and rancorous passions'" (Kerber 1976, 202). This idea of Republican Motherhood developed in the Romantic period, from about 1820 to 1860, when true women were expected to be passive, domestic, and virtuous but also had a republican responsibility to educate their sons (Palmieri 1987). Solomon (1985, 39) and Ryan (1981) argue that religious changes were necessary before the Republican Motherhood concept could be accepted. In particular, there had to be movement away from the idea of original sin and "infants' total depravity" (to use the title of a sermon published in 1815) in order for mother's influence to be seen as critical for children's development.

Clearly there was a spectrum of beliefs about the desirability of educating women, apparent even before the Civil War in the domestic literature written by women (Solomon 1985, 36). At one extreme were the dire warnings of people like Dr. Clarke about what higher education did to women's femininity. At the other end of the spectrum were people who were concerned that women were not able to receive sufficient education. The "Declaration of Sentiments," for instance, proclaimed at the first women's rights convention held at Seneca Falls, New York, in 1848, decried women's inability to obtain a "thorough education" and the lack of women teachers in "theology, medicine, or law" (Schneir 1972).

But the ideological realm may not be the most appropriate one for explaining why women's higher education became increasingly acceptable over the course of the nineteenth century. Social and political events revealed women's capabilities and created the need for more educated women. During the Civil War women performed many jobs formerly done mostly by men, including agricultural work and teaching, and demonstrated their ability to work under arduous conditions; for example, on battlefields where they served as nurses (Woody 1929 I, 8, 74; Solomon 1985, 45). After the war many people believed that there was a shortage of men, in the Northeast especially, and so not all women could count on getting married but rather, needed to be able to support themselves (Palmieri 1987).[5] At the same time public schools were increasing at a rapid rate, which had two effects: it meant that more girls could afford education to prepare them for college studies (Antler 1982), and that women were needed to fill the great demand for teachers. Over the course of the century the field of teaching became "feminized"; by 1870, 59 percent of teachers were women (Sicherman 1988, 147). Teaching was an occupation deemed suitable for women since it could be viewed as a natural extension of their maternal role. There was, as well, a practical reason for hiring women as teachers—they saved schools money as women were paid considerably less than men (Sicherman 1988).

The Founding of Wells Seminary

And so when Henry Wells began planning a collegiate institution for women in the rural village of Aurora, New York, he was doing something a bit controversial but not revolutionary. After all, Vassar College had already opened in 1865 and received much publicity for its claim of offering to women the same education that men were given at Yale and Harvard. Like Matthew Vassar, the founder of Vassar, Henry Wells was not a well-educated man, and he had little previous involvement with educational institutions. What both men had, however, were strong religious convictions and wealth from their business careers. Founding women's colleges was the way Matthew Vassar and Henry Wells made their secular activities meaningful.[6] Both men fit Jencks and Riesman's (1968, 3) description of college founders as men who were seeking "outlets for a variety of talents and dreams that could not be accommodated within either small business or the normal activities of the churches . . . men with unrealistic ideas about the demand for their services."

The son of a Presbyterian minister, Henry Wells (1805–1878) spent his early life first in Vermont and then in several towns in upstate New York. Unlike two of his brothers, Henry Wells did not himself go into the ministry, perhaps because he had a stammer. After intermittent education in local schools, Wells entered the commercial and business world, ultimately making his fortune in the express and telegraph industries. Besides his own rudimentary schooling, Wells's only other direct connection to the educational field were the schools he established for the treatment of speech defects (he himself had received treatment in a Rochester, New York, program). But Wells had many acquaintances in the business world, some of whom were involved with higher education. Ezra Cornell, the founder of Cornell University, located only about twenty-five miles from Wells College, became a close friend of Wells's through their work together on establishing a telegraph line in Canada. Henry Wells also met Samuel Morse through this same line of business; Morse was a charter member of the Board of Trustees at Vassar College (Vassar College Catalogues, VCA). Henry Wells's closest friend and business associate was Edwin Barber Morgan (1806–1881), who became the first president of the most famous express company that Wells and another business associate founded: Wells, Fargo and Company. Although E. B. Morgan's philanthropy had not previously been focused on higher education, he adopted Henry Wells's cause as his own and gave about one-third of a million dollars and a great deal of his time to the collegiate institution for women that Wells founded.[7]

It is not clear what led Henry Wells to give about seventeen acres and $200,000 to found an educational institution for women. Wells himself claimed that he had been motivated to build a college when he visited Philadelphia in the 1830s and saw Girard College being constructed.[8] In words quoted in every Wells College Catalogue of the first half of the twentieth century, Wells said to himself, "Standing thus alone, I thought I would rather be Girard, as he was thus represented, than the President of the United States . . . . It was there and then that I resolved that if ever I had the ability I would go and do likewise" (1900 to 1956 Catalogues, WCA). Presumably Wells was impressed by the size and beauty of Girard

College, and the generosity of the man who made it possible. Stephen Girard, an immigrant from France, became so rich as a merchant and financier that he was able to play a significant role in averting a major financial crisis in the United States during the War of 1812 by buying up the U.S. Bank. In fact, in the beginning of the nineteenth century he was the "wealthiest merchant in Philadelphia and, with the possible exception of his friend John Jacob Astor, in the entire nation" (Adams 1978, 6). Upon his death Girard bequeathed to the city of Philadelphia most of his property, worth a phenomenal six million dollars, to build a "college" for white male orphans (Arey 1877).[9]

One factor that undoubtedly influenced Henry Wells to found an educational institution was his friendship with Ezra Cornell, who was simultaneously involved in planning the university that bears his name. In trying to account for why Wells chose to found a seminary *for women*, other writers have pointed to his "reverence" for women (Temple Rice Hollcroft, "A History of Wells College," n.d., WCA), and the time period, which was favorable since colleges for women occupied "much of the best thought of the day," as an 1894 college catalogue sketch of Henry Wells put it (1894 Catalogue, WCA). A relative of Henry Wells by marriage, Louise Welles Murray, who attended Wells College from 1870 to 1872, wrote in later life that she had been told by Wells's daughter, Mary, that it was she who suggested "an institution for *girls* rather than *boys*." Interestingly, this same relative said that she had "had it from her [Mary's] lips" that Henry Wells mentioned this idea to Matthew Vassar, which "crystallized the thought in Vassar's brain that found expression in Vassar College" (Alumnae Bulletin 1918, WCA). The more usual version of Matthew Vassar's inspiration for the women's college he founded is actually somewhat similar to the story of Wells. Vassar, a brewer by business, visited Guy Hospital in London, which had been given by a distant cousin, and he wished to build a similar grand and useful building in the small city in which he lived, Poughkeepsie, New York. He was dissuaded by Milo Jewett, however, who made the pragmatic argument that hospitals need large cities. Jewett, an educated man who had been involved with educational institutions for women, including one in Poughkeepsie, suggested a women's college as a worthy use of Vassar's wealth (Elizabeth Daniels, "Matthew Vassar—More Than a Brewer," 1992, VCA).

When Henry Wells spoke and wrote about his goals for the women's collegiate institution he was founding, he revealed both conventional views of women, their abilities and proper social roles, as well as more progressive attitudes. In a major speech in 1868 that Wells wrote for the inauguration of the college, he stressed the inherent similarity of boys and girls, whose "minds" had "little distinction" until they were separated at the end of Common School instruction. Yet his arguments for giving women better "mental training" rather than conventional training that aimed at cultivating their "ornamental talents," rested at least partly upon the influence women might then have on "elevating the tone of social intercourse" and "refining" the "nature of man," rather than on what such education might do for the women themselves. Wells ended this speech with these stirring words:

> It is commonly said that it is not the province of woman to extend her researches to those finer and more beautiful lines of science; that woman's mind is not capable of attaining to a high order of discipline. Not acknowledging this, let me say, Give her the opportunity. (Hollcroft, n.d., 34–35, WCA)[10]

In private correspondence to Ezra Cornell in 1866, Henry Wells sounded more conservative about his aims for the educational institution he was planning. He clearly endorsed the Republican Motherhood goal when he wrote that he wanted his institution to have a "higher standard" so that it would prepare "young ladies to be Wives and Mothers to educate the rising generation . . . and direct the destinies of a great nation" (Hollcroft, n.d., 17, WCA). Moreover, he expressed his hope that by educating women, they would be able to fulfill their "mission without going to the polls or entering the arena of politics." As the second president of Wells College, S. Irenaeus Prime[11] wrote in the *Christian Observer* in 1870, Henry Wells "had no respect for the modern nonsense of women's rights," even though he had "the best and broadest ideas of the education that every mind requires" (quoted in Dieckmann 1995, 32).[12]

Again and again Wells emphasized that the collegiate institution he was founding should be Christian and should function as a "Home" for its women students. As Wells said in his 1866 address at the ceremony marking the laying of the cornerstone of the seminary, the college was not to be conducted as an "ordinary boarding-school" nor a "manual-labor school, where young ladies may obtain a knowledge of domestic duties . . . [n]or a 'fashionable' collegiate institute, in which dress and deportment claim chief, if not exclusive attention." Instead, Wells wrote, it was his "fervent wish" that the college "always be conducted on truly Christian principles." He noted that he appreciated "the value of secular education, but [was] not forgetful of its dangers when divorced from religious training." His ideal, he went on, was of a

"Home," in which, surrounded with appliances and advantages beyond the reach of separate families, however wealthy, young ladies may assemble to receive that education which shall qualify them to fulfill their duties as women, daughters, wives, or mothers, and to practice that pleasant demeanor . . . which so befit those whom our mother tongue characterizes as "the gentle sex." (Wells history file, A6, WCA)

Overcoming Objections to a Women's College: Wells as a Religious, Healthy Home

Henry Wells's concerns that the seminary he was founding should function as a home and that it should be Christian were evident in the institution's early years. In order to be like a home, Wells was planned as one large building, and it was kept very small (Wells opened with 36 students, compared to 353 at Vassar in its first year). Also, students and women faculty lived together in one building where all the instruction occurred, and students' lives were circumscribed by the kinds of rules believed to be appropriate for young ladies, including periods of silence, daily exercise and chapel attendance, and regulation of visitors. Henry Wells's English valet rang the bells that indicated the hours in which students were to do such things as rise, eat dinner, or turn off their lights at night. A member of the class of 1884, Anna Goldsmith, recalled that the rules at Wells were even stricter than the rules that governed the preparatory school she later ran in Aurora (Alumnae Bulletin 1918, WCA). Such living arrangements and rules were typical of boarding schools and seminaries of the time, but some people, especially young women, did not consider them appropriate for colleges. The first student to arrive at Wells in 1868, Lizzie Fish, wrote much later (in 1940), "It didn't seem like a College this first year but just like a girls school" (Wells history file, A7, WCA).

Wells was like virtually all other seminaries and colleges of the time in being Christian. It was less sectarian than some but definitely allied with the Presbyterian Church, not surprisingly as Henry Wells was the son and brother of Presbyterian ministers and an active member of the local church. Wells seems to have struggled with the issue of how closely his school should be connected with Presbyterianism. At the first meeting of the Board of Trustees in 1868, a Declaration about the Founder's Wishes for the Management of Wells Seminary was passed unanimously. This Declaration described Christianity as the "ultimate and definitive religion for all mankind," so that "all who . . . control or impart or receive instruction" should be Christian. Henry Wells asked that his preference for Presbyterian Church doctrines and rules of order and practice influence the choice of all succeeding Trustees and for there to be regular visitations from the Presbytery of Cayuga (the county in which Aurora is located) (Wells history file, folder A, WCA). There is a record of one such visitation, in 1872, in which the committee of the Presbytery concluded that Wells was successfully combining "refining culture" with depth and breadth of scholarship and "high moral and spiritual tone" (Wells history file, A18, WCA).

A direct tie between Presbyterianism and Wells College in the early years was avoided due to an outside body, the New York State Board of Regents. In 1873 E. B. Morgan—Henry Wells's friend, generous benefactor to the college, and college trustee—attempted to give $100,000 to the college in a fund named after his son, who died while studying to be a Presbyterian minister. The condition for this gift, however, was that the president of the college always be a member of the Presbyterian Church. The trustees unanimously acquiesced to this condition, but the Regents did not.[13] Nonetheless, up until 1946 all the presidents were religious men (either clergymen or laymen who had studied theology), and almost all were Presbyterian.

To the public, Wells College proclaimed itself a Christian institution that was "in no sense sectarian" (1879 Catalogue, WCA). The 1879 Catalogue, which contained more information than earlier catalogues about the college's "religious culture," said that students were expected to attend daily prayers (conducted by students), and additionally, on Sundays, a "Praise Meeting," the Bible classes given by teachers, and services at "either" of the churches in the village (earlier catalogues assumed the Presbyterian Church, but this Catalogue accepted that some students might want to attend the recently built local Episcopalian Church).[14] There were also some curricular connections to Christianity. The 1871 Catalogue said that natural science was taught to demonstrate the "exhaustive revelations of Divine wisdom and goodness" as well as to prepare students for more extended study. And similar to students at many other colleges of the time, seniors at Wells took a course in "Evidences of Christianity."[15]

The choice of location for the early colleges for women was a serious matter due to concerns about women's health (Woody 1929 I, 405). Milo Jewett, for example, in his work on plans for Vassar College, wrote a paper for Matthew Vassar, "Hints in Regard to the Proper Location of a College for Young Ladies" (1859). Jewett argued that a women's college should not be located in a large city but rather in a beautiful place, somewhat removed from "the eager gaze of the public eye," and where there was pure water, a system of "sewerage," and sufficient space for students' physical education and for the college to grow its own vegetable products (Jewett 1859, VCA). The village of Aurora, where Henry Wells and his colleague, friend and co-benefactor, E. B. Morgan, were living, met most if not all of Jewett's criteria for the location of a women's college. Aurora was (and still is) a small village in a rural area, located on the eastern shore of Cayuga Lake, one of the largest "finger lakes" in central New York State. In a letter Ezra Cornell wrote to Henry Wells in 1866, Cornell praised Wells for choosing "a beautiful and healthy location" for an institution "for the education of our females" (Dieckmann 1995, 3). Even as late as 1905, Mary Caroline Crawford, in her description of various women's colleges, noted that Wells students "spend a good deal of time on the water" as the location has "favorable health conditions" (Crawford 1905, 187).

Wells College officials were concerned to persuade the public that their students obtained proper exercise and diet and did not study so hard that they would jeopardize their strength. Early college catalogues had sections entitled "Health and Physical Culture," in which students' health was said to be "regarded as of the first importance." Students were required to exercise in the open air each day, their diets were monitored (milk was always in plentiful supply), and they were obliged to report to the Health Officer any "premonitory symptoms of illness" (1871 Catalogue, WCA). After describing the most rigorous academic program Wells students could study, the Collegiate course, the 1871 Catalogue added the following note of reassurance: "The fatal but too frequent error of requiring or allowing more studies to be pursued than can be properly attended to without injury, is studiously avoided."

A Seminary, a College, or a University?

A major issue for all women's colleges in the nineteenth century was whether their students should study the same curriculum as male college students. Even if a women's college offered the classical curriculum, there was the problem of whether there were enough young women whose academic preparation was adequate to undertake such studies. Vassar College, for instance, had to modify its original aims and offer a preparatory program for those students who needed more work before they could take the collegiate course (Horowitz 1984, 40–41).

In the case of Wells, the founder seemed unclear about whether he was establishing a full-scale collegiate institution. Before Wells opened, Henry Wells referred to it variously as an institute or college (in fact, in his earliest recorded mention of it, he called it Glen Park Institute, after the name of the house he lived in) ("Truly Yours," Letters of Henry Wells to E.B. Morgan, 1859–1867/1944–45, CUA). The charter from the state of New York described the "object" of Wells Seminary as being "to promote the education of young women in Literature, Science and the Arts" and enabled it to "grant and confer such honors, degrees and diplomas as are granted by any University, College or Seminary in the United States" (1871 Catalogue, WCA). The change in name from Wells Seminary to Wells College, which required petitioning New York State, occurred during the institution's second year. Students greeted this change with "jubilation," according to the reminiscences of Margaret Turner Sexton, who was a student at the time; the day was declared a holiday and students serenaded the founder (Alumnae Bulletin 1918, WCA).

A name change is one thing; changing an institution is another. Wells College was, and was perceived to be, a seminary more than a college even after its name was officially changed in 1870. To be equivalent to a college, the qualifications of its faculty, the academic preparation of its students, and the curriculum offered all needed to be upgraded. These changes gradually did occur—partly in response to the increasing legitimacy of women's higher education over the course of the nineteenth century; partly as a result of the direct pressure of the college's constituencies, including presidents, students, and alumnae; and partly due to the standards of an outside body, the Association of Collegiate Alumnae (ACA).

The first full-time faculty of Wells Seminary were eight women, none of whom had academic degrees, not even a bachelor's degree.[16] Almost immediately, however, these faculty were supplemented by a few men "professors," many of whom came from nearby Cornell University. Early college catalogues made it clear that the academic qualifications of the faculty were not the only characteristics of instructors considered important, when they noted the following: "The utmost possible care has been taken to secure the services of teachers not only of superior attainments . . . but of a personal character and manners adapted to wield a happy influence over the students" (1871 Catalogue, WCA). The first president who had academic as well as religious training was Edward Frisbee, D. D., who assumed the office in 1875. Under Frisbee the college began to upgrade its faculty as well as its curriculum. By 1879 there were thirteen faculty members, including the president (who had some teaching responsibilities, as was common at the time); five of these faculty had academic degrees, the highest of which was a master's degree (1879 Catalogue, WCA).

From the beginning Wells made provisions for students unable to enter the collegiate course, the majority of the students before 1880 (Kerr D. Macmillan, Wells College Bulletin 1926, WCA). Students in what later became the preparatory department studied what was essentially a high school program, including arithmetic, English grammar, geography, general history, and elementary French and Latin. Students in the Collegiate course had two options: the Regular course, which included Latin and French, or the English and Scientific course, which did not require Latin. Men's colleges of the time were questioning the value of studying Classics, Latin and Greek, and sometimes had a similar division of their programs of study. What was more telling at Wells was the absence of Greek, but by 1876 students in the classical course at least had the option of studying Greek as a replacement for Latin (Wells College Catalogues, WCA).

The curriculum at Wells also changed from being self-consciously tailored to fit what were believed to be women's aptitudes and needs, to being standard for the time for students of either sex. For example, the 1871 Catalogue said that the college's prescribed course in mathematics was "as extensive as is desirable for young ladies." The system used for teaching ancient languages was described as one that would "obviate many of the current objections to the study of the ancient languages particularly by young ladies" (1871 Catalogue, WCA). Such comments about the curriculum no longer appeared after the mid-1870s, and the program students followed, course by course, became clearly specified.

Given the preponderance of students in the preparatory department in the early years, and the nature of Wells's curriculum, it is not so surprising that in 1872, Henry Wells and E. B. Morgan, then vice-president of the Board of Trustees, approached the head of a school in Union Springs, a small village about ten miles north of Aurora, to see if he might be interested in a "union" between his school and Wells College. Howland School was a Quaker academy for girls that offered a collegiate course in classics, languages, and mathematics (E .B. Morgan diaries 1872, WCA). Its most famous pupil was undoubtedly M. Carey Thomas, who later became the second president of Bryn Mawr College and a well-known feminist (Horowitz 1994, 40). The head of Howland School declined Wells and Morgan's offer of a union, however, so Thomas never became associated with Wells College, despite having been a student at Howland School from 1872 to 1874.[17]

Just a year after Henry Wells and E. B. Morgan approached Robert Howland about merging Wells College with his school, trustees considered plans for turning Wells into a university (Minutes of the Wells College Board of Trustees, August 12, 1873).[18] A special committee of the trustees had been studying ways to raise the standard of scholarship and thereby to encourage support for an endowment. They submitted their plan to President Eliot of Harvard and President McCosh of Princeton and after receiving their "cordial approval," brought it before the board of Wells in 1873 where it likewise was approved unanimously "in its general features" (Hollcroft n.d., 109, WCA). The proposed university would have only sixty women students but would give them an education of "wide scope," one that was "flexible" in being able to adapt to "the individuality of the scholar, whether mental or physical," and having a curriculum that contained "all that is needed to perfect intellectually womanhood, and thus fit it for the individual orbit which the Providence of God may ordain." In addition to the usual degrees in arts or science, there were to be courses leading to three special degrees: Mistress of Architecture, Mistress of Painting, and Mistress of Sculpture (Minutes of the Wells College Board of Trustees, August 12, 1873). Nothing ever came of this plan, but it is interesting in revealing how much uncertainty surrounded the mission of Wells College in its early years.

The attempts to form a union with Howland School as well as to establish a university were clearly responses to Wells College's financial problems. Ezra Cornell had foreseen such difficulties. In 1866, two years before Wells Seminary opened, he wrote to Henry Wells with his own offer of union: why not, he suggested, build a "Wells Female Department of the Cornell University"? Cornell pointed out how expensive it was to build and maintain an independent institution and how such a female department would be able to benefit from Cornell University's "educational facilities, lectures, libraries, cabinets, museums, apparatus, and the perpetuity and support of the institution" (Hollcroft n.d., 16, WCA). Although Henry Wells turned down this offer, Ezra Cornell remained supportive of Wells Seminary. During a speech he gave at the inauguration of the seminary, Cornell offered to be one of a hundred gentlemen who would subscribe $1,000 for an endowment for scholarships (Dieckmann 1995, 10). Unfortunately Cornell's offer was not taken up, and scholarships were not established until much later, in the 1890s (Dieckmann 1995, 81).

Wells College's lack of endowment created problems that Henry Wells himself came to recognize. In his last address to the college, shortly before he died in 1878, Henry Wells referred to his "errors" and "shortcomings" as a "comparatively uneducated" man trying to "found, build, and put into successful working . . . the proper management of a woman's college." At the same time he took a "brighter view" of the future due to the "unstinted liberality" of his "neighbor, friend and brother," Edwin Barber Morgan (Hollcroft n.d., 147–48, WCA). And there is little doubt that his assessment was correct. Since Wells had been unable to continue supporting the institution he founded after he lost money during the panic of 1873, the college probably would not have been able to survive without the generous financial support of E. B. Morgan.

Born in 1806 in Aurora where he attended school and lived all his life, E. B. Morgan made his fortune from a variety of business and investment enterprises, including buying and shipping agricultural produce, boat building, express companies, gypsum beds in Michigan, and a starch-making company. He was also an original stockholder in the *New York Times* and served as a U.S. Congressman from 1852 to 1859, where he took a vigorous anti-slavery position. Morgan was given the nickname "Colonel" as a result of his financial support for colonels and volunteers in a regiment from central New York State during the Civil War (Dieckmann 1995, 32–39). Wells College was not the only institution E. B. Morgan supported; he was a trustee of Cornell University, and he gave money to the Presbyterian Church, Auburn Theological Seminary, and the school in Aurora he had attended, Cayuga Lake Academy. Yet Wells College became the institution "closest to his heart" (Dieckmann 1995, 37). It has been estimated that Morgan gave more than one-third of a million dollars to Wells, through major gifts, including the second college building, as well as through many small gifts, such as supplementing the salaries of particular faculty members whom he wanted to keep at the college (Hollcroft n.d., 179, WCA).

Students and College Life in the Early Years

The lack of endowment and scholarships may later have been recognized by Henry Wells as a mistake, but at the same time it was consistent with his aim for the college to be "consecrated" to the "ideal of true womanhood." Wells wanted students to have "well-trained . . . cultured . . . Christian minds," as he reiterated in his last address to the college (Hollcroft n.d., 148, WCA). His speeches frequently used such words as "refined," "elevating," and "the gentle sex" when referring to students. The Wells "college home" was, in fact, intended for a select group of privileged young women whose families could afford the high tuition without financial aid.

There are several indications that Wells College did attract the wealthy students it was created for. In 1868, at about the same time that nearby Hamilton College cost its men students less than $300 per year, Wells cost $450, plus extra for training in instrumental music, oil painting, or German or Italian instruction (Wells College Catalogues, WCA; Hamilton College Catalogues, HCA). Many students who attended had family connections to Henry Wells, E. B. Morgan, members of the Board of Trustees, or wealthy families of Aurora and other nearby communities. For example, one student was the granddaughter of a prominent local man, also related to E. B. Morgan, whose name was given to the township (Ledyard) that contains Aurora; this student's father was a career diplomat who spent time in Japan (Hollcroft n.d., 65, WCA). Henry Wells once joked that he established the college to give his nieces an education, and, in fact, at least one of his nieces did attend (Dieckmann 1995, 46). Fairly early on, a high percentage of Wells students came from out of state, another indicator that they were wealthy (Levine 1986). In 1871, for example, out of sixty-six students at Wells, sixteen, or 24 percent, came from out-of-state (compared to less than 10 percent of Hamilton College students at about the same time). And the out-of-state students did not come just from neighboring states, either; many came from as far away as Wisconsin, Michigan, and Illinois. Not surprisingly, given their wealthy family backgrounds, students tended to be conservative. An informal poll of the four women who graduated in 1870 found none in favor of women's suffrage, and none in favor of the recently formed women's club, Sorosis (Hollcroft n.d., 62, WCA).[19]

Evidence that the early Wells students were wealthy, and that their wealth was noticed by others, is also available from a report produced at the time. When a committee of the Presbytery of Cayuga visited Wells in 1872, they were pleased to see that the college was giving Christian education to "a large class of our most influential women." More specifically, the authors described the women as influential because of "the position they occupy, and the wealth and other resources they wield . . . [they are] women who do not engage in occupations for which they receive wages . . . . They find their most important sphere in elegant social life . . . they influence even their husbands and children and servants" (Wells history file, A18, WCA).

Wells college catalogues attempted to appeal to wealthy young women and their families by promising that students would become cultured and trained in graceful living. Such an emphasis on "social graces" was a usual focus of women's colleges at the time (Newcomer 1959, 112). The Wells curriculum emphasized art and especially music, which was said to be taught using the "most approved European methods" so that those wishing to complete their education abroad would be able to do so (1879 Catalogue, WCA).[20] Out of ninety-five faculty members between 1868 and 1894, more than one-third (33) had some sort of involvement with music at the college (General Catalogue 1868–94, WCA). In the early years Wells expected students to speak French, at least until after the noon meal, since this was seen as "indispensible to liberal culture" (1871 Catalogue, WCA). A member of the class of 1872, Louise Welles Murray, recalled this as a "foolish requirement" since "not half a dozen" students had even studied French. As this rule applied only within the college building, some students put their heads out of the window and talked English! Others just flouted the rule, confident that no one would report them, according to the recollections of a member of the class of 1873, Margaret Turner Sexton (Alumnae Bulletin 1918, WCA).

Some of the ways Wells College had a refining influence on its students were through its beautiful grounds, elegant furnishings, and the inclusion of students at dinner parties given by Henry Wells or E. B. Morgan. The reminiscences of early students mention the "stately homes and lovely gardens" in Aurora, the greenhouses, "wonderful gardens," and the many roses that "bloomed upon the lakeside lawns" (Alumnae Bulletin 1918, WCA). The main (and at first, only) college building was described by Margaret Turner Sexton '73 as having been designed by an "architect [who] with rare good taste, strove to have as many windows as possible command a view of the lake." When students went to dinner at the nearby home of Mr. and Mrs. Wells, they were served lunch or supper on "gilt-edged china with a big pink rose in the center." Margaret Turner Sexton recalled that when she first dined in "Colonel" Morgan's new dining room, she felt as though she were in "a baronial hall." She also remembered how frequently E. B. Morgan gave her flowers, including some he sent to her when she got married (Alumnae Bulletin 1918, WCA).

Alumnae's reminiscences of college life in the early days give the impression of many festivities, some of which included young men and many of which involved formal dress. Balls at Morgan's grand house, celebrations of Henry Wells's birthdays (Founder's Day), Halloween parties, Washington's birthday, and Commencement festivities were some of the regular social events at the college. When the railroad line through Aurora was completed in 1873, the college held a big celebration. More than one hundred of the visitors, some of whom had come from

Philadelphia and New York City, stayed to dine at the local hotel. A reporter called the visitors a "splendid looking . . . set of solid men . . . nearly all were millionaires" (Hollcroft n.d., 84, WCA). An event that reinforced the impression that Wells students were socially desirable was the engagement and subsequent marriage of one of its students, Frank (later called Frances) Folsom, to the president of the United States, Grover Cleveland. The age difference between them was large (she was 21, he 49), and the portly Cleveland was considered "ugly but honest" (Cashman 1993, 260).[21] Nonetheless their engagement and White House marriage in 1886 (a year after Folsom had graduated, which gave her time to take a trip to Europe with her mother) created great excitement at Wells (Dieckmann 1995, 74–76).

Wells students met some famous and influential people who came to Aurora as guests of Henry Wells or E. B. Morgan or to the college to give lectures. Millard Fillmore, the former U.S. president who was born in the county where Wells is located, gave the Commencement address in 1873 (Hollcroft n.d., 89, WCA). Other notables who visited in the early years included the conservative sociologist William Graham Sumner, the former governor of New York and secretary of state, William Seward (whose son was a college trustee), and the renowned English poets Matthew Arnold and Edmund Gosse (Hollcroft n.d., 190, WCA). Later, famous women came too. In 1899 Jane Addams lectured on the social principles of Tolstoi. Ida Tarbell, the muckraking journalist and historian,[22] and Ellen Swallow Richards, the first woman to study at MIT and nationally known for her work in home economics, also visited Wells.

On a daily basis, students' lives at college revolved around their classes, student organizations, and those with whom they shared the same living space: other students, women teachers, and the person primarily responsible for maintaining discipline and enforcing "lady-like manners," the Lady Principal (later called the Dean). At least some students at Wells during its first years were concerned about the quality of the academic training they were receiving. A member of the class of 1872, Louise Welles Murray, later described the faculty as a "heterogeneous collection," with the most "deplorable deficit" in the English department because the woman teacher taught them nothing in literature "outside the covers of the book." Yet Welles Murray had high praise for the woman who taught mathematics (who was also "the very heart of the religious life of the college"), whom she described as follows: "As an instructor of mathematics, she was unexcelled, and she was more strict in her requirements than any other teacher, thus elevating the standard of her department above the others" (Wells College Alumnae Bulletin 1918, 9, WCA). Students seemed aware of the distinction between the "teachers" (all women) and "professors" (all men), as their reminiscences never confused these titles. Margaret Turner Sexton '73, for example, recalled one professor who came to Wells from Cornell: "He brought not only erudition and discernment, but the true love of English literature and charming rendition" (Alumnae Bulletin 1918, 41, WCA).

The earliest student organizations at Wells were a literary society, a missionary society, and an alumnae association. Although little is known about the first years of the literary society since its records were burned in a major fire in 1888, students later wrote that originally it was "somewhat frivolous, making dramatics and literature rather the excuse than the end of its existence." In those years it was more concerned with its special and mysterious rings, its elaborate laws, and initiation rites (Cardinal Yearbook 1896, WCA). While Wells was still a young college, however, the literary society became more serious. It developed students' interest in literature through annual "public entertainments" and regular "literary exercises," and it also formed a library (1879 Catalogue, WCA). The other early student club, the Missionary Society, had as its stated aim the cultivation of "Christian benevolence" by acquiring knowledge of the "progress of evangelical truths throughout the world." It held monthly meetings and took up voluntary contributions for special needs of particular Christian missions (1879 Catalogue, WCA). The alumnae association was formed eleven years after Wells was founded, with the goal of maintaining "permanent interest in one another and in the prosperity of their alma mater" (1879 Catalogue, WCA).

More fun than these serious organizations, and perhaps more central to students' lives, were students' many informal get-togethers in each others' rooms or on picnics and walks. These occasions can be seen as marking the beginnings of college life, an "autonomous culture—characterized by independence and intense friendships" (Horowitz 1984, 5). Students clearly delighted in flouting rules, which sometimes involved improvising utensils for eating at times and places forbidden, as the following account illustrates: "Most inconvenient ventilators were over our doors, but these we covered with our waterproofs and, after . . . the last bell, gathered to make chocolate, holding the tin pail over the one gas jet. Sometimes the treat was oyster stew. A roast turkey that came in a box from home was carved with a pen knife and wire hair pin" (Margaret Turner Sexon '73, Alumnae Bulletin 1918, WCA). As a Vassar student exclaimed after describing similar types of activities: "Guess it must be sinful—this kind of life—for I enjoy it so much" (Letters from Old-Time Vassar, VCA).

As catalogues emphasized in their sections on the "College Home," Wells was intended to function as a family. Upon admission, catalogues throughout the nineteenth century stated, students were "members of the family." Until his death in 1878, Henry Wells functioned as the father with "a personal interest in his family of children," as he "delighted" to call the students (Louise Welles Murray '72, Alumnae Bulletin 1918, WCA). Like other rich, benevolent patriarchs, Wells brought back many gifts for his family when he returned home from his extensive travels. These gifts included marble statues for the college, a parrot, a monkey, seedless oranges and beetles from Brazil, and pearls from Italy for use in dramatic productions. In recognition of his benign authority, students complied with his request to serenade him upon his returns, and they celebrated his birthday on Founder's Day, one of the biggest events of the college year.

The early men presidents of Wells College had other jobs outside the college as well and so did not play a key role in the college's authority structure. Much more important was the Lady Principal (Dean), especially after a shrewd woman assumed this position in 1876. Helen Fairchild Smith, whose father had been the president of Wesleyan University, was described by a later president of Wells as dominating "the inner life of the College Home by her own high moral standards, wide interest in everything human, and her charming personality" (Kerr D. Macmillan, Wells College Bulletin 1926, 13, WCA). A scholar who has studied the activities of Helen Fairchild Smith found that her power derived from being the center of a female network: women faculty, the wives of men faculty, alumnae, and trustees' wives (Russ 1980). Although students probably were not aware of some of Miss Smith's machinations, which included activating her network to depose an ineffectual college president, they had a powerful example in her of a woman whose authority extended mostly over other women (the resident teachers and students) but also included some men. Despite the strictness with which Miss Smith regulated students' lives, some became close to her. Frank Folsom, for example, invited Miss Smith to her White House wedding. Helen Fairchild Smith also personified the importance of mother-daughter ties since her own mother lived with her at Wells College. A charitable student organization, the Catharine Guild, was named after Miss Smith's mother and celebrated her birthday by holding a "chocolatarium" (Russ 1980, 54).

A College Emerges from a Seminary:
Comparisons of Wells with Vassar

One way to assess the position of Wells College among institutions of higher learning for women in the mid-nineteenth century is to compare it to Vassar College. The similarities are obvious: both institutions were chartered in New York State, and Vassar opened only three years before Wells (although its charter dates from a few years earlier). Moreover, through their high tuition, stress on the cultivation of ladylike manners, and oversight of students' lives by having them live with women faculty in one large college building, both colleges show their connections to seminaries for women (Horowitz 1984). Yet Vassar, despite being founded before Wells, made a more complete and explicit break with seminary education.

Matthew Vassar was himself relatively uneducated, but he learned about higher education from two key people. The first was his stepniece, Lydia Booth, who after teaching in Virginia returned to Poughkeepsie, New York, to take over a "ladies seminary." The second, probably most important influence on Matthew Vassar was the educator Milo Jewett, who encouraged Vassar to have his college provide women with an education equal to that received by men at Yale and Harvard (Milo Jewett, "Origin of Vassar College," 1879, 5, VCA). A contemporary college historian considers the "maturing of his [Vassar's] ideas about women's education" to be one of the "most interesting aspects" of his life (Elizabeth Daniels, "Matthew Vassar—More Than a Brewer," 1992, 12, VCA). Henry Wells, in contrast, seemed unclear about the status of the institution he was founding. Although he had some associations with other people in higher education, notably Ezra Cornell, no one equivalent to Milo Jewett made it their job to educate him. Thus even though Vassar College had received much publicity as a real, endowed college for women, Henry Wells did not use it as a model to follow. Apparently, however, he was pleased when the name of Wells was officially changed from "Seminary" to "College," just as the students were (Alumnae Bulletin 1918, WCA).

From the beginning Vassar's catalogues were clear about admissions standards. Students had to be at least fifteen years old; the books in Latin that they were examined on were specified, and they had to take examinations in French grammar and algebra (First Annual Catalogue, VCA). Wells Seminary, strictly speaking, did not have a catalogue but a "prospectus," which did not specify admissions requirements. A student who entered Wells as a junior in 1870 later recalled that she had "merely" had "a verbal examination" about the studies she had pursued and "how far advanced" she was in them (Louise Welles Murray, Alumnae Bulletin 1918, 6, WCA). By 1871 Wells, by then called a college, did have a catalogue that specified admissions requirements. For admission into the Regular course, students were to take an examination in arithmetic, English and Latin grammar, Caesar's comments on the Gallic War, and "leading facts" in geography and history of the United States (1871 Catalogue, WCA).

From the outset Vassar College specified what students were to study each term and year. By 1867, one year before Wells opened, Vassar, like many men's colleges of the time, divided its Regular course into a classical and philosophical course, requiring the study of Greek as well as Latin, and a scientific and modern language course, which required Latin and French but no Greek (Vassar College Catalogues, VCA). Wells College made a similar division of its Regular course, beginning in 1871, but, as noted earlier, it required only Latin (no Greek) for its "collegiate-regular" course, and no Latin but some French for its "collegiate-English and scientific" course (1871 Catalogue, WCA).

In the 1860s and 1870s Wells's faculty were less qualified, in terms of having academic degrees, than were Vassar's faculty. For example, when Wells opened in 1868, none of its women faculty had degrees. By 1879, not including the president, there were twelve faculty, four of whom had degrees (three at the bachelor's level, one at the master's); five of the faculty were men (accounting for three of the faculty with degrees) (Wells College Catalogues, WCA). In 1868, by comparison, Vassar had thirty-four faculty members (not including the president, lady principal, a librarian, or the master of horsemanship), five of whom had degrees, and six of whom were men.[23] By 1879, Vassar already had several faculty with the Ph.D., something Wells did not achieve until the 1890s[24] (Vassar College Catalogues, VCA). The most famous member of Vassar's original faculty was Maria Mitchell, an astronomer who had discovered a comet for which she received a medal from the King of Denmark (Malone 1934). Even though Mitchell did not have formal academic credentials, she was hired as a "professor." Along with one other woman on the faculty who had a doctor of medicine degree (M.D.) and served as Vassar's physiologist, Mitchell broke the more usual pattern of the designation of women as "teachers" and the men as "professors," a pattern that existed also at Wells.

Another factor making Vassar a stronger collegiate institution from the beginning was the quality of its presidents. Milo Jewett, the first president, who was appointed when Vassar obtained its charter, had studied at both Dartmouth College and Andover Theological Seminary and had firsthand experience with three seminaries for young women. Although Jewett encountered opposition from some of Vassar's trustees and so was no longer president by the time Vassar opened, the next president, John Raymond, was also knowledgeable about higher education, as he had been head of the Collegiate and Polytechnic Institute in Brooklyn (Horowitz 1984). The early presidents of Wells College did not have backgrounds in higher education. The first president, William Washington Howard, was the pastor of the local Presbyterian church, a post he kept while serving as Wells's president. When this reverend resigned after only one year as Wells's president, he was replaced by a religious journalist, Samuel Irenaeus Prime, who resided in New York City (about 250 miles away). It was not until 1875, when Edward Frisbee, D.D., was hired as the fourth president of Wells, that the college had a president who devoted himself full-time to the work. Frisbee was also better qualifed in terms of his education, having graduated from Amherst College and studied at Union Theological Seminary (Dieckmann 1995, 60).

Thus despite such similarities between Vassar and Wells as their regulations of students' lives and their concern with cultivating ladylike manners in their wealthy students,[25] Vassar in the 1870s and 1880s had a stronger academic program and thus much more of a claim to the status of a true college. Many Wells students and alumnae felt strongly that Wells should improve its collegiate status, in particular, by disbanding its preparatory department. The trustees of Wells, however, were reluctant to refuse admission to those young women with insufficient academic preparation to do college work for fear of losing revenue from a reduction in the student body. The college almost came to an end when its original and major building burned to the ground in 1888. Insurance covered some of the cost of a new college building, but debts were incurred so that without the private donations of wealthy trustees, the college would not have survived.[26] Thus Wells at the beginning of the 1890s was in a very shaky financial state and more dependent on students' fees than was desirable (Kerr D. Macmillan, Wells College Bulletin 1926, WCA).

Concern about the preparatory department and the large number of students in it came to a climax in the late 1880s, when Wells alumnae were refused admission to the Association of Collegiate Alumnae (ACA). Marion Talbot, a graduate of Boston University and later a dean at the University of Chicago, founded the ACA in 1881 with her mother, Emily Talbot, an active educational reformer. ACA had two major purposes: to encourage young women who wanted to attend college, and to expand the opportunities for women graduates (Rosenberg 1982, 19), and it maintained strict criteria of admission. Alumnae were admitted as members only if they had graduated from schools approved by ACA's board, based on the "conviction that the prestige that came from meeting ACA membership standards would pressure colleges and universities to raise their standards for female students" (Levine 1995, 9). For example, by a vote of the members in 1896, institutions that had preparatory departments, fewer than fifty women graduates, or less than $500,000 endowment were not acceptable (Association of Collegiate Alumnae 1900). Even as late as 1908, only twenty-four institutions were judged adequate. These included all of the women's colleges that later came to be called the Seven Sisters, with the exception of Mount Holyoke (that is, Vassar, Smith, Wellesley, Radcliffe, Barnard, and Bryn Mawr), but still not Wells (Woody 1929 II, 189).

In 1889 a newspaper reported that Wells's most famous alumna, Frances Folsom Cleveland, had been turned away from a meeting of the ACA in Washington. The upset this caused some Wells alumnae led President Frisbee to write to one of them, Grace Carew Sheldon, Class of 1875, spelling out the facts of the matter and explaining why Wells was seen as not "really a college." He denied that Mrs. Cleveland had been turned away from the ACA meeting and pointed out that for Wells to belong to the Association, the graduates would have to make a formal application. But the rest of Frisbee's letter made it appear doubtful that such an application would have been accepted. He noted that until 1880 Wells's collegiate curriculum was much weaker than Vassar's or even those of Smith and Wellesley, the two women's colleges that had opened in 1875. He also noted that only about one in seven of students who entered Wells went on to graduate, over half stayed at Wells one year or less, and many never went beyond preparatory studies "though they pass as Wells College students." Thus, Frisbee concluded, "a very large proportion . . . of our students do not represent to the public the results of college training" (Frisbee 1889, History File, WCA).

Wells was changing, but not as fast as some alumnae or President Frisbee would have liked. In 1891 the alumnae presented a petition to the Board of Trustees to abolish the preparatory department (Kerr D. Macmillan, Wells College Bulletin 1926, WCA). This did not occur, however, until 1895, a year after President Frisbee resigned, because of the trustees' concerns that this would decrease enrollments by about one-third, with serious consequences for revenues (Dieckmann 1995, 81).[27]

Despite its shaky financial status, a lingering preparatory department, and a curriculum and faculty that only gradually achieved collegiate status, by the 1880s Wells was beginning to get recognition as a sound liberal arts college. In 1886 the U.S. Education Bureau classified Wells among 7 Division A women's colleges in the Northeast, compared to 152 Division B institutions (Woody 1929 II, 185). Although this classification was later criticized for being biased against southern schools (Durbin and Kent 1989), Division A colleges were meant to indicate those that were organized according to the "usual plan of the arts colleges" and that had small preparatory enrollments compared to college-level enrollments (Webster 1984).

The select students who were able to attend Wells, by virtue of their wealth, (Protestant) religion, and (white) race, were privileged to experience an institution that promoted the achievements of women like themselves. Wells was founded by one man and received critical financial support from several other men, but in terms of its day-to-day functioning, women dominated. Women formed the majority of the teaching staff; between 1868 and 1913, about 80 percent of the faculty were women (Russ 1980, 79). The dean, who held a key position in the college hierarchy that involved direct relations with the Board of Trustees and the president, was always a woman. And relatively early on, in 1887, only nineteen years after Wells was founded, the first two women were appointed to the Board of Trustees (Frank Folsom Cleveland and Dean Helen Fairchild Smith).[28] How much this situation contrasts with a men's college that became coeducational in the 1880s will be explored in the next chapter, when I discuss Middlebury College.

Notes

1 Toward the end of the nineteenth century some writers questioned the term "seminary." Clarke (1873, 65), for example, noted that women's collegiate institutions were "commonly but oddly called a seminary for girls." Seminaries began to seem old-fashioned, in contrast to colleges, which were expected to treat their women students as adults. Thus after Wellesley opened in 1875, faculty and students were dismayed by the "proliferating regulations and the constant religious exhortation," which they believed were appropriate only for seminaries, not real colleges (Palmieri 1995, 13–14).

2 The injunction for women to be happy or cheerful is long-lasting. In the early 1960s, a planning body for Kirkland College stated the following: "A woman's greatest need, like her greatest attraction, is *joie de vivre*. . . . The great purpose of a women's college should be the honing of women with a talent for the joy of effort and renewal" (Final Report on the Educational Philosophy of the Women's Coordinate College for Hamilton, September 1964, HCA).

3 About thirty years after Clarke's book was published, a well-known American psychologist, G. Stanley Hall, reiterated some of these same ideas, acknowledging his basic agreement with Dr. Clarke although he felt that Clarke had probably put his ideas "too harshly." The first volume of Hall's two-volume *Adolescence* contains an entire chapter on periodicity, which he described as "perhaps the deepest law of the cosmos [which] celebrates its highest triumphs in woman's life" (Hall 1904 I, 639).

4 There are interesting comparisons to be made between Dr. Clarke's views of what happens to women who receive the wrong form of education and Daniel Defoe's views, expressed about two hundred years earlier, of the effects of no education on women: She will be "Soft and Easy [if good temper] . . . Impertinent and Talkative . . . Fanciful and Whimsical . . . [and] If she be Passionate, want of Manners makes her Termagant, and a Scold, *which is much at one with Lunatick* . . . . And from these she degenerates to be Turbulent, Clamorous, Noisy, Nasty, *and the Devil*" (Defoe 1697 [1969], 295–296).

5 The demographic effects of the Civil War have been insufficiently studied by historians. While we do know that the war was the bloodiest in U.S. history, and that a greater proportion of Southerners died than Northerners, we do not know which groups of men fought, in which years, and from which communities (Vinovskis 1990).

6 As Milo Jewett expressed it when he was exhorting Matthew Vassar to found and endow a college for women: "If you establish a real college for girls and endow it, you will build a monument for yourself more lasting than the Pyramids; you will perpetuate your name to the latest generations; it will be the pride and glory of Po'keepsie" (Milo Jewett, "Origin of Vassar College," 1879, VCA).

7   For more information about the lives of Henry Wells and E. B. Morgan, see
     Dieckmann (1995), Russ (1980), and Malone (1934).

8   This institution was not a college in the conventional sense of the term. It admit-
     ted white orphan boys between the ages of 6 and 10 for training until they were
     14 to 18. The purpose was vocational, i.e., the boys were to be prepared to be
     apprenticed in such suitable occupations as agriculture, navigation, mechanical
     trades, or manufacture.

9   In several ways, Stephen Girard was a strange choice of a model for Henry Wells,
     a religious man interested in supporting women's education. Some people saw
     Girard as a difficult person with a violent temper (Burt 1963, 10). He married a
     servant girl but eight years later had her put in a hospital for the insane, where she
     eventually died. During Girard's lifetime rumors arose that he had had his wife
     institutionalized so that he could enjoy his mistress in peace. A recent biography
     of Girard, however, based on a detailed study of his voluminous correspondence
     and other records, argues that his wife was really insane (Wilson 1995, 107–
     109). The most unusual aspect of Stephen Girard, in terms of Wells's choice of
     him as a model, was Girard's attitude toward religion. His will contained detailed
     instructions about the college, not only how it was to be built but also who was to
     be kept out of it: any "ecclesiastic, missionary or minister of any sect whatsoever"
     (Monroe 1912). Such religious figures were not only prevented from holding a
     position at the college, but could not even be admitted as visitors (Arey 1877).
     This stipulation barring members of religious orders became well-known, as it
     was the basis of a court case brought by Girard's heirs. The U.S. Supreme Court
     ruled in 1844 that the City of Philadelphia could take the bequest and noted that
     Girard's will did not forbid the teaching of Christianity in the college by laymen
     (Arey 1877, 612). It is interesting that this controversy over Girard did not deter
     Henry Wells from citing him as a source of inspiration for founding Wells Semi-
     nary. Toward the end of his life Wells wrote that his attitudes toward Girard's
     intolerance of religion had changed somewhat: "I comprehended and appreciated
     all but his [Girard's] exclusion of Clergymen. Yet he may have been right, for our
     present age of progress is fast abolishing all sectarianism from our public schools
     and colleges" (Founder's Day Address 1875, WCA). Wells might have been re-
     lieved to learn that the orphans at Girard College were "steeped in religion,"
     being required to attend fifteen services a week, even though these services had
     to be led by laymen (Wilson 1995, 360). The ban of religious figures on campus
     has remained, but in 1968 the U.S. Supreme Court declared that the "college"
     could not continue to admit only white orphans, and in the 1980s, litigation
     resulted in the admission of girls, too (Wilson 1995, 364).

10   While to a late-twentieth-century mind, Wells's reference to women's ability to
     study science might seem surprising, according to Rossiter (1982) many people in
     the first half of the nineteenth century believed that the study of science increased
     people's respect for nature and thus brought them closer to God. Having women
     students study science was a way of reassuring the public that the intent of the
     educational institution was to produce women of high moral character, unlike
     what the study of literature and novels would produce. Veysey (1965, 133) also

notes that the meaning of the word "science" was changing in the mid-nineteenth century. It had meant any well-organized body of principles concerning any area of knowledge, able to serve as an "unchanging reflection of the divine." This was how the earliest catalogues of Wells described natural science—providing "exhaustless revelations of Divine wisdom and goodness [which] afford an ample field for interesting and refining study" (Wells Catalogue 1870, WCA). In the Age of Darwin "science" came to be associated with specific evidence observed in nature or studies confined to matter. This definition was threatening to traditional religions.

11   President Prime, D.D., was the editor of the *Christian Observer* newspaper in New York City. Prior to the Civil War, in the early 1850s, Prime had come into conflict with Harriet Beecher Stowe and her preacher brother, Henry Ward Beecher. A specific point of contention was Stowe's criticism in *Uncle Tom's Cabin* of a Presbyterian clergyman, Dr. Joel Parker, who had written that the evils of slavery were "inseparable from depraved human nature in other lawful relations." Prime defended Dr. Parker in his newspaper, known to be pro-slavery, as part of his campaign against a rival anti-slavery newspaper, *The Independent*, and also as part of his disagreement with Henry Ward Beecher's more liberal type of evangelical Christianity (Hedrick 1994, 226–230). The pro-slavery position of President Prime contrasted markedly with the vociferous anti-slavery stance of the great benefactor of Wells College and friend of Henry Wells, E. B. Morgan, who is discussed later in this chapter.

12   Henry Wells's hope that education would prevent women from wanting suffrage supports Palmieri's point that women's colleges were founded, in part, to prevent more radical social change (Palmieri 1987). Yet Matthew Vassar did support women's suffrage (Malone 1934).

13   Even though the college was prevented from accepting this gift, E. B. Morgan paid the college $7000 per year as interest on this fund during his lifetime, and the college obtained the principal after Morgan's death in 1881 (Temple Rice Hollcroft, "A History of Wells College," n.d., 114, WCA).

14   The village of Aurora also had a Roman Catholic Church, just completed in 1874, but probably few, if any, of the Wells students at this time were Catholic.

15   College catalogues continued to include references to Christianity for almost one hundred years. In 1960–61, under "Religious Life" the Wells College Catalogue stated: "Wells College desires to develop in each student the highest ideals of *Christian* life and service." By the following year this same section said: "the highest ideals of *religious* life and service" [my emphasis]. This change was apparently linked to a gift by the parents of an alumna, Helen Rosen Yellin '50, for an Interfaith Series. Yet Sunday Vespers were still held, conducted by visiting members of different denominations, as well as noonday Chapel, five times a week, led by members of the College.

16   This should not be considered too unusual, however, given the era. When Wellesley opened seven years later, for example, only two of its original women faculty had

bachelor's degrees (from Vassar); the others were "self-educated" (Palmieri 1995, 11).

17   It is also noteworthy that despite her proximity, M. Carey Thomas did not consider attending Wells College for her undergraduate degree, although she thought seriously about Vassar. A teacher of metaphysics and political science at Howland School advised "Minnie" to attend Cornell rather than Vassar or the two new women's colleges, Smith and Wellesley, scheduled to open in 1875. Minnie entered Cornell in 1875 as a junior, after spending a year at home preparing for the entrance examinations (Horowitz 1994, 50). There is no question that Thomas was an unusually academically ambitious woman; after graduation from Cornell she tried to attend Johns Hopkins University (which her own family had helped establish), but when she learned she was unable to get a graduate degree there, she went to Europe, ultimately earning her Ph.D. *summa cum laude* from Zurich in 1882 (Dobkin 1979). Even though Wells was called a college in 1870 and had a charter from the state of New York to give college degrees, it was still not perceived as being as academically serious as some of the other women's colleges of the time, and for that reason, presumably, was not interesting to a student as ambitious as M. Carey Thomas.

18   At the time there was an educational institution for women located in central New York (Le Roy, Genesee County) that called itself a university. Ingham University developed out of the Le Roy Female Seminary and the Ingham Collegiate Institute; it lasted for 35 years, before folding in 1892 (Wing 1991).

19   Sorosis, established in 1868 by Jane Cunningham Croly, in response to the exclusion of women from a New York Press Club dinner in honor of Charles Dickens, was joined mostly by career women in the arts and cultural fields who were trying to reconcile their careers with their private lives. Its founder wanted to avoid controversial subjects like religion and suffrage while providing a forum for women's intellectual stimulation and mental growth (Blair 1980).

20   Sicherman (1988) argues, however, that the early introduction of music into the women's colleges may have had a vocational impact, since women graduates classified by the 1870 U.S. Census were most likely to be working in music after teaching and nursing. On the other hand, students at Smith College objected when music and art courses were introduced into the curriculum in the 1880s, since they thought of such courses as typically female, not appropriate for their college, which was aiming to be as rigorous as the best men's colleges of the time (Gordon 1975).

21   The campaign for the 1884 election between Blaine, the Republican candidate, and Cleveland, the Democrat, was notoriously dirty, with a major contested issue being public morality. Blaine supported business and protective tariffs. Cleveland, the former mayor of Buffalo and governor of New York, was considered to have the "common touch" and was believed to be opposed to the power of monopolies. Yet Cleveland was supported by big business and had a mistress in the city of Buffalo, who had borne him an illegitimate child (Cashman 1993, 260–61).

22   Ida Tarbell was, however, "chagrined" at being called a muckraker, the term coined by President Theodore Roosevelt. Although she was sharply critical of the Standard Oil Trust and the secret railroad agreements that gave Rockefeller advantages, according to James (1971), she was "fundamentally" a "warm friend" of business.

23   Matthew Vassar was originally persuaded by Milo Jewett that his college should have men faculty, but as a result of a critical article by Horatio Hale, the son of the editor of *Godey's Lady's Book*, Vassar conformed to pressure to have Vassar mirror a home, which required women students to be taught by surrogate mothers. Thus beginning in 1864, Vassar favored hiring women faculty (Horowitz 1984, 37–38).

24   It is interesting to note that one of the women faculty at Wells in the 1890s with a Ph.D. (from Cornell) was Margaret Washburn (1871–1939), who became a famous psychologist after she left Wells to teach at her alma mater, Vassar. Washburn had a long, illustrious career at Vassar, during which she involved her students in many experiments described in one of her books, *Studies from the Psychological Laboratory of Vassar College*. Washburn also became the president of the American Psychological Association in 1921 (James 1971), and is mentioned in the famous fictional book about Vassar in the 1930s, Mary McCarthy's *The Group*.

25   Vassar's tuition and board was $400 when Wells's was $450 (Hamilton College's was about $250, by comparison), although Matthew Vassar from the very beginning referred to the needs of "indigent" students, whom he wished to support. Vassar's Catalogues contained a section similar to Wells's on the College Home in which it was written that the duty of the lady teacher who resided in the "College edifice" was to "enforce therein the laws of order, neatness, and decorum" (First Annual Catalogue, 1865, 33, VCA).

26   Horowitz (1984, 94) argues that after 1875, when Smith College opened with a "cottage plan" rather than with one large seminary-like building, "a college had to have cottages to be up-to-date." Vassar built "cottages" as soon as it had sufficient enrollment to create the demand for additional space. Despite the perfect "opportunity" to create a modern campus in 1888, due to the devastation of the fire, Wells built another seminary-like building, closely modeled on the one that had burned.

27   Vassar had abolished its preparatory department by 1884 (Vassar College Catalogues, VCA).

28   The first women on Vassar's Board of Trustees were also appointed in the 1880s. By 1888 there were three women on Vassar's Board (Yearbook, 1888, VCA).

Chapter 3

"Ladies on the Scene":
Women Enter Middlebury College

When Middlebury College opened its doors to women students in 1883, women's options for higher education were considerably greater than they had been just fifteen years earlier when Wells Seminary opened. In the Northeast alone, women could attend women's colleges (notably Smith, Wellesley, Wells, Vassar, Ingham University, and Elmira), several coeducational colleges and universities (Cornell University, Syracuse University, Boston University, University of Vermont, Colby College, Wesleyan, and Bates College) and the first coordinate institution, the Annex, which later came to be called Radcliffe.[1] Women could also attend many excellent seminaries for women, including Mount Holyoke, Wheaton, and Troy Female Seminary.

Middlebury's admission of women students occurred at a time when nationwide, women were more likely to attend coeducational than women's colleges. In fact, in terms of the number of women enrolled, only in 1870 did more women attend women's colleges (of all sorts, including many that were not degree-granting) than coeducational institutions. In 1880, 40 percent of all women enrolled in institutions of higher learning attended women's colleges; by 1890, this figure was down to 30 percent. (For the subset of private, four-year non-Catholic women's colleges, 28 percent of women were enrolled in 1880, 21 percent in 1890) (Newcomer 1959, 40). But these are national data; women in the Northeast were more likely than women in the West to attend women's colleges (Durbin and Kent 1989, 3).

The first generations of college women in coeducational institutions were full of "revolutionary" zeal in their attempts to demonstrate to the larger public that they were as intellectually capable as men. These pioneers recognized that future women's educational opportunities depended on their performance. Not surprisingly, then, women students developed a reputation for their seriousness and academic excellence (Palmieri 1987, 55; Solomon 1985, 95). This reputation was later turned against them, when some people came to fear—correctly, as it turned out—that they would outperform men students.

By the 1880s not only did women have more opportunities for higher education than in the 1860s, they also had a formal organization advocating for their educational interests, the Association of Collegiate Alumnae (see Chapter 2). Yet women's educational opportunities did not match their demands. Women in many locales, sometimes with men allies, struggled to get men's colleges to admit them. Middlebury was one such institution that women tried, initially without success, to enter.

Middlebury as a Men's College

In the nineteenth century, Middlebury was not a nationally known college but a small, struggling institution with a conservative classical curriculum. The college was founded in 1800 by local townspeople in Middlebury, Vermont, in competition with their northern neighbor, Burlington, which had obtained a charter for a university in 1791 but only managed to open at the same time as Middlebury (Stameshkin 1985, 36). Most of the men who attended Middlebury in its first eighty years came from poor or middle-class rural backgrounds.[2] Virtually all of them were white Protestants from New England and New York,[3] and many planned to enter the ministry.[4] Although not a sectarian college, Middlebury's relation to Congregationalism was similar to Wells's relation to Presbyterianism, in that a majority of its presidents, trustees, faculty, and probably even students, were Congregationalists.[5] Before the Civil War, the tone of the college was especially Calvinist and austere. Frivolities were frowned upon, sports were almost nonexistent, and the main extracurricular activity was a literary and debating club to which practically every student belonged (Stameshkin 1985, 173). Faculty and students alike were pleased when religious revivals swept the campus, which they did frequently—before 1840, there had been at least ten religious revivals (Allmendinger 1975, 119).

After the Civil War, Middlebury College gradually became less intensely religious and the usual signs of men's college life were manifest: students committed pranks, drank, played cards, and cut classes more frequently. Fraternities, which had first appeared in the 1840s, became much more popular and encountered less opposition from faculty and other students.

In fact, between 1869 and 1880, more than 85 percent of Middlebury students joined one of the three fraternities on campus (Stameshkin 1985, 177). Students occasionally engaged in athletic competitions with other teams in western Vermont and published a yearbook and somewhat later, a campus newspaper. But Middlebury's curriculum remained wedded to the early nineteenth-century ideal of what a man's college education should be. It continued to stress Greek and Latin and allowed for no electives, just as it had done when it was founded in 1800 (Stameshkin 1985, 168).

For much of its first eighty years, Middlebury was a fragile college. Its very small size[6] meant that it was vulnerable when one or two faculty members left or when events like the Civil War caused enrollment to decline still further. Moreover, its local character, the high percentage of students who came from nearby towns,[7] and its reliance on financial support from local residents, created a narrow resource base. Thus, for example, when Middlebury's president, Reverend Joshua Bates, allied himself with a controversial itinerant revivalist in the late 1830s, he alienated the college from some prominent Congregationalists in the area, who then switched their support from Middlebury to its rival, UVM (University of Vermont, in Burlington), an institution that had previously been perceived as too religiously liberal (Stameshkin 1985, 125–131). This was just one of several occasions in which Middlebury's very survival seemed in doubt.

Attempts to make Middlebury College less vulnerable included petitioning the state of Vermont for financial support and negotiating with UVM about the possibility of merging the two institutions. Neither attempt was successful, in part due to trustees' desire for Middlebury to be an independent college, free of state control (Stameshkin 1985, 39, 154). Middlebury remained dependent on private donations from county residents, and frequently ran up large annual deficits even though it paid its faculty and president low salaries, sometimes reducing them still further when financial conditions worsened (Stameshkin 1985, 160).

In the second half of the nineteenth century, many small colleges, like Middlebury, had difficulties with finances and enrollments.[8] The large university, perceived as being more in tune with the practical needs of the industrializing country for specialized skills in practical subjects, was becoming increasing popular (Veysey 1965). Middlebury's presidents joined with the heads of other small colleges in attempting to convince the public that small institutions were able to educate students more thoroughly than large universities were. Rev. Calvin Hulbert, president of Middlebury in the 1870s, referred to this as "perpendicular" power—the success of a college being determined "not so much by the number it may encompass and influence as by the thoroughness and depth of its work in those committed to it" (as quoted in Stameshkin 1985, 183). Not surprisingly, however, such verbal defenses of the value of small colleges did not translate into higher enrollments.

Women Gain Admission to Middlebury

After the Civil War Middlebury College's enrollments did not rise even though they did at nearby UVM. Thus while Middlebury's enrollments remained steady (52 students in 1866–67 and 51 students in 1874–75) UVM's enrollments increased from 31 to 87 students. From the vantage point of today, admitting women might seem an obvious way Middlebury College could have solved its enrollment problems and become more financially secure. But the college was on record as being opposed to admitting women. About sixty years earlier, one of the most famous woman educators of the nineteenth century, Emma Hart Willard, had tried to gain privileges at Middlebury. Willard was the head of a Female Academy in Middlebury and then opened a school in her own house. She asked to be allowed to take examinations at the college and for her students to audit college classes. She was refused, with the president calling it a bad precedent and "unbecoming" to Mrs. Willard (Stameshkin 1985, 117).[9]

For a while in the early 1870s, it did seem that Middlebury might admit women. Middlebury's trustees formed a committee to consider their admission, and faculty voted to meet with the faculty of UVM to discuss the "expediency" of opening colleges in Vermont to women. But after the trustee committee reported that a majority favored women's admission, the motion to admit women was tabled and not considered again (Minutes of the Corporation of Middlebury College, 1870–71, MCA).[10] To understand why trustees opposed the admission of women, it is necessary to realize how central was the image of Middlebury as a men's college. In the memorable words of Calvin Hulbert, who was president of the college between 1875 and 1880, "*Men* are in demand—not *homines*, animals that wear pants, but *viri*, plumed knights, with swords upon their thighs; scholars and specialists they may be, if back of scholarship and specialty there is manhood enough" (Hulbert 1890, *The Distinctive Idea in Education*, as quoted in Veysey 1965, 29).

Middlebury's enrollment dropped to a perilous low of 39 students in 1880 after unfavorable national press coverage of an incident at the college. A popular student had been suspended due to accumulating too many demerits, the last of which he received for violating the president's bans of informal football that students played between college buildings and traditional cane rushes (a ritualized physical struggle between the freshmen and sophomores). Students went on strike, and ultimately, the president and two faculty members resigned (Stameshkin 1985, 163–165). The college's desperate need for more students led local residents and alumni to pressure the college to admit women. In 1882 a woman graduate of Middlebury High School, May Anna Bolton, requested admission to the college, and the Alumni Association asked the trustees to consider admitting women students. The trustees once again discussed the issue but refused to admit women, saying that the "organization" of the faculty and money given to the college by people who "contemplated a different disposition and use of . . . [their] gifts" made them conclude that Middlebury should not alter the sex of its student body (Minutes of the Corporation of Middlebury College, July 4, 1882, MCA). The trustees changed their mind the following year, however, when enrollment fell even lower, to 38 students, and townspeople renewed their arguments that the college should be educating their daughters. Local people made the sensible argument that admitting young women would not increase the workload of faculty appreciably, and would not increase costs for the college, but would help fill empty seats in the classrooms (Stameshkin 1985, 202).

Thus women finally gained admission to Middlebury in 1883. They were not admitted out of trustees' ideological commitment to furthering women's opportunities for higher education, but rather as a way of solving the college's continuing financial and enrollment problems. Many specific issues concerning the integration of the women had yet to be decided, including the basic one of whether or not the women would be able to receive degrees (Stameshkin 1985, 218). The trustees voted to admit "young ladies" under "such regulations as the Faculty and Prudential Committee shall prescribe," and stipulated that "their names shall appear in the Catalogue in a separate list" (Minutes of the Corporation of Middlebury College, July 1883, MCA). Yet when the catalogue was published, under the president's directives, it merely stated that "the College offers the same privileges to young ladies as to young gentlemen" (1883–84 Catalogue, MCA).[11] Six women students entered Middlebury in the fall of 1883, including May Anna Bolton, the young woman who had been refused in 1882; three were admitted as freshmen, the other three as "specials," students who did not take a full load of courses (three men student were specials, too, for the first time). The women students were not listed separately in the catalogue but rather in the same alphabetical list as the men students (1883–84 Catalogue, MCA).

The First Years As a Coeducational College

The entry of the first women students did not change Middlebury College dramatically; in fact, the college changed hardly at all. Unlike many women's colleges at the time, including Wells, no preparatory work was offered; the young women had to be able to do advanced work in Latin as well as Greek. Middlebury did not provide the women with housing or even a place to study, so during the day the young women had to walk down the hill to the houses at which they boarded and then back again for other classes. It was not until winter 1885 that the college set aside a reading room for the exclusive use of women students. The women furnished the room themselves from the proceeds of a "Dickens Party" in which they and some women from the town portrayed characters from Dickens's novels (*The Undergraduate*, February 1885, MCA). Nine years later women students appealed to the trustees and obtained a larger room with a toilet and washbasin (Pollard, Class of 1896, "Women at Middlebury College," MCA).

Men students' responses to the announcement about the admission of women were at first anxious, then positive but guarded. In May 1883, when students knew that the trustees were seriously considering admitting women, an editorial in the student newspaper said that the "situation of the college" made it likely that "many" women would enter. This led the editorial writer to "question very much the propriety and advantage of making the change" (*The Undergraduate*, May 1883, MCA). But the next issue of the paper justified the decision, noting that the "experiment" did not indicate a "measure of last resort" since coeducation was "one of the urgent demands of the times" (*The Undergraduate*, July 1883, MCA).

Once women students were on campus, men students expressed relief about how little their presence affected the college. In an editorial entitled, "Appearance of Ladies on the Scene," the writer noted the "indifference" of the men students to the presence of the young women. At the same time he commended his fellow men students for their "hearty co-operation" in the admission of women, noting that Middlebury men had treated the women students in a "far more creditable manner" than UVM men had treated the women who entered their institution in 1871.[12] In a telling comment that indicated the desire for Middlebury to remain in essence a men's college, the editorial writer remarked that he did not see how the admission of "ladies" would "in the least alter the established order in our college in respects which will affect the rights of the masculine element" (*The Undergraduate*, October 1883, MCA).

While men students were concerned that their masculine "rights" be safeguarded, many clearly enjoyed the presence of women. In the same editorial that expressed relief that women had not altered the "established order," the writer "censure[d]" the proposal for separate library hours for the women students since this implied that "either the faculty or ladies" believed the men students were "barbarians." The following issue of the student newspaper contained a spirited letter from an unidentified "co-ed" correcting the statement that it was the women students who wished to have separate library hours. The co-ed noted sardonically that "the ladies feel highly complimented by the assumption that they have such influence with the faculty . . . still they have not yet been admitted as members of that august body." She concluded by recommending that in the future editorial writers should "find out the facts of the case before making such sweeping assertions." This letter produced an apology from the editors of the student newspaper, who noted that the desire to change the library hours was really due to "the stern decree of the faculty" (*The Undergraduate*, November 1883, MCA).

In addition to the issue of separate library hours for the women students at Middlebury, men writers in the student newspaper criticized the college's decision not to allow the "ladies" to appear on the college stage for the rhetoricals and not to let them compete for two academic prizes. The writer of the December 1883 editorial expressed his views directly: "The college is co-educational . . . yet it discriminates." He also criticized the freshman class for excluding the "girls" from class elections. "If the girls are excluded from class meetings, if they are not treated as if they were members of the class, they surely cannot be expected to pay any part" of class expenses for events such as Junior Exhibition, he argued (*The Undergraduate*, December 1883, MCA).

Thus although Middlebury's trustees may have thought that they were just experimenting by admitting a few young women to a men's college, students seem to have seen this step as making the college coeducational. With this change in the institution's identity, pressures developed for extending to the women students the same privileges that existed for the men. Articles in the student newspaper compared practices at Middlebury to other "mixed-schools in the country," and used such comparisons to influence college authorities to change procedures when they thought they were unfair. The students were successful in some but not all of their campaigns. Women were allowed to appear on stage to receive their degrees, and in 1891 women were permitted to compete for the same academic prizes as the men students. But the students' attempt to have men and women use the library during the same hours was not immediately successful, and women did not have a student government until they got their own association in 1912. Some college functions such as chapel, that were originally integrated by sex, became separate in later years.

No diaries or correspondence of the first women students at Middlebury exist, so direct evidence of their experiences is lacking. But since campus clubs and organizations were closed to them, and they did not live together, it would appear that at first, the women had few opportunities to enjoy college life. What is known about Middlebury's first women students is that they, like women pioneers at many colleges and universities, did exceptionally well academically. In December 1884 the student newspaper noted in its editorial that one of the "co-eds" got "a large share" of the prizes. The writer explained this by noting that many branches of study were "perfectly adapted to the fair sex" and in these they do "excellent work." In answer to the general question, how are the co-eds getting along, the editorial writer concluded, "We are inclined to think that there are many advantages in co-education, and we are also ready to admit that there may be some evils" (*The Undergraduate*, December 1884, MCA). What these "evils" might be, he did not specify, but their mention seems to indicate some resentment of the first women students, described in another editorial as "beyond the average in mental capabilities and poise" (*The Undergraduate*, June 1885, MCA). Yet when the first woman, May Belle Chellis, graduated in 1886 at the top of her class, the men students warmly applauded her "pluck and gut" (*The Undergraduate*, July 1886, MCA).

After three years of experimenting with coeducation, the trustees were convinced, both by the academic success of the women and by the increases in enrollment (from 36 in 1885 to 49 in 1886), to continue admitting women (Stameshkin 1985, 218). Paradoxically, at the same time that the trustees moved to make coeducation permanent, the women students were made more separate from the men students, at least symbolically. Women students' names in the catalogues no longer appeared in the same list as the men's; they were listed under a line after the men's names, and then in 1886–87, under the heading, "Lady Students" (Catalogues, 1883–84, 1884–85, 1885–86, 1886–87, MCA).

The Emergence of College Life for Women Students

At first the number of women students at Middlebury remained low; there were just 3 regular (that is, non-special) women students between 1883 and 1887, and then only 5 in 1888. The number of men students picked up slightly in 1886, however, when 46 men were enrolled, so overall enrollment continued to rise from when Middlebury became (provisionally) coeducational in 1883. Six years after Middlebury admitted women, in 1889, the numbers of women students began to increase steadily: 8 in 1889, then 11, 16, 23, and 30 in 1893 (Stameshkin 1985, 216). Concomitant with the rise in the number of women came the first organizations and housing for them and thus the beginnings of their college life.

In 1889 fraternity members encouraged women students to form the first sorority at Middlebury, Alpha Chi (Mary Pollard, "Women at Middlebury College," 1959, MCA). Although membership was open to everyone (until a student was "blackballed" in 1894), initiation ceremonies were mysterious and elaborate, as the following account of a freshwoman indicates:

> We were led blindfolded, one by one, up into the cupalo [sic] over the chapter rooms. There, in a little room, draped in black, each girl was made to kneel before a black robed judge, place her hand on a skull, and answer a list of what seemed to us most vital questions. A scribe on the left took down the answers while the four walls resound[ed] with heart rending groans. After this ordeal we were allowed to see and hear for the first time the most beautiful, the most sacred service in the Naon. ("History of Alpha Chi," undated, MCA)

Clearly part of the enjoyment in belonging to the sorority was a sense of secrecy. Members adopted Greek names, used a password, and appointed a committee to "decide upon a knock." By 1893 Alpha Chi held regular meetings one evening each week. Some aspects of these meetings were educational. The members studied such subjects as the lives of prominent American women, the heroines in literature, or the noted graduates of Middlebury. They gave papers on serious topics, and held debates on subjects considered less serious, for example, "Resolved that coeducation is a failure" or "Resolved that the greatest good a girl derives from a college education is its financial benefits." Sororities encouraged scholarship among their members not only through their programs of study and occasional sponsoring of lectures by professors, but also by noting members' achievements; for example, proudly announcing that they had "carried off" both the valedictory and the salutatory honors. With the establishment of a second sorority at Middlebury in 1893, competition for members during rushing began, with the consequent need to entice them through special off-campus trips, teas, and receptions for faculty and male fraternity members ("History of Alpha Chi," undated, MCA).

Sororities at Middlebury never achieved the status of fraternities, which dominated the campus's social and political life (Stameshkin 1985, 261–65), but they gave their members a sense of solidarity and experiences with organization and leadership that were unavailable to them in campus organizations controlled by men. Graduates established networks of women through the sororities; alumnae returned for some meetings, and members wrote a newsletter to "keep all the girls in touch" ("History of Alpha Chi," undated, MCA). Since the sororities served as a buffer between the male-dominated campus and the women's college life, the relatively few young women who did not get into one of Middlebury's sororities were doubly marginalized.[13] They were neither fully integrated into campus organizations at large, nor members of one of the only associations controlled by and centered around women.

Women students gradually came to have more of their own clubs and organizations and to join some of the men's associations. They established a chapter of the YWCA (Young Women's Christian Association) in 1894 and a Ladies Glee Club in 1899, but before that some women were on the staff of the newspaper and the yearbook. A hierarchical pattern for the mixed-sex campus clubs became established early and persisted, with only a few exceptions, until the late 1960s: men students had the kudos of the top position, while the women students worked as their assistants, in name at least.[14] Students sometimes noted the injustice of this situation. A woman member of the class of 1896, for example, later recalled her appointment as assistant editor of the yearbook "with the stipulation" that she "should do the work but Frank Davis have the name of editor-in-chief, because it did not look well to have a girl in higher rank than a man" (Pollard 1959, MCA).

Eight years after the first women students entered Middlebury, the college purchased a house, remodeled it as a dormitory for women, and appointed a matron to live with the women students, the first woman staff member employed by the college. The house could accommodate only eight to twelve women, however, and that year, 1891, sixteen women were enrolled at Middlebury. Since no additional housing for women students was built until 1909 (Stameshkin 1985, 220), some continued to board with families in town. Mothers of women students sometimes moved to Middlebury to ensure their daughters had a safe place to live; most took in other boarders as well, according to the recollections of a member of the class of 1896 (Pollard 1959, MCA).

The diary of Marion Elizabeth Dunbar, class of 1897, indicates that by the 1890s, Middlebury women students had a well-established college life. Miss Dunbar described many activities beyond the classroom, both formal and informal. She visited other women students in their rooms, to talk, play music with them, or to share such food treats as popcorn or sugar on snow. Her diary mentioned skating, sleighing parties, hay rides, receptions for faculty, picnics, walks, tennis, and attending baseball games between Middlebury "boys" and the Burlington YMCA. Some of the events involved women only, for example, sorority meetings, dancing with other girls at a YWCA reception, and attending a musical for "young women of the college and the wives of the members of the faculty." Miss Dunbar also did well in her studies, which included French, German, Latin, and Greek, and received encouragement to go on to graduate school from a (male) professor of rhetoric and English literature.[15] Somewhere between the serious and fun sides of college life were the exhibitions; upperclass men and women read their essays, and all who attended dressed up in fancy clothes. Miss Dunbar's comment that her father would have been "much shocked" by the "low necked and short sleeved" dresses that some of the women wore to the exhibition she attended suggests the sense of freedom and slight naughtiness that college life could produce (Mary Elizabeth Dunbar, class of 1897, journal, MCA).

Opposition to Women Students

As women students became more established at Middlebury, resentment against them grew. Not only did the proportion of women students increase, but their share of academic prizes was even greater. Men students began to fear that *their* college might become feminized or even a women's college. By 1890 women students comprised 20 percent of the student body; a mere three years later, they were more than one-third (30 women out of a total of 85 students) (Stameshkin 1985, 216). An editorial in the student newspaper sounded an alarm while painting an unflattering portrait of women students:

> If this rate of increase continues, in a few years the co. part will equal the rest of the college. Deeply as we admire the picturesque Oxford caps and wonder at the faultless recitations and pretty dignity of the well-known co-ed figure as she minces up and down the walks of old Middlebury, we should be deeply grieved to believe that this college is becoming a female college. . . . . The remedy does not lie in checking the inflowing of women, but in increasing the number of our men. . . . We would farther [sic] exhort the aspiring genius among our men to gird itself for the fray. The scholarship of the Middlebury co-ed is of a very high order, and, though we have no doubt of the ability of the men to carry off the palm, nevertheless

without mighty effort the honors will soon begin to go to co-eds even more than
in the past. (*The Undergraduate*, October 1893, MCA)

Thus at least in the 1890s men students' concerns about coeducation
did not translate into a desire for the college to revert back to a men's
college but rather to ensure that the proportion of men did not fall too
low. The contributions that the women could make to the college were
recognized. For instance, in the same issue of the student newspaper in
which the editorial writer worried that Middlebury might become a "female college," he noted that given the large percentage of "lady students,"
the women should have "several representatives" on the paper's editorial
board (*The Undergraduate*, October 1893, MCA).

The number of women students at Middlebury continued to grow, so
that by 1896 they constituted more than 40 percent of the student body.
During the next decade their proportion remained at about this level,
dipping slightly below 40 percent only twice, in 1901 when women were
38 percent of the student body, and 1906 when they were 39 percent. At
the same time the college itself grew, from 106 students in 1896 to 178
in 1906 (Stameshkin 1985, 216). Thus one of the earliest predictions of
editorial writers in the student newspaper was fulfilled: coeducation appeared to be "one of the urgent demands of the times" so that "many"
young women had entered Middlebury (*The Undergraduate*, July 1883,
MCA). At the same time, by the end of the nineteenth century and the
beginning of the twentieth, men students feared for the "rights of the
masculine element" that earlier, when there were so few women students,
they had believed would be secure even with coeducation (*The Undergraduate*, October 1883, MCA).

The early twentieth century was a period of anxiety in the country at
large about the feminization of American culture, which manifested itself
in part by an opposition to coeducation (Rosenberg 1988; Woody 1929
II). It is therefore not surprising that Middlebury's trustees shared men
students' anxieties about the increasing number of women students. In
1902, a year after the number of women entering Middlebury was greater,
for the first time, than the number of entering men, senior men at the
college founded a society for discouraging coeducation, and the (male)
student government sent a petition to each trustee urging them to do
something about the situation (Stameshkin 1985, 221). And so the
trustees did. Among themselves they quickly came to "a tacit understanding that, for the present, the number of girls should be limited" (Minutes
of the Board, June 1902, MCA), and they began working on separating

women from the men by establishing an annex or coordinate institution, using the models of Barnard at Columbia and Pembroke at Brown. By the end of the year the trustees had obtained from the state of Vermont a charter to establish the Women's College of Middlebury.

Insufficient funds prevented Middlebury from establishing a separate college for women.[16] Women students continued to attend the same college exercises as the men students, with the exception of freshman recitations beginning in 1904 and chapel in 1906. The college catalogues described a women's college, however, in an attempt to reassure prospective men students (Stameshkin 1985, 221–222). In 1908, for example, the catalogue had a separate section entitled "The Women's College," which included the following description of its history:

> In 1902 a charter was granted for an affiliated College for Women, and steps have been taken towards two coordinate institutions, one for men and one for women, as fast as resources have allowed. It is believed that both men and women are better for the distinct social life of a separate College, but that the greater economy in administration and instruction when the education of both sexes is conducted under the same corporate management and by the same Faculty justifies affiliated institutions in the same location. (1907–08 Catalogue, MCA)

Women students at Middlebury were concerned about these developments. While their complaints did not extend to some of the issues that women of today would fight against—the injustice of the college's spending a far greater proportion of its resources on men students' needs when women lacked such basic requirements as adequate housing—they did at first worry that a coordinate system would deprive them "of full rights and privileges." According to an article in the student newspaper, this reaction did not last. Instead, the women students soon developed "a spirit of unity and common interest" and came to believe that "under the new conditions, [they would obtain] a surer and more recognized place" (*Middlebury Campus*, February 1905, MCA).

Comparisons Between Wells and Middlebury Colleges

By the beginning of the twentieth century, women students at Middlebury College had demonstrated that they were capable not only of doing the same academic work as the men students, but excelling at it. Yet their institutional position was not secure. The college had admitted them for its own survival, not out of concern for women's education. To see whether and in what ways the lack of a college's commitment to its women students mattered, in this section I compare the turn-of-the-century experiences of women students at Middlebury with those at Wells, a college that was founded expressly for women.

Wells College did not easily break with its founder's assumptions about women's "nature" and education appropriate for women's "separate sphere." While over the years the college did change in a more academically serious, collegiate direction, it remained influenced by its founder's desires to impart Christian education of a refining nature to wealthy young women in a home-like setting. Tuition continued to be expensive, and until the end of the nineteenth century, enrollments were sufficiently low to permit students to live in one building under the supervision of the (woman) dean. Wells did finally eliminate its preparatory department in 1895, however, making it more similar to Vassar College, with which it was often compared. An article in *The Independent* newspaper in 1897 on eight women's colleges described Wells as "a dainty little college" but noted that its courses of study were "of the same grade as those of the men's colleges." The article went on to compare Wells with Vassar: "Here, as at Vassar, there is special training in home and social graces, the Dean in her lovely parlors having no other care than the cultivation of morals and manners of those in her charge" (Wells College Catalogue 1897–98, WCA).

Middlebury College, in contrast, struggled to maintain itself, in public image and in fact, as a men's college that happened to have some women students. Middlebury did not describe itself as a home, nor was it concerned with refining its women students, but rather it permitted women to attend a men's college and succeed if they could. Even after women were admitted, the president of Middlebury, Ezra Brainerd, referred to the aims of college in terms that applied better, if not exclusively, to men: "a school of general culture, of liberal education, such as any youth should have who aspires after the highest manhood" (*The Undergraduate*, July 1886, MCA).

Table 3.1 presents information to assess whether, by the end of the century, Middlebury was beginning to accommodate itself more to its women students, and whether Wells was giving its students sound academic training. It appears that the colleges had converged somewhat, but Wells had moved more in the direction of academic rigor than Middlebury had moved in the direction of support for its women students.

At the end of the nineteenth century, Wells and Middlebury Colleges were both small colleges, with total enrollments of less than 110 students. Wells was smaller than Middlebury, however, since it had only 59 full-time students and 31 part-time students ("specials"), whereas all of

TABLE 3.1 Comparisons of Wells and Middlebury College at the End of the Nineteenth Century

	Wells	Middlebury
A. Size		
No. of students	90 in 1898, including 31 "specials"	104 in 1898 (plus 3 graduate students), 45 of whom were women
No. of faculty	18, including the president, 1898	11, including the president, 1898
B. Indicators of wealth of students attending		
% out of state	1898–99: 62/90 or 69%	1898–99: 40% of all students; 37% of men, 47% of women
Tutition charged	$100 in 1898	$60 total for 3 terms, 1898
C. Academic rigor		
No. of faculty with Ph.D.	5 of 18 or 28%	1 of 11 or 9%
Admissions requirements	1898: tested on Latin & one other language; Math (algebra incl. quadratic equations, plane geom.); History (Amer., Greek & Roman); English. No exam if certificate of Regents.	1898: tested on Latin, (Greek for classical course); Algebra through quadratics, four books of plane geometry; History (Greek and Roman); Geography; English. For Latin-Sci. course, in place of Greek & Greek hist, Amer. Hist., Amer. Lit., French, or German. No exam if student had certificate from a school with a classical course.
Graduation requirements	1898: 1 yr. of Latin, 1 yr. of French or German, Math, English, Hygiene, Biblical Lit. (2 yrs.), Chemistry, History, Physics, Psychology, Ethics. Only B.A. degree.	Classical course required many hrs of Latin & Greek, fewer of German. Latin-Scientific course — Latin & more German. Both courses required Math, English, Philosophy, Logic, History, Poli. Sci., Physics, Chemistry, Natural History. French was an elective.
D. Support for Women Students		
Dean of women?	Yes	No, not until 1909
Women trustees?	Yes, 3 of 17 in 1898	No
Women faculty	13 of 18 (1898)	No women on faculty until dean of women who also taught sociology, 1909

TABLE 3.1 Continued

	Wells	Middlebury
Women students' activities	8 societies by 1898: a social sciences club with debates; a literary society; bicycling, tennis and basketball; student self-government; YWCA; boat club.	By 1899, 2 sororities, YWCA, Ladies Glee Club, tennis. Newspaper & yearbook staff mixed sex but women in lower positions. No student govt.
Scholarships for women students	Beginning in 1894, a "limited number" of annual scholarships of $30-$100. Several more scholarships by the end of the century.	Beginning in 1898, $100 annual scholarship from the Emma Willard Association for "deserving young women."
Women speakers on campus	Yes, including Jane Addams, Ida Tarbell, Ellen Swallow Richards. In 1899, 6 out of 11 campus speakers were women.	No record of any

Information comes mainly from college catalogues, supplemented by student handbooks and yearbooks. Trustees' and faculty's gender was determined by my inspection of their first names, as well as the institutions from which they received their degrees. In cases of doubt, I alternated assigned gender.

Middlebury's 104 students studied full-time. Yet Wells had a greater number of faculty—16 compared to 12 at Middlebury—supporting its claim that it fulfilled what a later president of Wells called "the duty of caring," provided by "the intimacy of contact of student with student, and student with professor" (Kerr D. Macmillan, "The College Home," Wells College Bulletin, October 1920, WCA).

Wells attracted wealthier students than did Middlebury. Table 3.1 shows that tuition costs were higher at Wells and a greater percentage of students came from out of state, especially beyond the Northeast area.[17] The family backgrounds of Middlebury's *women* students may have been closer to those of Wells's students than to those of Middlebury men students, however. Many Middlebury men students paid for their tuition by working part-time or even taking off brief periods from college in order to work, with the result that the average age of men graduates was higher than at colleges with wealthier students. Middlebury women, in comparison, had fewer job opportunities or scholarships available to them and so presumably came from families that could afford to pay for their education (Stameshkin 1985, 272). Nonetheless, even if Middlebury women did not have family backgrounds as modest as Middlebury men, their families were probably not as wealthy as Wells students' families. Middlebury was not attempting to appeal to the desire of wealthy families to "finish" or refine their daughters. It did not claim to provide training in social graces the way Wells College did.

The academic program of Wells College changed dramatically between 1868, when it opened as a seminary, and the end of the century. The original teaching staff had no formal academic credentials, but by 1898, one-quarter of the faculty at Wells had their Ph.D.s (excluding President Waters, who also had a Ph.D.). Such a change was not achieved solely by hiring men, as two of the four faculty with their Ph.D.s were women, one in mathematics. Yet seven of the sixteen Wells faculty did not have any academic degrees. Most of the faculty without academic degrees taught subjects where this might not matter—German language, for example, and art and music. But one woman without a degree taught chemistry, and another taught ancient and modern history. In comparison, only one of Middlebury College's eleven faculty in 1898 had his Ph.D., but all of the faculty had some degree (as they all had in 1868 as well). Two of the degrees were in law (LL.D.), one was in medicine (M.D.), and four were master's degrees (A.M.) (1898–99 Catalogue, MCA).

Requirements for admission to Wells, as well as the requirements for graduation, became more stringent between 1868 and the end of the century. Wells's requirements were still not as conventionally rigorous as those at Middlebury, however, since students at Wells never had to study Greek. Yet Wells students were assumed to have studied Latin before they were admitted, as well as another language (French, German, or Greek), and they had to continue taking Latin once at Wells. Similar to other women's colleges, Wells had always required students to study modern languages, since this was one of the ways young women were assumed to become cultured. At Middlebury, by contrast, modern languages were introduced into the curriculum at a somewhat later date and were not emphasized as much.[18] By 1898 Middlebury's classical course, leading to the B.A. degree, required the study of Greek, Latin, and some German. The Latin-Scientific course, first established in 1886 and leading to the B.S. degree, required Latin and more German, but French was an elective. One notable difference in the curriculum was that Wells, but not Middlebury, required students to study Biblical Literature during both their first and second years. Wells also offered many courses in art and music, especially music. Although these subjects were not required, "ladies" were assumed to want to increase their proficiency in such refinements. In comparison, Middlebury offered no art or music courses until the second decade of the twentieth century.[19]

How little Middlebury College supported its women students, and how much, therefore, their success was due to their own extraordinary efforts, is evident from the information presented in Table 3.1. Middlebury remained almost an entirely male environment, with no dean of women, no women on the Board of Trustees, nor any women faculty, for more than twenty years after the first women students were admitted. Women students did begin to forge a college life for themselves, however, especially once their numbers increased in the late 1880s, and some of them began to live together in college housing after 1891. They formed some of their own clubs, joined with men in others (even though they could not hold the top positions), and in their sororities, developed leadership skills and experienced solidarity with other women.

The situation at Wells contrasted markedly with that of Middlebury in terms of support given to women students. Partly because of the ideology about women's nature that was prevalent when Wells opened in 1868, many women staff and faculty were hired. Women had positions of power, too, especially the dean and, beginning in 1887, women trustees. Wells had many campus clubs and organizations, which meant that women students had practice at administration and leadership.[20] Some clubs were unusual for women at the time. The Social Science Club, for instance, which was founded in 1890, conducted debates using parliamentary procedures. In 1897 the issues debated included: "Is the expenditure of wealth for luxuries a benefit to society?" "Should women engage in professional or industrial pursuits?" "Does the Monroe Doctrine warrant President Cleveland's message to Congress in regard to the Venezuela question?" and "Does prohibition prohibit?" (1897 Yearbook, WCA). Before the end of the century, Wells women had the beginnings of self-government, although at first their power was limited to such relatively minor issues as the length and times for quiet periods, chapel attendance, and daily exercise (1897–98 Catalogue, WCA).

Another way colleges support their students is through scholarships and financial aid. Since Henry Wells planned the collegiate institution he founded for wealthy young women, it is not surprising that he did not provide for scholarships. Their lack became a major concern of the president and trustees in the late 1890s, however. A financial drive produced enough money for three or four scholarships, and in 1899 seniors established Wells College's first endowed scholarship (Dieckmann 1995, 53, 88).

Given the modest backgrounds of most Middlebury students, the college had long offered its men students financial aid. In fact, estimates are that Middlebury men paid only a small proportion of the tuition and fees, probably no more than 20 to 40 percent (Stameshkin 1985, 180). In keeping with the college's treatment of women students generally, they were not at first given scholarships nor allowed to compete for the same prizes (which had monetary value) as the men students. But in 1891 the trustees, at the urging of the president, increased the monetary awards for college prizes and allowed women to compete for them on the same terms as the men. Women began winning the prizes in numbers far greater than their proportion of the student body. In 1891–92, for example, women won six of the twelve prizes even though less than 24 percent of the students were women. In the 1890s Middlebury also obtained $2000 from the New York Emma Willard Association to endow a fund for women students' financial aid (Stameshkin 1985, 220). Thus Emma Willard, the famous woman educator who had begun her career in Middlebury, was finally mentioned in the college catalogue, if only in the list of scholarships.

Not surprisingly, special events at Wells were more tailored to the tastes and concerns of young women than they were at Middlebury. In the earliest years of Wells, well-known men were invited to give speeches, but beginning in the 1890s some nationally famous women came to campus (see Chapter 2). In contrast, the only mention of nationally known women at Middlebury during the nineteenth century appears to have been a joke. The student newspaper reported in 1884 that Victoria Woodhull and Frances Willard had participated in a mock election day convention. The idea of these controversial women, known to have pro-suffrage stances, coming to Middlebury was apparently considered intrinsically ludicrous.[21]

By the end of the nineteenth century Wells College was much stronger academically than it had been when it opened in 1868, and Middlebury College had begun to support its women students more than it had when women entered in 1883. Yet neither college had overcome its historical legacies sufficiently to be acceptable to the ACA (Association of Collegiate Alumnae). Alumnae of Wells were rejected because Wells had too few graduates of its collegiate course and had eliminated its preparatory department only in 1895; Middlebury's alumnae were rejected because Middlebury did not have a dean for the women students, any women faculty, nor any women on the Board of Trustees. These rejections so upset the alumnae of both colleges that they pressured their respective colleges to change in appropriate ways. Middlebury did not obtain a woman faculty member (who was also dean) until 1909, however, and rather than allowing women to become trustees, it set up an "advisory" board for women in 1913. Not until 1921 was Middlebury accredited by the national organization that developed from the ACA, the A.A.U.W. or American Association of University Women (Gertrude Cornish Milliken, "Brief History of the Advisory Board of the Women's College of Middlebury, 1913 to 1949," MCA).

To succeed at Middlebury College, women students had to be academically well-prepared, determined, and willing to forgo some of the pleasures of college life available at women's colleges. Middlebury's first women students were like pioneers at other colleges—serious, capable scholars. But their very success and their increasing numbers caused many men students and trustees to become concerned. How to keep Middlebury a men's college, even though the financial success of the college appeared to depend on having women students, was an issue that concerned trustees and presidents of the college for the next forty years. Middlebury never did find sufficient funds to establish a true coordinate college for women as permitted by its 1902 charter. Whether this was an advantage or disadvantage for Middlebury's women students can be better seen by comparing their experiences with those of women students at another college which was a coordinate of a men's college from its beginning—William Smith College, founded in 1908 as the coordinate of Hobart College. How women students fared under this coordinate arrangement is the subject of the next chapter.

Notes

1   In 1883 Columbia University, responding to women's petitions for entry, allowed women to take examinations and receive degrees, but no provisions were made for their study toward the degree (Woody 1929 II, 312). It was not until 1889 that Barnard College, the coordinate of Columbia, was formally organized.

2   One indication of how poor students were is the percent of mature students, since they had to earn money before or during college to support their studies. Like many other colleges in New England in the nineteenth century, Middlebury had a rather high percent of students over 21 years old. Between 1838 and 1850, 29 percent of Middlebury's students were over 21 years old, compared to only 8 percent at Harvard but 36 percent at Amherst and Brown (Allmendinger 1979).

3   Interestingly, one of the first black Americans to have graduated from college attended Middlebury. Alexander Twilight, class of 1823, apparently "passed" for white, "leaving only an ambiguous census return and a whispered legend to document his racial background" (Stameshkin 1985, 108–109). An openly black American, Martin Henry Freeman, graduated at the top of his Middlebury class in 1849; he later became the president of Liberia College in West Africa (Stameshkin 1985, 179). Lest Middlebury appear to have been an unusuallly progressive institution, however, it should be noted that in the mid-1840s, when a Philadelphia abolitionist tried to get some New England colleges to admit five black students, the president and trustees of Middlebury were opposed on the grounds that having more than one black student might scare away white students (Stameshkin 1985, 318). No other black student besides Freeman appears to have attended Middlebury between 1840 and 1880. In 1899 Middlebury's first black woman student, Mary Annette Anderson, graduated with a B.S. degree. She not only was elected to Phi Beta Kappa, but also was the class's valedictorian (General Catalogue of Middlebury College 1915, MCA).

4   Between 1800 and 1840, 42 percent of Middlebury's graduates entered the ministry; between 1840 and 1880, 23 percent did (Stameshkin 1985, 169).

5   Although records of students' religion were not kept, a historian who has examined the records of graduates who entered the ministry found that about 50 percent of them were Congregationalists (Stameshkin 1985, 90, 171).

6   Between 1811 and 1837, enrollment ranged from a low of 78 in 1816–17 to a record high of 168 in 1836–37 (Stameshkin 1985, 37). It then dropped precipitously, due partly to the dismissal of a very popular professor, so that there were only 46 students in 1840. Average enrollment figures for 1840–1854 were 60 students, and for 1855–60, 79 students (Stameshkin 1985, 137, 150). During the Civil War enrollments dropped again, averaging 63 students (Stameshkin 1985, 152) and did not pick up after, with an average of only 55 students between 1865 and 1879.

7   Even after the railroad made it easier for students to attend colleges farther from home, a surprisingly high percentage of Middlebury's students came from towns within its county—an average of nearly 30 percent between 1865 and 1876 (Stameshkin 1985, 184).

8   See, for example, Leslie, who discusses difficulties faced by three denominational colleges in Pennsylvania (Franklin and Marshall, Bucknell, and Swarthmore) between 1870 and 1915 (Leslie 1977).

9   Emma Willard left Middlebury in 1819 and shortly thereafter established her famous Female Seminary, first in Waterford, New York, then in Troy, New York. For more information about this famous educator, see Lutz (1964).

10   UVM did decide to admit women in 1871, which is presumably why its enrollment rose over the next decade while Middlebury's fell.

11   It may be that elderly President Hamlin wished to admit women on an equal basis with the men students, or it may be that what happened was a result of his deafness, as a popular story relates. A version of this story appeared in the student newspaper in 1932 under the eye-catching headline, "Women have never been officially admitted to Middlebury by Trustees." According to the unidentified author of this article, President Hamlin had thought that trustees had voted to admit women on the same standing as the men. But at the next annual meeting of the trustees, when the minutes of the previous meeting were read, "Dr. Hamlin pricked up his ears. 'What's that?' he said. And they read the vote to him as it had originally stood. 'But I thought—' and he didn't finish his sentence" (*Middlebury Campus*, Feb. 24, 1932, MCA).

12   Of course the UVM student newspaper could not ignore this challenge, considering the history of rivalry between the two institutions. Their responding editorial commented, "We might make a few cautionary suggestions to our friend [the "sister college" of Middlebury] but for fear of giving ourselves away we will refrain . . . . We think the editor (of *The Undergraduate*, Middlebury's newspaper] indiscrete [sic] and presumptuous. He seems to take great delight in slurring every paper that comes in sight" (*The University Cynic*, November 7, 1883, UVMA). Three weeks later, the UVM paper noted the following about their "chief," who happened to be reading "Exchanges" (the column with news from other colleges): "Presently a smile expressive of deep sympathy makes its appearance. He is reading *The Undergraduate* and sympathizes with that journal in the vexations to which it is subject, and is already enjoying (?), by the presence of the co-eds . . . he makes no comment upon the matter however" (*The University Cynic*, November 28, 1883, UVMA).

13   According to Stameshkin (1985, 333) the percentage of young women in sororities ranged from a high of 88 percent between 1889 and 1900 to a low of 59 percent between 1911 and 1920, approximately the same percentage as that of young men in fraternities.

14   In 1969 Maureen Crowley became the second woman since 1947 to hold the position of editor-in-chief of the college newspaper. The outgoing male editor-in-

chief, James Trombettta, said he "didn't usually approve of women being given positions of such responsibility" but in this case there was little choice (quoted in Eileen O'Brien, "The Myth of Coeducation: A History of Exclusion in Women's Higher Education at Middlebury College," Thesis submitted for Honors Degree in the Department of History, 1991, 60, MCA).

15 Marion Dunbar did continue her education after Middlebury, attending the Boston Law School and Cornell University, eventually getting both her LL.B. and J.D. from Boston University in 1905 (General Catalogue 1950, MCA).

16 The closest Middlebury came to having a coordinate women's college was actually much later, in the 1930s. Even then, however, the national depression and consequent lack of funds prevented the plan from being fully implemented. See Chapter 5 for a discussion of these developments.

17 While in 1898 only 2 of Middlebury's 43 out-of-state students came from beyond the Northeast (one from Chicago, the other from Cedar Rapids, Iowa), over 50 percent of Wells's 62 out-of-state students did (this number includes "special" students, but eliminating them changes the percentage very little).

18 At least on a continuous basis. In his history of Middlebury College's language schools, Stephen Freeman presents evidence that German was first taught in 1821, four years before Harvard introduced the subject. French and German were "continuously" offered at Middlebury only after 1880, however (Freeman 1975, 2–6). Middlebury students sometimes complained about the lack of foreign languages and the requirement to study Greek and Latin. In 1874, for example, members of the junior class petitioned the board of trustees to be able to study German (Minutes of the Corporation of the Board, 1874).

19 In 1912 Middlebury added Dramatic and Social Arts (as well as Home Economics) "to meet the special needs of women students." By the following year, the program had become "Fine Arts and Music" and was open to both men and women students (Middlebury College Catalogues, 1912–13, 1913–14, MCA).

20 The presidents of some Wells campus clubs were women faculty members, however. The president of the Social Science Club in 1897, for instance, was a woman professor of Latin (1897 Yearbook, WCA).

21 Other parts of the same article went to greater lengths to be funny, viz. about the idea of someone portraying Dr. Beecher, who in turn was representing presidential candidate Cleveland: "We would say here, that the doctor had missed his breakfast and was not feeling his best." But no additional comments were felt to be necessary about Victoria Woodhull, the notorious spiritualist and advocate of free love as well as women's suffrage (Underhill 1995), or Frances Willard, the former president of the Evanston College for Ladies, later president of the Women's Christian Temperance Union, which she transformed into a strong women's movement in support of women's suffrage (James 1971).

Chapter 4

"Free from the Drawbacks . . . Observed in Coeducation": The Coordinate College, William Smith

By 1908, when William Smith College was opened as an annex of Hobart, the men's college, women were well established in institutions of higher education—"as plentiful as blackberries on summer hedges," as M. Carey Thomas expressed it (Thomas 1908, 66). Over one-third of the nation's undergraduates were women (Newcomer 1959, 46), and a large majority of the women students were enrolled in coeducational institutions. Yet this was also a time of backlash against women (Palmieri 1987). Some educators feared that higher education was becoming "feminized," since women's enrollments at coeducational colleges and universities had increased more than sixfold between 1875 and 1900, whereas men's enrollments had increased only slightly more than threefold (Woody 1929 II, 251). It thus seemed possible that men might become a minority of students enrolled in colleges and universities. Equally alarming to some observers was that the women students often did better academically than the men students (Rosenberg 1988). The presidents and trustees of many coeducational institutions responded by trying to contain the influence of women, either by setting quotas on their admission, as, for example, Stanford University did (Solomon 1985), or by establishing a separate college for their women students, as Middlebury College tried to do.

Another contentious issue around the turn of the century was the effect of higher education on women's marriage and childbearing rates. Statistics showed that women college graduates were less likely to marry and had fewer children than their peers who did not attend college.[1]

Eugenicists charged that women's higher education was encouraging "race suicide," a term popularized in 1905 by President Roosevelt (Palmieri 1987, 57). As a Dartmouth sociology professor expressed it, the growth of the "college habit" among women was leading to the "comparative sterilization of superior stocks" (Wells 1909, 739). Critics debated whether it was higher education of women that caused their lower fertility, single-sex education in particular, or the content of the curriculum (cf. *Journal of Heredity*, Volume VIII, 1917, for articles representing these different views). While all were variously blamed, it is probably fair to say that women's colleges received most of the negative attention (Palmieri 1987).

Regardless of this backlash against women's education, more women were attending college to prepare themselves for the increasing number of professions open to them. The social activism that characterized the Progressive Era led women to press for an education that did not just provide them with general culture but also with practical courses and appropriate extracurricular experiences. The greatest issue for women's education became not whether women should attend college, but rather the relationship between a college education and women's postgraduate lives (Antler 1982). The practical field of home economics made inroads into the college curriculum, particularly after the founding of the American Home Economics Association in 1909.[2] While critics assailed this new field for its seeming lack of academic rigor, graduates were able to find jobs teaching home economics in high schools and colleges, or apply their knowledge to the increasing number of social work jobs in urban or rural communities (Solomon 1985, 86–87). Medicine and clerical work, which in the 1890s received higher remuneration than teaching, were two other fields that women began to enter in greater numbers and that affected some colleges' curriculums (Cookingham 1984).

This chapter looks at the experiences of women students at William Smith, a college that was established expressly for women but in coordination with a previously existing men's college, Hobart. The manner in which William Smith was established reflected concerns of the early twentieth century; in particular, educating women without "feminizing" a college, and providing women with some practical instruction. Women students' experiences at William Smith differed in significant ways from those of women students at Middlebury, a college that admitted women to survive but that did not adapt to women students' concerns. William Smith was a women's college but not to the degree that completely autonomous Wells College was. I begin with a description of Hobart College before William Smith was established as its coordinate institution.

Hobart College in the Nineteenth Century

Hobart College, named after the Episcopalian Bishop Hobart (1775–1830), developed from Geneva Academy in Geneva, New York. Its founding date is generally given as 1822, although technically this was only the year in which the New York State Regents gave it permission to change its status from an academy to a college, once certain financial conditions were met (Smith 1972, 42–43). A major reason for establishing Hobart, originally called Geneva College, was to prepare young men for the Episcopalian ministry. By the second decade of the nineteenth century, the town of Geneva had a population of over 1,200 and a small Episcopalian Church, many of whose parishioners were well-to-do families who had recently moved from Virginia with their slaves in search of good farmland (Smith 1972, 9–10). The city, on the northern shore of Seneca Lake, one of the largest of the "finger lakes," seemed a promising place to establish a college that although nonsectarian, could promote the development of the Episcopalian Church in western New York.

The Episcopalian leanings of Hobart meant that its atmosphere was distinctly different from the more severe and Calvinist environment at Middlebury College. Bishop Hobart had had negative experiences at Princeton, which he described as a "dark and dismaying . . . temple of Calvinism" (Smith 1972, 27). He therefore set his college in a "high church" direction through his opposition to presbyterianism and Bible societies (Smith 1972, 130). Religious revivals never occurred at Hobart as they did quite frequently at such evangelical campuses as Middlebury.

Although it is accurate to consider Hobart a nonsectarian college, in that students, faculty, and trustees were not required to be Episcopalian, and church doctrines were not part of the curriculum, the ties between the college and the church were quite strong. Periodically during the nineteenth century Hobart had an affiliated theological school (Smith 1972, 103–109), but undoubtedly the most important way the college benefited from its ties to the Episcopalian Church was financially. An annuity from Trinity Church in New York City prevented Hobart College from folding, as many other small colleges of the time did, but it also strengthened the church—college ties, making it clear that Hobart was a "church-related college" (Smith 1972, 98). After 1851, according to a college historian, Hobart was "almost completely dependent upon the Church for its support" (Smith 1972, 145). The choice of faculty became somewhat more restricted, favoring not only Episcopalians but among them, men favorable to high church ritualism.[3]

Hobart students were expected to attend chapel regularly. In the 1860s students had to attend morning and evening prayer and two full services in the chapel on Sunday, "unless excused in order to attend some other place of worship" (1865–66 Catalogue, HWSA). All presidents of the college were ordained ministers (until the 1930s), the Board of Trustees always contained clergymen (in 1868, for example, 8 out of 25 trustees were reverends), and many of the faculty were Episcopal clergymen (the greatest concentration occurred in the 1860s, when five of the faculty were) (Smith 1972, 137).

The men students who enrolled in Hobart College in the nineteenth century generally came from white, Protestant, well-to-do families in New York State.[4] Precise information on their family backgrounds is lacking, but observers at the time, as well as contemporary analysts, concur that Hobart was "a relatively aristocratic college" with many students from "distinguished" New York families (Smith 1972, 115–116, 131). In 1849 the future first president of Cornell University, Andrew Dickson White, studied at Hobart for one year before transferring to Yale. He later described the "majority" of students at Hobart at the time as "sons of wealthy churchmen, showing no inclination to work, and much tendency to dissipation" (White 1905, 18). The difference between the comfortable family backgrounds of Hobart's students in the nineteenth century, and the more modest backgrounds of Middlebury's students, is also suggested by the comparatively young age of Hobart students. Many Middlebury students, but few Hobart students, had to work before or during their college years (Smith 1972, 122).

College life, in the sense of students' solidarity through their pranks and rebellions, developed earlier at Hobart than it did at the sober and religious Middlebury College (Horowitz 1987). More than one recollection of college life mentioned cannonballs being rolled down corridors and a horse brought into college buildings. Andrew Dickson White's reminiscences of life at the college provide a vivid description of the "carousing and dissipation" that characterized college life prior to the Civil War. He observed

> a professor, an excellent clergyman, seeking to quell hideous riot in a student's room, buried under a heap of carpets, mattresses, counterpanes and blankets. . . . The president himself, on one occasion, [was] obliged to leave his lecture-room by a ladder from a window, and, on another, kept at bay by a shower of beer-bottles. (White 1905, 19)[5]

Over the course of the nineteenth century more student organizations appeared that helped to bring order into campus life. Notable among these organizations were fraternities (Hobart had four before the Civil War, as well as an "anti-secret" society) and, beginning in the 1860s, athletics, including a boat club with regattas, baseball teams, and lacrosse (Smith 1972, 181).

One way in which Hobart College was distinctive in the nineteenth century was in its curriculum. Besides having the usual classical course, requiring the study of Latin and Greek, it had a more practical course, called the English course (or later, the Scientific course). By the latter part of the century, other colleges, including Wells and Middlebury, also had a course of study that did not require students to study the classics, but Hobart established its English course very early, in 1824. The original prospectus of Hobart, written in 1824, aimed to convince state legislators that "Geneva College" would teach such sciences as chemistry, mathematics, and natural philosophy not only as "liberal sciences" in the classical course but also "practically" in the English course, which would be aimed at farmers and men in manual trades (Smith 1972, 46–48). The early establishment of the English course was a source of pride to Hobart. In the twentieth century Hobart College catalogues, in their brief histories of the college, noted that the establishment of the English course, oriented to "the practical business of life," had enabled students to bypass "a tedious course of classical studies" (1948–49 Catalogue, HWSA).

Another way Hobart College distinguished itself in the nineteenth century involved a woman. Elizabeth Blackwell studied at its affiliated medical school, becoming in 1849 the first woman in the country to receive a regular medical degree.[6] Although the historical record indicates that her admission may not have been intended, and although the Geneva Medical College afterwards admitted only one or two other women, this historical first was something the college later pointed to with pride (Blackwell 1895 [1977], 257; Smith 1972, 78). In 1949 Hobart and William Smith Colleges celebrated the centenary of Elizabeth Blackwell's graduation by giving awards to twelve women medical doctors, and in 1958 they established an annual Blackwell Award, which brings a woman of outstanding achievement to campus and honors her.

William Smith and the Founding of the Coordinate College

Despite the support of the Episcopalian Church, Hobart College continued to have financial problems throughout the nineteenth and early twentieth centuries. Faculty sometimes were not paid or their salaries were reduced. In the 1890s, during a period of national depression, women tried to enter the college. The trustees received two petitions in June 1894 on behalf of women students attending local schools. One petition requested only that women be allowed to take the college's examinations (and that the trustees "consider" the question of conferring degrees on those who passed), but the other petition asked that women be admitted as regular students "on equal terms and conditions with the men" (Trustee minutes, HWSCA). The trustees referred the petitions to a committee, which reported back in June 1895 "setting forth the impracticality of the proposed change in the present financial and other circumstances of the college" (Trustee minutes, HWSCA).

In the early twentieth century Hobart College's financial difficulties were getting worse but its needs were increasing. The college did not have the money to develop areas of the curriculum that many faculty, alumnae, students, and trustees believed to be necessary in an age when elective courses were becoming popular. In 1904 the President of Hobart, Rev. Langdon Stewardson, listed some of the college's needs, including more faculty and new equipment in order to add the fields of biology, physiology and hygiene, Romance languages, and economics; money to raise faculty salaries; and two new buildings, a gymnasium and a dormitory. President Stewardson estimated that the cost of the needed changes would be $500,000 (Stewardson file, HWSCA). This happened to be about the same amount of money that a local rich resident, William Smith, was planning to use to establish a school for women. Given William Smith's beliefs and the type of institution he intended to found, however, it did not at first seem that Mr. Smith's money could help Hobart College.

Like both Henry Wells and Matthew Vassar, William Smith (1818–1912) was a relatively uneducated but successful businessman. Born in England, Mr. Smith emigrated when he was in his twenties and went to Geneva, New York, where he and two brothers established what became a large, prosperous wholesale nursery business. Although he had not had much formal schooling, Mr. Smith was well-read, with a particular interest in astronomy. He never married—he had once been engaged to a woman who died—but lived with his mother in an "imposing" house in Geneva (Smith 1972, 188), which contrasted with his general reputation for being frugal. Mr. Smith's philanthropy included donating money to Hobart College and building an opera house in Geneva. He supported women's suffrage and so allowed the opera house to be used by speakers involved with the political equality movement.

Besides being rich and generous, William Smith was unconventional, at least in terms of his religious beliefs. After his mother died in 1872 he became a spiritualist, expressing his belief in the continued existence of individual souls after death (which many spiritualists preferred to call "transition") and in the possibility of direct communication with disembodied spirits. Like other spiritualists of the late nineteenth century, Mr. Smith saw these beliefs as compatible with scientific inquiry (Moore 1977, 22) and was anxious that fake mediums be exposed (Anna Botsford Comstock, "William Smith," undated, HWSCA). Moreover, Mr. Smith was similar to other spiritualists in being concerned about social injustice and sympathetic to such social reform movements as temperance, abolition, and women's rights (Moore 1977, 70–74). His beliefs and his lack of social polish caused Mr. Smith to experience "a certain ostracism" from conventional society in Geneva (Comstock, undated, HWSCA) which again was the way most spiritualists were treated (Moore 1977, 74, 90). At the same time he was welcomed into the circle of interesting, unusual, but well-connected people who gathered at the nearby home of Elizabeth Smith Miller and her daughter, Anne Fitzhugh Miller.

Elizabeth Smith Miller (1822–1911) was the daughter of the famous, wealthy abolitionist and philanthropist, Gerrit Smith,[7] and a second cousin of Elizabeth Cady Stanton. She became well-known in her own right as a supporter of suffrage, who (with her husband and father) signed the women's rights declaration at the 1850 convention in Worcester, Massachusetts. She and her daughter formed the Geneva Political Equality Club in 1897, and each successively held the position of honorary president. Although Amelia Bloomer's name is associated with women's reform dress, it was actually Elizabeth Smith Miller who was the first woman to wear "bloomers" on a continuous basis before the Civil War (Kesselman 1991).[8] The Miller mother-daughter combination was also known for their entertainment of reformers and progressives, in what could perhaps be described as a rural salon, in their beautiful house outside of Geneva. Elizabeth Smith Miller was, like William Smith, in favor of women's suffrage and sympathetic to spiritualism, at least toward the end of her life. Most importantly, in terms of her influence on the founder of William Smith College, Elizabeth Smith Miller was known to her contemporaries for her "passion" for the "broader education of women" (*Geneva Daily Times,* 1915, HWSCA).

One of the persons the Millers entertained and introduced to William Smith was Felix Adler (1851–1933) who later became one of Mr. Smith's trustees. Adler was well-known for establishing the Ethical Culture Society; he also founded the first free kindergarten in New York City as part of his concern for the plight of the urban poor (Wollons 1990).[9] It was also at the Millers' house in Geneva that Mr. Smith, then over 80 years old, met Anna Botsford Comstock, who was to play a critical role in the founding of William Smith College. An active, intelligent woman, Anna Botsford Comstock (1854–1930) was very different from the Millers in her educational background, beliefs, and political attitudes. She had studied at Cornell University in the 1870s when it first admitted women, overlapping with M. Carey Thomas, future president of Bryn Mawr.[10] Anna Comstock became a celebrated wood engraver, specializing in depicting insects; a writer of successful science books, some with her husband, John Henry Comstock (a well-known entomologist), and some on her own; and an instructor in normal schools, the Teacher's College at Columbia, the Chautauqua Institute, and Cornell University. In 1913 she was appointed assistant professor at Cornell, and later promoted to full professor (Comstock 1953). In 1923 the National League of Women Voters honored Anna Botsford Comstock as one of the "twelve greatest living American women."

Despite being neither a spiritualist nor active in the women's rights movement,[11] Anna Botsford Comstock became a close friend of William Smith's, someone he felt he could trust and who supported his general desire to do something for women's education. She admired him, too; she called him "a remarkable man . . . [who] had an exalted idea of the place of women in the world; he believed they should be educated and fitted in every way for motherhood" (Comstock 1953, 211).

When William Smith first met Anna Comstock, he was planning to build a spiritualist college for women, and in fact, had begun excavations for the building. The legal statement for this college, dated 1903, said that the college was to be strictly nonsectarian, with no denominational or sectarian clergymen to be appointed as trustees. The curricula of studies were specified; they included natural science, hygiene, music and art, and practical courses for women wanting to earn their own livelihood, but gave special prominence to the "science of psychology" which would reveal "the powers of the mind." The college would provide opportunities for professors and advanced students to do Psychic Research in order to "demonstrate, if possible, the continuity of life after death and of communion between the mortal and spirit realm" (William Smith file, documents, HWSCA). Six trustees of the college were named; one of them, Benjamin Austin, a Methodist minister who had been in charge of a female seminary in Toronto and who also claimed to be a spiritualist, was appointed president.

Anna Comstock agreed to help Mr. Smith with his project of establishing a college for women, but she and some of his trustees did not agree with all aspects of his plans. Comstock was dismayed by Austin, the minister appointed as president of the planned spiritualist college, who, with his daughter, had lived with Mr. Smith for a winter (Smith 1972, 189). Comstock later wrote, "He was no longer a Methodist nor could I discover in him any genuine signs of being a Spiritualist. I was very unfavorably impressed." Soon after Anna Comstock became involved with his project, William Smith "paid off" Benjamin Austin, appointed new trustees, and was persuaded to consider other options for an educational institution for women (Comstock, undated, HWSCA). Anna Comstock took an active part in negotiating with Mr. Smith. She understood "so clearly the practical problems," as a trustee remarked (Henry Graves correspondence, December 1903, HWSCA).[12] Comstock also knew how to ascertain Mr. Smith's views, which was not easy since he was "quite unused to expressing his ideas." Comstock developed the technique of talking about other people's ideas and eliminating those of which he disapproved (Comstock, undated, HWSCA). Eventually Mr. Smith had so much confidence in Comstock's understanding of him that he asked her to speak for him on public occasions.

Once William Smith had agreed to abandon his prior plans for a spiritualist institution, to undergo "the humiliation of covering up an unpractical foundation and laying a new one," as a trustee expressed it, new plans had to be formulated (Henry Graves correspondence, Dec. 1903, HWSCA). Mr. Smith's friends and advisors communicated with each other about their own ideas. Anne Miller, for example, favored an industrial coeducational school; Anna Comstock also liked this idea, although she did not object to its being for "girls" only, if that was what William Smith wished (Henry Graves correspondence, July 16, 1904, HWSCA). Other possibilities were not recorded, but a letter of Anna Comstock's indicates that people did not find it easy to make suggestions to Mr. Smith. Comstock commented that she had "several ideas" but was "afraid that the bright colors which characterize them . . . will fade out in the presence of Mr. Smith and his desires" (Henry Graves correspondence, August 4, 1904, HWSCA).

Planning came to a halt when trustee Felix Adler bluntly told William Smith that the building costs of a new institution would use up so much of the half-million dollars he had to give that there would be insufficient funds to endow instruction (Smith 1972, 192). It was at this point that the president of Hobart College, Rev. Langdon Stewardson, became involved. He had previously met Mr. Smith and tried to interest him in "rescuing" Hobart. But at that earlier time Mr. Smith had indicated that he was interested in doing something for women, the "mothers of the race" who deserve "everything their sons can do for them," and he was beginning excavations for a spiritualist college of his own (Stewardson file, 1928, HWSCA). When Stewardson later heard about the impasse in Mr. Smith's planning due to insufficient funds for an independent institution for women, he "made a personal call on each of the advisers" with the idea of using William Smith's money to educate women in conjunction with Hobart College (Smith 1972, 193).

William Smith's trustees agreed that taking advantage of Hobart College's facilities and faculty to educate women would be the best way to accomplish Mr. Smith's goals. They knew, however, that Mr. Smith would be concerned about the relationship between Hobart and the Episcopalian Church. The trustees decided that they needed to convince Mr. Smith that "Hobart College, far from being narrow or sectarian is one of the most liberal colleges in this country" (Worcester to Graves, August 11, 1906, Henry Graves correspondence, HWSCA). Although William Smith was persuaded to establish a women's college in connection with Hobart, he remained concerned about Hobart College's ties to the Episcopalian Church. He insisted that the educational institution for women that he established be strictly nonsectarian.

The form of the association between Hobart's men students and the women students, who would be educated as a result of William Smith's gift, had yet to be determined. Trustees were aware of two models: coeducation, like nearby Cornell University, or coordination, like Radcliffe, Barnard, or Pembroke. In the nation at large, many educators feared that higher education was becoming "feminized" and so had doubts about the wisdom of coeducation. William Smith's trustees were split on the issue of which form would be best in this case. They consulted with a member of Hobart's board of trustees, who expressed the view that "two independent schools with separate instruction for each" would be preferable to coeducation as "it would certainly arouse less opposition among the alumni and students" (Rev. Worcester, Oct. 22, 1906, Henry Graves correspondence, HWSCA). In the end it was Anna Botsford Comstock who made the decision. As she later wrote:

> I have always been a firm believer in co-education from the kindergarten through the university but I did not hesitate a moment to decide that a college for women at Hobart should be co-ordinate. I felt that to make Hobart co-educational would

alienate the alumni and antagonize the undergraduates and, like putting new wine in old bottles, would ruin everything. I know that both Mr. Smith and President Stewardson were glad of this decision. (Comstock, undated, HWSCA)

In December 1906 the trustees of Hobart College held a special meeting to consider a letter from William Smith's trustees that recommended the establishment of "The William Smith School for Women" to be operated "under the Charter of Hobart College."[13] This lengthy document included both general ideological statements, as well as practical arrangements, such as which courses should be taught and how women students were to be housed. One section contained the following statement of William Smith's goals, which shows his adherence to the Republican Motherhood idea (see Chapter 2), and indicates the kind of education he believed women should have—what he liked to refer to as producing "abundant life":[14]

Women are the mothers of the race, and upon them largely depends the character of the men and women of the future. If, in addition to a mental and moral training such as is offered by the regular course at Hobart College, they were given careful instruction in all the laws of life, by which their own physical, mental, moral and spiritual life might be developed harmoniously, not only would they learn to enjoy life themselves, but the effect of such training would result in untold blessing to future generations. (Trustee minutes, December 11, 1906, HWSCA)

William Smith and his trustees wanted the college to offer courses in hygiene, anatomy, biology, and experimental psychology. They specified a nearby estate that was to be bought for the women students, which included a house that could be renovated to create "a suitable home for young women and the female staff of the School." Mr. Smith's gift of about half a million dollars was also to be used to erect a William Smith Hall of Science for physiology, biology labs, and lecture rooms. These facilities were to be available for the use of Hobart's students in the same manner that Hobart's facilities were to be available to students of the "William Smith School." The usual college degrees, B.A., Bachelor of Philosophy, B.S., and master's degrees, were to be open to William Smith students, which, the trustees noted, was important for "attracting serious students." In (unstated) contrast to Hobart students, the women students were to have an entirely "voluntary" and nonsectarian weekday religious service (Trustee minutes, December 11, 1906, HWSCA).[15]

"William Smith School for Women" was established as a "department" of Hobart College, not as an equal partner, a status that did not change for almost forty years. Although the new school/department was not to have its own Board of Trustees, three trustees were to be appointed to Hobart's board to represent William Smith's interests, and one of these had to be a woman.[16] Two additional William Smith trustees were to be appointed as resignations occurred (Trustee minutes, December 11, 1906, HWSCA).

The faculty of Hobart had already unanimously endorsed the idea of a coordinate institution for women students. In a letter to Hobart's trustees the faculty opined that co-ordination would be "free from the drawbacks which have been observed in co-education." They also saw this "combination" as enabling the "women of Geneva and its neighborhood" to have the opportunity for liberal education; apparently they did not envision women coming from afar (Trustee minutes, December 11, 1906, HWSCA).

Thus the coordinate college for women that was founded with William Smith's money was a hybrid. It did not have its own faculty, facilities (except one dormitory), or trustees. But its interests were seen to be somewhat separate from Hobart's; it had its own representatives on the Board of Trustees, and the women students were to be supervised by a dean, at first called a warden, who was initially chosen from the Hobart faculty. William Smith College was not the spiritualist institution that its founder had originally envisioned, but it guaranteed its women students "complete religious equality," and, unusual for the time, made attendance at religious services entirely voluntary (Trustee minutes, December 11, 1906, HWSCA).

Planning the Coordinate College

About a year and a half transpired between the agreement to found the coordinate college, William Smith, and its opening. This time period contrasts with the rushed decision at Middlebury College and meant that a more orderly transition from Hobart as a men's college to a coordinate one was possible. Of course, the large monetary gift from William Smith also differed from the situation at Middlebury in the 1880s, where no money at first was given specifically for women students.

One aspect of planning occurred at the ideological level; that is, President Stewardson and the newly appointed "warden" (later called Dean) of William Smith College, Milton Turk, were careful to reassure Hobart's students and alumni that the projected change would not harm their college. In other words, they were careful to assert that what was *not* happening was a change to coeducation. In December 1906, for example, in an address to the alumni that was published in a college catalogue, President Stewardson first stressed the subordinate nature of the coordinate college: "The relation of the William Smith School to the men's college is . . . *simply* that of a co-ordinate *department* of instruction within the one institution known as Hobart College . . . to be clearly distinguished from what is commonly called co-education" (emphasis mine). He also noted that men and women would not be instructed in the same classes, except perhaps in small, advanced courses. And he pointed out the advantages for Hobart: it would receive the famous observatory (previously owned by William Smith), laboratories for biology and psychology, chairs for these subjects and perhaps also for political economy—"invaluable additions to our college faculty and college equipment." Moreover, the student body would become larger and more varied, and professors' salaries could be increased (Langdon Stewardson, 1906 Bulletin, HWSCA).

Milton Turk, the newly appointed dean of William Smith College, who was also a professor of rhetoric and elocution at Hobart, contributed to favorable publicity about the planned college by writing an article published in the *New York Tribune* in March 1907, entitled "The Ideal College for Women." Even though it was about forty years after some of the earliest women's colleges, including Wells and Vassar, had opened, Turk still felt it necessary to address the "troublous problem of the college woman's health," and claimed that the location of William Smith College would be an advantage in that respect. Turk used a version of the "best of both worlds" argument in this article when he wrote that the planned "'annex'—a co-ordinate department for women"—would make an association of men and women students "possible, but not necessary." Like President Stewardson, he drew a sharp distinction between the coordinate arrangement and coeducation, yet he also noted that "the isolation and 'exclusively feminine atmosphere' which have been complained of in the ordinary woman's college . . . [would] be harmlessly avoided." Turk also claimed a "first": the "first attempt" to try the coordinate arrangement with a "small country college for men" (Milton Haight Turk, "The Ideal College for Women," March 17, 1907, *New York Tribune*, HWSCA).

Other aspects of the planning for the new college dealt with more concrete matters: renovating and furnishing a house for the women students to live in, hiring a housemistress to live with the young women, building a new science hall with equipped laboratories, and finding faculty for the new positions in biology, psychology, and sociology. William

Smith and his trustees were involved in the decisions about housing the women students. Since they saw themselves as creating a new women's college, albeit as an "annex" of a men's college, they had Dean Turk consult "experts" on women's colleges from Radcliffe, Wellesley, Western Reserve, and Wells College. It was the nearby president of Wells, Rev. George Ward, who advised Dean Turk to make sure that the housing provided for the women students was small since mothers would object if their daughters lived in a large building, much of which would be empty for "some time" (Henry Graves correspondence, HWSCA).

A year before William Smith College opened, Hobart College published a bulletin divided into three sections: an address by the president to alumni, the William Smith College Catalogue, and the Hobart College Catalogue. The president's address, in an implicit attempt to reassure the alumni and men students that their college was not being "feminized," mentioned a gymnasium that was being built "to induce men to enter." The William Smith College Catalogue described the same curriculum and admissions requirements as did the Hobart College Catalogue, and there were only minor differences in degree requirements. Yet Hobart students could choose among three degree courses (a classical course, leading to the B.A.; a scientific course, leading to the B.S.; and a philosophical course, leading to the Bachelor of Philosophy degree), whereas William Smith students had only two options (a course in the arts, leading to the B.A. degree, and a scientific course, leading to the B.S. degree). Thus despite Mr. Smith's intentions to open the same courses to women as men students, a few differences did prevail. With respect to religious requirements, William Smith students were freer than Hobart students. While the men students had to attend daily prayers and two services on Sunday, the women students were to have an "unsectarian" daily service with "voluntary" attendance, in line with the stipulations of William Smith's gift (1907–08 Hobart College Bulletin, HWSCA).[17]

The William Smith Catalogue also contained a section that resonated with themes common in women's colleges. College authorities wanted the students to have the "refining influences of well-ordered homes . . . without imposing needless restraint" so that each student would get "such supervision as earnest young women absent from home should receive." True to the advice of the president of Wells College, readers of this prospective college catalogue were reassured that the houses being built "will not be large" as they were trying to be "like a private family" with a "competent lady as its social and domestic head" (1907–08 Hobart College Bulletin, HWSCA).

William Smith College opened to much fanfare in September 1908 with twenty-two students, including three "specials," enrolled in its first class. The mayor of Geneva, who had graduated from Hobart in 1862, gave a speech that expressed his ambivalence about women students. Despite the benefits of young women's "refining" influence, he noted the "strong prejudice against co-education in the mind of the average young person of the male sex . . . accentuated by the fact that the girls have a way of leading their classes and taking prizes." The mayor concluded that Hobart was "wise" not to become coeducational but to make "Smith School for Women . . . co-ordinate to the College proper" (1908–09 Hobart College Bulletin, HWSCA).

Anna Comstock also spoke at the college opening, as someone who understood the Founder's ideal: to give women "the fullness of life . . . to control life instead of being driven by it." She went on to describe what she had learned about the educational needs of women from her travels in Egypt as well as her thirty-four years at Cornell. Using sectarian referents despite William Smith's commitment to nonsectarianism, Comstock argued that women should avoid memorizing to the degree that the Muslims memorized the Koran, but they should learn more facts than did Catholic seminary students. She also noted that women needed to study some subject in depth and learn how to make a home, care for children, and build character (1908–09 Hobart College Bulletin, HWSCA).

Men students recorded their reactions to these events, and to the presence of women students more generally, in their student newspaper. They sounded bitter and a bit envious when they compared the "most elaborate send off" of the opening of "Smith College" to Hobart College's "severely plain" opening. They also made it clear that they were not delighted to see women on their campus:

> It is a very strange, and, to many men, very unpleasant sight to meet girls on the same footing of fellow-students either on recitation days or socially . . . . It is the strangeness and incongruity of their being permanently in spots that the man has held sacred to himself that shocks him. (Hobart Herald, October 1908, HWSCA)

Rather than accepting the argument of President Stewardson, whose written messages reminded students and alumni of the benefits to them of William Smith's large monetary gifts, the Hobart student newspaper stressed how indebted the women students should feel to Hobart. In the newspaper's words, the "Smith students" had entered a "full-fledged college" and as they were benefiting from "all the prestige of Hobart's name and traditions," they should not be "unmindful of this debt." Even when the "newness and perfect equipment" of the Science Hall were praised, writers in Hobart's newspaper did not feel it necessary to mention that the hall was a gift of William Smith (*Hobart Herald*, October 1908, HWSCA).

Some of the men students' reactions to women students were patronizing and sarcastic, hardly disguised by humor. Even before William Smith opened, an "original comic opera" called "The Invaders," written by a Hobart student, was performed at both the college and the town opera house. It included women characters named "Susie Simple, who giggles," and others suggestive of nearby cities—"Bessie Buffalo" and "Salome Syracuse" ("The Invaders" file, 1906, HWSCA). Shortly after Wiliam Smith students arrived, the Hobart newspaper reported on an "interview" with "Miss T. Twitty Twiggs of Smith College '12." The young woman talked at length about making fudge and being popular with boys; the reporter fell asleep. This was his fault, however, as he should have known better than to undertake such an interview without precautions against sleep (*Hobart Herald*, October 1908, HWSCA). Hobart students also expressed some positive feelings about the presence of women students, however. For example, at a reception marking the opening of the women's dormitory house, a reporter noted that it was "made more interesting by the presence of those mysterious coeds . . . [he] found them . . . just real girls" (*Hobart Herald*, October 1908, HWSCA).

In general, Hobart students' reactions to the entry of women students were more negative than the reactions of Middlebury's men students twenty-five years earlier. Several factors account for this difference. The first is simply that fewer women entered Middlebury initially (6, out of a total enrollment of 42, or 14 percent; or if "special" students are not included, 3 out of 36 or 8 percent) than was true of Hobart (22 women, out of a total enrollment of 105, or 21 percent). Secondly, Middlebury College was in a more precarious state before admitting women than was Hobart, so presumably Middlebury men were relieved to see the college's enrollment increase, even if this was due to women. And thirdly, times had changed over these twenty-five years; people such as the mayor of Geneva knew the reputation of women for outshining men academically and were worried that the masculine image of their college would be tainted. While Middlebury men had originally seemed confident of the ability to maintain the "rights of the masculine element" (see Chapter 3), by the time William Smith opened, Middlebury men students were also concerned about the feminization of their college. Middlebury trustees became worried to the extent of taking legal action to establish a women's college affiliated with Middlebury.

Women Students' College
Experiences at William Smith

The first class of William Smith was sufficiently large (22 students) to construct a college life for itself. Moreover, an institutional framework had been established that acknowledged these young women and at least some of their needs. Students resided together in a dormitory with a house mistress who lived with and supervised them. Although no women were on the regular faculty, Mr. Turk served as dean of the new college, and a few curricular innovations had been made in the name of women students. The college appointed a music instructor, for example, for a new department which was not open to Hobart students, and also established a department of domestic science (1907–08 Hobart College Bulletin).

William Smith students rapidly made their presence felt. At receptions given in their honor, they played cards and astonished Hobart men by their ability to parry their "sallies" with "sang froid" (*Hobart Herald*, October 1908, HWSCA). During the spring semester of the first year of the coordinate college, Hobart's newspaper mentioned a mysterious club at William Smith—"the A.B.I. literary, sewing and woman suffrage secret society" (*Hobart Herald*, February 1909, HWSCA). That same semester William Smith students made decisions not to allow "fraternities" (sororities) to "taint" their college elections and to issue a yearbook in their senior year (*Hobart Herald,* February 1909, HWSCA).

By June of their first year William Smith students had formed a student newspaper. This gave William Smith students, in contrast to Middlebury's women students, their own forum to express their views and to report on events of interest to them. The first issue, for example, included reports on class elections, the formation of a self-government committee, their first dramatic performance, and the beginning of construction of a new college dorm. William Smith students used their newspaper not only to report on local and college events but also to comment on national events which had direct relevance to them. For example, in 1912 a student responded to an article that had appeared in *The Atlantic Monthly* on the disappearance of the "lady." Rather than women no longer being ladies, this student argued, the notion of the lady had changed to include the notion of "social salvation" or philanthropy done by women like Jane Addams (*The Ridge*, May 1912, HWSCA). In 1914, an issue of the newspaper contained an essay that argued against many articles that had appeared in the national press criticizing "the college girl." This piece was followed by two essays, one in favor of women's suffrage, the other against, which were sophisticated in their use of statistics, information about legislation in various states, and writings of such national figures as Charlotte Perkins Gilman (*The Ridge*, April 1914, HWSCA).

In many ways William Smith functioned like an entirely separate women's college. It had its own student government, and the students ran many organizations on their own, which besides a newspaper and yearbook included a glee club, dramatics, and athletics (with class, rather than inter-collegiate, teams). William Smith students sponsored receptions and dances, and they developed their own traditions. As a member of the class of 1917, Elizabeth Durfee, later wrote, "Everything, except the dances, was for William Smith alone. We were a separate college and gloried in that fact. We had our own Dramatic Association, Christian Association, Athletic Association and Glee Club" (Durfee '17, "William Smith College in the Mid Teens," 1975, HWSCA). The sense of power that the William Smith students must have gotten from starring in their own dramatic performances and playing men's roles is evident from the comment of a student reporter concerning her peer who had the role of an emperor in an operetta: she "never for a moment forgot that she was 'Lord of all she surveyed'" (*The Ridge*, June 1910, HWSCA).

Women were prominent in the college symbolically, too. At the end of the first year, a painting of Elizabeth Blackwell, given to William Smith College by Elizabeth Smith Miller, was unveiled during a ceremony at the student dormitory, Blackwell House. A niece of Elizabeth Blackwell spoke about her aunt's life, including the difficulties she had as a medical student at Geneva College (*The Ridge*, June 1909, HWSCA). The second dormitory built for William Smith College students was also named for a woman— Elizabeth Smith Miller. At the ceremony for the laying of the cornerstone, trustee Anna Comstock gave a speech about Miller's life, explaining why it was "so fitting" that the new dorm should be named after her (*The Ridge*, January 1910, HWSCA). Anna Comstock herself was later honored in the same way, when another dormitory for women was given her name. Thus women's lives were placed at the center of William Smith College. Not only were outstanding women commemorated by having buildings named after them, but homage was given to them at ceremonies in which women played central roles.

In a manner that was somewhat similar to Henry Wells's paternalism, William Smith had personal ties with the students of the college he founded. Students occasionally visited him at his house, and he attended some of their functions at the college. A student of the class of 1913 later recalled how William Smith would send the students a bushel of pears from his own orchards (Teresa Stevens Kane '13, Founder's Day Address 1975,

HWSCA), a gift not as munificent as those Henry Wells gave to the students of the college he founded, but nonetheless, an expression of Mr. Smith's regard. By the time the college opened, William Smith was very old, however, and he died during the first class's senior year.

Trustees who represented the college on Hobart's board maintained close ties with the students, too. Correspondence between trustees Anna Comstock and Henry Graves shows that both of them remained vitally interested in the college's affairs, monitoring not only its academic program, faculty, and finances, but students' social lives as well. These trustees were both concerned, for example, about the propriety of the "new dances" that they had seen students do. Anna Comstock expressed herself strongly on this issue, first complimenting Graves on taking the "time and energy to fight the DEVIL in his guise of modern dances." She put herself on record as firmly against William Smith students doing these dances: "I'd rather see a girl of mine take Lady Godiva's ride than to see her dancing in that way. (Yes—even if her hair weren't so luxuriant—as was Lady Godiva's)" (Henry Graves correspondence, May 1913, HWSCA). These views did not prevail, however, and students continued to dance.

Women's issues, including suffrage, received attention during the early years of William Smith College. When the famous militant English suffragette, Emmeline Pankhurst, spoke in Geneva in 1909 at the opera house that Mr. Smith had built, students at William Smith were given tickets by Elizabeth Smith Miller to attend (Huff 1984, 339). In 1914 a professor from Cornell, Nathaniel Schmidt, who had been one of William Smith's original advisors, spoke on universal suffrage at the home of one of the trustees who lived in Geneva. William Smith students attended this event and were given a suffrage banner in the name of Elizabeth Smith Miller (who was by then too feeble to attend in person). This occasion inspired twenty William Smith students to form a college political equality club (*The Ridge*, January 1914, HWSCA).

College curriculum also reflected women's concerns. A sociology course in theory, which was open to students of both colleges, noted in its description that it would discuss "sex distinctions and woman's suffrage" (1907–08 Hobart College Bulletin). A professor of English used an extract from Defoe's *An Academy for Women* (1697) in the midyear exams she gave to first-year students (Henry Graves correspondence, Jan. 30, 1914, HWSCA). And once suffrage had been granted to the women of New York State in 1917, the sociology and economics departments developed a short course designed to increase women students' awareness of political issues (*The Ridge*, November 1917, HWSCA).

Yet while William Smith College functioned like a women's college in many ways, it was subordinate to the older and richer men's college, Hobart. Women students were clearly aware that men's needs and activities were given institutional priority, and presumably most accepted the situation since it fitted in with the larger culture's views of men's and women's positions. In the first issue of the William Smith newspaper, a student expressed her understanding of the colleges' relations in this poignant manner:

> We do not blame those who regretted that we were coming, but we hope that now, at the close of the first year of William Smith College, the students of Hobart find their college life unchanged. We appreciate the courtesy which the new college has received from the old, and are grateful for it. (*The Ridge*, June 1909, HWSCA)

Although William Smith's status as a "department" of Hobart was generally not recognized, since William Smith was referred to as a "college," the differential positions of the two colleges were emphasized in other ways. The number of William Smith students was kept to about one-half of Hobart students, except during wartime; the Board of Trustees, which had a total of nineteen members, had only three to five representatives of William Smith College (and they were not distinguished as such in catalogues); and the better facilities were located on the Hobart campus. Early students' reminiscences refer to Hobart as "the" campus, and mention the requirement that they be chaperoned if they walked there, with the result that William Smith students often had to go longer distances to avoid breaking this rule (Durfee '17, 1975; Rosalind Daniels '18, Recollections and diary, 1975, HWSCA). William Smith College's first crude gym, a remodeled barn, was furnished with old equipment from Hobart's. A couple of students from the earliest classes at William Smith recalled the smell of the gym. As one explained, "The college had been unable to evict one tenant when they took [the barn] over. It was the homestead of a family of skunks" (Durfee '17, 1975, HWSCA). Hobart, in contrast, had a new gym, an observatory obtained from Mr. Smith, a large chapel, a library, and several residence halls and classroom buildings (1907–08 College catalogues, HWSCA).

Comparisons Among William Smith, Middlebury, and Wells Colleges

William Smith shared many similarities with the two other private liberal arts colleges, Wells and Middlebury, that I have discussed in previous chapters. All three were small institutions, located in rural communities; they all offered primarily a liberal arts curriculum, despite occasional experiments in some more practical courses; and although nondenominational, they were affiliated with Christian churches. Yet the ways in which these colleges accommodated their women students varied; moreover, partly in response to the demands of women students themselves, the colleges treated women differently at different periods of time. In the final section of this chapter I will compare, for the period around World War I, the college experiences of women students at the three colleges.

Wells College was a strong women's college by the second decade of the twentieth century. In 1914 almost 200 students were enrolled, more than two-fifths of the Wells faculty had their Ph.D.s, requirements for degrees were rigorous, there was a full complement of courses for the liberal arts degree, and endowment was increasing (topping one million dollars by 1923). Themes from earlier years—that the college should function as a home for refined young women and should therefore remain small—were still prevalent, however. The president of Wells inaugurated in 1913, Kerr D. Macmillan, reiterated such themes again and again in his speeches and writings. In 1920, for example, in an open letter to trustees that was reprinted in the college catalogue, Macmillan argued that colleges should avoid the "lure of numbers" which resulted in "barrack-like structures called dormitories" and made students turn to fraternities and clubs to fulfill the "natural desire for a home." Macmillan believed that the ideal number of students was "in the neighborhood" of 200, just the number enrolled at Wells. This size would enable the entire academic community to function as a "family," in which it would be possible for "the regulations of the home" to be few in number, the "liberty" of students to be great, and an "esprit de corps" to develop naturally (Kerr D. Macmillan, Wells College Bulletin 1920, WCA).

Middlebury was still a coeducational college, despite having obtained permission in 1902 from the state of Vermont to establish a coordinated women's institution, yet women and men students were separated in chapel and freshman recitations. Even so, some trustees, administrators, and men students continued to be concerned about the presence of women students, especially as their numbers increased. In 1909 there were actually more women than men students enrolled, and the president of Middlebury learned that the General Education Board (endowed by John D. Rockefeller) might reject the college's application for funds since it seemed that it was on the way to becoming a women's college (Stameshkin 1985, 230). Trustees tried to increase the number of men students by raising funds to build a new gymnasium (the same tactic that was used at Hobart at about the same time) and by offering a scientific course of study that did not require the study of Greek[18] (College Catalogues, MCA; Stameshkin 1985, 213).

Although Middlebury lacked funds to establish the Women's College that existed on paper and was advertised in its catalogues, it did make some attempts to move in this direction. In 1909, with a gift from a wealthy donor and trustee, the college appointed a dean for women who taught several sociology courses only for women students. Thus twenty-six years after women were admitted, the faculty finally included a woman. Before World War I, Middlebury established academic departments believed to be suitable for women—home economics, fine arts and music, and household chemistry—and women students had their own student government.[19] In response to pressure from the forerunner of the AAUW, the ACA, to include women on the Board of Trustees, Middlebury created an advisory board for the Women's College in 1913 (Gertrude Cornish Milliken, "Brief History of the Advisory Board of the Women's College of Middlebury, 1913 to 1949," undated, MCA).[20] Even while such moves were being made to respond to women students' needs, however, some trustees were anxious to reclaim Middlebury as a men's college, if not by refusing admission to young women, then by developing a completely separate college for them (Trustee minutes, 1918, MCA).

William Smith College was similar to Middlebury College in that its policies concerning the degree of women students' separation from men students changed over time. Yet there was a critical distinction between the two colleges. Women students' institutional existence in the coordinate college was secure; there was never any discussion of reverting back to a men's college. Instead, discussions at William Smith were limited to less fundamental issues, also discussed at Middlebury, such as whether or not women's commencement exercises should be joint with the men's, or which classes women and men should take together, which separately.

While William Smith functioned in many ways as a separate women's college, it was always a women's college in relation to an (overbearing) men's college. An optimistic view is that it had the best of both worlds of single-sex and coeducation. It is, of course, also possible to argue that it had the worst of both worlds, that is, that William Smith students experienced the pressures to be refined and ladylike in a paternalistic setting characteristic of women's colleges at the same time that they were constantly reminded of men students' greater freedoms and privileges. Clearly the coordinate arrangement had both advantages and disadvantages, and the balance between the two varied over time.

In the period around World War I, the general direction of William Smith seemed to be greater separation from Hobart, despite the decision to hold joint commencement exercises beginning in 1922. The movement toward segregation can be seen most clearly in the curriculum which resulted in a greater number of departments of study for William Smith students (all of Hobart's, plus ones seen to be appropriate for women, such as music and domestic economy), but fewer elective courses in such "masculine" areas as economics, chemistry, or physics. Students saw their colleges as separate; men students, for example, wrote in their student newspaper about "our fair neighbors on the hill" (*Hobart Herald*, October 1911, HWSCA). In their newspaper column that reported on happenings in colleges around the country, William Smith students included news about Hobart.

The separation of William Smith from Hobart had benefits for women students in that they were in charge of almost all their own activities and women's issues were emphasized, as discussed earlier in this chapter. Even so, William Smith did not have as many women on the faculty and Board of Trustees as Wells, a completely separate women's college (see Table 4.1). In fact, at first the A.A.U.W. would not accredit William Smith alumnae because the dean of William Smith was a man (Smith 1972, 226). As at Wells and Middlebury, pressure from this association resulted in a positive change for college women; beginning in 1915, the college always had a woman as dean of William Smith.

Table 4.1 summarizes differences and similarities among these three colleges in the period around World War I. The two smallest colleges were Wells and William Smith. The small size of these two women's colleges fit with their emphasis on providing a "refined home" for their students. Wells continued to have the wealthiest students, apparent from the higher tuition costs and the percent of students who came from out-of-state. Women in positions of authority were much more in evidence at Wells than at the other two colleges, especially among the faculty but also on the Board of Trustees. Both Wells and William Smith had symbolic representation of women on campus in terms of naming buildings after women. Even in terms of scholarships Wells supported its women students, despite the fact that a high proportion of them were upper- and upper-middle-class.

In comparison to the other two colleges, Wells appears to have been at least as academically rigorous. Over two-fifths of its faculty had their Ph.D.s, somewhat more than at William Smith and considerably more than at Middlebury. Wells required students to study Latin, just as Middlebury did, and William Smith did for those students wanting B.A. degrees, but not

TABLE 4.1 Comparisons of Wells, Middlebury, and William Smith Colleges in the Period Around World War I

	Wells	Middlebury	William Smith
A. Characteristics of students			
No. of students; % women	195; 100% (1914)	339; 48% women (1914)	238; 40% women (1914)
% women students from out of state	65%	46%	5%
Tuition costs	$150/year	$100/year	$100/year
B. Female presence & support for women students			
% women on Board of Trustees	38% (of 21), 1914	0% of 22 trustees, 1914	1 of 19 (+ 2 ex-officio) or 5%, 1914
% women on faculty	73% (28 of 36), 1914	11% (3 of 28), 1914	8% (2 of 25), 1914
Dean of women students?	Yes, and from beginning, always a woman	Yes, beginning in 1909, always a woman	Yes, but a man until 1915 (then always a woman)
Symbolic representation of women on campus	Two buildings named after women by 1910	No buildings named after women	Two dorms for women named after women by 1910
Scholarships for women students	Five scholarships	Emma Willard Scholarship, and from 1912, eligible for state scholarship	1909, Elizabeth Smith Miller scholarships for 2 women per year
C. Academic standards			
% of faculty with Ph.D.	41% (11 of 27), 1914	14% (4 of 28), 1914	36% (9 of 25), 1914
Phi Beta Kappa chapter?	No (not until 1931)	Yes, since 1912	Yes, since 1912
Latin required?	Yes, both semesters, first year	One year for classical or pedagogical course, but not for scientific course	Yes for B.A. course, but for B.S. course, French or German instead
D. Curriculum oriented toward women			
Home economics?	No	Yes, beginning in 1913 (until 1960)	Yes, beginning in 1912 (until 1961)
Art?	Yes. In 1914, art history and archeology	Yes, a few courses in fine arts beginning in 1913	None except drawing (part of math dept.) until 1916, and then for women only

TABLE 4.1 Continued

	Wells	Middlebury	William Smith
Music?	Yes, even a bachelor of music degree from 1907 to 1915	Yes, a few courses beginning in 1913	Yes, for women only
Education?	Two courses (theory and history) 1913–1915 only	Yes; pedagogy course open to men, too, from 1908	Yes, beginning in 1910

E. Women students' campus organizations

	Wells	Middlebury	William Smith
Student government?	Self-government begun in 1895, but not much power in early years	Begun in 1912	Begun in 1915, a Board of Control with Dean and one professor, one alumna + eight students, but not much power
Suffrage club?	Yes, beginning in 1910	No	Yes, beginning in 1914
Publications?	Literary magazine & yearbook	With men students, newspaper & yearbook; women second-in-command positions	Women had own newspaper & yearbook
Sports/athletics?	1910, athletic association, basketball, tennis; 1911, swimming pool	Basketball, tennis, class teams; 1914, Athletic Association	Basketball, tennis, some hockey. 1916, Athletic Association
Sororities?	No	Yes	No
Clubs based on curriculum, e.g., languages, science, etc.	Science club, 1915; language clubs (German club, 1910; French club, 1914)	Mixed sex: language clubs–1914, German; 1915, Latin and French	Not in 1914
Political or current affairs clubs	Current affairs club, 1914	1917, all-women civics club	Current events club in 1910 but discontinued and not established again until 1924
Dramatics, music?	Much drama, many musical organizations	All-women glee club & instrumental clubs; drama with men; in 1917, one choir with men & women	Women had own drama & music clubs (glee club)

Information comes mainly from college catalogues. See note at end of Table 3.1.

for those taking a B.S. degree. The only indicator that Wells might have been less academically rigorous than the other two colleges was in not having a chapter of the prestigious national honor society, Phi Beta Kappa (which Wells did not obtain until 1931). Getting a chapter of Phi Beta Kappa was not straightforward, however, so the meaning of this absence is unclear. Existing chapters in a region had to support an application, and apparently some men opposed new chapters in women's colleges (Current 1990, 185).

Differences among the three colleges in curriculum traditionally designated as appropriate for women are interesting. Wells stressed the arts subjects more than the other two colleges did; it even offered a bachelor's of music degree for almost a decade in the early twentieth century. Such subjects clearly fit into Wells's aim of making its women students more refined, a goal that also characterized William Smith College, but to a lesser extent. William Smith offered some fine arts courses before World War I, but the catalogue said that while the college recognized the value of music in higher education, it should be "primarily cultural rather than professional" (1911–12 William Smith Catalogue, HWSCA). Middlebury displayed prejudice against the arts that was typical of many liberal arts institutions, particularly those that historically had been affiliated with evangelical Christian churches (Rudolph 1977, 266), yet by 1913 it did offer a limited number of fine arts and music courses to its women (and men) students. Wells, on the other hand, differed from the other two colleges in not offering vocationally oriented subjects typically associated with women: home economics and education. Before World War I both of these subjects were offered at William Smith and Middlebury.

The final section of Table 4.1 shows the how much college life had developed by the second decade of the twentieth century. At all three colleges, but particularly at Wells, students had many opportunities to participate in dramatics, music, language clubs, literary magazines, and athletics. But only at Wells and William Smith were activities geared specifically toward women. Both of these colleges, for example, had suffrage clubs before women obtained the vote, and in these two colleges, but not at Middlebury, women controlled their own publications. Wells students were also more likely to have clubs that in other colleges were the province of men—the science club, for example, or at an earlier date, the social sciences club (see Chapter 3). Middlebury, on the other hand, was the only college to have sororities, a helpful refuge in a male-dominated institution.

Conclusions

William Smith College, as a representative of a coordinate institution, does genuinely seem to have fallen between women's colleges on the one hand and coeducational colleges on the other. It offered its students some, but not all, of the advantages of women's colleges, falling short mainly in having few women faculty and trustees. William Smith also shared in some of the weaknesses of women's colleges, but again not to the same extent; for instance, while it stressed the cultivation of its "young lady" students and the importance of making the college a "home," these themes were not as pronounced as they were at Wells. Similarly, William Smith was a weaker version of the coeducational college, Middlebury, both in its positive and negative aspects. It did not demand quite as much academically from its women students as did Middlebury, given William Smith's fewer offerings in "masculine" subjects, but on the other hand, William Smith supported women to a much greater extent, in terms of having women represented symbolically on campus and having extracurricular activities oriented toward women's interests.

The coordinate structure of William Smith provided the college with flexibility. When it was expedient to emphasize its single-sex nature, it was able to do so, but when the larger culture began to view women's colleges with suspicion, then it could advertise itself as virtually a coeducational college. Such changes in emphasis over time will be traced in the following chapter when I summarize some of the major developments relevant to women students from the 1920s to the 1960s at all three colleges.

Notes

1   The statistics people generally used gave an exaggerated picture of the differences in nuptial and fertility rates since they looked at alumnae shortly after they left college, and college graduates tended to get married at later ages. Also, some of the critics did not take into account that the social classes college women came from had lower marriage rates than the general population. In any event, college women's marital and fertility behavior rose after 1900 and so increasingly converged with other women's marriage and birth rates (Cookingham 1984, 363).

2   The elite eastern women's colleges resisted the trend to offer home economics; while more than one hundred colleges and universities offered instruction in home economics in 1910, no such courses were taught at any of the Seven Sister schools at that time (Antler 1982, 26).

3   A specific example of the way faculty became restricted occurred in 1861. The president of Hobart, Rev. Abner Jackson, "declined" to have an alumnus, William Watts Folwell, come back on the faculty because Folwell was "not high church enough." Folwell, a convert to the Episcopalian faith, later became the first president of the University of Minnesota (Folwell 1933, 157).

4   A couple of exceptional students attended Hobart before the Civil War. One, Abraham La Fort, was a chief of the Onondaga tribe of the Iroquois Nation. He graduated in 1829, and then worked as an Episcopalian missionary among his people for a while. The other was an African American, Isaiah De Grasse, who attended Hobart from 1832 to 1835 but did not receive a degree. De Grasse later became an ordained deacon in the Episcopalian Church (Smith 1972: 112–114). No other African American is known to have attended Hobart until the mid-twentieth century (Grover 1994, 292).

5   Despite A. D. White's criticisms of Hobart College, he later became a trustee of the college, as were his father and uncle before him (Smith 1972, 125).

6   The qualifier "regular" is important for historical accuracy, since as Walsh notes in *Doctors Wanted: No Women Need Apply*, Harriot Hunt was actually the first woman to practice medicine in the United States. She and her sister opened a practice in Boston in 1835. Hunt, however, was an "irregular" whose training, like that of many men doctors of that time, took the form of an apprenticeship. Interestingly, when in late 1847 Hunt tried to attend lectures at Harvard's medical school to obtain scientific training, she cited the precedent of Elizabeth Blackwell at Geneva (Walsh 1977, 25–28).

7   Gerrit Smith (1797–1874) was the son of Peter Smith, who made his fortune with John Jacob Astor in the fur trade. Gerrit Smith graduated from Hamilton College, became famous for his involvement in many causes, not only abolitionism but also temperance, women's rights, and freedom for Cuba (Huff 1984, 326), and served one term in the House of Representatives. He believed in spirit

communication and was pleased to find that most spiritualists were reformers (Moore 1977, 70).

8   It was through meeting Elizabeth Smith Miller that Amelia Bloomer, editor of the *Lily* magazine, first saw and then copied what came to be called "bloomers." It is clear that both Elizabeth Cady Stanton, who also wore the reform dress for a while in the 1850s, and Elizabeth Smith Miller resented the notoriety that Amelia Bloomer got for what was Elizabeth Smith Miller's idea (see Elizabeth Cady Stanton's letter to Elizabeth Smith Miller, July 2, 1851, Elizabeth Cady Stanton's Papers, Box 1, VCA). Elizabeth Smith Miller wrote two slightly different versions of her reasons for adopting reform dress, but both attribute her dissatisfaction with the "shackle" of long dresses having come to a head while she was working in her garden (see Smith Family Papers, Box 1, #12, NYPL). The "Bloomer" costume, and its relation to the suffrage movement, is discussed in the *History of Woman Suffrage*, edited by Elizabeth Cady Stanton, Susan B. Anthony, and Matilda Joslyn Gage (see Vol. I, pp. 127–28, and letters between Stanton and Gerrit Smith in the Appendix for Ch. XIII, p. 843). Elizabeth Cady Stanton was one of the women critical of Gerrit Smith for reducing the "whole battle-ground of the Woman's Rights Movement" to dress, even though she herself had worn "bloomers" for a while.

9   The Ethical Culture Society promoted the idea of moral good within human nature, rejected the idea of a personal God, and encouraged people to be active in reform movements. Information on Felix Adler and this movement can be found in *Who Was Who in America*, Vol. 1; *Dictionary of American Religious Biography*. Susan B. Anthony was not as impressed by Adler as Elizabeth Smith Miller was; Anthony remarked on Adler's lack of support for women's suffrage, which she found disappointing since he did support "Negro" suffrage. "He [Adler] is a wonderful man. It is queer that he can see the negro should be a man and should have the right to vote while he cannot see that woman in order to be a full fledged human being should have the right to vote also. But human beings are made up so funny and you cannot find anyone who is thoroughly consistent in everything" (Anthony to Elizabeth Smith Miller, April 13, 1904, Smith family papers, NYPL).

10 In her autobiography, Anna Botsford Comstock noted that as a student at Cornell, M. Carey Thomas was "dignified and cold to all but a few" (Comstock 1953, 81).

11 In her autobiography, Comstock explained that she did not join the suffrage movement for two reasons: one, because she thought women would be more influential in municipal affairs, where they mostly had the vote already, than in national affairs; and two, because she "felt unequal to voting wisely." Yet she went on to explain, "I had always believed women should have the same political rights as men, as a matter of justice, but I did not feel like taking up the cudgels for the cause" (Comstock 1953, 55). Comstock's general concern with the treatment women received was indicated by her complaint about how "unfair" it was that no women were elected as alumni trustees of Cornell University (Comstock 1953, 262).

12   Although the "practical problems" are not specified, this probably refers to the great expense that would have been incurred by setting up a completely independent educational institution for women. At various points in their correspondence, trustees expressed their concerns about making a "too expensive beginning" (Henry Graves correspondence, HWSCA). It was later estimated that setting up William Smith College as an annex had cost only one-tenth of what establishing an independent institution would have cost (Trustee minutes, December 11, 1906, HWSCA).

13   The trustees of William Smith's estate, named in 1906, were Nathaniel Schmidt, professor of Semitic studies at Cornell University; Anna Botsford Comstock; Felix Adler; Anne Fitzhugh Miller; Theodore Smith (William Smith's nephew and business partner); and three businessmen from Geneva: Lewis Chase, R. G. Chase, and Henry Graves. They signed a statement that described Mr. Smith's "proposed philanthropy" as being (1) to secure "the most important educational advantages to women," (2) to instruct them in all studies which make for "the increase of life," and (3) to ensure that this will occur in an atmosphere of complete religious freedom (William Smith file, December 11, 1906 document, HWSCA).

14   The phrase "abundant life" comes from The New Testament, John 10, in which Jesus talks of himself as the "good shepherd" who would lay down his life for his flock. According to people who knew him at the time, Mr. Smith was particularly fond of this verse and kept his Bible open to it (Geneva Daily Times, June 17, 1912, HWSCA). He clearly saw himself as the good shepherd, and when planning for his original, spiritualist college, put it directly: "I have founded this college that the people might have life and have it more abundantly" (William Smith file, 1903 documents, HWSCA). It is interesting to note that other educators at about the same time spoke in similar terms. The president of Wheaton Female Seminary had the seminary's motto changed in 1911 to "that they may have life and may have it abundantly" (Helmreich 1985, 88, 96).

15   How unusual the entirely voluntary nature of chapel at William Smith was for the time period can perhaps be grasped by comparison to regulations at Barnard College. In 1914 Barnard students had to attend chapel only once a month, considered "very early for such liberality" (Kendall 1975, 161).

16   The three original trustees were a subset of William Smith's estate trustees: Theodore Smith, Anna Botsford Comstock, and Henry Graves. Anna Comstock was delighted with the choice of Graves, whom she called "an ideal of fairness and squareness" (Graves correspondence, December 19, 1906, HWSCA).

17   Although the voluntary, nonsectarian nature of William Smith College's chapel may seem progressive and modern, this is not necessarily how young women of the time saw it. One writer in the William Smith student newspaper referred to the "restrictions" their college faced with respect to chapel that "other colleges" did not have (The Ridge, January 1910, HWSCA). Later college bulletins noted that while the college was nonsectarian, "because of its coexistence with Hobart . . . it is often considered as allied with the Episcopalian Church" (1938–39 Col-

lege Bulletin, HWCA). Advertisements for the college were at times placed in Episcopalian magazines along with those for Hobart College (Smith 1972, 195).

18 This Latin-Scientific course was begun in the 1880s when it was open to both men and women. For a short while in the period before World War I, women students could take only the classical course, requiring the study of Greek as well as Latin, whereas men had the choice of the classical course or the Latin-Scientific course. The bachelor of science degree was eliminated in 1935–36 when the requirement of Latin or Greek was abolished.

19 Only home economics remained a women's department. After one year, fine arts and music were opened to men students, and household chemistry was discontinued.

20 The AAUW accredited Middlebury in 1921 but recommended that the college hire more women faculty and appoint a woman to the Board of Trustees. Not until 1947, however, did a woman become a trustee (Gertrude Cornish Milliken, "Brief History of the Advisory Board of the Women's College of Middlebury, 1913 to 1949," undated, MCA).

Chapter 5

Progress and Setbacks: Women Students' Experiences at Three Colleges, 1915–1965

By the middle of the twentieth century, higher education moved into the mainstream of American life (Levine 1986, 17). An increasing percentage of young people attended college as higher education came to be seen as relevant to their lives and careers. Between just 1900 and 1930, for example, the number of students in institutions of higher education in the United States grew by about 300 percent (Fass 1977, 407). In a 1949 national poll conducted by *Fortune* and Roper, over 50 percent of those interviewed said that it was "more true than false" that "You've got to have a college education to get ahead in the world" (*Fortune* 1949).

With more and more people able to afford college education at the less expensive state universities, the liberal arts colleges performed a new social function. By becoming selective in their admissions, they were able to check an "undesired democratization" process and preserve the "hegemony of white Anglo-Saxon Protestant upper middle class" (Levine 1986, 21). The status of institutions became dependent, at least in part, on their homogeneous student bodies. The numbers of Jews and blacks, even Catholics, were kept deliberately low, sometimes under the guise of obtaining "geographical diversity" (Gordon 1986, 515). Yet at the same time, most colleges were becoming more secular, with fewer direct ties to particular Protestant denominations and weaker chapel requirements (Fass 1977, 147).

How did women fit into this picture? On the one hand, women's presence in higher education was accepted; no longer was it seriously debated whether women's intellectual abilities made them unfit for collegiate study (although stereotypes of which subjects they were good at persisted). Yet many issues connected to women's college education remained unresolved, particularly at the increasingly prevalent coeducational institutions: Did women's presence lower the prestige of an institution, or did this occur only when and if "too many" attended? Should women study exactly the same curriculum as men and in the same classrooms? What kinds of extracurricular activities were appropriate for women? What form should social relations between women and men students take? What value was college education to the post-college lives of women and did the college have any responsibilities for preparing women for their future?

Although the percentage of women undergraduates who attended women's colleges dropped dramatically, from about 24 percent in 1910 to less than 10 percent by the end of the 1950s (Newcomer 1959, 49), women's colleges remained an accepted, even prestigious, option for undergraduate women, especially in the East. The "Seven Sisters" colleges (Smith, Vassar, Radcliffe, Mount Holyoke, Barnard, Bryn Mawr, and Wellesley), so named in 1926 at a meeting of these colleges called by Dean Gildersleeve of Barnard (Gordon 1986: 19), represented the top of this academic hierarchy. Yet many other women's colleges, such as Wheaton, Chatham, Goucher, Wilson, Agnes Scott, and Wells, were highly respected, too. What seems unthinkable today—the founding of new women's colleges—also occurred during this time period; Bennington and Sarah Lawrence as well as many Catholic women's colleges opened.

Women's colleges were prestigious, but they were also subject to criticism. The sexual revolution of the 1920s[1] and the popularization of Freud (Davis 1929; Horowitz 1984) meant that intense relationships between women no longer seemed as innocent as the acceptable "smashes" and "crushes" of the nineteenth and early twentieth century (Horowitz 1984: 277). Some people began to charge women's colleges with encouraging lesbianism, which led the colleges to take special measures to avoid such imputations (Bromley and Britten 1938, 118; Davis 1929, 245; Horowitz 1984, 314).[2] Another criticism, voiced by Vice President Calvin Coolidge, associated some of the eastern women's colleges with radicalism and Bolshevism (Coolidge 1921). A rather different view of women's colleges was that they were only "finishing schools" for rich young women, not in tune with the needs of contemporary students, who wanted rigorous academic training to enter professional schools or demanding careers (Durbin and Kent 1989; Kehr 1920; Newcomer 1959).

In this chapter I discuss developments at three colleges from the time of the First World War to the eve of the student movement days of the 1960s. For the two mixed-sex institutions—Middlebury and William Smith—

a major issue is how the tension between integrating women and segregating them from men students worked itself out over time. For the women's college, Wells, the basic question I address is the degree to which it adapted itself to the changing roles for women, or, in other words, how well it accommodated young women's needs for academic work that would prepare them for careers rather than "finishing." I conclude the chapter by comparing the three colleges in terms of changes in their enrollments, the percentage of women on the faculty and boards of trustees, and their curriculums, in order to assess how well each college responded to women students' concerns.

The Wells "Family" Grows

Given the original aim of Henry Wells to have his college function as a Christian family, its very success posed a dilemma.[3] With a "great number of young women knocking in vain at college doors," as Wells College President Macmillan put it in 1926 (Wells College Bulletin 1926, 38, WCA), how could the college remain small enough for the ties among students, faculty, and administrators to be intimate? If the college was not going to refuse admission to ever more young women, it had to change its definition of what a "small" college was, or it had to abandon its commitment to functioning like a family. In fact, the college tried both of these solutions to the dilemma.

The man who became president of Wells just prior to World War I and who remained until 1936, Kerr Duncan Macmillan, believed passionately that the best college education occurred in small, close-knit institutions. Referring to such excellent English colleges as Balliol and Oriel at Oxford, Macmillan argued in 1920 that small meant 200 or fewer students. This size would enable the student body to have a "common consciousness," according to Macmillan, which in turn would mean the college could have few regulations so that the individual would have "as much liberty as is consistent with the general welfare and comfort." The physical plant that Macmillan envisioned for such a "college home" did not exist at Wells or perhaps anywhere, as he wanted it to be "one building capable of housing the whole academic family comfortably, containing bedrooms, studies, a common dining hall, class-rooms, club rooms, recreation rooms, a gymnasium, swimming pool and general assembly hall" (Macmillan, "The College Home," Wells College Bulletin, October 1920, WCA). As small as Wells College was at the time Macmillan was writing, approximately

230 students, it had several different buildings; even housing the students took more than one building.

Less than a decade after President Macmillan expounded his views on the desirability of a very small college that could function as a "home," he appeared to have modified his views somewhat. He still referred to "the College home" when describing the residential nature of the college but noted that the students were "scattered" in four dormitories. Using language that may have reflected his strong Presbyterian faith, he consoled himself and his audience that "the evils" of this situation were minimized by having all the seniors and first-year students live in the same building. He still claimed, however, that it would be more "efficient" if all the students were in one building where there was "provision for all their interests." The "interests" he listed (dormitory rooms, dining hall, places for social gatherings, reading, study, and play) were somewhat less comprehensive than his earlier list, however (President's Report, Wells College Bulletin 1928, 12, WCA).

A clear indication that Macmillan's views on the appropriate size for Wells were shifting was his statement in 1928 that "there is not anywhere in the Wells College constituency any real objection to its growth." Although he admitted that there was "strong prejudice in favor of a small college," he went on to say "just what is meant by 'small' is not . . . defined" (President's Report, Wells College Bulletin 1928, 32, WCA). Moreover, President Macmillan had begun to recognize some of the disadvantages of the college's very small size, namely the lower prestige of small institutions; their "uneconomical" nature, both "academically and financially"; and finally the negative effects on the "esprit de corps" of the faculty, who desire "more numerous scholarly companions" (President's Report, Wells College Bulletin 1928, 32, WCA). Macmillan's preferred solution was a second unit or sister college in which 200 additional students could be admitted. He envisioned a coordinate arrangement fairly similar to Hobart and William Smith, with one faculty, one Board of Trustees, shared administration, but separate housing and dining. In 1926 the President's Report included an announcement of a second unit with an illustrated booklet of two different plans, one "less ambitious" in terms of the money it would require than the other (Wells College Bulletin 1926, WCA). Most importantly, such a coordinate arrangement would have made it possible to grow while remaining "true to the Founder's ideal of a college home that is at the [same] time a school" (President's Report, Wells College Bulletin 1928, 33, WCA). Although this second unit was approved by the board of trustees, it never materialized, presumably due to the difficulty of raising sufficient funds in the depression years (Dieckmann 1995, 139).

Enrollments at Wells College were less affected by the Depression than they were at many other colleges, primarily because many of the young women who came to Wells were the daughters of wealthy parents. Even in 1934, the year that President Macmillan said was "the first year of the depression seriously to affect Wells College," the college did not apply for any of the Federal Emergency Relief Administration funds that could be used by colleges to pay students for work done around the institution. According to President Macmillan, Wells did not qualify for these funds since one requirement was that students would not otherwise be able to attend college. As Wells had a national rather than a local constituency, Macmillan explained, its students "would be able to attend some other institution which was nearer home and where the fees charged were not so large" (President's Report, Wells College Bulletin 1933–34, 4, WCA).

Wells may not have been as affected by the depression as other colleges, but the effects were still apparent: enrollment decreased, from 272 students in 1930–31 to 228 in 1933–34; the number of students on scholarships almost doubled, which meant that the college could not meet the needs for assistance out of the income from endowments for scholarships;[4] and for the first time since at least 1920, less than 50 percent of the class of 1934 stayed until graduation (President's Report, Wells College Bulletin 1933–34, 19, WCA). To cope with this financial crisis, all faculty, administrators, and staff took a 5 percent cut in salaries, and sabbatical leaves were suspended.

By Macmillan's last year as president of Wells, in 1935–36, the college's financial situation had improved somewhat. The number of students had increased to 267 which, the treasurer noted in his yearly report, brought in additional income that was slightly more than the decrease in income from the college's endowment (Treasurer's Report, Wells College Bulletin 1936, WCA).

From this time on, increases in enrollment were seen as desirable, necessary for the college's financial well-being. In 1941, for example, the treasurer's report concluded with a prediction that the college's "financial position" would always be "critical" with an enrollment less than 300 and would "not be fully satisfactory without an enrollment considerably higher than 300" (Treasurer's Report, Wells College Bulletin 1941, 17, WCA). His predictions proved accurate. When Wells' enrollment was "only" 309 in 1948–49, President Greene spoke of the "even darker" financial days unless it increased (Wells College Bulletin 1948–49, 10, WCA), whereas when it reached 368 full-time students in 1955, President Long spoke of the "excitement" due to "operating at 102% of capacity!" (The President's Annual Report, October 1955, WCA). In 1959 the trustees approved the growth of Wells to 500 students, and President Long boasted that already Wells had 50 percent more students than it had had in 1951 (*Express*, November 1960, 4, WCA).

While Wells still considered itself a "small" liberal arts college for women, which it certainly was in comparison to other colleges, it no longer defined small as Macmillan had—200 students. Given that the primary motivation for growth was financial, it is not surprising that some of Wells's constituency, particularly alumnae, regretted the change. In 1962 when Wells finally enrolled what the president considered the "magic number" of 500 students, a poll of trustees, alumnae, parents, and friends of the college revealed that many were concerned that Wells was becoming too large. President Long, who had previously talked positively about "the possibility of Wells College growing to 750" (*Express*, January 1962, 6, WCA), found it necessary to defend his views by discussing the pedagogical disadvantages of being too small. He argued that when classes had "too few" students, there was insufficient "exchange of ideas," and when there were departments with only one faculty member, students did not get exposed to different perspectives (*Express*, October 1962, 5, WCA).

One consequence of the growth of Wells's student body was that it became somewhat more heterogeneous, at least religiously, ethnically, and in terms of social class background (but not race except for an occasional Japanese student). Early lists of students show an overwhelming number of "WASP" names, primarily English, Scottish, and German, but also a few Dutch. Gradually some Catholics, mostly from Irish-American families, attended. In 1927–28, President Macmillan described the religion of students then in attendance. Over 90 percent of the students were Protestant, with the largest numbers being Presbyterian (40 percent of the student body), Episcopal (21 percent), Congregational (11 percent) or Methodist (9 percent). Five percent were Catholics, and only one student was Jewish (President's Report, Wells College Bulletin 1928, WCA). The preponderance of Protestant students is not really surprising given the Presbyterianism of Wells's founders which affected such practices as holding the baccalaureate service in the Presbyterian Church (until 1961), and in the 1920s, requiring students to take a course on "the life and teachings of Jesus Christ" (President's Report, Wells College Bulletin 1928, 11, WCA). Students' religious backgrounds were not usually officially reported, but students' surnames indicate that WASPs predominated until after World

War II, when not only Irish but also Italian, Jewish, and even occasionally Polish or Greek names appeared.[5] Until the early 1960s, Wells' catalogues continued to advertise the college as a Christian, nondenominational institution, where participation in chapel and vespers was voluntary but "expected."

The fact that the proportion of students on scholarships increased, especially during the Depression, may indicate that Wells students became more heterogeneous in terms of social class, too. But family income and wealth, especially in a period in which many people experienced sudden financial losses, are not always reliable indicators of social class. Status differences among students during the late 1920s and early 1930s are illustrated by the situation of two students. A daughter of a university professor who attended Wells in the early 1930s, while clearly upper middle class, did not consider herself one of the wealthy students. She was aware that there were "two Morgans and one Dodge" among the students then at the college and also that her background was not as elite as those who had attended "prep schools" (Personal interview, number 1, June 1995). A wealthy student at college at about the same time, Alberta Prigge (Zabriskie) '32, known as "Allie," clearly recognized her superior social position and mostly made friends with students of similar backgrounds. Although she described herself in letters to her family as "so democratic and a friend to all humanity" (and one of only 30 people out of 250 at Wells who in a straw vote, cast their ballots for Democrat Al Smith), Miss Prigge was shocked when one of her best college friends, "a big deb in Milwaukie [sic] . . . [whose] family are the leading lights there," married a boy from a family with "absolutely no money." She characterized the situation as "perfectly ridiculous." Moreover, Allie Prigge (who had a fur coat) spent money conspicuously; for instance, she and a few college friends traveled by taxi to a restaurant in Aurora, about half a mile away, to celebrate one of their birthdays with a specially-ordered meal (Letters Home, Alberta Prigge Zabriskie '32, Class Folders, WCA).

Despite the increase in the percentage of students on scholarships, and the decrease in the percentage who had attended private (independent) schools,[6] Wells continued to advertise itself in a way designed to appeal to wealthy families, the kind who had always sent their daughters to Wells. In 1957–58, for instance, the college catalogue included for the first time a section on horseback riding, with rates given for boarding privately owned horses (an expensive $50 per month).[7] Also, for each entering class, students whose relatives had attended Wells were given special attention. In 1960 the alumnae magazine noted that the entering class had more alumnae granddaughters and daughters than probably any previous class (*Express*, November 1960, WCA). Yet a factor working against the college's tendency to be socially exclusive was its desire to be academically competitive, as I will discuss below. The scholarships that the college maintained for gifted students made it more likely that students would be more heterogeneous than they had been in the nineteenth or early twentieth centuries.

Was Wells Still a Finishing School?

Even while Wells was growing in size and developing a more heterogeneous student body, its curriculum and extracurricular activities reflected its "finishing school" past. More emphasis was placed on developing "ladylike" manners among the students and preparing them to fit into refined society than was true at coeducational colleges like Middlebury. Similar to students at William Smith, Wells students attended many teas, given by deans and faculty. Teas not only reinforced proper manners and gracious living, but gave students an opportunity to practice the hostess role, by making sandwiches or pouring, for example. Students had other occasions to practice these skills, too; for example, the faculty-senior bridge tournament in which seniors provided the refreshments for the first night and faculty reciprocated on the third evening (Jean Davis, "Facts and Folklore," 1970, 125, WCA).

Dining was quite formal at Wells. Until sometime during the Depression, dressing for dinner was required, which meant that students changed from a blouse, sweater, and skirt to a dress.[8] Some women faculty regularly presided at student tables in the dining room (Davis 1970, WCA), and the dean had a special table to which it was an honor for students to be invited. All were served by waitresses from the village, and good table manners were expected. One alumna from the class of 1933 recalled receiving a booklet before she entered college, "Welcome to Wells," that included such etiquette rules as, one never spreads a whole slice of bread but rather does it bit by bit (Personal interview, number 1, June 1995).

Close relations with faculty, particularly the unmarried women faculty who lived in the students' residence halls, meant that many aspects of students' lives could be supervised. "Allie" Prigge wrote to her parents in the early 1930s that an English teacher had commented on her nicotine-stained fingers as well as complimenting her on her "most charming voice." Yet this compliment was also an attempt at social control, since the faculty member went on to say that although her voice was sweet, low, and husky, she abused this gift by talking "stridently." The teacher begged this student "in the name of charming femininity, to cultivate a modulated voice" (Zabriskie, Class Folders, WCA).

The larger culture's ambivalence about women's higher education and its implications for their femininity found its way into Wells. Students' beauty not only mattered but was celebrated by such traditions as the May Day procession, pole dance, and crowning the queen. Some honors for students in which physical appearance might seem irrelevant apparently were influenced by their looks. Alberta Prigge '32, for example, wrote to her family that she had been elected president of the junior class and so would lead the prom. Her election surprised her since she was "certainly not the best-looking girl in the class by a long shot" (Zabriskie, Class Folders, WCA).

Related to the earlier emphasis on students' health, but also connected to an emphasis on beauty, was the attention paid to students' posture. Freshmen and sophomores were examined, their posture graded from A to F, specific defects noted, and corrective exercises prescribed. Alberta Prigge, for example, wrote to her family in 1928 that her physical exam had revealed that she had drooping shoulders, for which she was given special exercises (Zabriskie, Class Folders, WCA). At the end of the year, students were re-examined to determine how much they had improved. This subject was deemed sufficiently serious for President Macmillan to include a chart in his 1934–35 President's Report on the posture grades underclass women received in both September and June, noting that overall, sophomores had better posture than freshmen. The students' speaking voices were given similar attention, with the college Catalogue proudly proclaiming that over the course of a year, "forty per cent [of students who had been given voice remedies] . . . showed such a marked improvement that it would be noticed by the lay person" (1936–37 Catalogue, 13, WCA).

Wells's finishing school past influenced its curriculum, too. As discussed in earlier chapters, from the beginning Wells had emphasized the arts and did not offer such practical subjects as domestic science and education, since "ladies" were presumed to need refinement but not to work for a living nor to learn how to do their own housework. Such an anti-practical emphasis also fit in with the counter-attack on pragmatism after World War I. Many liberal arts colleges were then seeking to establish themselves as "elite" institutions, concerned not with the practical affairs of the world but rather with educating the mind (Levine 1986). One critic of liberal arts colleges' lack of practicality looked at curriculums of comparable women's and men's colleges in relation to the post-college lives of alumni and alumnae. A 1915 survey of alumnae of nine colleges (mostly women's colleges, one of which was Wells), showed that women's colleges were not preparing women well for their post-college lives, as they created "a limited and artificial environment often quite out of touch with the everyday world" (Kehr 1920,13). This researcher advocated more professional and scientific courses for women during their college years since many could not afford such training after college.

Wells took pride in its lack of practical courses. In 1918 President Macmillan praised students and faculty for the help they had given to the war effort, but at the same time he boasted that the college had not lowered its standards by introducing "emergency courses" (President's Report, 1918 Wells College Bulletin,WCA). More than forty years later, during the course of a review of some of the college's accomplishments, President Long mentioned how during the Depression, Wells resisted the pressure to open professional departments, a strategy that had been used by other small colleges (*Express*, January 1962, WCA).

Many students accepted this academic hierarchy and were proud that their college offered only pure liberal arts subjects—"a little snobbery there," as one alumna of the class of 1948 described it (Personal interview, number 2, Mrs. Davis Cutting, June 1995). But other students tried to get Wells to modify its curriculum somewhat. In the 1920s students requested that pedagogy be taught, but faculty rejected their petition, arguing that the course would not meet New York State teaching requirements (McKean 1961, 208). Students were more successful in their attempt to get vocational guidance; after years of struggle a Placement Bureau was established in 1928 (McKean 1961, 211), although for many years it was staffed by existing personnel at Wells rather than specially trained people. In 1950 President Richard Greene reported that to meet students' demand for typing instruction, his secretary conducted a noncredit course for thirty-four students that met twice weekly throughout the academic year (President's Report 1949–50, 8, WCA).

Over time Wells's emphasis on music declined. The bachelor of music degree that had been offered in the earlier part of the twentieth century lasted for less than a decade. It was reinstated, in a different form, in 1922 as a 5-year double course for a bachelor of arts degree and a bachelor of music degree, but this arrangement also lasted less than five years (Class Folders, 1922; Catalogues; WCA). Many students took music lessons, but fewer enrolled in formal courses and few majored in the discipline.

Rather than changing the curriculum in any fundamental ways to meet students' desire for career-relevant courses, Wells College administrators made the argument that the study of liberal arts had practical benefits. The 1957–58 Catalogue, for example, under the section entitled "A basic goal—liberal education," stated that "a liberal education is truly a highly practical education since it provides training in those basic principles and ideas which find wide and general application." But, it went on to note, "practical values" are "not our main interest" but rather a "by-product" of the college program, which seeks "the cultivation of a humane individual . . . the promotion of growth to maturity and freedom" (Wells College Catalogue 1957–58, WCA).

Thus although Wells College was influenced by its origins as a finishing school for rich young women, it did make some minor changes in its curriculum in response to students' demands. Over time subjects traditional for women to study, such as music, were emphasized less, and lipservice at least was paid to the idea that women needed a practical education suited to their anticipated careers. But as long as Wells was able to attract a sufficient number of wealthy students, it still paid to advertise itself as an elite college in which students studied the pure liberal arts.

Wells's Academic Program Becomes More Rigorous

During the twentieth century, particularly after World War I, Wells developed a strong academic program that appealed to academically well-qualified students. Since the late nineteenth century, Wells had been moving in this direction, by abolishing its preparatory program, hiring more faculty who had their Ph.D.s, and becoming more selective in admissions. But in the 1920s the efforts to become academically rigorous intensified under the direction of President Kerr Duncan Macmillan.

In 1923 Wells became one of the first American institutions to introduce the honors course. In its original form the honors course was so rigorous—involving studying independently under faculty supervision during the junior and senior years and having outside examiners for the 12-hour final examination—that few of the students who qualified were willing to apply. In 1934–35 out of 88 students whose special fields were known, only 9 were honor students (President's Report 1935–36, 18–19, WCA). President Macmillan was also instrumental in establishing comprehensive examinations for all students in every discipline. As Macmillan explained, the comprehensive examination "assumes that the student has acquired considerable knowledge during her four years and proceeds to inquire whether and to what extent she can handle it" (President's Report 1929–30, 9, WCA).

Wells's success in upgrading its academic program was evident from the acceptance of its application to Phi Beta Kappa in 1931, as well as the high scores Wells students obtained on national examinations. In 1930 President Macmillan reported that Wells freshmen had taken the intelligence test developed by Professor Thurstone and scored third among 131 institutions, coming behind only Haverford and Dartmouth (President's Report 1929–30, WCA). Up through the mid-1960s, there were other indications that Wells was an increasingly selective college whose students did well. For example, between 1953 and 1959, median scores on the verbal SATs went from 479 to 560; median scores on the math SATs similarly increased, from 456 to 531 (L. J. Long, "A Report of Progress, 1950–1960," WCA). More rigorous admissions criteria, as well as a more diverse student body that came from having a greater number of scholarships, improved students' academic qualifications. Between 1953 and 1963, just under 24 percent of Wells students received scholarships, but they accounted for 68 percent of Latin honors and 67 percent of the Phi Beta Kappa keys (*Express*, March 1963, WCA).

At Wells College students encountered a stimulating intellectual environment. Faculty members were well-qualified, according to the high percentage who had their Ph.D.s (see Table 5.1). Faculty publications were listed in President's Reports and while few faculty were very well-known, many published in respectable journals within their fields. Perhaps the most famous faculty between 1915 and 1965 were the poet Robert Tristram Coffin, who later went to Bowdoin College and while he was there, won a Pulitzer Prize; the musician Nicholas Nabokoff, cousin of the much more famous Vladimir Nabokov (or Nabokoff); the artist and book craftsman Victor Hammer; and the internationally recognized musicologist Paul Lang, who commuted from Columbia University. Lecturers, artists, and guests who came to Wells between 1930 and 1965 were truly outstanding, including poets Robert Frost and W. H. Auden, writer and political analyst Hannah Arendt, novelist Thornton Wilder, choreographer George Balanchine, composer Bela Bartok, opera singer Joan Sutherland, First Lady Eleanor Roosevelt, and the first woman to be a member of a U.S. President's cabinet, Labor Secretary Frances Perkins. During the 1930s Wells, like many other colleges, invited a few radical speakers to campus, including Norman Thomas, who almost "converted" wealthy Alberta Prigge to socialism, according to her own report (Zabriskie,

Class Folders, WCA), and Philip Randolph, national president of the Brotherhood of Sleeping Car Porters (President's Report 1933–34, WCA).

Thus in the mid-1960s Wells was a flourishing women's college, able to be selective in its admissions and offering an education comparable to other good liberal arts colleges. Although it was still smaller than most colleges, whether women's, men's, or coeducational, Wells had few vestiges of its finishing school past. Its student body had become more diverse, with a greater number of scholarships enabling students from a broader range of family backgrounds to attend. It was still close to 100 percent white (the first African-American student was not admitted until 1960), but it no longer was so overwhelmingly WASP, with a sizeable number of Catholic and a few Jewish students. The biggest changes still lay ahead.

"Seeking Men and Tolerating Women": Middlebury's Ambivalence about Women Students

Women students at Middlebury appeared to be a permanent and significant component of the college by the second decade of the twentieth century. Yet many trustees and top administrators remained troubled by women's presence in what they still considered a men's college. Due to the larger increase of women's than men's enrollment in institutions of higher education between 1890 and 1910, many coeducational colleges were like Middlebury in being "paranoid" about their "public image" (Levine 1986, 124). Although Middlebury's 1902 charter from the state of Vermont for an affiliated women's college had not been acted upon, it was used by some trustees to justify fitful attempts to "increase the segregation of the sexes" (Minutes of the Board of Trustees, 1913, MCA). Some classes were separated by sex, for example, and in 1913, it was decided to hold separate commencement exercises for men and women. The numerical dominance of women students as a result of the First World War increased trustees' anxieties. At a board meeting in 1918, when it was reported that the class of 1918 had 35 women and 15 men students, a committee was appointed to develop a plan for the "complete separation of the two colleges" (Minutes of the Board of Trustees, May 1918, MCA).

The chair of the trustee committee charged with developing a plan for the women's college was a very wealthy donor from the class of 1871, A. Barton Hepburn,[9] who favored excluding women entirely from Middlebury. Knowing this would not be acceptable to the majority of the trustees, Hepburn was willing to compromise on an annex college for women students that would be separately incorporated with its own Board of Trustees. Presumably to gather information that would support his views, Hepburn asked Carnegie's General Education Board, whose president was one of Hepburn's close friends and which was known for its anti-coeducation stance, to visit Middlebury and make recommendations. The report issued in 1919 by E. C. Sage of the General Education Board must have disappointed Hepburn, as it concluded that Middlebury was a co-educational college that had the approval of faculty and students. Moreover, Sage wrote that the facilities provided for women students were "inadequate"; among his specific recommendations were a gymnasium for women, residence and dining halls for women, and a women's educational building for home economics and related subjects (E. C. Sage, "Notes on a Visit to Middlebury College," General Education Board 1919, MCA).

Accompanying Sage's report was a paper by another alumnus trustee, Julian Abernethy '76, that summarized the results from a survey of twenty-seven faculty, the two deans, and several staff members. All favored the "continuation of women" (whereas two were not sure that *men* students should be continued); only about one-third favored an affiliated college for women; and slightly more than one-half wanted to "continue coeducation" with a student body of half women, half men. President John Thomas '90 also answered the same survey, expressing his wish for the college to remain predominantly "in the public mind a college for men." He argued that Middlebury did not have sufficient resources to establish an affiliated college for women and so was forced to continue the policy of "seeking men and tolerating women" (J. W. Abernethy, "Analysis and Summary of the Faculty Questionnaire," 1919, MCA).

When the trustees met to consider the Sage and Abernethy reports, they decided on a compromise. Middlebury would develop a "semi-detached institution" for its women students that in outline form resembled the situation at Hobart and William Smith: one board of trustees, one faculty, but separate sections of courses for women and men students as much as possible. Before pursuing this plan the trustees agreed that they should negotiate with the state of Vermont to see if it would establish a proposed teacher's college at Middlebury. If the state were prepared to do so, the women students would all attend this college and plans for a separate women's college at Middlebury would be abandoned (Minutes of the Board of Trustees, January 1920, MCA).

Hepburn was not satisfied with this compromise, as the proposed annex for women was, in his view, insufficiently separate from Middlebury. He confided to another trustee that he had between four and six million dollars that he wished to use to endow a women's college in New England (Thomas papers, February 21, 1920, MCA). If Middlebury had moved fast enough in a direction Hepburn approved of, the college would have received this enormous donation. But it did not, and as a result, Middlebury was cut almost entirely out of Hepburn's will. The failure to obtain these funds reinforced trustees' desire to develop the affiliated college. The next man appointed president of Middlebury, Paul Moody, was given explicit instructions to make the women's college a reality (Stameshkin 1996, 20, 37).

Middlebury's Men Students as "the Excluded Aliens"?

President Moody never managed to raise sufficient money to make the women's college a reality, but he certainly tried. In front of some audiences, at least, his motivations appeared laudable. When he gave his inaugural address in 1922, for example, he argued that separation would benefit women students:

> It is not because we do not believe in the higher education for women that we would exclude them from the corridors of a man's college. We prefer to state it another way. We believe in it so much that we desire to give them equal opportunities, which they can never have under the existing system. We would build a college for them, in which men are the excluded aliens. (*The Campus*, June 14, 1922, MCA)

In private correspondence, Moody sometimes revealed that his motivation for segregating the women students was less to benefit them than to benefit men or the prestige of the college. His thinking was based on a belief in sex stereotypes. Since women are "strong in work calling for detail and weak in work calling for a grasp of principles," and men are the opposite, Moody argued, separating the sexes is sound educationally (Moody correspondence, May 22, 1929, MCA). Moody preferred a coordinate arrangement because he viewed coeducational colleges as less prestigious than men's colleges, and even less prestigious than such women's colleges as "Smith, Wellesley, Vassar and Bryn Mawr." To back up his argument about Middlebury's status being lower due to the presence of women, he claimed to an alumna that before women were admitted to Middlebury, the college made "its greatest contribution," but after women entered, it "stood still" while men's colleges with which Middlebury "should be grouped" (Williams, Dartmouth, Amherst, and Wesleyan) have "gone on" (Moody correspondence, April 12, 1923, MCA). Given that Middlebury almost collapsed before women were admitted in 1883 (see Chapter 3), President Moody's version of the college's history seems self-serving at best. It is also interesting that Moody (and many other people) thought that men's colleges were more prestigious when it was the women at coeducational colleges, including Middlebury, who did the best academic work. President Moody knew that the college was able to be much more selective in admitting women than men which worried him but did not change his views of coeducation (Moody correspondence, May 22, 1929, MCA).

The desire to reclaim Middlebury as a men's college led President Moody to consider unusual, if not bizarre, proposals. At one point it was hoped that women students might all attend Bennington, the new women's college opening in the southern part of the state, and that it would become Middlebury's coordinate, even though the distance between the two places is about 75 miles. President Moody took seriously an administrator's suggestion that the freshman class of women be placed separately in the mountains in a campus used for the summer school to show the public that "we are dead in earnest . . . about this segregation." When Moody wrote about this idea, which he called "a particularly original suggestion," to a trustee known to be strongly in favor of segregation, the trustee was dubious, if not shocked. Putting the women in the midst of a forest in the Green Mountains six miles from the railroad would "be like sending them to Dannemora," a prison on the edge of the Adirondacks, the trustee noted. Besides, there were practical problems; the buildings were neither insulated nor heated, and where would Middlebury get the faculty to teach the women at that campus? (Moody correspondence, February 1922, MCA).

Despite machinations by President Moody and trustees to increase the segregation of women and men students, college life for women students seemed relatively unaffected. A woman student, Dorothy Tillapaugh Headley, who attended Middlebury during the early 1920s, wrote about her many college activities in letters to her family. Her description of these activities, including a sorority, the YWCA, glee club, mandolin club, choir, dramatics, and her courses in home economics and one-semester residence in a home economics practice house, indicate that she took women's place at Middlebury for granted. Some of Dorothy Tillapaugh's interests were focused on men students' activities, football in particular. She wrote excitedly in November 1922, for instance, when the college "allowed the girls to cheer. . . now they're even asking us to! Isn't that corking." She also said she was "delighted" when Middlebury tied Harvard in a football game, and she described the campus celebration that ensued, including a bonfire, a snake dance, cheers, singing, and speeches by the president, a couple of trustees and several professors (Headley '25, "Dorothy Goes to College: A Coed's Letters Home from Middlebury, 1921–1924," MCA).

Some of Miss Tillapaugh's other activities related just to women. She mentioned how she and friends went to a girl's room where they "popped corn on a grill, had fudge and a rare good time," and she wrote about the skits she and other women put on for each other, the party they gave in their rooms for women students as well as a librarian and a home economics faculty member, and the rules that (as freshmen) they were given by sophomores to emphasize their "inferior position" (Headley '25, MCA).

College officials, however, continued their planning for a separate women's college at Middlebury, despite the difficulties of raising funds as the nation went into a severe economic depression. Architects were hired to develop a blueprint of the women's campus, complete with chapel, library, new residence and recitation halls, a gymnasium, and buildings for art and music. Trustees thought about a name for the college but never agreed on anything more distinctive than the Women's College at Middlebury. The Advisory Committee of the Women's College was reactivated; it was empowered to make suggestions to the committee of the Board of Trustees concerned with the women's college, which could then bring proposals to the full board (Gertrude Cornish Milliken, "Brief History of the Advisory Board of the Women's College of Middlebury, 1913 to 1949," undated, MCA).

The Women's College at Middlebury

In 1930 the trustees voted that after the class of 1934, women would not be admitted to Middlebury but rather to a separate college. Until funds were procured for the women's college, Middlebury would "loan to the new college for women the recitation halls and labs and other facilities used at the present time" (Corporation minutes, June 21, 1930, MCA). Although this may sound like a stark statement of women students' marginal position, students seemed unconcerned. The student newspaper reported on the trustees' decision only when the class of 1935 entered, that is, in September 1931. An article on the first page noted that women members of the entering class were "officially considered as enrolled in The Women's College at Middlebury." The article went on to say that this was but a step in trustees' plans to segregate women and men students into "two institutions with separate curricula" (*The Campus*, September 30, 1931, MCA). The paper's editorial for that issue of the newspaper concerned an entirely different topic—fraternity rushing.

An attempt to prevent or at least influence the development of a separate college for women actually did occur, but it was earlier and, perhaps significantly, initiated by alumnae rather than women students themselves.[10] In the early 1920s several alumnae circulated a questionnaire on the implications of the proposed coordinate college for women students. When President Moody found out about this "misleading" questionnaire, he wrote to an alumna who he was hoping would get the others "to play fair." The separate college would not lead to women students' being "debarred from Chapel, Library or Gymnasium," Moody claimed. He justified a separate institution partly on financial grounds, noting that Middlebury had already lost between four and five million dollars because it had not put its policy of segregation into effect sooner and saying that it would be easier to obtain financial support for a separate institution. But Moody also argued that a coeducational Middlebury would never have the prestige it deserved and that women would not be able to get "a square deal until their college life is given a certain degree of entity of its own." And he supported his position by noting worse alternatives advocated by some others, such as excluding women entirely (Moody to Ellis, April 12 and May 31, 1923, Moody correspondence, MCA).

The moves toward segregation in the late 1920s and 1930s did not much have much effect on women students' academic work. No further special curriculum for women was added (home economics had been established earlier, and brief experiments with household chemistry and sociology courses for just women students had already disappeared). A few more classes were single-sex, but since the early part of the century, some had always been. In 1929 President Moody noted that out of 193 classes, 47 excluded women and 42 excluded men, which means that almost one-half were by then single-sex. Moody insisted that separation be carried out in students' first year, even when faculty wanted to combine small classes of men with small classes of women (Moody to Gifford, December 19, 1929, Moody correspondence, MCA). Besides women faculty in subjects designated for women, namely Physical Education and Home Economics, one woman was hired to teach mathematics only to women; no women faculty taught men, in line with President Moody's explicit intentions (Stameshkin 1996, 40).

The degree to which college authorities wished the larger public to define Middlebury as a men's college is evident from the attention—or lack of it—given to women students in college catalogues. In the early part of the twentieth century the college had one catalogue, with only a brief section toward the end on the "women's college." The main section could be read almost without recognizing that the college had women students.[11] Later the catalogues were divided, into sections or separate publications, sometimes with the titles "Middlebury College" and "The Women's College" (1921–22 and 1930–31, for example). But other times the titles were more symmetrical—"The Men's College" and "The Women's College" (and "The Summer School").[12]

During the decade that two separate catalogues were published, from 1929–30 to 1940–41, much more attention was given to the history of women at Middlebury. Previously Emma Willard's association with Middlebury was not mentioned, but the 1935–36 Women's College Catalogue noted that Middlebury was the site of one of the first "female academies" in the country, and that it was where Emma Willard experimented with her "Plan for Improving Female Education," which it described as probably the most influential brief for women's education ever written. The 1936–37 Women's College Catalogue added to this history of women at Middlebury by mentioning that women had made "repeated . . . appeals" to enter the college before they were admitted in 1883. Both the Men's College Catalogue and the Women's College Catalogue discussed the plans for "an entirely separate women's plant," but the men's catalogue did not discuss the history of women students at Middlebury except to mention the year they were admitted (College Catalogues, 1929–1940, MCA).

Although the attempts to segregate women students at Middlebury can be interpreted as regressive in that trustees were not very concerned about women's needs for higher education, in some ways women students benefited from the moves toward a separate coordinate college. A major vehicle for the improvement in women's position was the revitalized Women's Advisory Board, especially in conjunction with one of its ex-officio members, Eleanor Ross, the powerful dean of the Women's College from 1915 to 1944.

The Advisory Board had been established in 1913 to overcome A.A.U.W.'s concerns that Middlebury had no women on its Board of Trustees (see Chapter 4). At first it met only at the request of the president, but when President Moody reestablished the board in the mid-1920s as part of his move toward making a separate women's college become a reality, it began to meet annually. It had nine members: three alumnae, three trustees, and three prominent women as permanent members (in addition to the dean of women and president of Middlebury as ex-officio members). True to its name, it had no direct power but could work only in an advisory capacity, by making suggestions to the committee of the Board of Trustees concerned with the women's college, which took those suggestions of which it approved to the full (all-men) Board of Trustees. Nonetheless, this was the first time at Middlebury that there was a formal group whose responsibilities were to determine and lobby for women students' interests. During the approximately twenty years that the revitalized Board functioned, its recommendations that were acted on included hiring matrons for women's dormitories; adding courses in sociology and psychology, art, and music appreciation; modernizing admissions requirements; financing a mountain lodge for the women's athletic association;[13] hiring more women faculty; developing more scholarships for women students; having itself recognized by being listed in the catalogue; and obtaining a placement bureau (Milliken, undated, MCA).

Dean Ross, who herself had attended Middlebury at the end of the nineteenth century when there was no dean for the women students, did not oppose Moody's plans to develop the Women's College (Stameshkin 1996, 45). She appeared to believe that a separate college would enable women students' needs to be recognized and not always subordinated to men students' requirements. Functioning in many ways like a president of the women's college, as President Moody himself said (Stameshkin 1996, 44), she became an effective advocate for women students' interests. She was especially concerned about inadequate housing and brought this problem to the attention of President Moody, convincing him of the need to end "the discrimination of the past" (Moody correspondence, August 19, 1922, MCA). Despite Dean Ross's concern, the housing conditions for women students did not improve, however. In 1932 she recommended to the Board of Trustees that women's admissions be limited to 80 because of the "very bad" rooming conditions (Minutes of the Board of Trustees 1932, MCA).

Overall, Dean Ross, working with the Advisory Board, played a critical role in improving conditions for women at Middlebury. According to a graduate of Middlebury, Edgar "Cap" Wiley '13, who was himself dean of the men's college for nine years before becoming the director of admissions from 1927–1947, Dean Ross did not accept "the tendency [in a coeducational college] to plan curricula more for men and let the women adjust accordingly. . . . She battled for special consideration for courses, living accommodations, social life, and standards to meet the needs and interests of college women" (Middlebury College Newsletter 1953, 18, MCA).

Middlebury's Return to Coeducation

By 1940 Middlebury still had not raised sufficient money to build the women's college campus it had planned. Catalogues began stressing the college's coeducational nature rather than the separateness of the Women's College. The 1940–41 Catalogue, for example, said that the affiliated colleges were governed by the same Board of Trustees, had the same president, and occupied many of the same buildings. It also noted that there was one curriculum, and "where the subject or class registration do not warrant separate recitation periods, men and women attend the same classes." The Catalogue even mentioned that both colleges were commonly referred to as Middlebury. The major distinctions that the Catalogue pointed out were in admissions and in the dormitory and social regulations that governed the women students (1940–41 Catalogue, MCA).

The entrance of the United States into World War II in December 1941 dramatically changed campus dynamics. As women became the overwhelming majority of students, separating women from men students became a less salient issue. Even after a navy training unit was located at Middlebury, women dominated leadership positions. For the first time women were editors-in-chief of the student newspaper and yearbook, and according to June Brogger Noble '46, they dominated sports as well. Although parietal hours were still strict, and women students had to be chaperoned, the Navy men, older and more sophisticated, encouraged the women students to pressure the college to give them a place to socialize. For the first time, women who got married were allowed back in college. The loosening of rules, the sense during the war of being on "borrowed time," was reflected in more liberal politics. The famous controversial black congressman from Harlem, Adam Clayton Powell, spoke on campus, as did Granville Hicks, the Marxist author and literary critic. Students overwhelmingly supported the secret of the atom bomb being turned over to the United Nations, even at the cost of national sovereignty (June Brogger Noble, "Coming of Age in World War II," *Middlebury Magazine*, Winter 1974–75, 12–16, MCA).

As in the country at large, however, with the end of World War II came a return of women students to their more traditional places. Men students at Middlebury once again dominated in numbers as well as campus leadership positions and sports. Prewar enrollment figures indicate that women comprised about 46 percent of the undergraduates. The greatest imbalance during the war was in 1945–46, when women were 88 percent of the students, but by 1947, women were again 46 percent of the students and fell to 40 or 41 percent in the following years (Catalogues, MCA).

Almost half of the men students after the war were veterans, who affected the ethos of the college through their disdain for anti-democratic and elitist views (Stameshkin 1996, 86, 186, 304). But conservatism reigned again in the 1950s when the college sought to attract rich students, particularly young men from "prep" schools (Stameshkin 1996, 200, 305).

The Women's College of Middlebury came to an end in 1949, when the Women's College Advisory Board was abolished, considered unnecessary since women were represented on the Board of Trustees (Trustee minutes, Oct. 1948).[14] But women continued to be only a small minority of trustees; even when alumnae obtained the right to elect a representative on the Board, they had only one representative compared to four for the alumni (Catalogues, MCA). Housing for women students remained inadequate; in fact, in 1950, 145 women students had to be housed on the men's side of the campus, and still more had to live off-campus (Stameshkin 1996, 106–7).

After the end of the war but before the student protests of the late 1960s, a few changes did occur at Middlebury, mostly in the direction of relaxing some of the rules that were beginning to seem old-fashioned. These rules covered students' residential life, particularly women's, since a double standard prevailed. Elizabeth Kelly, who served as dean of women from 1950 to 1970, took pride in how "tough" a disciplinarian she was, noting that parents expected her to know where their "girls were . . . every hour of the day and night." She related an amusing but telling anecdote from her early years, when veterans were still studying at the college. A vet said to her, "I'm not bringing girls back by eleven." She responded, "Then you're not taking them out." The vet: "You're tough." Dean Kelly: "In New Guinea guys couldn't wait to get home to 'good girls.' These girls are going to stay that way" (taped interview with Elizabeth Kelly, January 31, 1986, MCA).

By the mid-1960s the rule changes that had occurred at Middlebury included lessening Chapel requirements, until attendance became entirely voluntary in 1961; slightly relaxing parietal hours for women; initiating mixed-sex dining for first-year students (in the mid-1950s); and, beginning in the early 1960s, having one student government association for both men and women students. The last change is a noteworthy one in that with a single student government came the rule that a man student had to be president (*The Campus*, November 10, 1966, MCA), just as men held the top offices of the mixed-sex student publications. This still represented some improvement for women students, however, since previously control of students' social life had rested with the male student government association at Middlebury, which in turn had been dominated by the fraternities.

Thus in the mid-1960s, on the eve of the student protest movement, Middlebury was not that different from a men's college, even though it had a (large) minority of highly qualified and highly socially regulated women students. Women students studied the same curriculum as men, yet male dominance was evident—in enrollments, student leadership positions, and in the faculty, administration, and trustees. The college's financial aid went mainly to the men students; for example, in 1957, men college scholars received $29,500, whereas women got only $10,725 (Stameshkin 1996, 199). A 1965 National Institute of Mental Health (NIMH) study of Middlebury chronicled the many ways men students dominated college life, including writing over 80 percent of the letters to the student newspaper and heading most clubs. The dean of the college, Dennis O'Brien, admitted in an interview that Middlebury was "a boy's college with women," a situation that was regretted by one professor but about which another professor said, "Maybe women don't need to be at the top. Maybe they subconsciously realize that some day they'll be homemakers . . . they would rather compete on more nebulous grounds, like appearance." The woman student, Maureen Buehler, who reported on these findings for the student newspaper did not seem upset about them, concluding that perhaps masculine domination was one of the "few ways in which the college resembles the outside world where our culture considers men more qualified for authority" ("Middlebury: A Masculine Image?" *The Campus*, November 10, 1966, MCA). Ten years later few women students would react with such complacency.

William Smith: Coordinate but Subordinate

William Smith originated as a coordinate college for the education of women, as I discussed in Chapter 4. The planned nature of William Smith and its origins in a large financial gift ensured that women students' interests received more attention than they did at Middlebury, yet relations between Hobart and William Smith Colleges were institutionalized in a way that reflected the subordination of women in society at large.

Hobart College trustees never intended that the number of women students enrolled in William Smith would equal the number of men students. Only in wartime did the numbers of women come close to or slightly exceed the number of men. In most years there were two to three times as many men as women students; for example, in 1928–29, Hobart had 310 students, William Smith 156; in 1938–39, the enrollments were 381 to 164; and in 1947–48 they were 924 to 295, more than a 3:1 ratio (Catalogues, HWSCA). The preponderance of men students was an open policy of which the trustees did not feel ashamed, as indicated by a statement in the 1957–58 Catalogue: "The normal enrollment is 750 men at Hobart and 250 women at William Smith" (1957–58 Catalogue, HWSCA).

One effect of limiting the admission of William Smith students was the same as at Middlebury—the college could be more selective so that women students were more qualified and performed better academically than the men students. In 1943 the regional college accrediting body criticized Hobart for admitting too many "prep" students and too many men who required "conditional" acceptances (Minutes of the Board of Trustees, 1943, HWSCA). The inequities produced by the numerical imbalance between Hobart and William Smith students were not addressed, however, until the early 1970s.

From the beginning William Smith College came under the jurisdiction of Hobart's trustees, but it did have its own five representatives on the Hobart board. Moreover, the founder, Mr. Smith, made it a condition of his gift that one of William Smith College's trustee representatives had to be a woman (see Chapter 4). Thus since the opening of William Smith, there was always at least one woman on the board. Yet similar to the numerical dominance of men students, the joint Board of Trustees always had a majority of men, most of whom were elected to represent Hobart College. Even when William Smith alumnae began to be elected to the board, at the relatively early date of 1924, they had only one representative, compared to five alumni of Hobart. It was not until 1947 that William Smith's alumnae representatives were increased to two (the alumni still elected five) (Minutes of the Board of Trustees, 1943, 1947, HWSCA).

Hobart's dominance over William Smith was also manifest in the way the coordinate arrangement was structured. As I discussed in Chapter 4, William Smith was legally not a separately incorporated college but rather a "department" of Hobart, even though most people, including faculty, trustees, administrators, and students, referred to it as a college.[15] In their diaries, for example, it was common for William Smith students to talk about "the colleges" or, even more specifically, the "two colleges" (cf. Helen Reid, class of 1919; Eleanor Heist Clise, daily diary notes, 1934, HWSCA).

According to two college historians, occasionally "mild complaints" surfaced about William Smith's being a "mere appendage of Hobart" before the situation was rectified in the 1940s (Walter Durfee and Otto Schoen-René, "William Smith College 1908–1958, A History," Hobart College Bulletin,1959, HWSCA). In 1943, the Board of Trustees, at the encouragement of Hobart's President John Milton Potter, revised the college charter to bring William Smith into "full parity" with Hobart. A new "corporation of colleges," called the "Colleges of the Seneca," came into being. Similar to what trustees of Hamilton College would contemplate about twenty years later, Hobart's "corporation of colleges" charter was written with the idea that additional colleges might "from time to time be constituted," if the Board of Trustees voted for them and the New York State Board of Regents approved (Minutes of the Board of Trustees, May 8, 1943, HWSCA). Although this charter revision created legal equality between Hobart and William Smith Colleges, it did not change the disparity in numbers of men and women students or the number of representatives on the Board of Trustees. Moreover, the name, "Colleges of the Seneca," never became widely known or accepted. It was mainly found on some official publications, although college guides like *Lovejoy's* did mention that "Hobart and its co-ordinate, William Smith College (for women)" formed the Colleges of the Seneca. Significantly, though, *Lovejoy's* listed both colleges under Hobart, which remained the better known institution, with William Smith described in an indented paragraph below Hobart.[16]

Remnants of a Women's College

Despite its relationship to Hobart, William Smith functioned in some ways like Wells and other women's colleges. More attention was paid to women students' social refinement than was true at coeducational colleges like Middlebury. Dining at William Smith, for example, was similar to Wells in its formality. Students sat at tables covered by white cloths, used cloth napkins and their own napkin rings, and were served by waitresses. Social occasions that required formal dress were common. A member of the class of 1916, Sarah Cumming, later recalled how at William Smith students "step[ped] into society" through many balls and receptions (Cumming '16, mss file, HWSCA). At a luncheon for the 1914 inauguration of a new college president, an article in the William Smith newspaper reported, women faculty "poured" and seniors "served" (*The Ridge*, 1914, HWSCA). Students attended many teas, which gave them practice in good manners and polite conversation. A member of the class of 1918, Rosalind Daniels, remembered a suffrage tea at a local farm owned by a trustee (Daniels '18, mss file, HWSCA), but more typically, the teas were with deans and professors (1933–34 William Smith Handbook, HWSCA). One indication that customs changed with the times comes from an alumna from the 1930s, who recalled a tea where the dean served students strawberry sundaes, cookies, and *cigarettes* (Eleanor Heist Clise, daily diary notes, 1934, HWSCA).[17]

Some William Smith students resented the kind of training that teas and receptions represented, at least in retrospect. Arleen Daniels Auerbach attended William Smith in the 1950s and majored in biology. She later described herself as having been a serious student who often felt lonely since she did not spend as much time socializing and attending parties as many of her classmates did. Her excitement was intellectual, rewarded by the encouragement one of her male professors gave her to pursue a career in science or medicine (which she did, but not until after she married and had children). When, as a researcher in medical genetics, Dr. Auerbach returned to William Smith in 1980 to give a Founder's Day address, she recalled her time as a student, specifically the teas on Wednesday afternoons. Students took turns at pouring—"training for the kind of life women were expected to lead after graduation." In this alumna's view, changes in the 1960s and 1970s that eliminated such functions made William Smith a better institution for the education of women (Arleen Daniels Auerbach, 1980 Founder's Day Address, HWSCA).

The curriculum of William Smith also reflected its status as a women's college, but not as emphatically as the curriculum of Wells College. William Smith had a music department with six courses when it opened in 1908, but art did not become part of the curriculum until later, and in 1917, only two art courses were listed. These subjects were viewed as only appropriate for women students, as Hobart students were at first not allowed to study them. In the early years of Wells College French was emphasized as necessary for women's refinement, but by the time William Smith opened, colleges of all types were de-emphasizing the classics and stressing modern languages, so it is not surprising that both Hobart and William Smith students had the same language requirements.

Similar to Wells, attention was paid to the posture of William Smith's "lady" students. Their physical measurements were taken each year and they were given "special corrective gymnastics, if necessary" (1918–19 Catalogue, HWSCA). Even as late as 1948, the catalogue listed "recreation" for William Smith students which, it said, worked toward their "better poise, carriage, and body movement." Hobart's analogous program was "athletics," which offered intercollegiate and intramural team sports (football, basketball, lacrosse, and baseball). William Smith did have an Athletic Association as well, however, which included tennis, golf, badminton, bowling, and swimming.

William Smith College opened during the Progressive Era, when the culture at large emphasized social amelioration through the application of specialized expertise. Scientific household management, taught in departments of home economics, fit this cultural ethos. Similar to many other colleges, William Smith established a department of home economics in 1912. For a period of time in the 1930s, students were required to take a two-semester course in the department.

In the early part of this century, women were increasingly engaging in remunerative work, at least before they married, and as the century progressed, such work became less exclusively associated with the working class and more characteristic of middle-class women as well (Tyack and Hansot 1990). And so, William Smith students were educated with their later work in mind, at the same time they were trained to be "ladies." William Smith added a secretarial work department in 1918 to "enable its graduates to take positions in the business world" (1918–19 Catalogue, HWSCA).[18] In this way William Smith was similar to Connecticut College for Women, which from its opening in 1915 had professional courses (Kehr 1920). Clerical work was, next to teaching, a major white-collar occupation for women, and one in which such middle-class attributes as good speech and writing skills gave applicants a decided advantage (Rury 1991). Thus William Smith College, despite having some of the characteristics of women's colleges devoted to training students in "social graces," had a practical bent as well.

Coordination and Adaptation

Flexibility was an unintended benefit of the coordinate structure between Hobart and William Smith (before and after the 1943 charter revision). When larger social conditions made it expedient to stress separation of women and men, the college was able to argue that it really was two single-sex colleges; on the other hand, when coeducation became more popular, coordination was downplayed and integration stressed. These changes were not simply rhetorical, either, as classes could become more or less mixed-sex, curriculum could be identical or different, and clubs could be single-sex or combined. During the period of time covered in this chapter, from pre-World War I until the mid-1960s, the general drift at Hobart and William Smith was in the direction of coeducation, but it was not always a smooth, uncontested movement.

In terms of curriculum, the greatest separation between what women and men studied occurred not during the earliest years of William Smith, but rather during the late 1920s. William Smith students had always been able to elect majors not available to Hobart students; for example, domestic science or music (and later secretarial studies and art).[19] Even within the same departments, different courses were sometimes offered for women and men students. In 1917–18, for example, William Smith offered an economics and sociology course on Woman's Education and Social Status, taught by a woman professor who did not teach Hobart students. The closest course to this for Hobart students was a course taught by a man professor on the history of institutions, whose description said that "the position of woman" would be discussed, including "the movements for industrial, political and educational emancipation of woman" (1917–18 Catalogue, HWSCA). But by the late 1920s, the course offerings of some departments differed dramatically depending on whether they were taught to women or men. Thus Hobart students were offered eight courses in economics while William Smith students had only three; Hobart had fourteen chemistry courses, including one on glass blowing, whereas William Smith had five chemistry courses, one of which was oriented toward teaching; and in mathematics and physics, Hobart had nine courses and William Smith seven (1928–29 Catalogues, HWSCA). Ten years later, however, when the country was still struggling with a national depression so that the economy of coeducation was more appealing, the curriculum at Hobart and William Smith was identical except for home economics (1938–39 Catalogues, HWSCA).

When William Smith opened in 1908, all classes were single-sex. Although some faculty were hired to teach in only one of the colleges, most faculty had to teach their classes twice. Stories from that time indicate that students, and perhaps faculty as well, considered Hobart and its students to be the "real" college. As a William Smith student from the class of 1919, Helen Reid, later said, "We used Hobart professors" (Reid '19, mss file, HWSCA). Faculty sometimes edited the lectures they gave to the women students, but the women heard the uncut versions from their Hobart friends (*Pultney Street Survey*, October 1982, HWSCA). Subjects less popular with men or women were offered less frequently; for example, physics for women students was taught every other year. A William Smith student in the class of 1917, Elizabeth Durfee, was counseled against taking physics when she wanted, her sophomore year. She was thus able to take only one year of physics before studying it in graduate school at Cornell University. Years later Durfee commented wryly,

"One couldn't teach boys and girls together in such a sexy subject as physics" (Elizabeth Durfee '17, "William Smith College in the Mid Teens," 1975, HWSCA).

By the mid-1930s many classes were mixed-sex. A William Smith student, Eleanor Heist (Clise) '36, recorded her day-to-day activities, noting the sex ratios of her classes: zoology had 9 "boys" and 2 "girls," genetics 8 boys and 5 girls, but her chemistry, education, and bacteriology classes were all women. Some large classes were also mixed; in her senior year Eleanor Heist reported that her large beginning German and large (28 students) sociology class were "co-ed" (Daily Diary Notes, Class of 1936, HWSCA). According to college historians, by 1938 all classes were co-educational (Walter Durfee and Otto Schoen-René, "William Smith College 1908–1958, A History," Hobart College Bulletin 1959, HWSCA).

Many student clubs and publications at William Smith became integrated with those at Hobart by the late 1930s or 1940s. In the 1930s, for example, the dramatic clubs merged; shortly after World War II, so did the international relations club, the debating clubs, language clubs, and the choir (Handbooks and Catalogues, HWSCA). After some debate, the student newspapers merged in 1942.

The combination of the student newspapers illustrates what frequently happened with integration. Both William Smith women and Hobart men favored combining their newspapers, according to an informal poll. Two weeks before the new merged newspaper was published, an editorial in the William Smith newspaper, *The Twig*, called the impending change "progress." The editorial's description of the new paper's design noted that four pages would be equally divided for important news of each college (*The Twig*, April 1, 1942, HWSCA).

When the combined newspaper was published, it looked very similar to Hobart's newspaper, *The Herald*, which had been much more professionally produced than William Smith's *The Twig*. The most noticeable change was a new heading with seals of the two colleges in the corners. The paper's editor-in-chief was a Hobart student; the managing editor was a William Smith student. The first issue had a large photo of a Hobart lacrosse game, but only a small article about the bowling of "Hill seniors" (William Smith seniors), and nothing about the other sports at William Smith that *The Twig* had reported on (badminton, lacrosse, and baseball). There was, however, a photograph of a physical education dance performance of William Smith students. A column on women students' clothes that had been a regular feature in *The Twig* did not appear. Yet the announcement of the merger of the two newspapers was described as "an event symbolic of the tendency towards progress which has so long been demonstrated by the local colleges" (*The Herald of Hobart & William Smith*, Apri 23, 1942, HWSCA).

The pattern of a man chief editor and a woman associate editor of the colleges' newspaper did not persist as it did at Middlebury. Two William Smith women were the chief editors during the war, and later the pattern varied. Many years, both a woman and a man served as editors-in-chief (1949 and 1950, for example). While the preponderance of articles on sports dealt with games at Hobart, short articles appeared on such events as the William Smith Athletic Association banquet.

Yearbooks of the two colleges remained separate for much longer than the newspapers—until 1962, in fact. And some college activities never merged; in particular, athletics, student government, and fraternities. Others changed form or purpose; the original William Smith newspaper, for example, became a literary magazine for both colleges. But starting in the 1940s, coordination was downplayed and the colleges tried to present themselves more as a coeducational institution. The descriptions in the college catalogues are one indication of this change in emphasis. Compared to earlier catalogues, more space was devoted to what students of both colleges had and did in common than to what they did separately. Not until the late 1970s would the pendulum swing back again and the colleges present themselves as uniquely coordinate.

In summary, even when William Smith College was moving in the direction of integration with its coordinate partner, Hobart, it never entirely lost its separate institutional identity. While students and college officials might not have recognized the benefits of some degree of separation, such advantages are apparent when one compares women students' position in the coordinate arrangement with that of women students in a coeducational college like Middlebury. Perhaps the clearest indicator of the difference is that at Middlebury, women students were in danger of being excluded entirely, whereas William Smith students were numerically underrepresented but secure.

Comparisons of Women Students' Experiences in the Three Colleges

Table 5.1 summarizes some quantitative information concerning Wells, Middlebury, and Hobart and William Smith Colleges over a period of about 40 years, from 1928 to 1965. All three colleges more than doubled their enrollment during these years, but Wells's enrollments increased somewhat less than those of Hobart and William Smith and Middlebury. Both Middlebury and Hobart and William Smith increased just under 300 percent, whereas Wells grew by less than 250 percent, despite presidents' and boards of trustees' attempts, beginning in the 1930s, to make Wells become a bigger college.

In all the years covered in Table 5.1, women comprised a larger percentage of the students at Middlebury (over 40 percent) than they did at Hobart and William Smith (never more than one-third). In some ways this seems surprising, since in comparison to Middlebury, the number of women who originally entered William Smith was much greater, and unlike at Middlebury, their entry was part of a planned process. But it was precisely due to this planning, in which it was specified that the desirable ratio of men to women was 3 to 1 (1957–58 Hobart and William Smith Catalogue, HWSCA), that Hobart and William Smith was able to maintain a rather steady, if lopsided, sex ratio. Middlebury, which admitted women students originally for financial reasons and only gradually became committed to their continuing presence, regulated the number of women students less strictly.

What is also apparent from Table 5.1 is that at Middlebury there was somewhat more equality in numbers between men and women in the earlier years covered by this table than in the later years; women comprised 46 percent of the students in 1928 but 41 or 42 percent in 1958 and 1965. This increase in numbers of men relative to women occurred at Middlebury despite the recognition that the men students who were being admitted were academically weaker than the women and that a greater percentage of men than women applicants was being admitted (Report of the President to the Trustees, 1959–60, MCA).[20] The ratio of men to women students at Hobart and William Smith became more unequal between 1928 and 1958; women comprised 33 percent of the students in 1928, but only 26 percent in 1958. By 1965, however, William Smith women were 41 percent of the students. Thus to the degree that the relative numbers of men and women students indicate which sex had the upper hand at these colleges, it appears that male dominance at Middlebury was slightly greater from 1948 to 1965 than from 1928 to 1938; at Hobart and William Smith, male dominance first increased, but then began to decrease in the early 1960s.

Information in Table 5.1 on tuition and the percentage of students from out of state indicates that at least until the mid-1960s, Wells College remained basically faithful to its founder's vision as an institution for young women from "good" homes. Even though the numbers of students on

TABLE 5.1 Comparisons of Three Colleges on Selected Dimensions, 1928–1965

		Wells	Middlebury	Wm Smith (& Hobart)
SIZE	1928	a) 237, 51%	a) 284, 64%	a) 156, 10%
a) # women			b) 337, 77%	b) 310, 30%
students,	1938	a) 313, 60%	a) 354, 77%	a) 164, 20%
% out-of-state			b) 423, 66%	b) 381, 25%
b) # men	1948	a) 305, 63%	a) 499, 70%	a) 295, 33%
students,			b) 682, 72%	b) 924, 29%
% out-of-state	1958	a) 383, 56%	a) 516, 77%	a) 250, 33%
			b) 748, 74%	b) 757, 32%
	1965	a) 552, 58%	a) 566, 91%	a) 360, 39%
			b) 786, 93%	b) 1014, 40%
TUITION	1928	$300/yr. tuition; $700 bd	$250/yr. tuition; $375 bd	$250/yr. tuition; $500 bd
& BOARD	1938	$1,000/yr. combined	$700/yr. combined	$950/yr. combined
	1948	$1,400/yr. combined	$990/yr, combined	$1020/yr. (or $820 if in coop. house)
	1958	$2,150/yr. combined	$1700/yr. combined	$1680/yr. combined
	1965	$2,700/yr. combined	$2400/yr. combined	$2650/yr. combined
FACULTY	1928	a) 40	a) 55	a) 36
a) Number		b) 47%	b) 15%	b) 31%
b) % Ph.D.		c) 70%	c) 20%	c) 17%
c) % women			including 11 instructors (11% w/o instructors)	
	1938	a) 52	a) 61	a) 47
		b) 52%	b) 15%	b) 36%
		c) 69%	c) 15%	c) 11%
	1948	a) 54	a) 75	a) 85
		b) 57%	b) 27%	b) 26%
		c) 69%	c) 13%	c) 22%
	1958	a) 52	a) 94	a) 85
		b) 60%	b) 39%	b) 33%
		c) 63%	c) 15%	c) 24%
	1965	a) 62	a) 107	a) 105, ft incl. instructors
		b) 60%	b) 46%	b) 39% of all ft
		c) 42%	c) 8%	c) 16%

TABLE 5.1 Continued

		Wells	Middlebury	Wm Smith (& Hobart)
BOARD OF	1928	21, 43%	23, none	23, 13%
TRUSTEES	1938	22, 45%	23, none	22, 9%
Number, %	1948	24, 50%	23, none	23, 17%
women	1958	24, 46%	24, 12.5%	25, 16%
	1965	24, 46%	25, 12%	22, 18%

Information obtained from college catalogues. See note at end of Table 3.1.

scholarships increased over time, Wells's high tuition and its tendency to enroll many descendants and relatives of former students meant that its student body was overwhelmingly white, Protestant (or at least Christian), and rich. The high tuition costs at William Smith in the earlier years, and its emphasis on training "ladies," suggest that, like Wells, it enrolled quite wealthy students. By the late 1950s, however, William Smith became relatively less expensive. On the other hand, although Middlebury's charges were lower in the early years, they became approximately the same as William Smith's by 1958. Moreover, a high percentage of Middlebury's students came from out of state, which generally indicates that a college has enrolled middle-class students (Levine 1986). Moreover, according to a historian who has studied Middlebury, after World War II, the college self-consciously set out to attract rich students; it was helped in this endeavor by having its own ski slopes, since skiing was a boom sport for the wealthy (Stameshkin 1996, 282). Middlebury was successful in recruiting wealthy students; in 1960, more than one-third of entering freshwomen, and close to one-half of the entering freshmen, had attended private schools (Report of the President, 1959–60, MCA). Thus by 1960 Middlebury's students seem to have come from backgrounds at least as privileged as Wells students, since fewer than one-third of students entering Wells in 1955 had attended private secondary schools, a figure that was lower than in previous years (President's Report, October, 1955, 2, WCA).

Faculty at Wells differed significantly from the faculty at the other two colleges. As Table 5.1 indicates, a much higher percentage of faculty at Wells were women than was true at either Hobart and William Smith or Middlebury. At Wells and Middlebury, the percentage of women on the faculty decreased over time—at Wells from a high of 70 percent in 1928 to 42 percent in 1965, and at Middlebury from 20 to 8 percent. The decrease in the number of women on Wells's faculty appears to have been the result of a conscious decision by President Long in the 1950s to increase the number of men faculty in order to enhance the academic reputation of the college (Dieckmann 1995, 330). The trends were not consistent at Hobart and William Smith, where women comprised as much as a quarter of the faculty in 1958, but as few as 11 percent in 1938.

When the majority of Wells's faculty were women, these intellectual, mostly unmarried women struggled to create a satisfying community for themselves. An economics and sociology professor, Jean Davis, wrote about her experiences at Wells from 1928 to 1946. She described the discrimination faced by women faculty, not only in terms of pay but also in terms of extra expectations and restrictions. Unmarried women faculty at Wells (and almost all were single) originally were expected to live in student housing and to take their meals with students. It took "financially courageous women" to break away from this "living-in system," but some, probably those who were independently wealthy, finally did. A few bought houses together, and later two groups established cooperative housekeeping, calling themselves "the Women's Faculty Club of Wells College," a name which they had printed on stationery (Jean Davis, "Facts and Folklore," 1970, WCA).

What has been called the "family wage" system prevailed at Wells. Men faculty were given the basic salary for their rank, and then $1,000 more for their spouse and $250 for each child under twenty-one years of age (President's Report, 1927–28: 6, WCA). But when a couple of women faculty at Wells tried to apply this logic to their own situations, they were refused. One who had adopted a child and asked for the extra $250 was told by the president that she did not have to have the child. She let it be known, at least to other women faculty, that she could never forgive the president for this response. Another woman faculty member married an unsuccessful writer, and applied for the $1,000 for her spouse. The president was "outraged," as he believed it was husbands' duty to support their wives. In this latter case, however, a "compromise" was worked out and the faculty member received $500 (Davis 1970, WCA).

The opportunities for women faculty at Middlebury and Hobart and William Smith to form satisfying communities were much fewer than at Wells since there were so few women on these faculties.[21] The women faculty at these two colleges were almost entirely in fields considered appropriate for women:[22] foreign languages, music and art, education, and until the major was eliminated, home economics.[23] Although women faculty at Middlebury and Hobart and William Smith were not expected to live with women students, they were paid less than the men faculty.[24] To the degree that such sex discrimination had to be justified, presumably the arguments made were similar to those at Wells: women did not have families to support, and even single men faculty could not live as cheaply as single women faculty since, unlike the women, the men could not do their own laundry, sew on buttons, or make their own clothes during summer holidays (Davis 1970, WCA).

Table 5.1 also shows that a higher proportion of Wells's faculty had their Ph.D.s than was true of either Middlebury or William Smith. More than 50 percent of Wells faculty had their Ph.D.s from 1938 on, whereas even in 1965, somewhat fewer than half of Middlebury's faculty had their Ph.D.s. It is revealing that even though Wells had a faculty that was highly qualified academically, as long as the faculty were predominantly women, the college felt it was not perceived to be as prestigious as it might have been.

Women were better represented in the governing structure of Wells than they were at Middlebury or Hobart and William Smith. Table 5.1 shows that between 1928 and 1965, women comprised close to half of Wells's Board of Trustees, whereas they remained less than 20 percent of the trustees of Hobart and William Smith and were not present at all on Middlebury's board for most of these years (and then there were only three women on a board of 24). Even at Wells, however, the chair of the board was always a man, and the college continued to appoint men as president.

Did it make a difference to women students how many women were on the faculty or Board of Trustees at their colleges? I would argue that it did, but not in a simple or straightforward way. To assume that the more women were on the faculty, the more women students would "model" themselves after these women and elect majors that were not traditional for women is putting too much weight on a single causal factor.[25] Women students arrived at college with ideas about what women should do and many already had interests in particular academic subjects. Also the popularity of faculty members, whether women or men, affected the likelihood of students' majoring in these faculty members' areas, especially as all three of these colleges were small. But it seems reasonable to believe that the more young women saw other women in responsible positions, doing scholarly work, the more subtle encouragement they were receiving for taking themselves and their ambitions seriously.[26] And having women on the board served the same kind of purpose that including representatives of any particular group would: it increased the likelihood that issues of particular concern to that group would be recognized. The record at

Middlebury does seem to indicate that women students' interests were given more attention when the Advisory Board of the Women's College functioned. Even though this board was not part of the Board of Trustees, it did have representatives from the board who could bring its concerns to the full board.

The letters of the Wells student "Allie" Prigge in the early 1930s give some idea of the kinds of relationships women students were able to form with faculty. She mentioned going to the apartments of women instructors, having picnics or going out to dinner with them, even going to the movies in a city about twenty miles away with a group of friends and two women faculty. When one of these women faculty members had a serious accident, Allie visited her in the hospital. Allie was also friendly with a man on the faculty, the poet Robert Tristram Coffin, whose children she frequently minded. When Robert Frost visited the college, Allie was invited to Coffin's house for a reception. Coffin also asked Allie to work on a collection of Wells' students' prose and poetry. Before she graduated, Allie and a few of her friends took Dr. Coffin and his wife out to a restaurant: "We must do something for them after all they've done for us all these years," she explained to her parents. Given these varied experiences, it is interesting to read Allie's reactions to the announcement of new faculty: "Four men among them, thank God" (Letters Home, Alberta Prigge Zabriskie '32, Class Folders, WCA). And so, despite this student's warm relationships with some women faculty, she seemed to accept the verdict of society at large: having men on a faculty is somehow better or more prestigious.[27]

Many letters and reminiscences of William Smith students also mentioned close relationships with faculty. Students reported canoeing with faculty, having teas with them, sharing meals in their homes, and babysitting for their children. Elizabeth Durfee '17 called Professor Muirheid, a Shakespeare scholar, "one of my best life-long friends" (Durfee 1975, HWSCA). Several factors may have led women students at Wells and William Smith to form closer relationships with their faculty than women students at Middlebury did: the colleges' smaller size (considering William Smith separate from Hobart), the students' wealthier backgrounds (making the social distance from faculty seem less), and the many informal interactions between faculty and students that women's colleges encouraged. The few extant diaries or letters of Middlebury women students make it difficult to know about the quality of their relationships with faculty, however.[28]

Another way in which Wells and William Smith Colleges were more supportive of women during the half century under consideration was in bringing famous women to campus. From the late 1890s on, Wells College had women speakers quite frequently. In 1948–49, for example, seven of twelve special lectures were by women. It is interesting that in this postwar year, the women gave lectures on career opportunities or scholarly subjects, whereas all the men spoke on issues connected with marriage and childrearing (1948–49 Catalogue, 113, WCA). William Smith used the centenary of Elizabeth Blackwell's graduation in 1949 to bring twelve outstanding women physicians to campus to honor them. About a decade later it instituted the Elizabeth Blackwell Awards, in which almost every year such well-known women as Margaret Mead and Marian Anderson have received honors and spoken on campus. Middlebury, by contrast, brought very few women to campus to speak or to honor them. Most years after World War II, for example, out of about six or seven people given honorary degrees, only one was a woman (in 1950, 1 woman and 6 men received honorary degrees; in 1956, 1 woman and 5 men; in 1961, 2 women and 12 men).[29]

Considering the overall situation for women students at these three colleges by the mid-1960s, I conclude that Wells, and to a lesser extent William Smith, supported their women students without being in any way feminist. The overt message women students received most of the time reinforced ideas that marriage and motherhood were their most important roles. Yet women at Wells and William Smith, to a much greater extent than women students at Middlebury, were able to see learned women in respected positions. They also led their own clubs and cheered each other on (as well as competed with each other) in sports and, at Wells, in academic work. Thus at least during their college years, Wells and William Smith students observed and experienced the pleasures of being competent and successful women.

In the next chapter I describe the founding and ultimate demise of a coordinate women's college in the turbulent mid-1960s. Kirkland, Hamilton College's coordinate, was unlike Wells, Middlebury, and William Smith in that it did not have a traditional legacy to overcome. The major question I will address is, was this new women's college successful in avoiding stereotypical assumptions about women's "nature" and in establishing an environment which met women's need for a supportive yet challenging academic institution?

Notes

1   Some historians argue that changes in sexual mores originated earlier (cf. Palmieri 1995), but in any event some of the most obvious manifestations of women's sexual liberation, for instance, short skirts, bobbed hair, sexually suggestive dances, and smoking, occurred after World War I (Fass 1977; Horowitz 1984; O'Neill 1973). It may be, as Smith (1973) suggests, that the sexual revolution occurred later for educated women than it did for less educated women.

2   In *Odd Girls and Twilight Lovers* Faderman (1991: 49) notes that between 1740 and 1895, only one article on lesbianism appeared in the Index Catalogue of the Library of the Surgeon General's Office, whereas almost 100 books and 566 articles appeared in the same source between 1896 and 1916 on women's sexual "perversions," "inversions," and "disorders" (Faderman 1991, 49). Faderman also mentions one article in a 1902 medical journal that described women's colleges as a "great breeding ground" of lesbianism, but she argues that for the most part, medical journals focused on sexual "disorders" of working-class women and that most middle-class American college women were naive about lesbianism, as witnessed by the poetry society at Oberlin, which until the 1920s, called itself the Oberlin Lesbian Society (Faderman 1991, 51).

3   A 1927–28 President's Report addressed this dilemma directly: "The most distressing thing about Wells College is also a cause of congratulation; namely its crowded condition" (President's Report, 30, WCA).

4   In 1933–34, 75 students (about 33 percent) received scholarships, compared to only 46 students just the year before (President's Report 1933–34, WCA). Overall, about one-quarter of the 1936–1940 classes at Wells received scholarships. For the 1941–1944 classes, the percentage increased to over 30, and then dropped down to about 22 for the class of 1945 (President's Report 1943–44, WCA). In the 1950s about 25 to 30 percent of students received scholarships or grants-in-aid (L. J. Long, "A Report of Progress, 1950–1960," 10, WCA).

5   Although it is not possible to be certain about ethnicity based on surnames, they can provide a rough indicator. In 1946–47, for example, students listed in Wells catalogues had such Jewish-sounding names as Abraham, Bernhard, Goldstein, Jacobson, Klein, Levy, Rosen, Rubin, and Weintraub, as well as Italian-sounding names like Caruso, Facciolo, and Pestalozzi. Ten years earlier their names were overwhelmingly WASP-sounding, for example, Hunter, Campbell, Norman, and Livingston, with most of the "unusual" ones being Irish—Kennedy, Conners, McMillen, McHugh, O'Brien, for instance—and one or two possibly Jewish (Levine, Lazarus).

6   In 1950 the Wells Director of Admissions reported that about 50 percent of the entering class had prepared in public schools (Alumnae News, October 1950, WCA). In 1955, 19 percent of the entering class came from private schools, 9 percent had attended both public and private schools, while the remaining 72

percent came from public schools. President Long described this as a "trend" of more students coming from public schools and said that it was a trend experienced at other Eastern women's colleges as well (President's Report, October 1955, 2, WCA).

7   Earlier, a 1934–35 President's Report said that many students had signed up for riding but Wells College was unable to secure riding horses. President Macmillan added that he hoped the college would eventually have its own horses (President's Report 1934–35, WCA).

8   Some alumnae recalled dressing for dinner only on Sundays. One from the class of 1948 said that was when students wore heels (Personal interview, number 2, Mrs. Davis Cutting, 1995).

9   Hepburn was the president of the Chase National Bank, "a financial wizard" whose friends included such industrial giants as Andrew Carnegie (Stameshkin 1985, 233). By 1919 he had already given over one hundred thousand dollars to Middlebury (Stameshkin 1985, 245).

10 In the 1920s, however, articles in the college newspaper indicated a diversity of student opinions on the subject of coeducation. One informal poll of 48 students, 24 women and 24 men, found that more than two-thirds of each favored educating men and women together (Stameshkin 1996, 39). Yet an editorial posed a "conundrum": "Why does the average woman favor coeducation, while the average man does not?" (*The Campus*, November 28, 1923, MCA). Letters by men students did tend to favor single-sex education; for example, one man student argued against a previous letter by a woman, saying, "What would be a "better contribution . . . to the strength of any institution" than "250 serious-minded deep thinking women" would be "250 additional m-e-n, MEN" (*The Campus*, November 28, 1923, MCA).

11 The main part of the 1908 Catalogue, for instance, mentioned women students only when it noted that they could take just the classical course, whereas men could elect either the classical or scientific course, and when it listed the Y.W.C.A. as one of the student clubs. The two-page description of the Women's College appeared at the end of the Catalogue (1908 Middlebury Catalogue, MCA). In 1911–12 the Catalogue said that there were special courses for women students in P.E. and art (combined into one department) and home economics, but the description of the Women's College was still only two pages and found toward the end of the Catalogue.

12 Similarly, the separate diplomas that were issued between 1935 and 1949 were for Middlebury College and for the Women's College at Middlebury (Eileen O'Brien,"The myth of coeducation: a history of exclusion in women's higher education at Middlebury College." Thesis submitted for Honors Degree in the Department of History, 1991, MCA).

13 This house, the Marion Young cabin, was the first building of Middlebury named after a woman. It was the "dream" of Ms. Young, an alumna who was an athletic instructor at the college for twenty years (1918–38). At the time of her death in an automobile accident, the lodge or "mountain shelter" had been built and she

was reviewing the final plans for its interior decoration. A brief note in the *Middlebury College News Letter* about the lodge concluded that it would "stand as a significant and appropriate memorial to Miss Young" (December 1938, Vol. 8, #2, page 5, MCA).

14   The first woman was elected to the Board of Trustees in 1947; the first alumna on the board was elected in 1949 (Catalogues, MCA).

15   Newcomb, the women's coordinate college of Tulane, was similarly considered a department, even though it had its own faculty (Solomon 1985).

16   This *Lovejoy's* listing remained essentially the same until the mid-1980s, when the Colleges of the Seneca was no longer mentioned and the heading became "Hobart and William Smith Colleges" (Lovejoy's Guides, 1960–85).

17   Only by the end of the 1920s had smoking become acceptable for middle-class women. The first college to lift its anti-smoking ordinance was Bryn Mawr in 1925, in what became a *cause célèbre* (Fass 1977, 294).

18   William Smith's secretarial work department lasted until 1925, so it existed for only seven years (Catalogues, HWSCA).

19   Education was at first an option only for women students, but due to men students' demand, it was soon available for them to study, too (Smith 1972, 194).

20   For the entering class of 1960 at Middlebury, the median verbal SAT score for women was 628, whereas for men it was 585; the medians on the math SATs were closer but women were still higher—600 vs. 595. Only 19 percent of women applicants to Middlebury were accepted, whereas 40 percent of men applicants were (Report of the President to the Trustees, 1959–60, MCA).

21   In the 1920s President Moody of Middlebury made it a policy not to hire women faculty and to discourage their applications. He argued that since women faculty could not teach men students, they were too expensive to hire, even though their salaries would be lower than men's. Moreover, he was concerned that they would inculcate "a certain kind of feminism" in the women students (Stameshkin 1996, 41).

22   This statement is true in comparison to women faculty at Wells, but there were exceptions. A woman taught (women) students mathematics at Middlebury in the 1920s and 1930s, for example, and by the late 1940s, some of the women faculty of Hobart and William Smith taught sciences (chemistry and biology), psychology, and English as well as subjects more traditional for women.

23   Middlebury eliminated its home economics major in 1960; William Smith did this in 1961.

24   Stameshkin (1996, 41) notes that at Middlebury in 1930, women were paid less than men for entry-level positions and the maximum salary for women (excluding the dean of women) was only one-half the maximum salary for men.

25   Using college yearbooks, I did examine the proportion of senior women who majored in math or the sciences for the years majors were presented. The propor-

tions at Wells in 1958 and 1968 were slightly higher than at the other two colleges, but overall the percentages were approximately the same, around 12–15% at all three colleges in both years (at Wells in 1958, 17% majored in math or science).

26   The concept of "role model" has not been clearly defined in the research literature. Some investigators assume that all women faculty in a college are *ipso facto* role models for women students (cf. Tidball 1973). Other researchers have asked students questions to determine who serves as their role models; at least some of these studies of women *graduate* students found that students did better if they had same-sex faculty role models (Gilbert 1985). For critical overviews of the concept, its measurement and use, see Jung (1986) and Speizer (1981).

27   Another factor that may have led to some Wells students' preferring men to women faculty was that many women faculty lived with students and hence supervised more aspects of their lives. It is not unreasonable to imagine that such supervision led to students' negative or at least ambivalent reactions. One example comes from Allie herself who, as I described earlier in this chapter, reported being criticized for smoking.

28   A letter of one Middlebury woman student written in the 1920s does mention having a party in her room to which twenty women were invited, including two faculty members (Dorothy Tillapaugh Headley, "Dorothy Goes to College—a Coed's Letters Home from Middlebury, 1921–1924," MCA).

29   One exception to this general pattern is found with commencement speakers. None of the colleges had many women before the 1970s. William Smith held its graduation ceremonies separately from Hobart until 1921; during that decade of separate commencement ceremonies, two speakers for the William Smith graduation were women (one was Anna Comstock). For almost the next 50 years, until 1970, all the speakers were men. Wells's and Middlebury's patterns were almost identical until the 1970s: both had their first two women commencement speakers in 1954 and 1959. Since the 1970s Wells has had more women as commencement speakers than either Hobart and William Smith or Middlebury.

Chapter 6

Women's Struggle for Equality Continues: The Story of Kirkland College

In the 1960s, students' involvement in the civil rights and anti-war movements broke down barriers between universities and communities. This had happened before, during the Depression of the 1930s, but for the first time in the 1960s the students who engaged in protest were much more likely to be those who had previously been the backbone of collegiate life (Horowitz 1987, 235).[1] Colleges and universities thus could not ignore students' demands, and their responses changed the quality of higher education in fundamental ways. Students won the right to be treated as adults, allowed to manage their own personal lives rather than be governed by parietal rules. To a varying extent they also obtained a say in college committees, formerly controlled solely by faculty and administrators, and became freer to determine what courses they would study as undergraduates. Particular groups whose needs had not been recognized or met—African-American, gay, and women students—struggled to establish their own academic programs, campus clubs, and sometimes special housing.

The most widely publicized student protests occurred at large universities, beginning in the early 1960s at the University of Michigan. Students for a Democratic Society (SDS) worked to mobilize students to participate in the civil rights movement as well as the national campaign against nuclear testing (Flacks 1971, 3). A few years later, the Free Speech Movement at Berkeley began; for the first time students used the direct action tactics of the civil rights movement to change the policies of university administrators (Lucas 1994; Flacks 1971, 82).

Many protests occurred at smaller institutions as well. In fact, by 1969 over one-half of campuses nationwide had experienced some kind of demonstration (Horowitz 1987, 221), mostly in protest of the United States' involvement in the Vietnam War. When the United States invaded Cambodia in 1970, student protests grew, especially after national guardsmen and police killed some protestors at Kent State and Jackson State Universities. In May and June, campuses exploded in "an unprecedented general strike . . . one of the largest protests in American history," involving "millions" of students (Flacks 1988, 167). But by the beginning of the next academic year, campuses had already become quieter. Several factors appear to have been responsible for the more sober mood: the increasing opposition to the Vietnam War by the larger public, a growing concern about the economy, and a switch in tactics by militant youth to organizing and educating uncommitted people rather than using direct confrontation (Flacks 1971, 92–93).

In 1968, when student protests were about at their apex, a small college for women opened in the rural village of Clinton, New York. Planned in the early 1960s as an innovative coordinate of the men's college, Hamilton, Kirkland College lasted only a decade before being taken over by its coordinate partner. Its brief institutional life coincided with the second wave of the women's movement, which in higher education resulted in allowing women undergraduates into such all-male prestigious colleges as Yale and Dartmouth. Kirkland's story is useful for showing both how far women's higher education had developed in the century since Wells College opened and yet how much institutions designed specifically for women were still constrained. At the end of the chapter I examine the situation for women students at Wells, Middlebury, William Smith, and Hamilton Colleges from the mid-1960s until the mid-1980s, comparing them on such characteristics as the presence of women among faculty and administration, women students' leadership of campus activities, and programs designed to support women students.

Hamilton's Century and a Half as a Men's College

Like Hobart College at approximately the same time, Hamilton College originated as a religiously inspired academy. The Hamilton-Oneida Academy was chartered in 1793 through the heroic efforts of Samuel Kirkland (1741–1808), a Congregational missionary who worked among the Iroquois and learned several of their languages. Although the academy was named for Alexander Hamilton, the first secretary of the treasury of the United States, who was one of the academy's trustees, he did nothing for the school except give it his "moral support" (Pilkington 1962, 29).[2]

Samuel Kirkland had intended for the academy to serve mainly Indian interests, enrolling white youths just for the purpose of enabling the Indian youths to learn English by hearing it spoken (Pilkington 1962, 19). Instead the academy enrolled almost entirely white boys, and some white girls. It flourished, however, serving the educational needs of a growing population in this region of New York State (south of Utica, about seventy miles east of Wells College). Its success, and the desire for greater prestige, led its trustees to apply to the Regents for a change of status from academy to college; the fourth application was finally accepted in 1812 (Pilkington 1962, 43–55). Although Samuel Kirkland had already died, many people consider him to be the "real founder of the College" (Pilkington 1962, 184).

In some ways the early history of Hamilton College sounds similar to that of Middlebury College. Like Middlebury, the first presidents of Hamilton were Congregational ministers, although before the Civil War, Hamilton became distinctly Presbyterian. Also like Middlebury (but in contrast to Episcopalian Hobart College), Hamilton experienced several religious revivals which, according to one college historian, helped to "calm" the college down (Pilkington 1962, 94). A direct tie between Hamilton and Middlebury came in the form of Hamilton's second president, Henry Davis, who had previously been president of Middlebury. After surviving a crisis during President Davis's tenure (in the late 1820s) that almost closed the college, Hamilton became a larger college than Middlebury. Between 1865 and 1885, for example, Hamilton's enrollments were generally three to four times greater than Middlebury's, with Middlebury's ranging from a low of 38 to a high of 65, and Hamilton's ranging from a low of 139 to a high of 210 students (Stameshkin 1985, 200). Hamilton was also a richer institution than Middlebury; in 1885, when Middlebury's endowment was $130,000, Hamilton's was $277,000 (Stameshkin 1985, 225).

Similarities existed between Hamilton and Hobart Colleges as well in the nineteenth century, although again Hamilton was larger, generally having more than twice as many students. Both Hamilton and Hobart received financial assistance from the churches with which they were affiliated, eventually finding such assistance more burdensome than helpful. In Hamilton's case, the divorce between the college and the Presbyterian Church came in 1892 with the first appointment of an alumnus as president, Melancthon Stryker. Although Stryker was a Presbyterian pastor, he recognized that the college was too dependent on promised church funds that had not materialized. Stryker convinced alumni to donate money to their alma mater. Hamilton grew in campus size, enrollment, and number of buildings, so that Stryker's tenure came to be seen as the college's "golden age" (Pilkington 1962, 214–20).

While it is difficult to know about students' socioeconomic backgrounds, it seems that most Hamilton students were wealthier than Middlebury's but poorer than Hobart's. Some very wealthy students, for example, Gerrit Smith (the son of fur trader, Peter Smith), did attend Hamilton. Yet the college was aware of many students' needs to earn money, by teaching school, for instance, and allowed students to be absent from the winter season for such reasons (1868 Catalogue, HCA). Hamilton students were on average slightly older than 22 years when they graduated, another indication of their need to work as well as study, but not as old as students at many New England colleges like Middlebury. The average age of Hamilton's class of 1889 when they graduated, for example, was 23.7 years (Hamilton Literary Monthly, May 1889, HCA).

Fraternities were very popular at Hamilton, as they also were at Middlebury and Hobart. As early as 1840, about half of Hamilton's students belonged to one of four secret societies, and by the time of the Civil War, there were six well-established fraternities to which almost two-thirds of the students belonged (Pilkington 1962, 130–33).[3] Although some of the motivation for students to join fraternities was lessened with the establishment of athletic and social programs, the fraternities continued to have influence at the college through their ties to the Board of Trustees (Pilkington 1962, 138). When enrollments at Hamilton increased during the twentieth century, the college relied on fraternities for housing. Before World War II, about three-quarters of Hamilton students belonged to fraternities.

Hamilton College had a reputation for loyalty to tradition. It was one of the colleges that supported the Yale Report of 1829, a manifesto for the classical curriculum. Hamilton did not develop such new academic programs as fine arts and economics, but rather emphasized mathematics, foreign languages, English composition, and particularly oratory and public speaking (Pilkington 1962, 157, 248, 251).

In the early 1960s Hamilton College was still a conservative, but academically sound, liberal arts college for men. The layman who had been president during World War II, William Cowley, tried unsuccessfully to liberalize the college, which he described as a "staunch and even reactionary Republican" institution (Pilkington 1962, 256).[4] Women were seen on Hamilton's campus only during the weekends, but then so many came for house parties that part of the college's infirmary "served as a dormitory for the overflow" (Pilkington 1962, 201). Many of these young women came from Wells College, considered Hamilton's "sister" college, presumably because Wells women were compatible in terms of religious and socioeconomic backgrounds. Hamilton students were quite homogeneous: almost all white, Protestant, and middle-class. Given the changes in society at large and at other colleges and universities, Hamilton looked increasingly anachronistic.

Coordination: To "Disturb" Hamilton "the Least"

The 1960s were not only a time of protest; they were also a boom period in higher education. In the words of Clark Kerr, former Chairman of the Carnegie Commission, "the decade of the 1960s was characterized by the most rapid growth and development of institutions of higher education in American history" (Cheit 1971, vii). Hamilton College had increased from 550 students in 1953 to almost 800 students in 1961, and in response to a Ford Foundation challenge grant, authorities were planning for its future growth. The president, Robert McEwen, favored Hamilton's developing a cluster of colleges along the Claremont model. Each college in the cluster would be separately organized, with its own faculty, administration, board of trustees, curriculum, and definition of purpose. In this way, the President argued, Hamilton would grow while retaining the advantages of a small college. "Educational flexibility" was another perceived advantage to such a cluster of coordinate colleges. Although people connected with Kirkland later debated how much innovation McEwen was seeking (his premature death prevented his views from becoming fully known), as early as 1961 he did state that new colleges in the cluster would be able to have a "lively impact" on Hamilton (McEwen memo, 1961, historical documents of Kirkland College, HCA).

The college cluster idea took root. Administrators and trustees planned to establish a new college every ten years, but needed to decide which types of colleges should be in the cluster, and which should be established first. An early planning document discussed several types of institutions, raising objections to all except a women's college. The reasons other possibilities were rejected reveal assumptions and concerns of Hamilton planners. For example, one possibility was a denominational college for Friends or Presbyterians. But, the planners noted, the Society of Friends would probably not be interested in establishing a college that "would basically be subordinate to Hamilton." It is interesting in light of later events to note that a proposal for an experimental or progressive college, "College John Dewey," was rejected because it would "by definition" be "prickly—perhaps exasperating—as a neighbor" and besides, why not just pick and choose the better features of the experimental college for Hamilton itself? ("The Cluster," undated, Hamilton Long Range Planning Committee, HCA).

The Long Range Planning Committee that considered these different options developed a list of "guidelines" to follow. Planning was to be from the perspective of Hamilton, these guidelines made clear, and the well-being of the college was to be the preeminent consideration. Furthermore, Hamilton College was to "remain the dominant institution of the cluster . . . although the College might not state it this bluntly and in public." To ensure this dominance, the coordinate colleges were to be smaller than Hamilton, with a limit of about 400 for a single-sex school, and perhaps 650 or 700 for a coeducational college. Yet it was considered important for the coordinate colleges to maintain the status of Hamilton, by being liberal arts and having high admissions standards. "Hamilton does not want a second rate institution in its backyard," the guidelines stated ("The Cluster," undated, Hamilton Long Range Planning Committee, HCA).

Many factors favored establishing a women's college. Besides the demographic ones—a rise in the number of 18-year-olds and a faster rate of increase in the proportion of women attending college than of men—most reasons proffered concerned the welfare of Hamilton and its men students. In the memorable words of a report of a faculty committee on long-range planning, "the presence of a girl's college would end the isolation and 'civilize' the men . . . [and] would provide a more normal and a healthier social life . . . [it would be] easier to regulate girls in the new college than to regulate transients imported from hither and yon."[5] At the same time, Hamilton would not have to change much: "A women's college would strengthen Hamilton where it is weakest—a proper social environment—[but] disturb it the least as far as curricular matters are concerned" (quoted in "Draft, Proposed Units for the Hamilton Cluster," HCA).

Trustees believed that a women's college would make Hamilton more academically competitive. They expected the quality of the men students to improve, since Hamilton's isolated male character was seen as discouraging more first-rate men applicants than it attracted (Interim Report of Long Range Planning Committee, April 1963, HCA). Moreover, based on the experiences of such nearby selective coeducational liberal arts colleges as Middlebury and St. Lawrence, trustees were confident that the women students who applied to the new women's college would be "first-rate."

Changing any long-established college inevitably threatens alumni, but perhaps even more so in the case of a conservative college like Hamilton. Certainly alumni's reactions to the idea of a women's college were considered as planning proceeded at Hamilton, as they had been at Hobart sixty years earlier. An alumnus member of the faculty's long-range planning committee, David Ellis, favored coordination over "pure coeducation" because he thought alumni would be less resistant to a coordinate college and would not object to some joint instruction of men and women students in advanced courses. Another reason he gave for favoring coordination over coeducation was that if the coordinate college failed, it would be easier for Hamilton to back away from close cooperation (Ellis's memo to Long Range Planning Committee, 1961, HCA).

While Middlebury admitted women students in 1883 with no advance planning and Hobart spent two years developing its coordinate college, Kirkland College did not open until seven years after the first planning group had been appointed at Hamilton. And not only were faculty, administrators, and trustees involved in the planning, but also people outside of the college, including presidents of women's colleges, faculty from other institutions, educational commissioners, and recent graduates of women's colleges.[6] The key planning group, appointed in March 1964, consisted of ten distinguished people, six women and four men, from outside Hamilton. The chair of this advisory committee, who later became one of the first trustees of Kirkland, was Millicent McIntosh, past president of Barnard College and niece of M. Carey Thomas.

The advisory committee's views about the type of student who should be enrolled in the women's college were quite traditional. They envisioned a woman

> of superior academic ability . . . [but] not exceptional. This means that she will not think exclusively in terms of a career. She will anticipate marriage and motherhood as a likely part of her life. . . . It must be an essential part of her training that she be able to understand the "black-out period" of child bearing and child-rearing and emerge as a vital individual ready and able to use her later, productive years effectively.
>
> (Summary of 2-day River Club Meeting,
> March 25–26, 1964, HCA)

Planning for Hamilton's coordinate college for women was based on the assumption that most of the women students would marry and bear children. The unusual phrase, "black-out period," was referred to several times, meaning the time of life in which women stayed at home with their children and did not have any vocational commitment. The advisory committee wanted the coordinate college to teach young women to "enjoy the process of learning" so much that they would be able to develop further on their own, perhaps during their spare time when they were homemakers. Yet in a more contemporary vein, the committee saw the need for the new college to "train women, more than at present, to assume important roles as leaders in society" and to train them for careers "at whatever time or times in their lives seem appropriate" (Summary of 2-day River Club Meeting, March 25–26, 1964, HCA).

Whether women's education should be identical to men's was the subject of some debate. Members of the advisory committee agreed that although they did not want the new college to teach women how to change diapers, "we would put in any course, whether Hamilton had it or not, which was of direct bearing on the living of a good life for a woman." This type of reasoning led the committee to consider what was best for the women's college itself, not just in relation to Hamilton. In contradiction to later developments and criticisms of Kirkland, the advisory committee made the following strong statement about the women's college curriculum:

> For the women's college it is particularly important to see that its course offerings have an integrity and purpose of their own. . . . It does not offer courses primarily to round out delinquencies in the short course list of Hamilton.
> (Summary of 2-day River Club Meeting,
> March 25–26, 1964, HCA)

The advisory committee favored a largely separate coordinate college for women rather than a more integrated coordinate institution on the lines of Hobart and William Smith. Their recommendation was not really surprising considering that Millicent McIntosh, who had been president of Barnard College for seventeen years, chaired the committee. McIntosh described herself as "the worst feminist on the Barnard faculty," but she did appreciate the importance of "a separate life for a women's college," seeing it as a structure that permitted women to "fulfill themselves in unconventional ways" (Transcript of interview with M. McIntosh by Peggy Farber, September 6, 1977, HCA). Thus while other planning groups at Hamilton mostly stressed the benefits to Hamilton College of having a women's coordinate college, the advisory committee saw the advantages of separation from the perspective of the women students: the coordinate institution would have "identity and pride," women students would be "a first concern" to faculty, it would permit the introduction of courses designed especially for the new college, it would encourage experimentation and research in the area of education for women, and finally, it would preserve the virtues of smallness (Summary of 2-day River Club Meeting, March 25–26, 1964, HCA).

Other planning bodies concerned with general philosophy or aims of the new college made traditional assumptions about women's roles that sound quite similar to statements of Mr. William Smith sixty years earlier (see Chapter 4). In 1964 the chairman of the trustees' Planning Committee, Walter Beinecke (who later became chairman of Kirkland's board), submitted the final report on the educational philosophy of the women's coordinate college. It included the following generalizations:

> No one would deny that a married woman owes her first allegiance to her husband, her children and her home; nor that she finds her greatest happiness and the fullest expression of her talents in meeting her responsibilities to them. . . . A woman's greatest need, like her greatest attraction, is *joie de vivre*. . . . The great purpose of a women's college should be the honing of women with a talent for the joy of effort and renewal.
>
> (Final Report on the Educational Philosophy of
> the Women's Coordinate College for Hamilton,
> September 1964, HCA)

This same report did say that the new college should train women for leadership by preparing them for the professions which "minister to the deepest needs of our society." But the training that the planners mentioned mostly involved traditional occupations for women: teaching, medicine, social and welfare work, library work, and nursing.

"Ready and Willing to Experiment": Kirkland College Takes Shape

As early as 1964 a planning group thought about the characteristics they would like the president of the new college, Kirkland, to have. The group favored hiring a woman for president, or even a husband-and-wife team, but felt that a good woman might be "hard to find." More important was finding someone "not too old—somewhere in the neighborhood of 40" who was "ready and willing to experiment" (Minutes of a July 9, 1964 meeting of the advisory sub-committee, HCA). After more than a year of searching for a woman for the presidency, McIntosh and McEwen heard about Samuel Babbitt through the Dean of the Graduate School of Yale.[7] Babbitt had excellent academic credentials and relevant experience. His undergraduate degree and his Ph.D. were from Yale, he had administrative experience at Yale as well as Vanderbilt, and he had briefly been in charge of college recruitment for the Peace Corps.[8] President McEwen and Dr. McIntosh were relieved when Babbitt accepted the offer of the presidency.

As the new college president, Samuel Babbitt was certainly "ready and willing to experiment." Some people, not surprisingly, found his ideas too radical. Millicent McIntosh, for instance, later said that Sam (as he was usually called) was so "beguiling" that she and McEwen did not realize "how much of a rebel" and how "fed up" with conventionality he was (Transcript of interview with M. McIntosh by Peggy Farber, September 6, 1977, HCA). Yet many faculty and students—even people more distant— appear to have adored him. The wife of a Hamilton faculty member re- called that Sam "had charisma in spades. Young, self-assured, handsome, articulate and witty, he snowed everyone he met" (1996 Class and Char- ter Day Address, E. Wertimer, HCA).

Under Babbitt's leadership, the plans for Kirkland developed in ways similar to other reform colleges of the 1960s. Characteristics of these innovative colleges included a sense of mission, a devotion to commu- nity, an egalitarian spirit, a commitment to interdisciplinary study, and a desire to make students responsible for their own education (Grant and Riesman 1978, 33–35). Babbitt also appreciated the modern architec- ture planned for the new college, which symbolically emphasized the campus's difference from the older stone buildings of traditional Hamilton (Transcript of interview with S. Babbitt by Peggy Farber, March 3, 1977, HCA).

Out of all the planning and discussions of what the new college would be like, the college chose to present itself in its first catalogues as based on four "educational assumptions":

1. That selected, motivated students can assume major responsibility for their own education;
2. That a college educates best when it starts with the individual stu- dent . . . rather than starting with tightly categorized specialties and molding students to fit academic requirements.
3. That teaching is an exchange between an experienced learner and an inexperienced one . . .
4. That the college years are a significant and vital period of explora- tion . . . which should be enlightened not only by formal curricular work but by every aspect of life in the college community.

(1968–69 Kirkland College Catalog, HCA)

The Kirkland Experience:
"A Very, Very Family Kind of Thing"

In September 1968, Kirkland opened its doors to 172 young women students, all but five of them freshwomen. The caliber of the students was very high; in the words of one faculty member, they were "dynamite—energetic, purposeful, bright, well-trained, resourceful" (Transcript of interview with Bill Rosenfeld by K. G. Russell, June 1992, HCA). Conventional measures like SAT scores showed that the academic qualifications of Kirkland students in the first few classes were comparable to those of Hamilton students.[9] But the first Kirkland students also were self-selected for their desire to be pioneers in an innovative educational experience. Babbitt had warned prospective students in the catalogue that they "should be someone who is not afraid of a new situation" since the college would require their "participation to define itself." He encouraged them by describing the type of student who, he imagined, would do well at an experimental college: "If you're looking for tradition and well-worn paths, don't look here. But if you want the chance to find your own paths and to learn and to grow with a new college, I hope we will see you at Kirkland" (S. Babbitt in Kirkland College Catalog, 1969–70, HCA).

It appears that the message came across. In comparison to national samples of women students, the first Kirkland students were politically liberal. For example, in 1968 only 7.5 percent of Kirkland students agreed that a college has the right to ban extreme speakers from campus, whereas 27.8 percent of a national sample of women students agreed with this. Similarly, in 1968 fewer than half as many Kirkland students as women students nationally said that they felt that colleges had been too lax in dealing with student protests (21.5 percent, compared to 49.7 percent) (C. Schneider, 1975 Report to Trustees, HCA).

Although Kirkland students as a whole presented a stark contrast to traditional Hamilton men students, they did, of course, differ among themselves. Connie Strellas, who attended Kirkland in its early years, later said that Kirkland students used their dress, their music (rock or folk), and whether they preferred drugs (pot and LSD) or alcohol as "badges to identify which group they were." She also noted that Kirkland did have a "cheerleader element," and some students were interested in such Hamilton traditions as Homecoming Weekend (Transcript of interview with Connie Strellas by Peggy Farber, April 1978, HCA). Faculty member John O'Neill, who was hired in 1972 by Hamilton but who described himself as actually more sympathetic to Kirkland's ideals, recognized diversity among Kirkland students but said that "Kirkland women were, for the most part, very politically aware." He also noted that some Hamilton students distinguished between "Kirkies" and "Kirkettes"—those who really wanted to go to Hamilton but could not since it was a men's college, "the female versions of Hamilton students" (Transcript of interview with John O'Neill by K. G. Russell, Summer 1992).

The original Kirkland faculty was not half women, as hoped, but women comprised slightly more than one-quarter of the appointments. This contrasted markedly with Hamilton's faculty, however, which had only one woman, a visiting professor in philosophy (1968–69 Hamilton Catalogue, HCA). The first dean of Kirkland, Inez Nelbach, described qualities of the new faculty in ways that made them sound similar to the students. In an article in Hamilton's alumni magazine the summer before Kirkland opened, Nelbach talked about how the twenty-three faculty who had been hired were attracted to the new college because its "experimental curriculum" encouraged "freedom and innovation." (*Hamilton Alumni Review*, Summer 1968, HCA). A faculty member hired in 1975 vividly described the thrill of having such freedom to design his courses and to do what he wanted in the classroom. "I thought I had died and gone to heaven," he said (Transcript of interview with R. Werner by K. G. Russell, Summer, 1992, HCA).

Kirkland opened in an unfinished state. Three dormitories had only recently been completed, and other buildings were still being built, so that arriving students encountered a "sea of mud," as someone later recalled (1996 Charter Day Address by E. Wertimer, HCA). President Sam Babbitt responded to this difficult situation with characteristic panache: he gave entering students green hardhats. More important for student life than buildings was the yet-to-be-determined way Kirkland would function. Many members of the first classes found this lack of definition exciting, seeing themselves as "pioneers." Ellen O'Brien, who transferred in 1969 from William Smith College, later contrasted Kirkland with her previous college, where she had been required to dress for Sunday dinner and to sign out if she left the dorm after 7 P.M., even if she were going to the library. While she recognized that all colleges, including William Smith, were changing at that time, she noted that at Kirkland students "had the opportunity to build something new without stopping to tear down the old" ("A Kirkland Retrospective," *The Spectator*, May 12, 1978, HCA).

The new college's commitment to non-hierarchical decision-making meant that rules could not be imposed but rather had to emerge from intensive discussions and debates. When Kirkland opened, students decided on the "rule" that they would have no parietal hours. According to one of the original Kirkland faculty members, the situation "became scandalous" after about a semester because Hamilton students were staying overnight in the dorms, a practice that was not generally accepted in 1968. Kirkland began to have the reputation of being "a trifle too libertine and bohemian," which upset Hamilton trustees and administrators. As a result, President Babbitt met with his advisors, the chairs of the academic divisions, and the college "reversed" itself on this original principle (Transcript of interview with E. Putala by K. G. Russell, Summer 1992, HCA). Other accounts of this story indicate that it was students themselves who reversed the original decision about no parietals.

The student-faculty assembly was the major forum for both legislation and the discussion of issues at Kirkland (1970–71 President's Report, Kirkland College, HCA). Students and faculty representatives were elected in approximately equal numbers in order to "substitute equality for the usual hierarchy and bring faculty and students together in a community of shared interests" (Robin Krasny, "Kirkland College Today: an Experiment Stabilized," undergraduate thesis in Sociology, Princeton University, 1973, 47, HCA). Meetings were frequent and long, but as Millicent McIntosh said, "never dull." Students discussed issues that in traditional institutions only faculty would debate in private, especially when student interest groups tried to use the assembly as an open town meeting (Krasny 1973: 48, HCA; Middle States Evaluation Report 1972, HCA). Many other meetings besides those of the Assembly took place, so that overall people at Kirkland spent a great deal of time in meetings. While inevitably this led to frustrations, it also created a strong sense of "community," a word many students and teachers used to characterize their experiences at Kirkland. Sam Babbitt's role appears to have been critical in making these experiences successful. As student Connie Strellas later described him, he made Kirkland "a very, very family kind of thing" (Transcript of interview with Connie Strellas by Peggy Farber, April 16, 1978, HCA).

Some faculty at both Hamilton and Kirkland criticized Kirkland's governance. Common complaints were that the assembly took too much time, especially over unimportant details; it was chaotic, argumentative, and inefficient. Some faculty went further in their criticisms, however, noting that due to the cumbersome nature of the assembly, and due to the high proportion of Kirkland's faculty who were untenured and inexperienced, power tended to concentrate in Sam Babbitt's hands. "Dictatorial" was how some faculty described him, although others, including Carol

Bellini-Sharp, disagreed, saying he did "practice what he preached" (Transcript of interview with Carol Bellini-Sharp by K. G. Russell, Summer 1992, HCA). Sam Babbitt's magnetic personality appears to have played a role in his overwhelming influence on the college, a characteristic common in "communal-expressive" colleges, according to Grant and Riesman's research (1978). Various faculty, administrators, and trustees noted how much students and other women adored "Sam," which probably contributed to his being able to make decisions that at Hamilton were made by committees (Transcript of interviews with John O'Neill and E. Putala by K. G. Russell, Summer 1992, HCA).

Many aspects of Kirkland's educational program, particularly in its early years, distinguished it as an experimental college. Small classes based on discussion, written evaluations rather than grades, multidisciplinary core courses in the first year (which did not last, due to students' protests), and senior projects, were some of its key characteristics. Given that Hamilton continued to have a traditional academic program, and students at each college could take courses at the other, problems were bound to develop. Hamilton faculty, for instance, sometimes complained about the small size of Kirkland classes (necessary if written evaluations were to be feasible) since this meant that Hamilton students could not always get into the Kirkland classes they wanted (Transcript of interview with J. Williams by K. G. Russell, Summer 1992, HCA). The clear differences between the contiguous colleges also made comparisons inevitable. One Hamilton faculty member, Russell Blackwood, said that he felt that the written evaluations "too often" turned into "amateur psychoanalysis of the student" (Transcript of interview with Russell Blackwood by K. G. Russell, Summer 1992, HCA). Yet most Kirkland faculty and students liked the written evaluations, despite the occasional need to transform them into grades for professional or graduate schools (C. Locke, "Senior Interviews and Questionnaires," Kirkland College, May 1974, HCA).

Kirkland was not only a progressive college but a women's college, too. Yet some critics, including a Middle States evaluation team that visited in 1972, felt its significance as a women's college was never realized. The Middle States team concluded that Kirkland had given insufficient thought to the development of its student services, particularly academic and personal counseling, to be able to direct its students into professional, managerial, governmental, and political opportunities opening up to women. Middle States also pointed out that for a women's college, Kirkland did not have enough women on its faculty (Middle States Evaluation Report 1972, HCA).

In the mid-1970s, a woman faculty member wrote a memo to a member of the Board of Trustees (also a woman) about the insufficient number of women faculty at Kirkland, arguing that retention of women faculty was more of a problem than recruitment. Her own estimate was that between 1970 and 1975, turnover had been 67 percent for women faculty, compared to only 43 percent for men faculty. She described the subtle ways women had been discriminated against, including the reluctance of men faculty to discuss scholarly ideas with them, the use of such phrases as "faculty and their wives," teasing with sexual overtones, and the scheduling of meeting times that did not take into account women's domestic responsibilities. The high turnover of women faculty meant that women were not able to provide support for each other, particularly important as there was "some genuine fear of being identified as an outright feminist" (Memo from Sandra DeMyer-Gapin to Iola Haverstick, 1975, HCA). Presumably in an attempt to deal with these problems, a committee was formed in 1975 whose stated goals were "to ensure that Kirkland lived up to its responsibility as a college for women" (Mimeo from the chairperson of Kirkland as a College for Women Committee, May 1975, HCA).

Comparisons between the same students as freshwomen and as seniors showed that although most had not come to Kirkland because it was a women's college, over time they saw the importance of its single-sex status. In 1975, for example, 38 percent of the seniors said they attached "very much" importance to the fact that Kirkland was a women's college, whereas when they were freshwomen, only 1 percent had felt that way (Schneider, "Kirkland as a Women's College," October 1975, HCA). In 1976 almost half of the seniors (45 percent) said that Kirkland had helped them develop self-confidence and assertiveness, and close to one-third (31 percent) reported that they had become better able to relate to other women. And yet seniors still wanted Kirkland to do more, particularly by hiring more women faculty, by teaching more courses on concerns of women, and by placing more emphasis on career counseling (Schneider and Wittmaier, "1976 Senior Questionnaire: Summary and Commentary," HCA). One senior summarized the prevailing sentiment bluntly: "Kirkland needs to fish or cut bait on the women's issue: that is, whether we are a women's college by virtue of anything other than female enrollment" (Locke, Summary Report of Senior Interviews and Questionnaires, 1974, HCA).

Another criticism of Kirkland College was its failure to become a racially diverse institution. Despite the efforts of an assertive woman in charge of admissions, described by one of Kirkland's original faculty members as "very much committed to . . . look for activist women . . . minority women . . . students who came from the barrio" (Transcript of interview with E. Putala by K. G. Russell, Summer 1992, HCA), the college's students were almost all white. A Middle States evaluation team attributed the college's failure to attract minority students to the college's lack of Black or Puerto Rican faculty members (Report of the Middle States Association evaluation team, October 1972, HCA).

Not surprisingly, given their small numbers, African-American students generally did not feel comfortable at Kirkland. One used her senior interview to talk about the "hostility" she felt from white students who wanted her to justify why black students chose to live together. As a result she spent most of her free time in the city of Syracuse (Kirkland senior interviews, 1975, HCA). Racial issues were not ignored at Kirkland, however. The first social science core course, which all entering students had to take, focused on race relations but was criticized by students for the dispassionate way the issue was handled. One of the president's Annual Reports mentioned how a black student had used the open microphone that was part of the graduation exercises to speak "violently and disturbingly" about her experiences at Kirkland. President Babbitt did not attempt to excuse or deny what this student described but rather said, "She brought to our ceremony a sudden awareness of realities which cannot be avoided in our world . . . . It was good tonic, no matter how saddening, given its setting" (1971–72 President's Report, Kirkland College, HCA).

Kirkland did manage to attract Jewish students, however. By the early 1970s, Jewish students comprised almost one-third (31 percent) of the student body, according to an acting director of admissions (Krasny 1973, 118, HCA). Kirkland students thus contrasted with the predominantly WASP Hamilton students, which dismayed some Hamilton trustees, one of whom said the ideal Kirkland woman would be "the Wells student of 1932" (Baker, *Change*, May 1978, HCA). Another trustee expressed his hostility crudely by referring to the new college as "Kikeland" (Transcript of interview with N. Rabinowitz by K. G. Russell, July 1, 1992, HCA).

Given the sexism in the society at large as well as all the differences between Kirkland and Hamilton Colleges—in characteristics of their students, their educational philosophies, governance structures, and institutional ages—it is perhaps not surprising that many Hamilton students viewed Kirkland women as "second-class citizens" (Transcript of interview with I. Nelbach by Peggy Farber, August 1977, HCA). Even as alumnae, members of the first classes were "rankled" when they recalled how

Hamilton students believed Kirkland courses were not academically rigorous and assumed that the women students were "promiscuous" (Krasny 1973, 122–123, HCA). The prejudice against Kirkland apparently did not diminish over the decade of its existence. In spring 1978, as the college was coming to an end, a Kirkland student went public with her anger about its being viewed as inferior. In an op-ed piece for the college newspaper, titled "Anatomy of Disillusionment," this Kirkland student noted that for a "long time" both Kirkland students and faculty had been "condescended to" (*The Spectator*, March 3, 1978, HCA).

Relations between Kirkland and Hamilton faculty were similarly difficult. A survey of Hamilton faculty in 1972 showed that most considered their institution superior to Kirkland, although newer faculty were more likely to recognize Kirkland's important contribution (Krasny 1973, 96, HCA). Bill Rosenfeld, a professor at Kirkland who chaired a committee on curricular coordination, observed competition and tension between the faculty of the two colleges. It was not just one-sided, either, he argued. Kirkland professors tended to think that they were the better teachers, capable of showing Hamilton faculty "what education is really about" (Transcript of interview with Bill Rosenfeld by K. G. Russell, June 1, 1992, HCA).

Kirkland was not a calm institution; it was an exciting one that required, and for the most part obtained, students' commitment and loyalty. As a summary of interviews with seniors in 1974 noted, "Clearly . . . the seniors care about Kirkland" (C. Locke, "Senior Interviews and Questionnaires," Kirkland College, May 1974, HCA). Most of the faculty likewise were deeply committed to Kirkland, despite their acknowledgment of its "chaos." Faculty member Eugene Putala characterized the college as a "ferment . . . constantly bubbling" due to its many publicly aired disagreements. Yet he added: "We may have been squabbling, but we all did it in the sense that we were acting in the name of the spirit of Kirkland" (Transcript of interview with E. Putala by K. G. Russell, Summer 1992, HCA).

Kirkland's Problem of Survival

The relationship between Kirkland and its parent college, Hamilton, was very different from that between Hobart and William Smith. Kirkland had its own president, Board of Trustees, faculty, and physical plant; William Smith had none of these (except dormitories for its women students). A disadvantage of this independence was that Hamilton did not share its endowment with Kirkland (Letter to alumni, President McEwen, November 2, 1964, HCA). Kirkland was not even allowed to use Hamilton's constituencies for fund-raising (Transcript of interview with W. Beinecke by Peggy Farber, March 1978, HCA). And yet, Kirkland was not an entirely independent college; it would not have existed without Hamilton. Not only was Hamilton responsible for the original idea of the coordinate college, but Hamilton gave Kirkland land (about 60 acres of an apple orchard) to build on and underwrote its financial existence by giving it a million-dollar loan, interest-free, and a later loan of $800,000 on which Kirkland did have to pay interest (Transcript of interview with M. McIntosh by Peggy Farber, September 6, 1977; "A Statement on Kirkland," January 1, 1978, Kirkland trustees, HCA).

Hamilton's initial financial support of Kirkland was insufficient, as right from the beginning Kirkland had monetary problems. Its separate plant, faculty, and some administrators were expensive. Moreover, its educational philosophy required a low student-faculty ratio, another costly factor. And until the new college built up a reserve of older alumnae, it could not expect annual fund-raising drives to produce much money. As early as 1971 President Babbitt wrote about the need for "new funds from as yet untapped private sources," which he said were necessary for "the very survival of the college" (1970–71 President's Report, Kirkland College, HCA).[10] This message became more insistent with the passage of time. Just three years later, Babbitt called it "a time of retrenchment," a view shared by the Hamilton Board of Trustees, who were giving up on the five-college cluster idea. The need for a large endowment for Kirkland became ever more clear, as Babbitt had to spend a great deal of time engaging in "incredible annual fund-raising . . . [necessary] to avoid budget deficits" (1974–75 President's Report, Kirkland College, HCA).

By 1975 Kirkland owed Hamilton almost two million dollars, was paying close to half a million dollars annually for "debt service" on the loan from Hamilton and on a large loan from the New York State Dorm Authority (for which Hamilton College had cosigned), and had a deficit of a little more than one hundred thousand dollars (Appendix, 1974–75 President's Report, Kirkland College, HCA). Yet Babbitt remained optimistic, at least in his official writings; he noted, for instance, that the Council on Financial Aid to Education had rated Kirkland eleventh among eighty-five women's colleges in fund-raising (Appendix, 1974–75 President's Report, Kirkland College, HCA). Some big donations had been received, notably $500,000 from the Milbank Fund with permission to use the money for current expenses (Transcript of interview with M. McIntosh by Peggy Farber, September 6, 1977, HCA). In 1976 Kirkland announced a "Campaign for the Second Decade," with a goal of raising $20 million (1975–76 President's Report, Kirkland College, HCA).

The type of people on Kirkland's Board of Trustees may have been another factor contributing to the college's monetary problems. President Babbitt later said that in "hindsight" he saw that there were problems with some of the trustees: lawyers and women who were for the most part "well-to-do, but not millionaires and [who did] not . . . [have] extensive corporate ties." Generally the college attracted to its board people who were interested in progressive educational institutions (Transcript of interview with S. Babbitt by Peggy Farber, March 3, 1977, HCA). Yet Millicent McIntosh noted that of all the boards she had served on (and she had served on at least eight), none had ever "given more time, enthusiasm and money than the Kirkland Board" (quoted in letter to Musselman by President Babbitt, March 1, 1977, HCA).

In addition to the external problem of insufficient funds Kirkland experienced internal problems. These stemmed from structural tensions between Kirkland and Hamilton as well as problems inherent in Kirkland itself. While it is unlikely that any of these problems alone would have been sufficient to close Kirkland, they contributed to the belief of many people that the college could not last. As one Hamilton faculty member later said, "Kirkland was really doomed . . . it could have lasted a few more years, but I don't think that, really, it was ever going to go" (Transcript of interview with J. Williams by K. G. Russell, Summer 1992, HCA).

Right from the beginning Kirkland was defined in relation to Hamilton. The curriculum, for example, complemented Hamilton's so that it did not have the coherence of an independent institution. The social sciences and arts, in which Hamilton had been weak, were emphasized at Kirkland, whereas its science courses consisted mainly of history of science and botany. Thus the curricular strengths of each college reinforced traditional gender distinctions. It was also easy for people to move from the view that Kirkland's courses were complementary to the position that they were unnecessary since, after all, had they been needed, they would have been taught at Hamilton all along (Dean Gulick to President Carovano, February 21, 1977, HCA; Babbitt letter to Musselman, March 1, 1977, HCA).

Such curricular problems did receive official recognition. Beginning in 1976, the deans of Kirkland and Hamilton, under the direction of their presidents, began a review of the colleges' curriculum, with the goal of identifying ways of making coordination more rational and the overall curriculum stronger (Coordinate Academic Planning Statement, 1976, HCA; Academic Coordination, Kirkland and Hamilton Colleges, April 7,

1977, Deans Frazer and Gulick, HCA). Their joint statement on ways to improve coordination called for changes at *both* Hamilton and Kirkland to preserve each institution's "autonomy." A principle guiding their recommendations was to locate some of the disciplines at the colleges in a manner that contradicted sex stereotypes; for example, they recommended that Kirkland expand its offerings in computer science and statistics while Hamilton reduce such offerings (Academic Coordination, Kirkland and Hamilton Colleges, April 7, 1977, Deans Frazer and Gulick, HCA). These recommendations were never implemented, however.

The differences in educational philosophies between the two colleges caused problems, despite the arguments of Dean Frazer and others that such differences were a strength. Some Hamilton faculty argued that Kirkland students got course credit for experiences that were not sufficiently academic. Kirkland faculty were believed to publish less than Hamilton faculty, not surprising given the large amount of time Kirkland faculty spent in meetings and the intensive work they did with students. Since publications are generally used as an indicator of scholarly status, Kirkland faculty's presumed poorer publications record reinforced the general sense that Hamilton was the more prestigious college (Transcript of interview with John O'Neill by K. G. Russell, Summer 1992, HCA).

Some faculty believed that one reason for Kirkland's demise was that Hamilton's trustees were frustrated that it was not settling down and becoming the kind of college they thought appropriate for a coordinate partner for Hamilton (Transcript of interview with E. Putala by K. G. Russell, Summer 1992, HCA). A more specific version of this hypothesis was that the women students were not seen as suitable wives for Hamilton students, and that this had been the real reason for Kirkland's founding. Some of the unflattering epithets by which Kirkland was known—"the Jewish Whorehouse on the Hill," the "Lesbian College"—contradicted each other yet captured the notion that Hamilton men would not or could not marry Kirkland women (Transcript of interview with R. Werner by K. G. Russell, Summer 1992, HCA). In fact, of course, many Kirkland students did not conform to the stereotype of a protesting hippie feminist, likely to be a lesbian, especially by the mid-1970s, when Kirkland students, like students nationally, were becoming more conventional. Yet even a decade after Kirkland's demise, a faculty member noted how people's "reflexive" response when students demonstrated was to say, "Oh, that's a Kirkland type" (Transcript of interview with Bill Rosenfeld by K. G. Russell, Summer 1992, HCA).

Coordination presented its own problems; it was difficult to understand, especially for outsiders, and perhaps as a consequence, difficult to implement (Dean Gulick to President Carovano, February 21, 1977, HCA; Babbitt letter to Musselman, March 1, 1977, HCA). Several faculty at both colleges said that how well coordination functioned varied with the particular disciplines and how well the faculty at each college got along (Transcript of interview with R. Werner by K. G. Russell, Summer 1992, HCA; transcript of interview with R. Blackwood by K. G. Russell, Summer 1992, HCA). President Babbitt believed that the "creative friction" of coordination was worth the efforts it required and agreed with Millicent McIntosh that it was the best structure for developing "autonomous, thinking women." President Carovano of Hamilton did not share this view, however; according to Sam Babbitt, Carovano was impatient with the inefficiency of coordination and believed that a single institution could be "better controlled" (Babbitt to Hamilton's Board of Trustees, May 5, 1977, HCA).

The distinction between being a coordinate college of Hamilton as opposed to a single coeducational institution was not easy to maintain. Over time some student clubs, such as the choir and theatre, became mixed-sex, and only a minority of students took all their courses at Kirkland.[11] The colleges developed joint majors in American Studies and Life Sciences, and there were even a few mixed-sex dormitories.

Thus while Kirkland did have severe financial problems, lack of money was not the only reason its survival was threatened. As time passed, the need for a *separate* college for women seemed less convincing. Hamilton alumni were presumed to have become accustomed to women at their college, so coordination began to be viewed as a helpful stage for the ultimate goal of coeducation (Letter to Hamilton students, M. Carovano, June 23, 1977, HCA). Moreover, Kirkland's characteristics as a progressive college seemed more annoying than beneficial, calling to mind the early planning document that predicted that a hypothetical "John Dewey" College for the proposed cluster would prove to be "prickly" and "exasperating."[12] President Carovano of Hamilton and many Hamilton trustees believed that coeducation was the answer to all these problems.

"A Misogynist Fairy Tale": Hamilton Takes Over the Women's College

In the spring of 1977, when Kirkland was completing only its ninth year in operation, Hamilton College announced that it was going to withdraw the financial support its coordinate partner needed to survive. Kirkland did not die a quiet death, however. Many students on both campuses, alumni and alumnae, parents of students, faculty, and trustees, held rallies—

including one on Fifth Avenue in New York City—demonstrated, circulated petitions, held interviews with the press, and organized letter-writing campaigns.[13] When the president of Hamilton gave a talk in the chapel in December 1977 on the details of the "merger," two Kirkland students used a dramatic method of protest: they pushed an apple pie into his face (*Observer Dispatch*, Dec. 6, 1977, HCA). While this degree of intensity did not last, it took years for the protest to end completely.

The immediate cause of the crisis was that Kirkland could not meet its operating expenses and borrowing more money was not feasible given its ongoing capital campaign to raise $20 million. Kirkland asked Hamilton for a demonstration of commitment to coordination by guaranteeing up to $600,000 a year for five years.[14] Although the Hamilton trustees at first "seemed receptive to the request," ultimately they accepted the recommendation of Hamilton administrators to give only "limited aid" to Kirkland ("A Statement on Kirkland," January 1, 1978, HCA). They agreed with President Carovano of Hamilton that Kirkland's financial situation made it appear "very unlikely" that the women's college would become "financially independent in the foreseeable future" (Letter to Hamilton students, M. Carovano, June 23, 1977, HCA).

President Carovano gave other reasons for his belief that Kirkland and Hamilton should be consolidated. Kirkland's applications had declined, whereas at other men's colleges that had become coeducational, applications of women had risen (Letter to parents of Hamilton alumni, M. Carovano, June 23, 1977, HCA). Kirkland women were not as academically well-qualified as Hamilton men in terms of their SAT scores.[15] And in a phrase that his opponents often referred to in order to demonstrate that Hamilton's president was unsympathetic to the very nature of Kirkland, Carovano characterized the progressive women's college as a "remnant of the '60s without present validity" (Babbitt to Kirkland trustees, May 12, 1977, HCA).[16]

President Babbitt defended Kirkland eloquently in many memos and letters. Over and over again he stressed the benefits of a "coordinate pattern" over a coeducational environment: two small colleges meant students had educational alternatives due to the institutions' "differing philosophies"; women had a "supportive environment";[17] and there were two different constituencies for fund-raising, public relations, and admissions. He also pointed out what Hamilton had already gained from Kirkland: a $13 million college campus, including a performing arts center much needed by the men's college. Kirkland had been successful in fund-raising, too; each year of its existence, about $1 million of funds had been

raised. Babbitt attributed Kirkland's financial problems primarily to insufficient funding at the outset; he pointed out that it was a "lean educational
operation—if anything, too lean" (Babbitt letter to Musselman, March 1,
1977, HCA).

Babbitt also described the negative consequences that would ensue if
Hamilton and Kirkland were to become a single coeducational institution:
standardization of the educational philosophy in a "conventional mode,"
"male domination of student, faculty and administrative leadership," reduced competitive advantage in losing its unique market position as a
coordinate arrangement (Babbitt letter to Musselman, March 1, 1977,
HCA), and the loss of many of the pledges to Kirkland (at least $1.5
million worth) from the ongoing capital campaign (Babbitt to Hamilton
trustees, May 5, 1977, HCA). Babbitt believed that if coordination was to
work, both colleges had to be autonomous. He compared Hamilton and
Kirkland's positive differences to the contrasting situation at such supposedly coordinate arrangements as Hobart and William Smith or Brown
"and what was Pembroke." In Babbitt's view, "these are not models of
two institutions, but only one and its shadow—hardly worth the hassle."
Babbitt wanted to obtain from Hamilton a "recommittment [sic] to coordination, updated" which he believed would be "a stunning public fulfillment of a task undertaken in 1965 . . . [and would] put this Hill in the
forefront of undergraduate education at its richest" (Babbitt letter to
Musselman, March 1, 1977, HCA).

Some people believed that the real reason Hamilton would not give
Kirkland the money it needed to weather its crisis was that it wanted more
control over its "brash young offspring" (Letter of resignation from the
Hamilton Board, Clifford '41 in *The Spectator*, April 28, 1978, HCA).
And in fact, Hamilton administrators had said that the college would give
the money to Kirkland if they were given the right to approve Kirkland's
budget. Babbitt's counter-proposal was to have a "joint finance subcommittee" that reviewed the budgets of both colleges to identify "possible
cutback areas . . . which could be effected in tandem" ("An Outline of
Issues Related to Current Relations Between Hamilton College and Kirkland
College," May 1977, HCA). Babbitt was unwilling to allow the "judgment
of the Hamilton Board" to control Kirkland's "basic policy document,"
even if that meant Hamilton "might" loan Kirkland the money it needed
(Babbitt to alumnae, May 17, 1977, HCA).

Despite the protests of students, faculty, alumni/ae, trustees, and parents, Hamilton's board voted to extend Kirkland only limited financial
support. By early August 1977, Kirkland's board had accepted that if the

college were not going to "close immediately," it had no choice but to agree to "consolidate" Kirkland with Hamilton (Babbitt to Kirkland people, August 1, 1977, HCA). The two deans, Dean Frazer of Kirkland and Dean Gulick of Hamilton, began meeting to work out the specifics of the consolidation agreement.

Negotiations did not last long. At its October meeting, the Hamilton board passed a resolution stating that it was "no longer" negotiating but rather that it was making decisions from the perspective of Hamilton as the "continuing institution," taking into account the viewpoints of Kirkland's constituents (Resolution of Hamilton Board of Trustees, October 8, 1977, HCA). On a matter of great concern to Kirkland, the fate of its tenured faculty, Hamilton's board rejected a compromise worked out earlier by the two deans. President Babbitt wrote "with profound sorrow" to the people of Kirkland, saying that Hamilton's board's action indicated "a deterioration in the relationships" between the two colleges and that the "rhetoric" of the "best of both colleges" as the goal was "just . . . rhetoric" (Babbitt to Kirkland people, October 12, 1977, HCA).

The specific arrangements of the takeover were more favorable to Kirkland's students than faculty. Continuing Kirkland students (classes of 1979, 1980, and 1981) were promised automatic admission to Hamilton and were given the choice of graduating under Kirkland's or Hamilton's requirements (Agreement between the trustees of Hamilton College and Kirkland College, December 8, 1977). Tenured faculty were not automatically granted tenure at Hamilton but rather were given four-year appointments, at the end of which time they had to go through another tenure review using Hamilton's criteria. Non-tenured Kirkland faculty were given two-year appointments. A faculty member at Hamilton, John Williams, who at the time was Chair of the Committee on Appointments, argued that the policy of Hamilton's president and dean of not accepting Kirkland's standards for tenure was "a big mistake" and meant that Kirkland's faculty were, as they felt, "knifed in the back." Because faculty from Kirkland emphasized teaching more than publishing, Hamilton lost "some very good people," which "caused a great deal of grief" (Transcript of interview with J. Williams by K. G. Russell, Summer 1992, HCA).[18]

In addition to the fate of Kirkland's tenured faculty, another controversial issue was the meaning of "consolidation." Apparently, as the Hamilton board became apprised that legally, consolidation involved dissolving its (as well as Kirkland's) charter and establishing a charter for a new institution, it realized that it did not intend to "consolidate." President Carovano argued that his former use of the term was informal. The legal term for Hamilton's intentions was "dissolution" of Kirkland, with Hamilton assuming its assets and debts (Memo to Kirkland Board of Trustees from law firm, Sue Stern and David Lascell, June 15, 1977, HCA).

Even after the legal agreement for the "dissolution" of Kirkland had been signed in December 1977, and plans to make Hamilton coeducational were proceeding, protests continued, not only among students but also trustees and alumni/ae. An alumnus member of Hamilton's Board of Trustees, Dr. Maurice Clifford '41, resigned, stating that he believed a "principle of historical commitment" had been violated. Two distinguished alumni also withdrew their support from Hamilton: Philip Jessup, a former World Court judge, who said he was "shocked" at the way trustees and President Carovano had handled the affair, and Charles Root '40, a Kirkland trustee whose family had been involved in Hamilton for generations (*The Spectator*, April 28, 1978, HCA).

The takeover of Kirkland raised many people's fears about the quality of education for young women at the future, coeducational Hamilton. One concession to this concern was that Hamilton agreed to use Kirkland's endowment, about three-quarters of a million dollars, for a foundation to endow scholarships for women and programs of special interest to women (Carovano, letter to Hamilton College faculty and administration, Dec. 5, 1977, HCA). Nonetheless, a Kirkland student wrote about her worries that when Hamilton took over Kirkland, men would dominate student government and the women students would lose their "firm sense of female identity":

> We will not have the fierce sense of female solidarity, of being a woman's school in conjunction with—and opposed to—a men's college. . . . We will have the larger responsibility of continuing to prove receptive to the specific problems that attend being a oman in a male-oriented culture. (*The Spectator*, Sept. 23, 1977, HCA)

The takeover radicalized several Kirkland faculty members. Professor Carol Bellini-Sharp described the experience as a "very hostile take-over," in which Hamilton attempted to "obliterate any idea of Kirkland." She learned what it meant to be "working for the man" and so became a feminist (Transcript of interview with C. Bellini-Sharp by K. G. Russell, July 1992, HCA). Another woman on the Kirkland faculty, Nancy Rabinowitz, claimed that they all became "radical feminists" because "the face of the enemy was so clear" in President Carovano. She compared the ending of Kirkland to "a misogynist fairy tale":

> You start the women's college but you don't give them . . . an inheritance, you give them an allowance . . . pin money. You keep them begging for money and dependent on you . . . You allow them to plant a flower garden. Comp. lit., all the

other frills, but you don't given them anything that's like a field where they could grow their own sustenance. (Transcript of interview with N. Rabinowitz by K. G. Russell, July 1, 1992, HCA)

Hamilton after the Takeover:
Better for the Men but Not the Women Students?

Making a formerly all-male institution a coeducational one was a more self-conscious act in 1978 than it was in earlier historical periods. The second wave of the women's movement meant that concepts like sexism, patriarchy, and male dominance were widely discussed. Moreover, Hamilton had the example of other formerly all-male institutions in New England to guide it, and certainly the women students and women and men faculty from Kirkland put pressure on Hamilton College to keep women's interests in mind. During the first year of coeducational Hamilton, a planning subcommittee of trustees, students, faculty, and administrators visited three comparable colleges (Vassar, Williams, and Middlebury) to evaluate for the trustees the adequacy of Hamilton's extracurricular activities as a coeducational institution (*The Spectator*, March 2, 1979, HCA). Later the college conducted other studies to assess Hamilton's strengths and weaknesses as a coeducational college. Even though these groups inevitably found that men's interests were better represented than women's, it is significant that monitoring and critical self-examination occurred.

Hamilton College did not seem to suffer as a result of announcing its decision to dissolve Kirkland and become a coeducational institution. In fact, the spring after this decision was made public, Hamilton's fundraising increased (Self-Study for Commission on Higher Education of the Middle States Association, 1980, HCA). Hamilton's budget deficit, expected to be half a million dollars as a result of taking over Kirkland and its debts, was reported to be only $300,000 in the spring semester of the first year of coeducation (*The Spectator*, February 6, 1979, HCA). By the following year, President Carovano announced that there was a "modest surplus" in the budget.

Applications and enrollments at the newly coeducational Hamilton were also strong. Over one-third (39 percent) of the 1,010 students accepted into the first coeducational class were women, with the quality of the women judged by admissions staff to be "a little higher" than that of the men (*The Spectator*, April 14, 1978, HCA). By the third year of coeducation, in the fall of 1980, Hamilton had a record-breaking number of applications (Self-Study for Commission on Higher Education of the Middle States Association, 1980, HCA).

People were curious about what the women students admitted to the newly coeducational Hamilton College were like. According to a newspaper report for which twenty-four entering students were interviewed, the new Hamilton women said they were more conventional than Kirkland students. "I never would have gone to Kirkland" was their "most consistent remark" (*Utica Press*, "Hamilton greets its first coed class," September 1978, HCA). The college newspaper ran a similar article in October about the "views" of the class of '82 in which two freshwomen explained why they would never have applied to Kirkland. One said that she believed Hamilton was "academically more challenging," and the other felt that she was a blend of the two colleges' strengths (*The Spectator*, October 27, 1978, HCA). Three letters from former Kirkland students (who were now Hamilton students) appeared in the next issue of the college newspaper, disputing that Hamilton was more academically challenging and pointing out that the freshwomen had no evidence for their beliefs about Kirkland. "We resent being stereotyped, and we always have. We resent the insinuation that we attended a second rate institution, we did not" (*The Spectator*, November 3, 1978, HCA).

The quality of life for the women students at the new coeducational Hamilton College is difficult to assess. On the positive side, some women students did hold top leadership positions—the president of the student assembly, the editor-in-chief of the student newspaper (*The Spectator*, April 21, 1978, HCA), and the president of a new debating group (*The Spectator*, November 10, 1978, HCA). The Women's Center that had existed at Kirkland, where perhaps the need was less, continued to be maintained. By 1981 the interdisciplinary minor of women's studies had been established (1981–82 Hamilton College Catalogue, HCA). Funds from the Kirkland endowment were used to sponsor campus events related to women's concerns, including during the first coeducational year, a talk by the well-known feminist author and activist, Robin Morgan, and a debate between Phyllis Schlafly and Karen De Crow on the ERA. During the second coeducational year, the funds were used for a two-day conference on women and education, at which one of the featured speakers was Florence Howe, a feminist author who is known for her argument that coeducation is not the same as equal education (*The Spectator*, November 16, 1979, HCA).

On the negative side, the top administrators and the trustees of Hamilton continued to be all men; about 80 percent of the faculty were men (1978–79 Hamilton College Catalogue, HCA); men's sports continued to receive the most coverage by far in the student newspaper;[19] and fraternities continued to dominate the college's social life. In spring 1979, an event held in the chapel included a woman stripper, which administrators decried as "degrading and exploitive" of women. Men students, at least those who wrote to the student newspaper, defended the stripper, arguing that anyone who was offended could have left the chapel and that a campus play had contained more nudity (*The Spectator*, May 11, 1979).

Numerical representation of women on the Board of Trustees and among the students improved quite quickly. Within two years, the board went from having no women to having 5 women out of 35, and women students increased from 32 percent to 42 percent of the entering classes (1979–80 Hamilton College Catalogue, HCA). The faculty did not change as rapidly, however; two years after Hamilton became coeducational, women still had only about one-fifth (22 percent) of the regular faculty appointments, up just slightly from 19 percent in 1979.

Probably the most sensitive issue for newly coeducational Hamilton was the role of fraternities. A self-study report prepared for the Middle States accrediting body shortly after the colleges combined devoted a lengthy section to fraternities, including a survey of students' attitudes and information about the position of fraternities at other colleges. Fraternities entailed sex discrimination, the report noted, since men had greater opportunities to live in non-college-owned residences as well as more opportunities to eat outside the college board contract. Perhaps most importantly, women had no say in planning that part of campus social life sponsored by the fraternities. "Women become strictly invitees, never the ones to do the inviting" (Self-Study for Commission on Higher Education of the Middle States Association, 1980, 55, HCA).

Despite faculty and administrative opposition and despite their decline in membership (from about 85 percent of men students in 1962–63 to 42 percent in 1979–80), fraternities continued to exist at Hamilton. And even though few women students had expressed interest in sororities, a couple of sororities were established, the first one in 1984, the same year that women's studies was upgraded from a minor to a major field concentration (1984–85 Hamilton College Catalogue, HCA).

The change from two coordinate colleges with different philosophies, curriculum, faculty, and student bodies, into one coeducational college was the dominant concern of Hamilton from 1977 until the end of the period being discussed in this chapter. While the role of fraternities fit into this larger concern, other issues that might have been given more attention tended to be pushed aside. This may explain why in the period before 1985 Hamilton did not pay much attention, at least on an official level, to minority students. Although students occasionally expressed concerns about the situation of minorities at Hamilton (cf. *The Spectator*, December 1, 1978, HCA), college officials did not. Hamilton's self-study report prepared in 1980 for the Middle States Association, for example, mentions the number of minority students at the college but does not express concerns about them or discuss programs to recruit them. In fact, the decline in the percentage of minority students, from only about 5 percent in 1977–78 to even lower, about 3 percent in 1978–79, was not commented upon (Self-Study for Commission on Higher Education of the Middle States Association, 1980, HCA).

Table 6.1 shows that in comparison to the other three colleges, Hamilton College's enrollment increased the most between 1965 and 1985.[20] The number of students more than doubled, not surprisingly since a new college was added. The percentage of women students increased after Hamilton became coeducational, from 37 to 43.5 percent—lower than Middlebury but slightly higher than Hobart and William Smith. The percentage of women on the faculty (25 percent in 1984) was about the same as Middlebury and Hobart and William Smith (but considerably less than Wells), but the percentage of women on the Board of Trustees was lower (just under 20 percent). Like Middlebury and Hobart and William Smith Colleges, Hamilton had a low percentage of women in top administrative posts. Women were not well represented in the student newspaper, in terms of the number of photos with women in them, but Hamilton did develop a major in women's studies within six years of becoming coeducational.

Faculty who had been at either Kirkland or Hamilton before the takeover and remained at Hamilton after it became coeducational were not always convinced that the combination of the colleges had preserved all the advantages of each of the independent colleges. While the curricular opportunities for students remained, the progressive features of Kirkland—for example, evaluations rather than grades and a participatory governing structure—were dropped. As a faculty member from Kirkland, Nancy Rabinowitz, commented, "We tried to make something of the women's college stay more than we tried to make something of the innovative college stay" (Transcript of interview with N. Rabinowitz by K. G. Russell, July 1992, HCA). She noted various ways Hamilton had benefited from Kirkland—"vigorous" arts and a strong women's studies program, a caucus for women faculty's concerns, and the Kirkland endowment—but still concluded that the demise of Kirkland was not equally advantageous to all groups:

TABLE 6.1 Comparisons among Four Colleges, 1965–1985

	Wells	Middlebury	Hobart & Wm Smith	Hamilton
Number of students				
a) Total				
b) % women				
1964–65	a) 552	a) 1352	a) 1355	a) about 800
	b) 100%	b) 42%	b) 27%	b) 0%
1969–70	a) 674	a) 1612	a) 1550	a) 1193[1]
	b) 100%	b) 43%	b) 30%	b) 25%
1974–75	a) 510	a) 1878	a) 1740	a) 1640
	b) 100%	b) 45%	b) 40%	b) 39%
1979–80	a) 510	a) 1914	a) 1816	a) 1621
	b) 100%	b) 48%	b) 40%	b) 37%
1984–85	a) 472	a) 1995	a) 1784	a) 1687
	b) 100%	b) 48%	b) 42%	b) 43.5%
% women on faculty				
1964–65	42%	12.5%	17%	3% (all were visiting fac.)
1969–70	28%	10%	17%	Kirkland: 30% Hamilton: 2%
1974–75	36%	13%	18%	Kirkland: 31% Hamilton: 10%
1979–80	42%	21%	28%	19%
1984–85	44%	25%	27%	25%
% women on board of trustees				
1964–65	46%	12%	17%	0%
1969–70	50%	9%	16%	Hamilton: 0% Kirkland: 35%
1974–75	52%	29%	23%	Hamilton: 0% Kirkland: 38%
1979–80	45%	31%	31%	14%
1984–85	58%	29%	30%	19%
# women top administrators				
1964–65	1 of 3 (dean of students)	1 of 5 (dean of women students)	1 of 4	None
1969–70	1 of 3	1 of 5	1 of 4	Hamilton: 0 Kirkland: 1 of 3
1974–75	1 of 3 (dean of students)	1 of 6	1 of 4	Hamilton: 0 Kirkland: 2 of 5
1979–80	3 of 4	1 of 5	1 of 4	0 of 6
1984–85	2 of 4	0 of 6	1 of 4	1 of 6

TABLE 6.1 Continued

	Wells	Middlebury	Hobart & Wm Smith	Hamilton
1st year of women's studies—minor/major				
	1979: a "special acad. opportunity" 1980-81: a minor, no course of own	Not by 1985	1974: a "program," more developed by 1979	1981 minor 1984 major
Photos in coll. newspaper—% with some women				
1st issue in Oct. 1964	6/8 or 75%	4 of 8 or 50%	3 of 10 or 30%	2 of 9 or 22%
1st issue in Nov. 1969	0 of 1 (issue mostly on war protests)	0 of 1	0 of 3	1 of 7 or 14%
1st issue in Feb. 1974	Missing; 1st with photo, Mar. 15, 1974, 3 of 4 or 75%	2 of 5 or 40%	3 of 15 or 20%	6 of 14 or 43%
1st issue in Mar. 1979	3 of 4 or 75%	7 of 20 or 35%	5 of 10 or 50%	4 of 14 or 29%
1st issue in April 1984	15/15 or 100%	8 of 18 or 44%	9 of 29 or 31%	2 of 11 or 18%

Information obtained from college catalogues and student newspapers. See note at end of Table 3.1 about determination of gender of trustees and faculty.

[1] Exact enrollment figures for Kirkland College were unobtainable. The 1969-70 numbers are based on an estimate of 300 students at Kirkland, somewhat less than double the entering class number of 168 since in 1969 the college was only in its second year of existence. The 1974-75 figures are based on 640 students at Kirkland, a number between 625 that college publications gave for 1972 and 655, the number newspaper accounts gave for 1977.

> Hamilton is better off, but women are worse off, and I still feel sad about that. . . . Women got a better education at Kirkland than they do at Hamilton, and men are getting a better education at the new Hamilton at the expense of Kirkland. . . . (Transcript of interview with N. Rabinowitz by K. G. Russell, July 1992, HCA)

Wells College, 1965–85: A Time of Major Changes

Wells College, like Hamilton, benefited from the boom period for higher education. In 1963–64 Wells had more than 500 students for the first time in its history (Temple Rice Hollcroft, "A History of Wells College," n.d., 352, WCA), and in 1969 its largest incoming class ever, 236 entering students (Self-Evaluation Report prepared for the Middle States Association, 1979, WCA). Like Hamilton at about the same time, Wells thought about expanding by building a coordinate college for students of the opposite sex. A self-evaluation report written for Middle States in 1967 mentioned, on its first page, that "active consideration" was being given "both by the Trustees and by the Faculty" to the admission of men students, perhaps through a coordinate college (Self-Evaluation Report prepared for the Middle States Association, August 1967, WCA).

The politics of Wells students also reflected larger social trends. By the mid-1960s, students were no longer staunchly Republican: while in 1960, Nixon had been favored "overwhelmingly" over Kennedy, a student poll in 1964 found Lyndon Johnson was an almost 2 to 1 favorite over Goldwater (*The Courier*, November 1, 1960; October 15, 1964, WCA). Some students became involved in the civil rights movement, with a few attending Spelman College for a semester and others participating in spring voter registration projects (*The Courier*, February 25, 1965).

Starting in the mid-1960s, Wells students protested the Vietnam War (cf. Letters to the Editor, *The Courier*, December 16, 1965, WCA), not as vehemently as at some campuses but in marked contrast to the decorum of earlier Wells cohorts. The largest campus rally took place in October 1969; about half the student body, thirty-one faculty members, and twenty-three village residents signed a petition to end the U.S. involvement in South Vietnam (*The Courier*, October 23, 1969, WCA). After protestors at Kent State were killed in the spring of 1970, some Wells students took over a faculty coffee hour and attempted to strike. Since the majority of the students wanted to resume classes, however, the protestors had to modify their demands (*The Courier*, editorial edition, November 19, 1970, WCA).

Diversity of the Wells's student body became more evident in the late 1960s. Minority students formed a Black Women's Society in 1969, one of whose members, Clara DeLaCruz, became an articulate spokesperson for revolutionary change. At a campus anti-war rally, for example, she addressed the "racial overtones" of the war (*The Courier*, October 23, 1969, WCA). Rather predictably, the visibility of African-American students and their student organization caused a backlash, with some white students decrying a "fall in standards" (*The Courier*, October 23, 1969, WCA).

The nationwide trend toward coeducation also had an impact at Wells. When John Wilson became the president of Wells in 1969, just as many of the most prestigious men's colleges in the East began admitting women, he used the occasion of his installation to predict that "if the present preoccupation with co-education continues for very long, it may well close off the possibility of sustaining a first-class, single-sex undergraduate college." But at the same time Wilson commented favorably on the "special character of women's colleges" (*The Courier*, November 13, 1969).

The decade of the 1970s marked the beginning of the decline of Wells College, most notably in terms of enrollment but also financially.[21] First-year classes dropped 41 percent between 1969 and 1977 (from 236 to 139). To achieve even these smaller classes, Wells had to be less selective: whereas in 1967 the percentage of applicants who were accepted was slightly over two-thirds (69 percent), ten years later almost 90 percent (89 percent) of applicants were being accepted.[22] The academic qualifications of entering classes also declined. Combined SAT scores went from a total of 1168 in 1970 to 1065 in 1977 (Self-Evaluation Report prepared for the Middle States Association, January 1979, 124, WCA).

Another major consequence for Wells of the decreasing popularity of single-sex education was that students no longer came from predominantly wealthy families. More often students came from rural communities in New York State,[23] many from families in which they were the first to attend college.[24] Financial aid became one of the major ways Wells attracted students. A large percentage of the budget had to be used to assist students, which in turn put pressures on the college's budget. In fact the budget for financial aid increased by about 300 percent between 1967 and 1975 (Self-Evaluation Report prepared for the Middle States Association, January 1979, 124, WCA). By 1977–78 about half of the students received financial aid from Wells, with each of the 256 aided students getting, on average, $1,900, for a total of $500,000 expended by the college (Self-Evaluation Report prepared for the Middle States Association, January 1979, 127, WCA).

Rather predictably trustees attempted to deal with this changed financial situation by cutting back on curricular offerings and reducing faculty.[25] By order of the trustees, the academic dean and faculty committees worked together to produce a "Report of Programmatic Directions for 1977–1980," commonly referred to as "the Blueprint," which recommended cutting about five faculty positions. As an already very small faculty grew smaller, and faculty tried to compensate by teaching an even wider range of courses, "an intangible yet real erosion of Faculty morale" occurred (Self-Evaluation Report prepared for the Middle States Association, January 1979, 10, WCA).

At the same time that Wells was becoming more financially troubled, it became a more visibly female-dominated institution. "The Blueprint" was carried out under the first woman academic dean, Dr. Nenah Fry, who was appointed in 1975. In 1976 the trustees appointed the first woman president, who was also the most famous president in the college's history: Frances ("Sissy") Tarlton Farenthold, a lawyer and former member of the Texas House of Representatives, the first woman nominated (by the Democrats) for Vice President in 1972, and the first chair of the National Women's Political Caucus (Dieckmann 1995, 213). Another woman, Dr. Patti McGill Peterson, became president of Wells when Sissy Farenthold resigned in 1980. While the percentage of women on the faculty had declined during the 1950s and 1960s, it began to rise again in the mid-1970s, so that while women were 37 percent of the faculty in 1967–68, they were close to half (44 percent) in 1984–85 (Wells College Catalogues, WCA).

The increase of women at Wells in higher administration and among the faculty occurred while the women's movement in the country at large was active and visible. A consequence of both trends was that women's issues received more attention in Wells's curriculum and extra-curricular activities. Students established a Women's Resource Center in 1973, which maintained a library to inform students about health and reproductive issues, showed films, and sometimes brought speakers to campus to talk about women's issues. Under President Farenthold's leadership, Wells and several other women's colleges, supported by a Carnegie Corporation grant, formed PLEN, Public Leadership Education Network, which sponsored seminars on women's policy issues (Dieckmann 1995, 216). President Farenthold appointed a women's studies committee in the late 1970s. When minors were introduced into the Wells curriculum in 1980, women's studies became a minor field using existing courses in the curriculum that focused on women's issues (1979–80 Wells College Catalogue, WCA).

Table 6.1 summarizes many of these trends at Wells College, showing a 14 percent decline in enrollment between 1964–65 and 1984–85, at a time when the other three colleges grew in size; a relatively high percentage of women on the faculty, especially beginning in the late 1970s; a very high percentage of women on the Board of Trustees (more than 50 percent in the mid-1970s as well as the mid-1980s); and a good representation of women in top administrative positions. Thus Wells was truly coeducational in all respects except its all-women student body. The only surprising datum of Table 6.1 is, perhaps, that Wells College was not the first of these four colleges to establish a women's studies program.

While the change from the expansion of higher education during the 1960s to the tightening during the 1970s affected many colleges, the impact on Wells was particularly great due to the decreasing popularity of single-sex education. Those women's colleges like Wells that remained single-sex found it difficult to convince young women, particularly academically talented young women, that an environment without men students had unique advantages. Declining enrollments and finances inevitably became the college's major preoccupations.

Struggling to Become "Truly Coeducational": Middlebury College, 1965–85

Similar to Hamilton and Wells College, Middlebury benefited by the 1960s boom in higher education, but unlike Wells, Middlebury continued to prosper in the 1970s. Middlebury's endowment and student body increased, at the same time that it was able to be selective about the students it admitted.[26] While the college as a whole flourished, women students still struggled to achieve equal treatment in admissions and in student life. The legacy of being a men's college was very visible in 1965, and even twenty years later, after the second wave of the women's movement, Middlebury's men students were more privileged than the women students.[27]

A major way men students' privileges were maintained was, as at Hamilton, through the fraternities. Even before the student revolts of the late 1960s, the role of fraternities was being questioned at Middlebury, sometimes by students themselves, who became concerned about the discriminatory policies of their national organizations. Although fraternities became much less popular in the late 1960s and 1970s, as they did in most colleges (Stameshkin 1996, 229), their membership began to increase again in the mid-1980s when college students nationally became more conservative. Thus while only 17 percent of men students were members in 1979, 40 percent belonged in 1983 (Stameshkin 1996, 237). The administration and faculty generally saw the fraternities as problems, not solely or even primarily because of their gender discrimination but rather because of their anti-intellectual focus, their encouragement of disruptive and offensive behavior, and the unsightly appearance of their houses. Fraternities were weakened, however, when the college purchased all fraternity properties in 1979–1980, and students lost the right to dine in them (Stameshkin 1996, 236).

It might be thought that Middlebury's women students could have countered fraternities' dominance through their own organizations, in particular, the sororities. But sororities were not as influential as fraternities, and they did not have nearly equivalent resources, such as their own houses. Sororities became less popular with women students in the student movement days of the late 1960s, when exclusive organizations of all sorts became suspect, and they disbanded in 1969 over concern about racial and religious discrimination in the national organizations (*Middlebury Campus*, January 16 and February 20, 1969, MCA).

Women's social situation at Middlebury altered quite dramatically beginning in the late 1960s as students successfully protested the strict social regulations governing their college life. Rather than having one set of rules for women, and a different, more liberal set for the men, women and men came to be treated equally, at least formally. These changes occurred simultaneously with the integration of women and men—in dining, housing, student government, athletics, admissions, and valedictory and salutatory awards. The fraternities were, of course, one exception, but even some of them had started allowing women students to eat and live in their houses (Stameshkin 1996, 234).

Indicative of the changes then occurring at Middlebury, the woman who replaced Dean Kelly in 1970, Erica Wonnacott, was appointed not as the dean of women but rather, dean of students. Although she was one of the first women in the country to serve as dean of men as well as women students, Dean Wonnacott described herself as not having "a particularly feminist consciousness" (Taped interview with Erica Wonnacott, February 1989, MCA). Integration of women and men students occurred rapidly during her tenure, from 1970 to 1988. As she explained it, her "first task" was "consolidation," represented concretely by putting "men's and women's files . . . into the same drawers for the first time" (*Middlebury College Magazine*, Spring 1988, MCA). Mixed-sex housing began in the language dormitories in order to justify it to the trustees on the grounds that men students would be able to have academic opportunities previously available only to the women students (Taped interview with Erica Wonnacott, February 1989, MCA). By 1975 only two single-sex residence halls remained at Middlebury (Stameshkin 1996, 411). Such rapid change, along with the end of parietal hours and the integration of athletics in 1977, led Dean Wonnacott to warn an administrator at Lowell Technical Institute that Middlebury was probably "not a good model" for their policies since Middlebury was "super-liberal" (Eileen O'Brien, "The Myth of Coeducation," thesis submitted for Honors Degree in History, 1991, 82, MCA).

Presumably also influencing Dean Wonnacott's description of Middlebury as "super-liberal" were the student protests, which climaxed during the early years of her tenure. While from the perspective of the country at large events at Middlebury were not very dramatic, they did shake up the bucolic campus. After the United States invaded Cambodia in May 1970 and student demonstrators at Kent State and Jackson State were killed, Middlebury's students engaged in a six-day strike. More dramatically, a building was set on fire, although it turned out that the arsonist was a former student who was considered to have psychological problems (Stameshkin 1996, 311).

Another way in which Middlebury College changed between 1965 and 1985 was in the composition of its student body. Students played a key role in pressuring the administration and trustees to admit more minority students, to increase the number of women students, and to hire more women and minority faculty. While the numbers of minorities, in particular, black students, did increase, they remained very low; there were only three African-American students in 1960, 23 in 1967, 36 in 1969, and about 60 in the early 1970s. From then until 1987, black students remained at about 3 percent of the student body (Stameshkin 1996, 203–205). Recruitment of black faculty was even less successful. In 1983, for example, an article in the student newspaper noted that there was only one black faculty member that year—a visiting assistant professor of philosophy (*Middlebury Campus*, October 14, 1983, MCA).

In marked contrast to its early history, Middlebury College by the mid-1960s was seen as a "preppy" college for students from upper-class families. The lack of diversity in the socioeconomic backgrounds of students became a cause for concern, but until 1975, less than one-fifth of Middlebury's students received financial aid, a percentage that was significantly lower than the colleges Middlebury liked to compare itself to—Bates, Bowdoin, Colby, Wesleyan, and Williams, for example. In 1982 Middlebury, at the urging of its president, changed to an aid-blind admissions policy, and the percentage of students receiving financial aid increased to 25 percent by 1985. At the same time the average grant went from $1,760 in 1974–75 to $3,406 in 1979–80 (Report to the Board of Trustees, Middlebury College, 1975–80, Olin Robison, MCA; Stameshkin 1996, 210).

Thus in the mid-1980s Middlebury was a flourishing coeducational college. Although its student body was mostly rich and white, and slightly more than 50 percent male, it was less rich, less white, and less male than it had been in the mid-1960s. Students had taken a leading role in calling for changes that improved women's position at the college and increased the numbers of minority students somewhat. It may have seemed like Middlebury had finally become a genuine coeducational college (if still a mostly white and rich one), but as can be seen from information presented in Table 6.1, there were other signs that this was not so, in particular, the virtual absence of women in key administrative positions, the low percentage of women on the faculty and the Board of Trustees, and the lack of a women's studies program. While representation of women in photographs in the student newspaper seems quite good, according to the information in Table 6.1, men's sports still received much more attention than women's sports. For example, examination of these same issues for sports coverage shows that in the February 1974 issue, *all* articles on sports, spread over three pages, were on men's sports; in the March 1979 issue, two of four pages on sports were solely on men's teams, the other two pages had articles on men's and women's sports; and in April 1984, articles on and photos of men's sports still dominated by a ratio of about six to one. These and other, more sensitive issues such as sexual harassment had yet to be fully discussed at "coeducational" Middlebury.

Struggling to Retain a Separate Identity: William Smith College, 1965–85

In contrast to Kirkland's relation to Hamilton, William Smith College never tried to be different from Hobart in its educational mission or philosophy. Rather than distinctiveness, what William Smith College struggled for was parity. Legal parity was established in 1943 when William Smith's status changed from being a "department" of Hobart to being an equal college in the corporate entity, Colleges of the Seneca. But Hobart's dominance was still evident from the disparate numbers of students admitted to each college. In 1964–65, for example, there were close to 1,000 Hobart students and only 360 William Smith students (27 percent of the total number of students at the affiliated colleges). A report of an accrediting body in the early 1960s called attention to this issue and recommended that as Hobart "expanded its enrollment," it should "increase the present ratio of women to men" (Middle States Association of Colleges and Secondary Schools, Evaluation Report, February 1963, HWSCA).

In the early 1970s some administrators, faculty, and students tried to do something about the unequal ratio of men and women students. A faculty committee recommended to President Allan Kuusisto that fewer men students should be admitted to Hobart and more women students should be admitted to William Smith to move the colleges "toward parity." Faculty favored this on the grounds that the admission standards for women students were higher and so such a move would improve the quality of the students overall. Dean Zimmerman of William Smith argued further that the inequality in numbers of men and women students made it "very clear to every William Smith student that education for women is considered to be less important than, though not qualitatively different from, education for men at the Colleges" ("Toward Parity at Hobart and William Smith Colleges," Zimmerman 1972, HWSCA).

Students at William Smith were also concerned about the inequality in their numbers compared to those at Hobart. According to the 1971 president of William Smith's student body, Mary Helen Hawthorne, the predominance of men in classes tended to produce an "adverse classroom situation" in which the women felt "intimidated." Moreover, on any college-wide decision, the "female point of view" was barely recognized since the women were "always outnumbered two to one" (Memo to Dean Speer, October 21, 1971, "Toward Parity," HWSCA). The student government of William Smith held a referendum that asked the women students whether they preferred the status quo in the male-female ratio or a move to parity by 1978—almost two-thirds of the William Smith students voted for parity. Slowly the situation changed. In 1974 President Kuusisto reported that the ratio of women to men students had improved slightly, but only from 2:3 to 7:10 (President's Report, 1973–74, HWSCA).

During the period of student unrest, other concerns besides the issue of the numerical dominance of Hobart over William Smith students were raised. Students protested social restrictions, eventually getting the right for William Smith dormitories to establish 24-hour parietals (*The Herald*, February 13, 1970, HWSCA). Their protests also led to student representation on faculty and trustee committees and to some changes to the curriculum to make it more relevant to the mid-twentieth century. Diversity of the student body was another major issue that received attention.

By the end of the 1960s African-American students at Hobart and William Smith had organized a club for themselves. One article in the student newspaper in early 1970 listed all the reasons black students were "not happy" at college, including the fact that they comprised only 2 percent of the student body and that there were no black faculty members and only one black administrator. They also talked about attitudes they encountered, including "hopeful assimilation expected by the colleges" and "teachers knowing about our personal capabilities before we enter class" (*The Herald*, January 16, 1970, HWSCA).

Interestingly, one way the colleges addressed diversity was by using Hobart's links to the Episcopalian Church. In 1962 the Association of Episcopal Colleges was founded at Hobart; one of the colleges that joined was Voorhees, a historically black college in South Carolina. In the late 1970s Hobart received a grant to establish a student exchange program with Voorhees. While the president of the colleges saw this as a step in the right direction, he acknowledged that more financial aid was needed as a "vital tool in promoting diversity" (President's Report 1979–80, HWSCA). In the early 1980s the colleges established a minority affairs office to address the concerns of minority students and to try to increase minority student enrollment. By 1985 President Brewster claimed that the office had been a notable success. In contrast to national trends, minority students had increased, so that they were now about 8 percent of the student body. Moreover, the retention rate for junior minority students was 80 percent, while nationally, the retention rate for minorities was 41 percent (President's Report 1984–85, HWSCA).

In the mid-1970s an outside review body noted that Hobart and William Smith were not as serious academically as they might be. A report of visitors for the Middle States Association encouraged the colleges to be clearer about their mission since there seemed to be "confusion" between the goal of "academic excellence" and the goal of college life traditions (vigorous athleticism, health and well-being, etc.). Some faculty and administrators responded to this report, mostly disputing the idea that these two aspects of the colleges represented a dichotomy. A faculty committee report admitted, however, that although the colleges had a good academic reputation, they also had the "reputation of being a party school." This committee was concerned about the dominance of athletics and asked what the "attitude toward fraternities" should be (Middle States Evaluation folder, 1974, HWSCA).

Faculty at Hobart and William Smith, like faculty at Middlebury and Hamilton colleges, were generally hostile to the fraternities, but they did not make fraternities the object of a sustained campaign. During the period of student unrest, many students at Hobart and William Smith expressed anti-fraternity sentiment,[28] but even then, about half the freshmen submitted bids (*The Herald*, January 30, 1970, HWSCA). It is interesting to speculate whether part of the reason fraternities were not seen as more threatening—to campus unity and to the status of women—was a result of the relatively independent and secure position of the women students at William Smith. While men students did dominate campus life, they did not do so to the degree that they did at coeducational colleges like Middlebury.

At times Hobart and William Smith seemed on the road to becoming an ordinary coeducational college, especially during the 1960s when integration—first of races and then of women and men—was generally equated with progress. An editorial in the student newspaper expressed this view directly: "Hobart and William Smith are one college . . . we're friends no longer; we've been lovers for years, it's time we got married" (*The Herald*, January 9, 1970, HWSCA). But perhaps due to the history of William Smith, its separate name and endowment, and perhaps also due to the vision of some key administrators, a complete merger did not occur. When the women's movement developed during the 1970s, William Smith was able to take advantage of the recognition of some benefits to women of separatism and strengthen its identity as a *coordinate* college.

Official rhetoric about the coordinate system claimed that it was equally beneficial to women and men students. Clarence Butler, as acting dean of Hobart, called the arrangement a "three-in-one school: two single-sex institutions and one coeducational institution." The dean of William Smith, Rebecca Fox, similarly argued that under coordination men and women had the opportunity to come together "as equals," and it was easier than under coeducation for both men and women to achieve a "distinct identity" (*The Pulteney St. Survey*, October 1982, HWSCA). Yet students and alumni/ae generally recognized that women benefited more than men from coordination. For instance, a small poll of seniors in 1983 found that while only 40 percent of the Hobart men were in favor of coordination, 70 percent of the William Smith seniors were. Those in favor of coordination noted the strong independence fostered in women by the coordinate system and argued that maintaining the tradition was in and of itself positive. Those against argued that coordination created negative relations between the sexes, was not cost effective, and led to certain inequities (Self-Evaluation Report for the Middle States Association, 1984, HWSCA).

One of the most eloquent defenders of coordination was Susan Connally, who had been president of the William Smith student government in her senior year, 1969–1970. When she returned to campus to give a Founder's Day address in 1977, the demise of Kirkland was imminent, as she soberly mentioned. Ms. Connally listed the benefits of coordination, including many leadership opportunities, women role models, students' having their "own territory" and being "part of a community of women." She even claimed that William Smith students were free from "dating and mating rituals" (Connally, Founder's Day Addresses, 1977, HWSCA).

Thus despite William Smith College's having been overwhelmed numerically by Hobart, and despite its not having been a very distinct institution, it did seem to provide its women students with some of the advantages of separation from men: a chance to develop their own capabilities in a supportive institution created specifically for them. As the data in Table 6.1 show, William Smith was not nearly as much of a women's college as completely separate Wells, in terms of the representation of women on its faculty,[29] trustees, or top administrators. It did develop programs like women's studies quite early, however, and occasionally women students had top positions in the mixed-sex student activities, such as the editor-in-chief position on the student newspaper. Yet men's sports at Hobart, even after Title IX, were given more attention and newspaper coverage, a fact that members of the colleges' community themselves sometimes noted (*The Pulteney St. Survey*, March 1977, HWSCA).[30] Even though Hobart and William Smith might have desired to distinguish themselves from coeducational colleges, the larger public did not necessarily recognize the distinction,[31] which may be one reason why William Smith did not have the enrollment problems of Wells College. It grew between 1965 and 1985,[32] even though it did not achieve parity with Hobart, as many people associated with William Smith thought it should.

Tensions Between Separatism and Integration

Equality of opportunity for women appeared to have been achieved by the early 1970s as the last prestigious colleges for men opened their doors to women undergraduates and as discriminatory social regulations for women at coeducational institutions ended. With the acceptance of integration as an ideal, for women and racial minorities, separate colleges lost their apparent justification. Women's colleges such as Wells were put on the defensive, despite research, reported first in the early 1970s, that their graduates were more successful in later life than women graduates of coeducational colleges. Women's colleges increasingly found it difficult to attract students, with the result that many decided to admit men and others closed down.

Kirkland was one of the "disappearing" women's colleges. Like women's colleges of about a century earlier, Kirkland was founded for a variety of reasons—some reflected women's needs, but many originated from the needs of Hamilton College's men students. Moreover, Kirkland was set up in a way that virtually guaranteed failure: insufficient funding, restrictions on fund-raising, and an unbalanced curriculum. Other external factors contributed to the demise of Kirkland, including the year of its opening, 1968, just at the time that the most prestigious men's colleges began to admit women and single-sex education became less popular. Radical or progressive institutions like Kirkland did not have the same appeal, either, a decade after Kirkland opened. While these factors may have made it inevitable that Kirkland would not succeed, the takeover by Hamilton College did not have to occur in the manner it did. The treatment of tenured Kirkland faculty made it very clear that key people at Hamilton viewed Kirkland as inferior, the traditional way that any women's institution has been perceived. Had Kirkland College received the financial support it needed and had it been treated as an equal partner in its relationship with Hamilton College, it seems likely that it would have evolved into a more integral, less distinct coordinate institution.

It is ironic that just as single-sex education declined in popularity, research evidence mounted that coeducation has disadvantages for women while single-sex education has advantages. Such research stemmed from the women's movement's probes into the various facets of what began to be called "sexism." Previously hidden, or not discussed, ways in which (white, middle-class, heterosexual) men perpetuated their privileged positions began to be challenged. Within colleges, for example, the relatively greater amount of resources devoted to men, including such difficult-to-quantify resources as faculty time, came to be questioned. Men students' dominance in classroom discussions and campus leadership positions, the extent to which traditions and even curriculum were defined by and for men, and men's sexual harassment of women, were all seen as ways in which women were disadvantaged. Women's colleges rightfully claimed that these problems were absent or considerably less in their institutions and thus that they presented a supportive environment in which women flourished. But given that women's colleges were going against the more accepted cultural belief that equates integration with progress, this argument was not always heard but rather remained "news."

Such was the situation when the class of 1988 entered college. The next part of this book follows women students at all four colleges from their entry in 1984 until the spring of their senior year, and for a subgroup, six years after their graduation. I also discuss developments at each of these colleges from 1985 to the late 1990s. Before turning to my survey findings and recent changes at the colleges, however, I review arguments, made both historically and in contemporary times, for and against separate education for women.

Notes

1   Flacks (1988, 118) discusses three waves of "collective intellectual leftism," in which the 1960s were the third. He argues that unlike the earlier waves, prior to World War I and in the 1930s, the sixties left did not depend on left parties among the workers but rather was "the property of intellectuals themselves," with a mass base of students rather than workers.

2   One man who supported the academy financially was Peter Smith (Pilkington 1962, 28), the fur trader and father of Gerrit Smith, the abolitionist, philanthropist, and advocate of women's suffrage. Gerrit Smith later attended Hamilton College, married the daughter of the college's first president, and served on its Board of Trustees (Pilkington 1962, 99). Gerrit Smith's daughter, Elizabeth Smith Miller, was the suffragist who had a great influence on William Smith, the founder of William Smith College, as discussed in Chapter 4.

3   By comparison, over 80 percent of Middlebury men belonged to fraternities between 1865 and 1905 (Stameshkin 1985, 262), and an "overwhelming majority" belonged at Hobart (Smith 1972, 270).

4   A woman who came to Hamilton in 1952 as the wife of a faculty member estimated that the college community was about 75 percent Republican before she and five other Democrats moved there (Ellie Wertimer, 1996 Class and Charter Day Address, HCA).

5   A Hamilton faculty member who was involved in long-range planning later described the specific ways that a women's college was expected to "civilize" men. The faculty and trustee planners thought that the men would begin to shave every day, and the houseparties would lose some of their "stridency" so they would not be "quite so gross" (Transcript of an interview with David Ellis by Peggy Farber, June 1977, HCA).

6   A matter of later dispute was the extent to which Hamilton faculty were involved in the planning and kept apprised of developments. Some faculty later claimed that they had been insufficiently consulted during the planning, although they did vote unanimously for Kirkland's founding (Transcript of interview with Jay Williams by K. G. Russell, Summer 1992, HCA).

7   A more specific version of how McIntosh heard about Samuel Babbitt is that on her trips through New England to search for a woman for president, she often stayed with a good woman friend in New Haven. This woman knew Babbitt because she happened to have been his eighth grade teacher. Thus, Sam Babbitt quipped, he had obtained his appointment through the "old girls' network" (*The Spectator*, May 12, 1978, HCA).

8   An interesting fact about Babbitt, apparently not known by anyone at the time of his appointment, was that he was the great-great-great grandson of the sixth

president of Hamilton College, Samuel Ware Fisher. Babbitt himself realized this when he saw an etching of Fisher in an office at Hamilton where he was working (Transcript of interview with S. Babbitt by Peggy Farber, March 3, 1977, HCA).

9   According to the Kirkland College profile of the class of 1974, the average SATs were 663 verbal and 605 math. For the Hamilton College profile of the class of 1973, the average SATs were 643 verbal and 673 math. Kirkland's average SATs were very close to those of Vassar, slightly higher than those of Bennington and Sarah Lawrence, but about 50 points lower (for the totals of math and verbal) than Barnard, Smith, and Wellesley (Mimeo, June 5, 1970, HCA).

10   Many colleges in the early 1970s were in financial difficulty, leading one researcher to call the period the "new depression" in higher education. It is interesting, however, that this researcher, who studied 41 institutions across the country, classified Hamilton College in 1970 as one of the minority of institutions *not* in financial trouble (Cheit 1971, 140).

11   In 1973, according to research done by two Kirkland students, only 10 percent of Kirkland students had not taken any courses at Hamilton and more than one-quarter (28 percent) had taken six ("An Examination of Coordination, Single-sex and Coeducational Models of Higher Education: Should Kirkland Alter Its Status?" December 1973, paper for Psychology 301, HCA). The majority of Hamilton students also took some of their courses at Kirkland. In 1976 only 14 percent of seniors at Hamilton had *not* taken any course at Kirkland (Memo from Dean Kinnel to Hamilton faculty, April 1976, HCA).

12   In 1977 Dean Gulick of Hamilton also concluded that Kirkland's philosophy had been more attractive to women in 1968 when it was founded. Nine years later the Kirkland undergraduate, according to Gulick, had "yearnings" that "are more easily satisfied traditionally" (Dean Gulick to President Carovano, February 21, 1977, HCA).

13   According to President Babbitt, Hamilton administrators and trustees had intended to make the decision about Kirkland over the summer to avoid such protests, but "the Kirkland Board, once it sensed how imminent such an action might be, forced the matter into the open" (Babbitt, letter to alumnae, May 17, 1977, HCA).

14   Kirkland people did not feel that asking for $3 million from Hamilton was unreasonable given the following: Hamilton's endowment was over $30 million; over the years, Kirkland had paid Hamilton almost that amount, about $2,750,000, in debt service and its share of administrative expenses; and $600,000 per year was just slightly more than Kirkland paid to Hamilton each year (for administration and interest on loans) ("A Statement on Kirkland," January 1, 1978, HCA).

15   Babbitt did not deny that the gap in SAT scores between Hamilton men and Kirkland women students had widened, but he did question its relevance, noting that Kirkland women received, on average, approximately the same grades in Hamilton courses, and as seniors, Kirkland students actually performed better than Hamilton men (Memo of Babbitt to the Hamilton Board of Trustees, May 5, 1977, HCA).

16 Another indication of President Carovano's lack of concern about Kirkland emerged later that year. President Babbitt "startled" a meeting at Kirkland with the announcement that Hamilton had "recently engaged in conversations" with Wells College "in which a merger between the two schools was contemplated." Apparently President Babbitt himself had just heard about this merger idea from one of Kirkland's lawyers, David Lascell, who was at the time chair of the Wells College Board of Trustees. President Babbitt reported that as a result, he felt himself in an "untenable position" (*The Spectator*, December 9, 1977, HCA).

17 Babbitt was clearly influenced by the second wave of the women's movement and, in particular, by studies of such researchers as Tidball that demonstrated the superior outcomes for women educated in single-sex environments (see Chapter 7). His views had changed from when he was appointed in the mid-1960s, since at that time, according to his own admission, he had not previously thought much about women's education or women's colleges (Transcript of interview with S. Babbitt by Peggy Farber, March 3, 1977, HCA).

18 The top administrators at Kirkland, Sam Babbitt and Dean Frazer, took leaves of absence until their contracts ended on July 1, 1978. Babbitt ran an office from his home in Clinton, helping students who were thinking of transferring and getting archives in order. Many years later, at a reunion, Babbitt referred to his "exile" as one of the events that left a "bad taste" (Babbitt, speech given at Kirkland reunion, June 7, 1997). Some other, but not all, Kirkland administrators and staff persons were offered jobs at Hamilton, although the jobs were not necessarily ones compatible with their interests or abilities.

19 The March 2, 1979 issue of *The Spectator* devoted less than one-half page to women's sports compared to one and a half pages to men's sports; even more extreme, the March 16, 1979 issue had about four pages on men's sports but less than one-half page on women's sports (HCA).

20 Anderson's study of single-sex colleges that did or did not become coeducational (and religious colleges that did or did not become secular) between 1965 and 1975 also found that men's colleges that added women experienced the largest increases in enrollment (Anderson 1977).

21 Anderson's comparisons of a sample of women's colleges that admitted men in the 1965–75 decade with those that remained single-sex found that those that became coeducational were weaker at the start of the decade (Anderson 1977). In many ways Wells fits the pattern for women's colleges that remained single-sex. Its enrollment declined slightly (while those that admitted men grew), and in 1965 Wells accepted fewer than 75 percent of its applicants (while those that admitted men accepted about 85 percent). But unlike the optimistic picture that Anderson paints for women's colleges that remained single-sex, by 1975 Wells had to accept a much higher percentage of applicants to obtain even smaller entering classes, and its financial problems had gotten worse. Perhaps a key reason Wells's problems were so severe was that it was small, even by women's colleges standards, and in this way was more like the women's colleges in Anderson's study that admitted men during this decade.

22   Wells College also had to spend more money on admissions to achieve these smaller classes; between 1973 and 1977, the amount spent more than doubled (Self-Evaluation Report prepared for the Middle States Association, January 1979, WCA).

23   Whereas in 1964–65, 58% of Wells students came from out of state, by 1984–85, only 43% did (Wells College Catalogues, WCA).

24   In 1984, 43 percent of the mothers of Wells students had graduated from college, and 54 percent of the fathers had (Report of the Committee for the 21st Century, WCA).

25   These cuts would seem to indicate that by the mid-1970s Wells was an institution in financial trouble, at least according to the criteria used in the 1970 Carnegie Commission study of the financial condition of 41 institutions of higher education. A college or university was defined in the 1970 study as "in financial difficulty" if its "current financial condition" resulted in a loss of services that are "regarded as a part of its program or a loss of quality" (Cheit 1971, 36).

26   Between 1975 and 1980, Middlebury's endowment increased 100 percent, from $31 million to $62 million; by 1984 the endowment was $100 million (Stameshkin 1996, 170, 174). Increase in enrollment was planned; specific numbers are presented in Table 6.1. In 1977 33 percent of men applicants were admitted, 29 percent of women applicants (Admissions Report, 1977, MCA).

27   The historical legacy of fears of feminization of Middlebury were still evident in the mid-1970s, at least in the views of the man who served as the director of admissions from 1964 to 1990. In his annual report for 1976–77, this admissions director wrote about his concern that "for a long time a number of factors combined to give Middlebury something of a 'girly' image." He believed that this image was changing due to "considerable athletic success" for a few consecutive years, so that Middlebury's "identity as a college for women and for MEN" had been more "clearly" established (Admissions Report, 1977, MCA).

28   See, for example, the editorial in the October 10, 1969, college newspaper, in which the writer sarcastically noted how the head of the inter-fraternity association had denied the existence of "bigotry, anti-semitism, house stereotypes," or the editorial a few months later that acknowledged that some students were complaining about the "absence" of anti-fraternity editorials (The Herald, October 10, 1969 and January 16, 1970, HWSCA).

29   A carefully done senior honors thesis by a sociology major investigated why the Colleges did not have a higher proportion of women faculty. Between 1975 and 1979 about 39 percent of faculty hired were women, and yet despite the increase in hiring of women that this represented, the proportion of women on the faculty was still only about 21 percent, and they were clustered at the bottom ranks. Similar to the conclusion being reached at Kirkland at about the same time, this study argued that women faculty were not sufficiently supported, for example, through maternity leave policies or child care facilities, so that many chose to leave (David B. Porter, "With Best of Intentions: An Impact Analysis of Equal

Opportunity Policy at Hobart and William Smith Colleges, 1964–79," Senior Honors Thesis in Sociology, 1982, HWSCA).

30   Title IX of the Educational Amendments of 1972, 20 U.S.C. Sec. 1681 prohibits sex discrimination in education. It has had far-reaching effects on many programs in colleges and universities that receive federal financial assistance, but particularly athletics. For a good discussion of the original legislation, the most significant court cases connected to it, and subsequent modifications, see J. Ralph Lindgren and Nadine Taub, *The Law of Sex Discrimination*, 1993.

31   Even the admissions department of Hobart, unlike its counterpart at William Smith, did not stress to prospective students the distinctiveness of the coordinate arrangement. According to Hobart's director of admissions, the Hobart staff first talked to high school boys about "all the aspects of the Colleges that are shared" (*The Pulteney St. Survey*, March 1977, HWSCA).

32   The figures of Table 6.1 show that overall, Hobart and William Smith's enrollment declined just slightly (by 2 percent) from 1979–80 to 1984–85. Since William Smith increased its share of enrollment from 40 to 42 percent, however, in absolute numbers its enrollment increased by 23 students. Hobart's enrollment, on the other hand, decreased by 55 students. Intentionally or not, then, parity was being approached by slightly decreasing the numbers of Hobart students.

Illustrations

Boat club, with professors, on Cayuga Lake, described in catalogues as "a delightful source of recreation and health." Wells College, 1876. *Wells College Archives.*

Dean Helen Fairchild Smith, with cap, back right; the Dean's mother, front right; alumna Frances Folsom Cleveland '85 in center with child; and other alumnae, Wells College, 1890s. *Wells College Archives.*

Women's Study—The "Phronisterion" (Deep-thinking place), Old Chapel, with students from classes of 1896, '97, '98 and '99, Middlebury College. *Middlebury College Archives.*

Home Economics class at the practice house, the Homestead, 1913–14, Middlebury College. *Middlebury College Archives.*

Yearbook (*Kaleidoscope*) board, 1918, with man student as editor-in-chief and woman as assistant editor-in-chief, Middlebury College. *Middlebury College Archives.*

Typing class, William Smith College, around 1920, *Hobart and William Smith Archives.*

Trustees, Hobart and William Smith College, 1922, with Anna Botsford Comstock on left. *Hobart and William Smith Archives.*

Senior comprehensive in art, in front of faculty and other students, 1939, with Nicholas Nabokoff on sofa to right, Wells College. *Wells College Archives.*

May Day, 1939, Wells College, with the queen and her attendants posing in front of a Wells, Fargo & Co. Stagecoach. *Wells College Archives.*

Tea at Comstock House, William Smith College, 1958–59. *Hobart and William Smith Colleges Archives.*

Opening procession of Kirkland College, still under construction, September, 1968. *Hamilton College Archives.*

Kirkland College class with Professor Raybeck, early 1970s. *Hamilton College Archives.*

Open "mike" at Kirkland graduation, 1973, with President Sam Babbitt in background.
Hamilton College Archives.

Community meeting, Kirkland College, May 1977, when the community heard about Hamilton College's takeover. *Hamilton College Archives.*

Student demonstration, 1970s, Hobart and William Smith Colleges. *Hobart and William Smith Colleges Archives.*

Moving-up Day celebration, May 1979, with students from the class of 1982. *Hobart and William Smith Archives.*

Rally in support of remaining a single-sex, Wells College, 1987. *Wells College Public Relations Archives.*

May Day Celebration, Middlebury College, 1990. *Eric Borg, Middlebury College Archives.*

Hamilton students, September 1997, on newly constructed bridge connecting the new and old sides of the campus. The bridge is named after former Hamilton President J. Martin Carovano; the building behind is named after former chair of the board of trustees of Kirkland College, Walter Beinecke, Jr. *Hamilton College Archives.*

Protest, April 1998, Middlebury College, after publication of racist "joke" in college newspaper's April 1st issue. *David Barreda.*

PART TWO

THE SINGLE-SEX VERSUS COEDUCATION DEBATE: EXPERIENCES OF WOMEN STUDENTS AT WELLS, MIDDLEBURY, WILLIAM SMITH, AND HAMILTON COLLEGES

Chapter 7

Separate or Together? Myths, Facts, and Research on How Girls and Women Should Be Educated

Separatism can be promoted, both historically and today, for progressive or reactionary reasons; that is, for the benefit of women or for the maintenance of traditional social arrangements that benefit men. Likewise with coeducation. In this chapter I am going to summarize the arguments for single-sex education (or, against coeducation) and for coeducation (or, against separate education) for girls and women. These rationales should not be equated with the reasons schools and colleges became (or have remained) single-sex or coeducational, however, as often practical and financial factors have been more important. Nonetheless, the reasons people give for being for or against single-sex education are interesting for what they reveal about assumptions concerning women's and men's abilities and appropriate roles. My goal is to show some of the historical roots of the contemporary debate between advocates of single-sex and coeducation, and how people have often made claims about the superiority of one or the other form of education despite lack of evidence. I conclude the chapter with a summary of recent empirical research that compares women's experiences in coeducational and single-sex institutions.

Separate Education to Accommodate Differences between the Sexes

The argument that men and women are inherently different has deep historical roots and was a major reason women were excluded from higher education (see Chapter 2). By the mid- to late nineteenth century, most people were no longer maintaining that women should not receive any higher education. Instead, those who claimed that women were different from men in important respects believed that women needed their own type of education that was compatible with their nature as well as their future lives as mothers and teachers. Henry Wells, for instance, insisted that his college be small so that women could be educated in an appropriate homelike setting.[1] Such intellectual disciplines as mathematics were to be taught in ways that would not be too taxing for Wells's students, and teachers were chosen with concern that they be able to exert a "happy influence" over the students. Yet Henry Wells did admit that many of the apparent differences between women's and men's intellects resulted from a lack of educational opportunities for women.

Versions of this argument can be found throughout the twentieth century as well. G. Stanley Hall, the first president of the American Psychological Association, promulgated such views early in the century. He argued that menstrual functions cause a "distinction" that is "absolute" (1904, I, 581), leading him to advocate education for women in separate colleges so that their "intuitions" would be encouraged, nature study and religion would be emphasized, and mathematics would be taught "only in its rudiments" (1904, I, 639). In the 1920s and 1930s, educators like President Moody of Middlebury College (who favored segregating the women students in their own coordinate college) wrote about the different talents of women and men, with women being good at memorizing and doing detailed work, men students being better at creative, intellectually challenging studies (see Chapter 5). Even as late as the 1960s, when Hamilton College was planning to establish a coordinate college for women, stereotypes of women's abilities and proclivities influenced some of the plans (see Chapter 6).

Recently some people have argued that because women and men have different learning styles (Belenky et al. 1986), use different forms of moral reasoning (Gilligan 1982), or develop mentally and emotionally at different rates (Fox-Genovese 1994; Riesman 1991), they benefit from separate education. This line of reasoning has sometimes led to the argument that women should be educated by the principles of "feminist pedagogy," which stress the participation of all students, collaboration rather than individual competition, and connecting emotions with the intellect.[2] A few public (and private) high schools concerned about the generally poor performance of girls (and minority males) in math and science courses have risked lawsuits by establishing single-sex classes, or even single-sex schools ("Single-sex education: a public policy issue" 1995, 13–14).[3]

Some of the single-sex classes attempt to use pedagogical techniques designed to match the way girls are believed to work.

If the argument is that single-sex education is needed to accommodate *differences* between the sexes, then it follows that not only women's colleges should be supported, but men's colleges as well. This was the argument that David Riesman[4] and Elizabeth Fox-Genovese each made separately in 1994 when the United States Supreme Court considered the case of women who were trying to gain entry into one of the last state-supported, all-male military institutions, V.M.I. (Virginia Military Institute). An irony for those who favor single-sex education for both men and women on the grounds of differences in their aptitudes or rates of development is that some of the scholars whose work they cite, in particular Carol Gilligan (1982), do not themselves believe that men's colleges should be continued. Thus while Fox-Genovese cited Gilligan in her testimony in favor of V.M.I.'s remaining all-male, Gilligan herself signed a brief on the opposite side that argued, in part, that "the purpose and import" of her work had been "misconstrue[d]" (A.A.U.P. et al. brief, posted November 27, 1995).[5]

One basic problem with favoring single-sex education to accommodate the different learning styles of women and men is that there is no evidence that teaching is different in most single-sex colleges. It is difficult to imagine how it could be when faculty at such colleges are not given special training and have obtained their higher degrees from the same universities as faculty at coeducational institutions. While "feminist pedagogy" has been discussed as a way of making classes more relevant to marginalized groups (cf., Maher and Tetreault 1994), there is no reason to believe that such pedagogy is applicable only to single-sex settings. Faculty who try to put such principles into practice are probably a minority at any college and mostly confined to such fields as women's studies and some of the humanities and social sciences. Perhaps faculty at women's colleges and girls' schools could learn alternative pedagogical techniques, but at present, this advantage of single-sex education remains in the realm of possibility, not actuality.

Coeducation Because Female Connotes Inferiority

Women's colleges in the United States can rightfully be seen as having developed because women were not allowed to study in the same institutions as men. And yet the existence of these schools was not applauded at the time by many women concerned with women's rights, who tended to view them as educationally inferior to men's colleges (Butcher 1989).[6]

Lucy Stone, speaking at the Seventh National Women's Rights Convention in New York City in 1856, when there were only a few women's colleges that later historians would consider to be true colleges, described women's colleges as "petty" and predicted that they would eventually perish. She also believed that it would take only "a little more time" for Harvard and Yale to admit women (Solomon 1985, 43). M. Carey Thomas,[7] Alice Freeman,[8] and Marion Talbot[9] all chose coeducational universities over Vassar and other women's colleges such as Elmira and Wells. Susan B. Anthony, one of the most famous suffragists, was "always a firm believer in coeducation" and helped open the University of Rochester to women, raising the final $8,000 for the endowment for that purpose (James 1971). Likewise, her great friend and collaborator, Elizabeth Cady Stanton, favored coeducation over women's colleges (Harper 1899, 142–43).

Not surprisingly, most nineteenth-century feminists were more concerned with obtaining the *right* for women to attend men's colleges than with criticizing the treatment of women within these institutions. Even when such prominent women's rights periodicals as *Woman's Journal*, published in Boston, reported that women students were receiving hostile treatment in some coeducational institutions, they "continued to promote coeducation" (Butcher 1989, 44).[10]

The early women's colleges were generally poor, struggling institutions. There were thus good reasons for seeing them as less educationally rigorous and less prestigious than some coeducational or men's colleges. The editor of the Chicago women's rights periodical, *Agitator*, argued in 1869 that the "whole system of government" was based on the assumption of women's "inferiority," which meant that "the best educators" did not take positions at women's colleges. "The best and the most of everything is provided for the male college—the female college is left to shirk for itself" (as quoted in Butcher 1989, 39).[11]

Some nineteenth- and early twentieth-century feminists did recognize benefits to female-controlled space, even though most were more concerned with opening men's colleges to women. Having rejected single-sex education for herself, M. Carey Thomas became the president of Bryn Mawr College and worked hard to make it academically (and socially) superior (Horowitz 1994). Marion Talbot made mostly unfavorable comparisons of Vassar College to the University of Wisconsin in *The Education of Women*. She argued that women's colleges were too rigid, hampered by attempts to prove themselves by emulating traditional men's colleges. At the same time, Talbot did note that when men are present, women are less likely to control social affairs in which they are interested (Talbot 1910, 203).

A few nineteenth-century feminists favored separate education for women.[12] Frances Willard[13] became the president of Evanston College for Ladies in the early 1870s. She resigned because it did not evolve into an independent coordinate institution within Northwestern University but rather was used as a steppingstone for coeducation (James 1971, 615). Jane Addams[14] wanted to attend Smith College but had to follow her older sisters to Rockford Illinois Female Seminary, known as the "Mount Holyoke of the West," which she attended from 1877 to 1882 (James 1971; Addams 1910/1960).

In their early years some women's colleges, like Wells, undoubtedly were academically weak, but before the end of the nineteenth century many became at least as strong as most men's and coeducational liberal arts colleges. Faculty at women's colleges were usually highly qualified, as they have been at Wells College throughout this century (see Tables 3.1, 4.1, and 5.1), and the curriculum of women's colleges, if not innovative, has generally been standard. It is true, however, that women's colleges have received less financial support than men's colleges, partly because their alumnae are not as rich as the alumni of men's or coeducational colleges (Newcomer 1959). Women's colleges may not provide many connections to other elite institutions, as one British researcher found distinguished girls' from boys' secondary schools (Walford 1983). On the other hand, many coeducational colleges are not rich institutions, either, nor are they able to give their graduates a head start in prestigious graduate or professional schools or in professional occupations.

Thus it is difficult not to conclude that views of women's colleges as educationally inadequate are based on prejudice. Anything that is identified with women or girls continues to be seen as inferior.[15] Stereotypes abound: women's colleges are seen as "soft," "coddling" their students, called "spinster factories" or "nunneries." These are not just nineteenth- or early twentieth-century views, either. Kirkland College students of the late 1960s and 1970s were frequently made aware that Hamilton College students, and many faculty and administrators, did not believe they were receiving a rigorous education (see Chapter 6).[16] Kendall (1975, 257) argued in her informal and quite hostile history of the Seven Sisters Colleges that single-sex education implies that "women may still need special treatment and accommodation." Kendall believed that once the Ivy League colleges admitted women, women's colleges became unnecessary; they were no longer just "eccentric" but "bizarre" (Kendall 1975, 30).

In both the nineteenth and twentieth centuries, the question seems to have been raised as a dichotomy—should women be educated in single-sex *or* coeducational institutions—rather than recognizing that it would be better to support both options.[17] Even if one could demonstrate that women's colleges were inferior in ways that mattered, it does not necessarily follow that they should be eliminated. Another response would be to lobby to increase support for them. But of course, this would only make sense if there were reasons to believe that women's colleges possess advantages over coeducational institutions. Some recent research supports this point of view, as I discuss later in this chapter.

Separate Education Is Not Realistic—Coeducation Leads to Normal, Healthy Relations Between the Sexes

Even during the nineteenth-century heyday of the belief in "separate spheres" for women and men, some people worried that too much separation for women and men might make subsequent intimate relations between them difficult. The founders of Oberlin, for instance, were concerned that without the company of women at a critical period in their lives, future ministers might develop deviant sexual practices and unrealistic, too romantic, views of women's character (Hogeland 1972–73). As a professor at Oberlin later explained to English visitors, "Nothing acts as a better antidote to romance than young men and women doing geometry together at eight o'clock every morning" (as quoted in Solomon 1985, 85). Such well-known feminists as Elizabeth Cady Stanton, Matilda Joslyn Gage, and Susan B. Anthony made similar arguments from a "hygienic-scientific" standpoint—being educated together would make relations between the sexes healthy and natural rather than "morbid" or too intense (Leach 1980, 75–80).

The concern that men students in single-sex colleges would become homosexual was probably one, unstated, reason why some men's colleges admitted women. Conway (1983) argued that evangelical educators of the nineteenth century were so worried that the imbalance of the sexes in frontier areas like Ohio would lead men to become homosexual that they took the risk of mixing the sexes in the first coeducational college, Oberlin.[18] More than a century later, before women were admitted to undergraduate study at Yale in 1969, researchers noted a "marked fear" of homosexuality. A survey of students showed that almost two-thirds (61 percent) believed there was a higher rate of homosexuality at "non-coeducational" schools (Lever and Schwartz 1971, 167).[19]

After Freudian ideas gained acceptance, and women's sexuality was acknowledged, same-sex pairings among women were looked upon as homosexual, hence "morbid and pathological" (D'Emilio and Freedman 1988, 194). In the 1920s some educators worried about the association between lesbianism and women's colleges after campus leaders at a few of the well-known women's colleges made "out-and-out" homosexuality "something of a fad" (Bromley and Britten 1938). According to a woman who did research in the 1920s on the sexual behavior and attitudes of over 2,000 women, deans of women's colleges acknowledged that serious problems could develop from the "uncontrolled 'crushes'" that arose "from time to time" among the women students (Davis 1929, 121).

The concern that single-sex education was not "natural" was not always explicitly sexual, however. Some critics argued that since most of social life is not sex-segregated, separate education did not prepare women and men for the rest of life. Some people argued further that the sexes are complementary and hence need each other for a complete education. As Amelia Bloomer wrote in 1851 in the women's rights periodical *Lily*, "Bring the sexes together and mutual benefit results—man is refined— woman is stimulated and inspired with a higher, nobler ambition. Each sex contributes to elevate and develop the other" (as quoted in Butcher 1989, 34). A *New York Times* series on women's education in the early 1930s contrasted the "softer and smaller" co-ed with the "young Amazon" of the women's colleges, arguing in part that the co-eds were superior in "poise, *realistic attitude* and in emotional maturity" [emphasis mine] (Barnard 1933). This belief continues. Katha Pollitt, generally considered a feminist, progressive columnist, has gone on record as being against women's colleges because "the future is coed." Single-sex institutions, according to Pollitt, are the "counsel of despair"; they are based on the idea that the sexes "can't be friends and colleagues and do serious work together" (Pollitt 1994). Similarly Kaminer, herself a graduate of Smith College, has argued that "collegiality is crucial to social equality" (Kaminer 1998).

Given the pervasiveness and duration of these beliefs, it is interesting that little or no research has been done to test them. Part of the problem may be how unclear or value-laden the terms are. What does it mean to have "realistic" views of the opposite sex or for the two sexes to relate "naturally"?[20] In earlier historical periods the evidence used to demonstrate the "unnaturalness" of higher education for women generally, and single-sex education in particular, was that it lowered marriage and childbearing rates (Hall 1904; Wells 1909).[21] About half of the women who graduated from Bryn Mawr between 1898 and 1908, for example, never married (D'Emilio and Freedman 1988, 190).[22] Even when these proportions were corrected for the social class factor, that is, women who attended college were generally from higher social classes whose marriage rates were lower even if they did not attend college, the evidence still showed college women had lower marriage and birth rates.

Today, however, some feminists believe the question should be turned around: given the sexism in society at large, in which men dominate social and economic life, do we want college women to learn how to relate "naturally" to men? (Shaw 1985). In their defense of single-sex education for women, Sarah, Scott, and Spender (1980, 56) argued that men need to be excluded, at least temporarily, so that women can learn to take each other seriously and to confront rather than to defer to men and men's "version of reality."

A recent challenge to the idea that coeducation promotes "natural," nonromantic views of the opposite sex comes from a study of two Southern coeducational institutions, one enrolling primarily African-American students, the other predominantly white students (Holland and Eisenhart 1990). The researchers found that fewer than one-third of the women students lived up to their occupational and educational goals, primarily because they came to be obsessed by the "culture of romance." What concerned the women students more than academic work was how they fared in the "dating and mating" arena. Perhaps when society at large is sex-segregated, as the United States was in the nineteenth century, coeducation might be useful for de-mystifying members of the opposite sex. This lesson, however, may not be needed today, when men and women mix in almost all social situations.

Coeducation for the Benefit of Men Students

Quite often when people make arguments about the benefits of coeducation, they are implicitly thinking about how *men* do better in coeducational schools or environments. The founders of Oberlin College, as I noted above, believed that men would become better ministers if educated in a college where women were also students.[23] In the past as well as today, people often say that boys and men are less rowdy, more considerate—better behaved in general—when they are in classrooms with girls or women (Jencks and Riesman 1968, 301). David Starr Jordan, the first president of Stanford, argued in the early part of this century that "the young men are more earnest, better in manners and morals, and in all ways more civilized than under monastic conditions" and, moreover, with coeducation there was "less of drunkenness, rowdyism and vice" (Jordan 1902, 102).[24] In England, R. R. Dale (1969, 1971) concluded on the basis of his research comparing single-sex schools with new coeducational, comprehensive secondary schools, that among the many benefits to mixed-sex schooling were boys' calmer and politer behavior. According to Dale, "time after time the opinion is expressed [by teachers at boys' schools] that the presence of girls has a 'refining' influence on the conduct of the boys" (Dale 1969, 61).[25] Similarly, when Hamilton College was debating the merits of establishing a coordinate college for women in the early 1960s, some faculty believed that having women around on a regular basis, rather than just for party weekends, would help civilize the men students (see Chapter 6).

The perceived benefits of coeducation for men students extend into the academic realm, too. In the nineteenth century, some people, faculty in particular, favored opening up men's colleges to women because they thought that men's academic performance would improve if they had to compete with women. John Bascom, who later became president of the coeducational University of Wisconsin, gave a speech printed in 1868 in *Revolution* (the women's rights periodical published by Stanton and Anthony) that put this position forcefully: "The young lady is quicker, more enthusiastic. . . . Her lively memory and imagination and perception would enter like yeast into the heavy, torpid mass, . . . arouse the sluggish young men to a better use of their powers, and cause a little light to find its way into their spirits" (as quoted in Butcher 1989, 36).

As I noted in Chapter 4, by the beginning of the twentieth century some people had come to see women's intellectual prowess as a threat. Women outperformed men students, which then led to fears of the "feminization" of education and cries for women and men to be separated, as happened at Middlebury College. Stanford President David Starr Jordan called this one of the "least worthy" arguments against coeducation: the dislike of the "idle boy to have his failures witnessed by women who can do better" (Jordan 1902, 104).

More recently the academic benefits of coeducation for boys has received a little research backing. A few studies that have compared the academic performance of boys and girls in single-sex and coeducational schools have concluded that boys (but not girls) perform better and are more likely to achieve their degrees in coeducational schools than they are in boys' schools (Dale 1974; Sutherland 1961). This is a minority viewpoint, however, with most studies finding that coeducation makes no difference (Marsh 1989 a,b; Riordan 1990), or even that boys' academic performance is better in single-sex schools (Lee and Bryk 1986; see also Riordan 1990 for positive outcomes for minority male students).

Recent Research: Coeducation Is Harmful to Girls and Women

Just as women's colleges were declining in number in the late 1960s and early 1970s, research studies began to be published showing that coeducational institutions systematically favored men and that women benefited from single-sex education. As Florence Howe argued, coeducation has not created a "model of equality between the sexes" but rather has meant "the admission of women to a male-initiated, male-centered, male-controlled institution" (Howe 1984, 209). It is not entirely a coincidence that the decline in the number of women's colleges occurred at the same time as research on their advantages, since both can be connected to the second wave of the women's movement. As young women gained entrance to virtually the last, and some of the most prestigious, men's colleges and universities, they were less interested in attending women's colleges. The subsequent decline in enrollment and students' academic qualifications led many women's colleges to admit men and hence become coeducational. Contemporaneously, women (and some men) scholars, influenced by the women's movement, began to investigate the relation between gender and social institutions and scholarship itself. The many subtle but deleterious effects of male dominance began to be recognized, with one result being a reevaluation of single-sex institutions for girls and women.

"Women and men in the same classroom have very different experiences," concluded Bernice Sandler on the basis of her summary of studies of women's and men's classroom experiences (Sandler, 1987, 121). Hall enumerated many, often unnoticed, ways the classroom climate can be "chilly" for women students, including faculty members' giving men students more attention (knowing their names, calling on them, asking them more profound questions, etc.), using sexist humor, attributing women's success more to luck or external factors while attributing men's success to their intelligence and motivation, engaging in more informal interaction with men students, and failing to encourage women to continue their studies (Hall and Sandler 1982).

In their well-known book, *Failing at Fairness*, Sadker and Sadker (1994) argued that the higher one goes in the educational system, the worse the situation becomes for women. They estimated that twice as many women as men are "voiceless" in college classes (170). Specific studies have found that men students dominate classroom interactions, talking more often and at greater length than women students, although they dominate less in classes with women professors (Karp and Yoels 1975; Sternglanz, and Lyberger-Ficek 1977). More recently, an observational study of classroom interactions at Vassar found, however, few differences between men and women students' participation. This study also reported that students' sex did not affect the way men and women professors responded to them (Constantinople, Cornelius, and Gray 1988). Another recent study of 86 classrooms in three types of independent non-Catholic secondary schools (boys', girls', and coeducational) found the "most problematic forms of sexism in single-sex environments"—explicit sexuality in the boys' schools and encouragement of dependence in girls' schools (Lee, Marks, and Byrd, 1994, 114). It is always difficult to know how to interpret inconsistent research findings. It could be, for instance, that Vassar, a former prestigious women's college, remains a better atmosphere for women students than other, more typical coeducational colleges.[26] Alternatively, it could be that since research like Sandler's and Sadker and Sadker's has received wide publicity, classroom climates have improved, at least in some institutions.

Some feminists who recognize the problems that coeducation creates for girls and women nonetheless oppose single-sex education because they believe it implicitly blames women for gender inequality. Madeleine Arnot's aptly titled article, "How Shall We Educate Our Sons?" argued that a single-sex strategy fails because it only tries to change girls but not boys (Arnot 1984). Similarly, columnist Katha Pollitt wrote that it was up to "grown-ups" to "read . . . the riot act" to boys who dominated classes or put down girls' contributions to class discussions. "Will it really be so difficult as all that?" she asked rhetorically.[27] Kenway and Willis (1986) expanded on these points by saying that single-sex advocates' "victim-blaming" was connected to their limited, individualistic goals of getting more women into male-dominated occupations.

It is essentially an issue of social policy or strategy whether sexism in education can be combated better in single-sex or coeducational institutions. None of the writers arguing against single-sex schools on the grounds that they do not deal with problematic male behaviors would deny that male dominance is a problem. They do seem to believe, however, that people in coeducational institutions can be made to recognize and then change men students' offensive behavior. Other people disagree, or at

least recognize that to do so is more difficult than Pollitt and others make
it sound (Shaw 1984).

Single-Sex Education Leads to Positive Long-term
Outcomes for Women Students

The researcher who over the last quarter-century has undoubtedly stirred
up the most interest in the benefits of single-sex education for women is
M. Elizabeth Tidball. Not a social scientist but a physiologist, Tidball follows a long line of women physiologists who studied at women's colleges.
In an interview she acknowledged the important mentoring she received
as an undergraduate at Mount Holyoke College from her "personal ideal
of a female role model," Dr. Charlotte Haywood (Appel 1994, 54).

Although Tidball's research into the success of graduates of women's
colleges is relatively recent, she has studied women who graduated as
early as 1910. Tidball's method, often referred to as baccalaureate origin
research, has been similar from study to study: she consults published lists
of successful women, usually editions of *Who's Who of American Women*
(but also the *Doctorate Records File*), recording where and when (what
decade) a random sample of these women received their degrees. Using a
selected list of institutions (for example, a list of institutions that have been
"productive" as sources of doctoral candidates), she computes the number of achievers per 1000 women graduates of each type of college (single-
sex or coeducational) for each decade. On the basis of several studies,
Tidball has concluded that women who graduate from women's colleges
are about twice as likely as graduates of coeducational colleges to become leaders in their fields, to receive their doctorates in science, or to
enter medical school (Tidball 1973; Tidball and Kistiakowsky 1976; Tidball
1980; Tidball 1985; Tidball 1986).[28]

Tidball's main explanation for these findings is that in contrast to coeducational colleges, women's colleges have many more women faculty
who can serve as role models of successful women (just as a woman
professor was her role model at Mount Holyoke). To back up this claim,
Tidball also compared attitudes of men and women faculty at both single-
sex and coeducational institutions (Tidball 1976). Not only did she find
that women faculty have attitudes sympathetic to difficulties faced by
women students (an awareness of practices that discriminate against
women, for example), but also that men faculty who taught at women's
colleges were more supportive of women's issues than men faculty who
taught at coeducational institutions. Tidball argued that other factors also

encouraged women students' success: if institutions enrolled large numbers of women students, and if they offered strong academic preparation in several areas of study. A "favorable climate" for capable, motivated women students, Tidball and Kistiakowsky concluded in 1976, is one that "conveys to them a sense of being in an environment where there are many other women seriously involved in a variety of academic pursuits" (Tidball and Kistiakowsky 1976, 652).

Tidball's research has not been without its critics, however. Oates and Williamson (1978) argued that Tidball's results were due mainly to the superior achievements not of the graduates of women's colleges in general, but to the graduates of the prestigious "Seven Sisters" colleges (see also Block 1984, 219–22). Oates and Williamson used methods similar to Tidball's, but with one major difference: rather than using *Who's Who of American Women*, they obtained their list of women achievers from *Who's Who in America (38th Edition, 1974–75)*. They separated out the graduates of the Seven Sisters colleges from the graduates of all other women's colleges, and focusing on the 1930s decade (the decade that most of the women achievers that Tidball studied had graduated), they found that the rate of achievers was approximately equal for women graduates of small coeducational colleges and graduates of non-Seven Sisters women's colleges (18 per 10,000) but that the Seven Sisters colleges produced achievers at a much higher rate (61 per 10,000). Oates and Williamson suggested that the greater success of alumnae of the Seven Sisters colleges might be due not only to the colleges' greater selectivity but also to the higher socioeconomic status of the students' parents (Oates and Williamson 1978).

As is common in academic disagreements, the argument did not end there. Tidball (1980) defended her data source and conclusions, and then Oates and Williamson (1980) defended their original criticisms and different conclusions. Tidball pointed out that in the data source used by Oates and Williamson (*Who's Who In America*), only about 4 percent of the entries were women, partly reflecting "the long exclusion of women from professional hierarchies and the failure to acknowledge women's accomplishments as regularly as men's" (Tidball 1980: 505). In contrast, Tidball noted, her favored data source (*Who's Who of American Women*) contained eight times as many women.

In order to check Oates and Williamson's contention that the Seven Sisters colleges were mainly responsible for the apparent greater success of women's colleges in producing achievers, Tidball reanalyzed her own data. She found that for each group of colleges *of comparable selectivity*, women's colleges were "twice as productive of achievers" (Tidball 1980, 512). Oates and Williamson (1980) in turn defended their choice of *Who's Who in America* as a data source, arguing that this avoided a "double standard" in defining success since it was applied as rigorously to women as to men. They clarified their position: it was not that "only" the Seven Sister colleges produced women achievers, but that these prestigious women's colleges held a "dominant place," comparable to the place held by the Ivy League colleges in producing men leaders (Oates and Williamson 1980, 344). Oates and Williamson pointed out that logic alone indicated that women faculty and an all-women environment were insufficient to produce successful alumnae, as then all women's colleges would be found to have similar success rates (and they do not, as the Seven Sisters colleges produced achievers at more than twice the rate of other women's colleges). And finally these researchers took issue with the idea that women faculty were necessary as role models: "It has not been determined that they (faculty role models) must be female or even preponderantly female. The key factor may be not the sex of the mentor but rather the achievements and encouragement he or she presents" (Oates and Williamson 1980, 345).

Other researchers have used baccalaureate origin studies to examine the educational backgrounds of more recent cohorts of women achievers. Rice and Hemmings (1988) compared the number of achievers who had graduated from women's colleges to the number who had graduated from coeducational colleges for the four decades between 1940 and 1979. Using *Who's Who of American Women* (WWAW) as Tidball had done for earlier cohorts, Rice and Hemmings found that graduates of women's colleges were proportionately more likely to appear in WWAW than graduates of coeducational colleges for both the earlier and later decades, but not during the 1960s—what they called "partial support" of Tidball's findings (Rice and Hemmings 1988, 555). A serious criticism of Rice and Hemmings' study, however, was its failure to control for the declining proportions of women who attend women's colleges (Jacobs 1996).

A study of even more recent cohorts of women, those who graduated since 1965, disaggregated data for groups defined by race (Wolf-Wendel 1998). Regardless of institutional selectivity, the researcher found that in comparison to coeducational colleges, predominantly white women's colleges were more productive of successful European-American women (those who subsequently received their doctorates or were listed in one of the *Who's Who* books). For African-American women and Latinas, colleges that served these racial groups, in particular women's colleges and colleges that had formerly been women's colleges (women's change col-leges), outproduced other institutional types in graduating successful women.

Tidball herself, in collaboration with other researchers, has extended her work to more recent cohorts of women, those who received baccalau-reate degrees in the 1970s. Moreover, her new research compares six types of institutions (women's colleges, private universities, men's change colleges, women's change colleges, coed colleges, and public universi-ties) by eight levels of selectivity and for doctorates classified by area (education, humanities, social sciences, life sciences, and physical sci-ences). The findings still show that women's colleges, adjusted for the number of graduates, are the most productive of doctorates in all fields (Tidball et al. 1999, 47–53).

Baccalaureate origin research cannot control for women students' so-cioeconomic background. Yet Tidball and other researchers who use this method have recognized how entering students' characteristics could be confused with the *impact* of college experiences.[29] Recently some re-searchers have used longitudinal data to examine the impact that the type of undergraduate institution attended has on students' postcollege lives. One study, not intended for the specific purpose of comparing single-sex education and coeducation, found that women who had attended women's colleges earned substantially more income later (Conaty et al. 1989). Using the National Longitudinal Study of the High School Class of 1972 and the Postsecondary Education Transcript Study, these researchers stud-ied a sample of women and men in 1986, most of whom had been out of college for seven to nine years. Controlling for students' family back-grounds (their parents' income and education, their SAT scores, their religion, etc.), their college majors, and even their occupations, Conaty et al. found that women who had attended women's colleges earned on average 20 to 25 percent more than women who had attended coeduca-tional colleges.

Another study by Riordan (1994) reached similar conclusions but dis-tinguished women who had *graduated* from women's colleges from women who had attended variable numbers of years, between 1972 and 1979. Riordan found that just one year of attendance positively affected women's post-graduate education. Further years of attendance at a women's college did not affect postgraduate education, but did result in women's obtaining higher-status occupations and higher income.

The results of one longitudinal study contradict these positive findings. Stoecker and Pascarella (1991a) used CIRP (Cooperative Institutional

Research Program) data from 1971–80, which enabled them to control for students' individual characteristics. They did not find that women who graduated from women's colleges had significantly higher postcollege educational, occupational, or economic attainments. They did note, however, that the women students in their sample had not been out of college for many years (only about six) when the follow-up data were collected, so that it is possible that "the impact of attending a women's college is manifest somewhat later in an individual's career" (Stoecker and Pascarella 1991a, 403).

More Immediate Benefits of Single-Sex Education for Girls and Women: Academic Experiences and Attitudes[30]

Academic success has been linked to single-sex education, for boys and girls, but especially girls. Lee and Bryk (1986) studied a random sample of about 1800 male and female students in seventy-five Catholic high schools in the United States. Even after controlling for family background, curriculum track, and school social context, they concluded that compared to students in mixed-sex high schools, students in single-sex high schools gained more in academic achievement between their sophomore and senior years. Riordan (1985) also reported that white students in Catholic single-sex schools, particularly the girls, did better academically than students in Catholic or public coeducational schools. Similar findings on the secondary or middle-school level have been reported in other countries, too—Australia (Carpenter and Hayden 1987), Ireland (Sutherland 1961), Thailand (Jiminez and Lockheed 1989), and in a three-country comparison of England, Sweden, and the United States (Finn, 1980; Finn, Dulberg and Reis, 1979). One researcher, Herbert Marsh, who has studied Catholic high school students in the United States, disputes these conclusions, however, arguing the methodological point that researchers like Lee and Bryk have not used sufficient statistical controls for "all preexisting differences" between students who attend single-sex versus coeducational schools (Marsh 1989a, 81). Marsh's own studies found no differences between the academic performances of Catholic students educated in single-sex or coeducational schools (Marsh 1989 a,b).

On the higher education level, Astin (1977) reported somewhat contradictory findings. His study used CIRP data, based on surveys of about 200,000 students in over 300 colleges and universities several times during their college years. Astin found that while men in men's colleges were more likely than men in coeducational colleges to participate in honors programs and to obtain good grades, women in women's colleges were less likely than women in coeducational colleges to show these signs of high academic achievement. Astin's explanation of these findings is that women's "superior level of academic performance" means that they do worse if they have to compete only with other women (Astin 1977, 232).

Women who attend women's colleges have been found to raise their educational aspirations more than students in coeducational institutions (Astin 1977, 114). Smith (1990) found that women who attended women's colleges were more likely than women in coeducational colleges to obtain their degrees and to plan to further their education because they were more involved and satisfied with academic components of their undergraduate education. Brown (1982) studied changes in the educational goals of a national sample of white college women who attended college between 1966 and 1971. Among her complicated findings, she reported that women in selective women's colleges and women in unselective sectarian women's colleges were more likely than women in other types of colleges to raise their aspirations between their first and last years from a bachelor's or master's degree to the Ph.D. or professional degree (Brown 1982, 324).

Another often-reported academic benefit to single-sex education for both boys and girls is that they are more likely to study and do well in subjects nontraditional for their sex. Girls, for example, are reported to be more likely to choose science courses and boys to choose English or a foreign language. This result has been reported for both secondary school pupils (Carpenter 1985; Foon 1988; Lee and Bryk 1986; Ormerod 1975) and college students (Carnegie Commission 1973; Newcomer 1959; Tidball and Kistiakowsky 1976). It may be historically true as well. Giele (1987) studied alumnae who had graduated between 1934 and 1979. Those who had attended a Seven Sisters college were more likely than alumnae of Oberlin to have majored in such male fields as science and mathematics. Bressler and Wendell (1980) reported a related finding for white students in selective residential colleges: the occupational aspirations of men students were somewhat more likely to become "feminized" (switched to fields associated with women), and women's occupational aspirations were much more likely to become "masculinized" if they attended single-sex rather than coeducational colleges.

Recent data compiled by the U.S. Department of Education, however, show rather small differences between the percentages of women who majored in "traditionally male-dominated fields" according to whether they attended private four-year women's colleges or "all" private four-year institutions. Looking at just "Baccalaureate I" private colleges in 1992–93, 5.5 percent of the women at all such institutions majored in male-dominated fields, compared to 7.2 percent of women at women's colleges. For the less prestigious Baccalaureate II institutions, it was women at all institutions who were slightly more likely to major in traditionally male-dominated fields than women at comparable women's colleges (U.S. Department of Education 1997, 73–74).

Many people believe that a key benefit of single-sex education is that in settings where men are not present to dominate and perhaps belittle them, girls and women can gain in self-confidence. Astin (1977) reported that in women's colleges students increased more in intellectual self-esteem than women in coeducational colleges and related to this, were more verbally aggressive in interactions with faculty and other students (41, 88–91). Likewise, Lee and Bryk (1986) found that girls in single-sex secondary schools had more positive self-concepts and more internal locus of control,[31] although once again, Marsh (1989b) disputed these findings because when he added more statistical controls, the differences disappeared. Rowe (1988) used a different method to investigate self-confidence and its relationship to math achievement. Students in a large postprimary school in Victoria, Australia, were randomly allocated to either single-sex or mixed-sex math classes. The most significant results were found for girls in single-sex classes who gained the most in self-confidence, regardless of their math achievement. This higher self-confidence led the girls to take more math courses.

A concept related to self-confidence is (lack of) fear of success, first identified by psychologist Matina Horner (1972). On the basis of a study she carried out at Harvard and Radcliffe, Horner argued that women do not fear failure and desire success, but rather fear success due to its anticipated negative social consequences, such as loss of friends, particularly male friends; unpopularity; even inability to marry. Horner's research led her to question coeducation, because the proximity of men would seem to exacerbate women's fears of social rejection if they are academically successful. Horner saw such a dynamic as worrisome since she found that fear of success was particularly strong among the most academically gifted women.[32]

One study tested the hypothesis that girls would exhibit less fear of success in single-sex environments (Winchel, Fenner, and Shaver 1974). The 252 girls (and boys) studied had similar backgrounds in that they were all high school seniors attending Jewish private schools in their middle- to upper-middle-class Brooklyn, New York community. The researchers looked not only at the students' current school but also whether they had attended a single-sex or coeducational primary school. Their results supported Horner's argument that "increased cross-sex competition increases fear of success in females" in that more than twice as many girls in coeducational high schools as in all-girls schools exhibited fear of success. Moreover, they found that the type of primary school girls had attended continued to have an important effect; only one girl who had gone to an all-girls primary school showed fear of success among seniors at both single-sex and coeducational high schools.

Some studies have investigated how satisfied students are with various aspects of their educational experiences according to whether they attend single-sex or coeducational institutions. Astin's large-scale study of students who attended college during the decade of the mid-1960s to mid-1970s found that women who attended women's colleges were more satisfied than women students at coeducational colleges about the quality of instruction, curricular variety, and academic demands (Astin 1977, 183–84). Smith (1990) also found that women in the class of 1986 who attended women's colleges were more satisfied than women who attended coeducational colleges with many aspects of their college experiences (overall quality of instruction, opportunity to talk to professors, career counseling, etc.); the only dimension in which women at coeducational colleges were more satisfied was social life. Similar findings for secondary school students have also been reported by some investigators; that is, girls at single-sex institutions are more positive about their experiences (Trickett et al. 1982; Jones, Shallcrass, and Dennis 1972). Other researchers, however, have found that it is students at coeducational schools who are the most satisfied with their experiences (Dale 1971; Schneider and Coutts 1982).

Mixed results have been found for comparisons of political attitudes of women in single-sex versus coeducational institutions. Astin (1977) found that women who attended women's colleges increased the most in political liberalism. Trickett et al. (1982) and Lee and Bryk (1986) found that girls in single-sex secondary schools were more supportive of the women's movement and less likely to believe in sex-role stereotypes than were girls in coeducational schools. On the other hand, Giele (1987) found that graduates of one of the Seven Sisters colleges were more likely than graduates of Oberlin to give traditional answers to what is the ideal division of labor in the home. In Australia first-year university students who had attended single-sex high schools were no more likely than students

who had attended coeducational high schools to have nontraditional gender-role attitudes (Harris 1986). I also obtained similar results in a comparison of the gender-role attitudes of women students at a women's
college to those of women students at a coordinate college (equated with
a coeducational college since classes and most campus organizations were
mixed-sex): neither in 1974 nor in 1982 did women students at the
women's college have more liberal gender-role attitudes (Miller-Bernal
1989).

Theoretical Reasons to Expect Single-Sex Education
to Confer Benefits to Girls and Women

While much recent research has demonstrated the long- and short-term
benefits of single-sex education to women, less attention has been given
to understanding the processes by which these benefits occur (Komarovsky
1985; Miller-Bernal 1993). There are, however, theoretical reasons to
predict that separatism would benefit women, stemming from one of the
two main approaches to gender inequality. A common perspective on
gender inequality, but one *not* particularly suited to understanding why
single-sex education might benefit girls and women, is sometimes referred
to as "dispositional." This approach focuses on how individuals at a relatively young age learn gender roles that are internalized as traits. These
traits, such as nurturance or passivity, are believed to influence how women
and men perform in a wide range of situations. This approach to gender
inequality tends to "blame the victim," as it assumes that if we want to
improve women's social position, we have to change women's gender
role traits, by making them more competitive, for instance.

A different approach to gender inequality, one that I favor and believe
is more hopeful for social policy, assumes that most behavior associated
with women or men is due to their differences in status rather than to
traits learned much earlier. This "situational" approach suggests that if
we were to put women and men in positions of equal status, then most of
the behavior now associated with each gender would become as likely to
be expressed by one as by the other (Wagner, Ford, and Ford, 1986). A
specific example of a study that supports this perspective is one that
tested whether interpersonal sensitivity is a female trait or a trait of whichever sex happens to be in a subordinate position. Psychologist Sara
Snodgrass varied the sex of the leader in two-person teams and found
that women were no better than men in understanding the impression
they were making on their partner. "'Women's intuition'" should perhaps
more accurately be referred to as 'subordinate's intuition,'" wrote Snodgrass

(Snodgrass 1985, 152). Epstein (1988) discusses many studies that support the situational approach (although this is not a term she uses), which she summarizes by saying that they demonstrate that "social circumstances can change the individual's personality or an unchanging social environment can reinforce personality attributes acquired earlier" (Epstein 1988, 90). If a situational approach to gender inequality is largely correct, then what is important about women's colleges is that they allow women to assume high-status positions and thereby learn behaviors and motivations usually learned by men by virtue of their gender's higher status (Miller-Bernal 1991).

Single-Sex Education and Role Models

Perhaps the most common explanation of why women students in single-sex institutions fare better, both in the short and the longterm, is that they are in an environment replete with successful women, in positions of authority, who thereby serve as role models (Tidball 1973, 1980; Ehrhart and Sandler 1987; Finn, Dulberg, and Reis, 1979; Riordan 1985). The concept of role model is based loosely on the psychological theory that argues that one way people become socialized is to identify with people in their environments. Block (1984, 144) points out, however, that psychologists differ in terms of the characteristics they believe effective models must have. Some psychologists, for example, argue that to be successful as a model, a person must have power over resources, while others stress the importance of a model's warmth and affection.[33]

There are many other unresolved questions about the concept of role model (Jung 1986; Speizer 1981). How many characteristics do role models have to share with the person they are meant to influence in order for them to be effective models? Of specific interest in the case of women is the question of whether men can serve as role models, but it is also unclear whether people need to be of the same race or ethnicity.[34] A related question is whether the role model has to be achieving in the particular field the person who is being influenced wants to enter. For example, can women faculty serve as role models for young women who do not want to become academics? Another unresolved issue is the nature of the relationship between role models and those they affect. Must there be direct contact, and must the role model encourage specific behavior? Or is it sufficient that the role models are visible, in which case could they be historical figures?

Many researchers have not asked women students about who, if anyone, are their role models but rather have assumed that the more women on the faculty, the more role models women students will have. Since women's colleges have about double the percentage of women on their faculties that coeducational colleges do, women students at women's colleges are presumed to have more role models. This difference between the two types of colleges is then given as the explanation of why graduates of women's colleges are more successful in later life than graduates of coeducational colleges. Oates and Williamson (1980), as noted previously, questioned this assumption, arguing that encouragement of students was more important than the gender of the faculty member. When researchers have used surveys to learn from women themselves who their role models are, results have been mixed. Lunneborg (1982) found, for example, that women college graduates who were working in fields nontraditional for women had received career encouragement from both their mothers and fathers and male and female siblings, teachers, friends, and other adults. Some studies have found that for undergraduate women, parents are more important as role models than faculty of either sex (Basow and Howe 1980). One study of graduate students found that women students who named women professors as role models had higher self-esteem, work commitment, and career aspirations than those who named men faculty (Gilbert, Gallessich, and Evans 1983). These conflicting research results indicate that for undergraduate women students' career and educational objectives, faculty may not be as important as they think they are—what Rossi (1987) calls a "humbling message." Perhaps role models are more relevant to women when they are further along in their career paths.

Leadership Opportunities in Women's Colleges

A different explanation for why single-sex education is favorable for women is that it enables them to assume positions of leadership that in most coeducational institutions are taken by men. Women's colleges were among the earliest institutions of higher education to establish student government, which researchers have credited with teaching women important skills.[35] As Horowitz explained, the early women's colleges may not have intended to encourage women to become independent and act like men, but through the development of college life and the "all-around girl" ideal, this is what many young women did learn: "the forcefulness and direct stance of men rather than the tilts and smiles that marked female subordination" (Horowitz 1984, 169). Stories about college life at the women's colleges, immensely popular from the 1890s to the 1930s (Inness 1993), made it clear that college was not just about classroom learning. The excitement of working all night to get out an issue of a college magazine or newspaper; the camaraderie that came through working together in clubs, music and theatrical performances; the informal socializing in each others' rooms; the team spirit developed through athletics, particularly "basket ball"—all were described as the "fun" of "college life." Students who insisted on just studying were sanctioned as "grinds."[36] Thus women were expected to become involved in many aspects of college life, and through this encouragement, they undoubtedly learned skills ordinarily associated with men. As a 1933 *New York Times* article on women's education pointed out, at women's colleges, women were "fitted for leadership" (Barnard 1933).

The benefits to women of learning how to organize, administer, govern, and lead continue to be recognized (Carnegie Commission 1973; Astin 1977, 117–118). While it is obvious that women at women's colleges must take up positions of leadership since there are no men students to hold these posts, what has not been clearly demonstrated is that this makes a difference for later-life achievement or even for more immediate benefits such as self-confidence or academic performance. These links seem plausible, but the research evidence is lacking.

Supportive Environments of Women's Colleges

Another under-researched explanation of why women and girls benefit from single-sex education is the supportive environment that can develop in a "room of one's own." In colleges designed for and presided over by women, programs and courses central to women's lives are more likely to be offered. A related aspect of a supportive environment is the types of relationships among students that women's colleges encourage. Rather than competing with men for resources, including faculty members' time, and competing with each other for attention from men, women in single-sex colleges may learn to appreciate women's strengths and to depend on each other. Sarah, Scott, and Spender (1980) argued that single-sex schools have "subversive potential" because in them women learn from each other, not from men. Thus male authority is not reinforced and a "sense of solidarity" among women is able to "flourish." Kenway and Willis (1986) disagreed, however. Their study of a private girls' school in Australia led them to conclude that the sense of "sisterhood" that developed among the students never generalized beyond women of similarly privileged backgrounds. The hypothesis that women's colleges have more supportive environments has not been adequately tested, nor have such environments been shown to matter in terms of producing proximate or long-term benefits.

Conclusions

In contrast to the nineteenth century, when most feminists favored coeducation over women's colleges, the second wave of the women's movement of the 1970s has brought about a positive reevaluation of these single-sex environments. Empirical research of the past thirty years has generally indicated that coeducational colleges favor men students and present women students with an environment that is "chilly" to their academic, social, physical, and emotional development. Many researchers have found that women who graduate from women's colleges are more likely to become leaders, receive their doctorates, particularly in the sciences, and earn more money than women who have graduated from coeducational colleges. Even while they are still students, women at women's colleges, in comparison to women at coeducational institutions, tend to become more self-confident, raise their academic aspirations, and express views supportive of egalitarian gender roles and feminism, according to the findings of some studies. Where the research is lacking, however, is in understanding what specific aspects of the environments of women's colleges encourage these positive developments among their students.

I have suggested three major ways in which women's colleges may benefit their students: by enabling them to have women faculty as role models, by providing them with leadership opportunities, and by supporting their interests and encouraging them to develop female solidarity. In the following three chapters I describe a longitudinal study of students, class of 1988, at the four colleges focused on in this book, designed to test whether Wells College (and to a lesser extent, William Smith College) differed from the coeducational colleges (Middlebury and Hamilton) in the ways I suggest. I also wanted to see whether these differences were related to benefits for the women students. The next chapter describes how I conducted my longitudinal study and what the students at these four colleges were like when they entered college in September 1984.

Notes

1 Many women's colleges and seminaries were concerned with providing students with a home. Wheaton Female Seminary, for example, was kept small to function as a home (Helmreich 1985, 61, 88), and although Vassar was much larger, in its early years it maintained a section in its catalogues on the "college family" (Vassar College Catalogues, 1865, 1868, VCA).

2 This type of pedagogy has deeper roots than contemporary feminism; it is indebted to Paolo Freire, who has addressed the educational needs of oppressed groups (Higgins 1982).

3 A recent AAUW report, "Separated by Sex," criticizes these initiatives, arguing that the initiatives are so varied as to defy generalizations and moreover, there is insufficient evidence that single-sex education is "better" than coeducation (American Association of University Women Educational Foundation 1998).

4 Riesman argued differently in the late 1960s, however. At that time, at least when writing with Christopher Jencks, he was more favorably disposed toward women's colleges than men's colleges because the latter were "likely to be a witting or unwitting device for preserving tacit assumptions of male superiority" (Jencks and Riesman 1968, 298).

5 And yet this interpretation of Gilligan's work is not unreasonable. Since the publication of her study, people have interpreted Gilligan as arguing that women and men have different styles of moral reasoning. Tavris (1992) summarizes and critiques Gilligan's work, concluding that "many (but not all) of the qualities associated with 'women's voices' prove to be qualities associated with women or men who are powerless" (Tavris 1992, 87).

6 Butcher's study of eleven women's rights periodicals, carefully chosen to represent different regions of the country, the seven decades of the women's rights movement, and the array of issues these papers covered, shows that they were all in favor of coeducation but "not unified in their opinions about all-female schools" (Butcher 1989, 35).

7 M. Carey Thomas chose Cornell University in the mid-1870s, as she was urged to do by one of her woman teachers, rather than Vassar College (see Chapter 2). After receiving her Ph.D. from Zurich University, she became the second president of Bryn Mawr College. She was renowned for her feminism and the high academic standards that she applied at Bryn Mawr (Horowitz 1994).

8 Alice Freeman, who became one of the University of Michigan's first woman undergraduates in 1872, dismissed Vassar and Elmira as "merely female academies." In 1881 she became the president of Wellesley College, where she worked hard to change it from a college with many of the "trappings" of a seminary into a true liberal arts college (Palmieri 1995, 22–35).

9   Marion Talbot received her bachelor's degree from Boston University, and later studied with Ellen Richards at M.I.T. She became involved in the development of the new field of domestic science and taught in this field at Wellesley College. She helped found the Association of Collegiate Alumnae, becoming its first secretary and its president from 1895 to 1897 (see Chapter 2). She taught at the University of Chicago, where she was also appointed dean of undergraduate women and later, dean of women (James 1971).

10   According to Leach (1980, 370) the *Woman's Journal* is the best source for learning about nineteenth-century feminist ideas of coeducation.

11   Sixty years later Virginia Woolf elaborated on this theme, comparing the poverty of the women's college, Girton, with the luxurious, well-endowed men's colleges of Cambridge University. "Intellectual freedom depends upon material things . . . that is why I have laid so much stress on money and a room of one's own" (Woolf, 1929/1977, 116–117).

12   Occasionally advocates of coeducation have accepted single-sex institutions as a necessary but temporary, transitional form. In 1879, three suffragists who favored coeducation—Lucy Stone, Mary Livermore, and Antoinette Brown Blackwell—accepted an invitation to visit Wellesley, after which Stone declared: "I am grateful to Mr. Durant [Wellesley's founder] that he has established this institution for those whose parents are not yet ready for the school, which like the family, does not separate the sexes" (as quoted in Butcher 1989, 42). About one hundred years later, Hamilton College used the same sort of argument that Kirkland College had paved the way for true coeducation (See Chapter 6).

13   Frances Willard later became the feminist, pro-suffrage president of the Women's Christian Temperance Union.

14   Although known mainly for her work in establishing Hull House, the preeminent settlement house in Chicago, Jane Addams (1860–1935) worked for women's suffrage, becoming the first vice president of the National American Women's Suffrage Association in 1911, in addition to other political and peace work (James 1971).

15   The social psychological experiment that asks women (or, women and men) to rate the same article, half of the time purportedly written by a man and half of the time by a woman, demonstrates the lower evaluation given to women's work. See Goldberg (1968) as well as a summary of replications of his study, some of which indicate that women, but not men, may be coming to see other women's work more equitably (Frieze 1975).

16   As I discussed in Chapter 6, views of Kirkland College were complicated by the fact that not only was it a women's college, but it was a progressive one as well. Coeducational progressive colleges are undoubtedly also seen as less rigorous than conventional colleges.

17   Sharp (1991) makes a similar argument about the women's movement of the 1970s when she questions why women's advocates could not see, for the educa-

tional field, the benefit of separatism as well as the need to open up opportunities to women, whereas they could recognize the benefits of a dual strategy in such other institutional structures as banking. She argues that the answer involves the importance of the prolonged fights over Title IX and the Equal Rights Amendment, neither of which was seen as relevant to women's colleges. Sharp feels, as I do, that it is unfortunate that the "reforming mind" could not seem to recognize "the importance of supporting women's colleges and the importance of opening up a larger arena of opportunity" (Sharp 1991, 4).

18   Conway (1983) also described the lengths educators at Oberlin took to "domesticate the forces of sexuality," including enforcing bland, vegetarian diets since meat and condiments were believed to stimulate sexual appetites.

19   Even slightly later, in 1981, ethnographic research at a boys' boarding school in England found that the staff were afraid that the boys would become homosexual. But countering the pressure to become coeducational was the loss of status that would ensue if girls were admitted (Walford 1983).

20   One study in Australia did look at first-year university students' *views* of coeducation versus single-sex education at the high school level (Harris 1986). Overall these students believed that coeducation led to "natural attitudes towards the opposite sex." See Marland (1983, 184) for criticisms of studies like this one and Dale's that use retrospective accounts of schooling.

21   The famous psychologist G. Stanley Hall attributed the decline in marriage and child-bearing rates not to single-sex education but coeducation. His argument might be summarized by the aphorism, "Familiarity breeds contempt." In his words: "There is a little charm and bloom rubbed off the ideal of girlhood by close contact, and boyhood seems less ideal to girls at close range. In place of the mystic attraction of the other sex . . . familiar *camaraderie* brings a little disenchantment. . . . This disillusioning weakens the motivation to marriage" (Hall 1904 II, 620–21). On the other hand, the president of Stanford at that time, David Starr Jordan (whom Hall quotes), noted that some people argued *against* coeducation because it *led* to marriage! In defense of coeducation, Jordan wrote that usually such marriages were not "premature" and were the best sort, "founded on common interests and intellectual friendships" (Jordan, 1902, 107).

22   Cookingham (1984) favors an economic or labor market explanation for these trends, arguing that women delayed marriage or did not marry at all in response to their job and income opportunities.

23   It is relatively easy to criticize Oberlin from the perspective of today's standards for gender equity, but Ginzberg (1987) argues that some criticisms are unjustified. The college's founders not only opened up important educational opportunities to women and African Americans of both sexes, but their evangelical and domestic worldview also led them to believe that men should live up to women's standards. On the other hand, an early alumna of Oberlin wrote an article in 1874 for the Boston women's rights periodical *Woman's Journal*, in which she said, "While Oberlin may justly claim to be one of the pioneers in coeducation, it has always

striven to show that it by no means considered the sexes equal" (as reported in Butcher 1989, 41).

24 Jordan did see women as benefiting from coeducation, too, but he emphasized more how men students gained from the company of women. With respect to women he argued that with men present in the classroom, there was "less of silliness and folly where a man is not a novelty," and the tendency to emphasize "expression" more than "action" is mitigated (Jordan 1902, 101–3).

25 Dale's writing is replete with assumptions about women's and men's different natures. To take just one example, he suggested that the reason that women teachers received less favorable evaluations than male teachers from ex-pupils was because "the female personality may not be ideally suited to the traditional class teaching situation—where there is some need for dominance, which comes more naturally to a man than to a woman" (Dale 1969, 95). For other criticisms of Dale's work, see Cross (1985) Laviguer (1980), and Bone (1983).

26 Constantinople, Cornelius, and Gray (1988) admit that their results may be unique, or nearly so, to Vassar. They point out that in none of the 48 classes in which their student observer-participants recorded interactions (three times for each class) were men students a majority.

27 One *Nation* reader did believe that it would be "so difficult." A letter writer, apparently a professor at Mills College, called Pollitt "naive" to think that boys' dominance of classes can be easily stopped. She also pointed out that it "never occurs to many grown-ups to read the riot act to their sons" (Letter of Carolyn Kizer, *The Nation*, October 24, 1994).

28 For an excellent review of the methodology and findings of baccalaureate origin studies see *Taking Women Seriously* by Tidball et al. (1999). This book also contains useful summaries of other forms of research on the single-sex vs. coeducation debate and contains qualitative information about two women's colleges, Bryn Mawr and Bennett.

29 Tidball et al. (1999, 57) note, however, that the question of whether women's colleges are successful "merely" because of students' self-selection "reveals a troubling bias." In most contexts people accept that prestigious institutions such as Harvard are "successful, in part because of the elite students who attend." Why then, Tidball et al. ask, do people require women's colleges or historically black institutions to demonstrate that their success does not depend on characteristics of their students?

30 Two points about the following section should be noted: (1) I combine research findings from secondary schools and colleges, the United States and other countries. While I know other researchers believe that at least some of these should be separated—Block (1984), for example, does not deal with studies in other countries, and Shmurak (1998, 18) points to the importance of the "differences in developmental levels" between high school and college—I would argue that the overall pattern of results is consistent enough to warrant their inclusion, although I do note which studies pertain to which level of education. (2) Some of the

"immediate benefits" might also be considered mechanisms by which single-sex education affects girls and women in the longrun. In other words, if single-sex education leads to better academic performance, as some research indicates, then women should be able to get better jobs later in life and be more likely to appear in the lists of achievers consulted by Tidball.

31 Locus of control, a concept developed by psychologists, refers to whether people believe that they themselves have control over what happens to them (internal) or believe that their lives are at the mercy of chance or fate (external).

32 The idea that women exhibit fear of success has been subject to much critical evaluation. For a good summary of these critiques, see Paludi (1998, 252–56).

33 A recent study suggests that women teachers are better role models if they are "empowered." A key factor that affects women teachers' empowerment is whether they work under a woman head, since women principals tend to create more participatory environments (Lee, Loeb, and Marks 1995). If this is true, then women faculty at women's colleges may be better role models than women faculty at coeducational colleges, since women's colleges are more likely to have women presidents.

34 Regardless of how academics resolve such issues, I find it interesting that the concept of role model has entered popular culture (even to the extent of appearing in the lyrics of a Neil Simon song, "Call me Sam"—"Will you be my role model?") and now people *expect* to have role models. This point was brought home forcefully to me in the late 1980s when I led a discussion on the concept at a one-day conference on women and education at Cambridge University. I shall never forget a young woman, a graduate student in mathematics, who expressed fury at the lack of women role models in her specific subfield. She seemed to believe that she had a right to such models and their lack was a deprivation.

35 Student government was established at Wells in 1889, whereas at Middlebury women students did not have their own government association until 1912.

36 Many of these stories about college life made one exception to their generally negative views of "grinds"—young women from poor families who had to achieve high grades so that they could teach after college. See, for example, *Brenda's Cousin at Radcliffe* (1903, 73) by Helen L. Reed or Gallaher's *Vassar Stories* (1900, 37).

Chapter 8

The Class of '88 Enters College

This chapter looks at a particular group of women students in depth. I compare those who in 1984 entered the women's college, Wells, with those who entered the three other private liberal arts colleges that I have focused on in this book: Middlebury, the long-time coeducational college; William Smith, the women's coordinate college; and Hamilton, the recently coeducational college. By the time the class of 1988 entered college, there were some distinct differences among these colleges, as I summarize briefly below (see Chapter 6 for a more complete description).

By the mid-1980s Wells was responding to its financial and enrollment difficulties in part by emphasizing the advantages of single-sex education for women but also by cutting back on academic programs. The student body had changed markedly from wealthy students to students requiring financial aid. Wells's faculty, administration, and Board of Trustees had many women, and the college had established programs focusing on women's issues. Middlebury College had just finished celebrating its centenary of coeducation, during which it was rightly noted that in contrast to the recent past, women students were treated equitably in terms of social regulations. Problems of fraternities persisted, however, even though Middlebury had bought the fraternity houses, and students could no longer dine in them. William Smith's lower enrollment than Hobart's remained a focus of concern for women on that campus, although the proportion of women had grown over the previous fifteen years. How a coordinate structure rather than coeducation benefited students, particularly women students, continued to be discussed. Hamilton College was still adjusting to the demise of Kirkland; while no women who had attended Kirkland were still students, there were still many faculty who had taught at Kirkland. The campus appeared divided between a modern, "artsy," political "Kirkland" side and a traditional, fraternity-dominated "Stryker" side.

How the Women of the Class of 1988 Were Studied

I began this study in the first week of fall semester 1984, when *all* women students entering Hamilton, Hobart and William Smith, Middlebury, and Wells College received surveys. The cover letter explained that since I was studying "women students' attitudes and plans and how they change while students are at college," I would need to contact them again (and so each questionnaire was numbered). The questionnaires covered students' family backgrounds, their academic goals, and attitudes toward such issues as the women's movement and appropriate gender roles. The response rate was gratifying, with 88 percent of the 793 entering women returning the questionnaires.

Before I surveyed the sophomores, I sent them a report based on the findings from the first-year questionnaire. Besides providing participants with feedback about the original survey's findings, I hoped that receiving such a report would encourage them to complete the sophomore questionnaire. In the spring of 1986, I sent a new survey to most of the 698 students who had completed the first questionnaire (some, of course, had left college or transferred; these women were not contacted). This survey covered some of the same issues as the first-year questionnaire but also contained questions about students' activities at college and their relations with faculty. Sophomores were more resistant to filling in the questionnaires; only 55 percent of them (348 sophomores) returned their surveys, despite having received the report of findings from the first-year survey and reminder letters about the importance of a high response rate.

During the students' junior year, I selected a random sample of about ten students at each college (of those who had completed the first two surveys) for intensive interviews.[1] I explored such issues as their beliefs about what influenced them the most at college, their description of their social lives, their feelings about role models, and their attitudes toward the women's movement, in order to obtain more qualitative information about students' college experiences. The interviews also helped me design the final questionnaire for the senior year.

I distributed the third questionnaire in 1988, during students' last term at college. Seniors answered questions about their attitudes toward the women's movement and gender roles and wrote definitions of feminism; they also described their college experiences and their career and educational plans. A high rate—84 percent—of those women who had completed the first two questionnaires and were still at the colleges returned this third survey, not surprisingly since they had already demonstrated their willingness to take part in a longitudinal study.

The 260 women students who completed all three questionnaires represent 47 students from Wells, 57 students from William Smith, 77 students from Hamilton, and 79 students from Middlebury. Some readers might question whether these students' attitudes or experiences at college are representative of their cohorts, given the rather high rate of attrition during the various "waves" of the study.[2] This is an important issue, but fortunately, it is relatively easy to answer in a longitudinal study of this kind. I compared students who answered all three questionnaires with those who answered only the first one and found few differences in family background or original attitudes. I therefore feel quite confident that the final sample, on which there are data from 1984, 1986, and 1988, is representative of all women students who entered these four colleges in 1984.

Entering Students' Educational and Family Backgrounds[3]

The women students who entered these four liberal arts colleges in 1984[4] were, on the whole, highly qualified academically. Slightly more than two-fifths (43 percent) had high school grade point averages (GPAs) of at least 90. The GPAs did vary somewhat by college, however, with Middlebury's entering women more likely to be the best academically qualified (51 percent of them had GPAs of 90 or higher), and William Smith's the least likely to be so qualified (28 percent had such high GPAs). (See Table 8.1.)

About two-thirds (67 percent) of the entering women students had attended a public coeducational high school. As expected given the changes since the late 1960s in the backgrounds of students who attended Wells (see Chapter 6), more entering Wells students had attended public schools[5] than was true of first-year students at the other three colleges: 83 percent of Wells students versus 70 percent of William Smith students, and 61 percent of both Middlebury and Hamilton students.[6] The converse of this is that Wells students were the least likely to have attended private non-religious high schools: only 11 percent of Wells students had gone to such expensive high schools, compared to 16 percent of William Smith students and a high 29 percent of both Middlebury and Hamilton students.

One consequence of these social class differences, in terms of the kinds of high schools students attended, is that students entering Wells were the *least* likely to have gone to a single-sex high school (whether religious or non-religious). Only 6 percent of Wells students did, compared to 10 percent of both Middlebury and Hamilton students and 16 percent of William Smith students. It is clear that having attended a single-sex high school was not a major factor leading young women to choose a women's college, or, more accurately, young women who had attended a girls' high school were less likely to attend Wells than to attend the other three colleges. Private girls' high schools were clearly beyond the financial means of most Wells students' families.

Differences in social class backgrounds of students entering these four colleges came out even more clearly from information on the education and occupation of students' parents, shown in Table 8.1. While overall, 48.5 percent of students' fathers had graduate or professional degrees, Wells students' fathers had much less education than the fathers of students at the other colleges.[7] Only 21 percent of Wells students' fathers had graduate or professional degrees, whereas between 48 percent and 59 percent of the fathers of entering students at the other colleges had such degrees. Similarly, the fathers of Wells students were much less likely to be major professionals (such as lawyers or doctors) or business executives of major firms than the fathers of women students entering the other three colleges: only 15 percent of Wells fathers had such occupations, compared to 44 percent of Hamilton fathers, 54 percent of William Smith fathers, and 59 percent of Middlebury fathers.

Characteristics of students' mothers varied by college, too, but less than they did for their fathers, and the differences were statistically significant only for their educational level (see Table 8.1). Slightly more than one-third (35 percent) of Wells students' mothers had no more than a high school degree, whereas this was true of only 23 percent of Hamilton students' mothers and 10 percent of both Middlebury and William Smith students' mothers. A quite high and relatively constant percentage of mothers' occupations were described by their daughters as housewives: 38 percent of Hamilton students' mothers, 33 percent of Wells students' mothers, and about one-quarter of both William Smith and Middlebury students' mothers. While the percentage of mothers who were major professionals or top executives fit the pattern of the fathers' occupations, with Wells students' mothers being the least likely to have these high-status jobs (24 percent) and Middlebury students' mothers being the most likely (42 percent), these differences were not as dramatic as the differences for the fathers. It is also interesting that the percentage of mothers with such prestigious occupations was higher than the percentage of fathers only for the students at Wells (15 percent of the fathers were top executives or major professionals versus 24 percent of the mothers).

TABLE 8.1 Entering Students' Background Characteristics by College, 1984

	Wells	Middlebury	Wm Smith	Hamilton
High School GPA: A or 90s	43%	51%	28%	48%**
High school type[a]:				
a) Private, non-religious	11%	29%	16%	29%
b) Single-sex	6%	10%	16%	10%
Father's education: graduate or professional degree	21%	59%	56%	48%***
Father's occupation: major professional or bus. exec.	15%	59%	54%	44%***
Mother's education: graduate or professional degree	17%	29%	33%	22%+
Mother's occupation: major professional or bus. exec.	24%	42%	40%	34%
Religion[b]:				
None	11%	15%	12%	14%
Catholic	47%	29%	32%	37%
Jewish	4%	4%	12%	8%
Protestant	38%	44%	44%	34%
Religion "very important"	28%	15%	12%	15%
Very satisfied with self	30%	38%	32%	50%
Mothers employed full-time since children	38%	32%	30%	36%
Family decision-making				
Mothers more influence on day-to-day decisions	56%	61%	52%	76%
Fathers more influence on major decisions	25%	31%	27%	33%
Family division of labor— mothers do most of traditional domestic work	74%	63%	62%	75%
Planning on Ph.D.	35%	20%	19%	35%
Specific career goals	57%	30%	30%	37%**
Want career, marriage, and family in 10 years	51%	51%	43%	49%+
Liberal political leanings	31%	31%	21%	21%
Support all aims of women's movement	22%	15%	2%	9%
Consider themselves feminist	46%	24%	24%	29%*
Man's interest in marriage would be negatively affected by:				
a) uninterrupted career	64%	62%	59%	52%
b) feminist values	57%	57%	52%	62%
c) work in traditionally male field	42%	29%	30%	26%

[a]These do not represent all the types of high schools but rather the types most relevant to this study.
[b]These percentages exclude a small percent of "other" religion at Middlebury and Hamilton Colleges.

+ significance <.10 but >.05	** significance <.01 but >.001
* significance <.05 but >.01	***significance <.001

With respect to religion, Table 8.1 shows that most students at all four colleges were Christian, but Wells had the highest percentage of Catholics (almost half—47 percent—of the students), and Middlebury had the lowest percentage of Catholics (29 percent). Wells and Hamilton had more Catholics than Protestants, but the reverse was true for Middlebury and William Smith. Jews were a minority: only 4 percent at Middlebury and Wells, 8 percent at Hamilton, and 12 percent at William Smith. No religious preference was indicated by slightly more than 10 percent of students at all four colleges. When asked to rate their religious feelings, somewhat under one-fifth (17 percent) of the women entering these colleges said religion was "very important" to them, slightly over one-half (54 percent) said it was "somewhat" important to them, and not quite one-third (29 percent) said it was not important to them. Students entering Wells were the most likely to say religion was very important to them (28 percent said this); William Smith first-year students were the least likely to consider religion very important (12 percent said it was). This difference was largely a result of Catholics being the most likely to consider themselves religious, and a higher percent of Wells students were Catholic, as noted above.

Students at all four colleges were quite racially homogeneous. While literature at all four of the colleges emphasized the desirability of diversity, and there were more women of color than earlier in these colleges' histories, still the overwhelming majority of students were white. With 10 percent or fewer of the students being women of color, it was not possible to analyze students' college experiences separately for racial groups. I did, however, make special note of whatever women of color said on their questionnaires that pertained to their racial backgrounds.

To measure entering students' global self-esteem, I asked them whether they strongly agreed, somewhat agreed, somewhat disagreed, or strongly disagreed with the following statement about "how you see yourself as a person": "On the whole, I am satisfied with myself." A majority of these young women, 54 percent, indicated they were "somewhat" satisfied with themselves, and over one-third (39 percent) said they were "very" satisfied.[8] Virtually all the rest (17 students) were somewhat dissatisfied with themselves; only two students were strongly dissatisfied with themselves (which means a total of 7 percent were dissatisfied, somewhat or strongly, with themselves). Students' level of satisfaction with themselves did not vary by which college they attended (see Table 8.1) or their family backgrounds, but satisfied students tended to have had the highest high school grade point averages, indicating the importance of academic success for good self-concepts.[9]

Family Life

Given the possible role model effects on daughters of having an employed mother who takes an active role in family decisions, I asked students a few questions about their family lives. Most students said their mothers had been employed outside the house since having children: only 48 students (19 percent) had mothers who had *not* been employed at any time since having children, and 69 more (27 percent) had mothers whose employment had been solely on a part-time basis. This means that a majority, 55 percent, had mothers who had worked full-time at least some years (34 percent had mothers who had always worked full-time, 21 percent had mothers who had worked full-time some years and part-time other years). While I had expected that Wells' students' mothers would be the most likely to have worked, given their less economically privileged situations, this did not turn out to be the case (38 percent of them had worked, always on a full-time basis, but 30 percent or more of the mothers at the other three colleges had also worked full-time).[10]

Entering students were asked two questions about which, of the adults they had lived with most of their childhood, had more influence in their families. The first question asked about the relative influence over running the household on a day-to-day basis; the other question concerned influence on making major decisions about the family. For the first question, most students (62 percent) responded that their mothers had more say on daily household matters, following the traditional pattern; virtually all the rest (33 percent) said that their parents shared these tasks about equally; only 5 percent said their fathers had more influence on running the household. Students' answers about who made major decisions, such as whether the family should move or purchase a new car, indicated that in most families (63 percent) these decisions were made jointly by both parents. In about one-third of the families (30 percent), the traditional patriarchal pattern prevailed, with fathers having more influence on these major decisions. In only 7 percent of the families with two parents did the mother have the most say in such major decisions. These family decision-making patterns did not vary significantly according to which college the students attended (see Table 8.1).

When these same students were seniors, they were asked a few other questions about their family life. One concerned the division of labor in household tasks: whether their mother (or stepmother) did most of women's traditional chores (cleaning house, cooking, child care, etc.) while their father (or stepfather) did most of men's traditional chores (yard work, garbage removal, car maintenance, etc.); or whether the tasks were mixed, not all along traditional sex-linked lines; or whether the division of tasks was almost completely opposite of a traditional division, with their mother doing mostly "men's" tasks and their father doing mostly "women's" tasks. Slightly more than two-thirds (68 percent) said their parents' division of household labor was traditional; 31 percent said the division was mixed; only 1 percent said the division of tasks was the opposite of the traditional pattern. Table 8.1 shows that a slightly higher percentage of Wells and Hamilton students reported their parents' division of labor was along traditional gender lines, but the reported pattern varied more according to whether the mothers were employed outside the home after having children. Ninety-three percent of the families in which the mothers never worked after having children had a traditional division of labor, whereas this was true for only 57 percent of families in which the mother had been employed full-time after children.[11]

Another question I asked seniors was whether they felt closer to one of their parents. A slight majority (51 percent) said no, but a much greater percentage (40 percent) felt closer to their mother than to their father (9 percent).[12] This suggests that if a parent is going to serve as a role model for these students, it is most likely to be the mother, and thus her employment may make a difference in terms of the goals these students set for themselves.[13]

During interviews in students' junior year, I asked how similar or different from their mother's life they believed theirs would be. A common theme was that they expected their lives to be different, often because they did not intend to have children until later in life and, related to this, because they wanted a career, not just a low-status job as many of their mothers had had. Thus in order to serve as role models for students wanting a serious career, mothers probably would not only have had to work, but also to have worked at a satisfying job. Not that these students saw their lives as simple; on the contrary, those planning on having children often appeared to worry how they would be able to have interesting work yet be good mothers with close, loving ties to their children. One student expressed this tension clearly when she said she expected her life to be different from that of her mother, who had been married when she was the student's age and had had a baby the next year. Although her mother is "amazingly talented," producing great meals, putting up shelves, etc., she lacks confidence in her abilities and has worked only as a secretary. This student expressed anger at her father's role: "I won't let my husband get away with what my father does." Yet she ended up emphasizing the importance of family to her. She was planning to go into social work because she believed this would give her the flexibility to be with her family. She noted that in some ways she does want to be like her mother, who would give up anything for her children and in this way, "shows her depth of loving."

Entering Students' Plans for Their Futures

A minority of these first-year women students (17 percent) planned on ending their formal education when they received their bachelor's degrees. The greatest number (56 percent) planned on obtaining a master's degree, but more than one-quarter (27 percent) intended to get a Ph.D. or higher professional degree. It is interesting that the women entering Wells, whose parents had the least amount of formal education, were, along with students entering Hamilton, the ones most likely planning to continue their education to the highest level: 35 percent of Wells and Hamilton students, compared to 20 percent of Middlebury and 19 percent of William Smith students planned to get their Ph.D.s, although these differences were not statistically significant (see Table 8.1). Similarly, overall, 37 percent of these first-year students said they already had specific career plans. But Wells students were more likely to say that they had such plans: a majority of Wells students (57 percent) said this, compared to between 30 and 37 percent of the incoming students at the other three colleges.[14] What first-year students considered "specific" plans ranged quite a bit, however. One student wrote spiritedly: "I know that at some point I wish to write; I know I must *try* to be a dancer; I would like to be a caterer, and study volcanoes." But most students were more specific than this, mentioning such goals as law, medicine, social work, or their intentions to become a veterinarian, teacher, or psychologist.

In general, women entering Wells in 1984 appear to have been different from the women entering the other colleges in terms of their motivation to get further education and in terms of already having formulated specific career objectives. As other researchers have suggested, women attending women's colleges in recent years may be more serious about their careers than women choosing coeducational colleges (Lentz 1980). Wells students also fit a pattern noted decades ago of women from lower-middle-class, less educated families being the most serious about their education and futures (Douvan and Kaye 1962; Brown, 1962).[15]

Entering students were asked to indicate what they wanted to be doing "ten years from now" by placing themselves into one of four categories: involved in a career; involved in a career and marriage (no children); involved in a career, marriage, and family (children); or involved in marriage and family.[16] Almost half (49 percent) of the entering students said they wanted to do it all (career, marriage, and children), and slightly more than one-third (36 percent) said that within the decade, they hoped to be involved in a career and marriage. One out of ten students said they wanted to be working at (just) their career, and the lowest percentage, 6 percent, said they wanted (just) marriage and family. As I show in Table 8.1, students' answers to this question did not vary much by college, but Wells and William Smith students were slightly more likely to say they wanted just a career (16 and 18 percent of them, respectively, compared to 7 and 3 percent of Hamilton and Middlebury students), and Hamilton and Middlebury students were somewhat more likely to say they wanted a career and marriage (42 and 40 percent) than were Wells and William Smith students (27 and 30 percent). Clearly most of these women students of the 1980s did not see higher education as incompatible with family life; they wanted, or at least expected, to combine a career with marriage and in most cases, children.

Political Attitudes, Including Attitudes Toward Feminism and the Women's Movement

Students entering these four liberal arts colleges were evenly split between being Republican or conservative and being Democrat or liberal. Almost one-third (32 percent) described themselves as middle-of-the-road Republican, and another 18 percent called themselves conservative (including one who said she was "far right"). Twenty-four percent considered themselves middle-of-the-road Democrat, and almost the same percentage, 26 percent, called themselves liberal (including one who said she was "radical left"). Interestingly, it was both Wells and Middlebury students who were slightly more liberal than William Smith and Hamilton students, although these differences were not statistically significant. Thirty-one percent of both Wells and Middlebury students considered themselves liberals, compared to 21 percent of both Hamilton and William Smith students. Wells (and Middlebury) students seem to have changed from earlier times when they were more conservative, whereas today women at Hamilton are probably more conservative than Kirkland students were.

When asked about their attitudes toward the women's movement, a large majority (73 percent) of these freshwomen said they supported "some" of its aims but believed "parts of it are going too far." Slightly more than 10 percent (12 percent) said that they supported all or virtually all of the aims of the women's movement, exactly the same percentage who said they did not support the movement because it is no longer necessary—"if a woman wants to be successful, she can; there's nothing to stop her." Less than 5 percent of these entering students said they did not support the women's movement because they felt it was "misguided—women and men are inherently different so women should *not* try to be 'just like men.'" Thus most of these women began college with quite favorable attitudes toward the women's movement and did not accept the conservative view, most often associated with the religious right, that women and men are fundamentally different and therefore women should fulfill different (subordinate, family-based) social roles.

Yet when asked if they would describe themselves as feminists, a large majority, 71 percent, of these women said no. Women entering Wells were most likely to say they considered themselves feminists (almost half, 46 percent, did so, compared to between 23.5 and 29 percent of the women at the other colleges).[17] And yet even the percentage at Wells was lower than the 56 percent of women willing to call themselves feminists in a national sample taken by Gallup only two years later (Boles 1991). As I show in Table 8.1, the differences in the percentage of students who said they supported all of the aims of the women's movement (22 percent of Wells students, compared to 15 percent of Middlebury, 9.5 percent of Hamilton, and 2 percent of William Smith students) was not as dramatic as the differences for considering themselves feminists, but in both cases, Wells students had the highest percentages.[18]

It is not surprising that such a large percentage of these young women did not want to call themselves feminists. Interviews during their junior year (and written definitions they gave in their senior years) revealed that many held to the usual stereotypes of feminists: radical, man-hating, hairy-legged, and perhaps "even" lesbian. It may actually be more surprising that almost half of the women entering Wells did call themselves feminist. One explanation may be that as single-sex higher education has become more rare, those women willing to make this "deviant" choice already had pro-women, feminist inclinations or were responding to the publicity concerning the benefits of women's colleges. It may also be that the decision to attend a women's college, for whatever initial reason, had a radicalizing effect. During casual conversations with first-year students at Wells, I have frequently heard them say that their friends from home could not understand why they chose a "girls' school." I am suggesting that in having to defend this decision, some young women may have come to see themselves in a more radical, feminist light.

Given the concerns about how young women may be caught between being perceived as feminine and being successful, I asked students questions about how three hypothetical conditions "would affect a man's interest in marrying a woman." These questions were also inspired by Parelius's earlier research, in 1969 and 1973, at Douglass College, which had found that even a majority of feminist women did not believe that men would want to marry women like themselves, that is, women who intended to work all their adult lives or who believed that wives' careers were as important as husbands' (Parelius 1975). I asked entering women students whether they thought a woman's "plans to have a serious, uninterrupted career" would have a negative effect, no effect, or a positive effect on a man's marriage interest. A majority of these students, 59 percent, said they thought such career plans would have a negative effect; 25 percent believed they would have no effect (and the rest, 16 percent, thought they would have a positive effect), results which fit Parelius's findings of more than a decade earlier. I also found that a woman's "feminist values and attitudes" were believed to be no more damaging to men's marriage interests than women's uninterrupted careers: 57 percent of students judged feminist attitudes to have a negative effect on a man's marriage interests, and 28.5 percent thought they would have no effect. Entering women students felt that a woman's "plans to work in a field traditionally dominated by men" was seen as the most benign in terms of its effects on a man's interest in marriage, perhaps because such work would put a woman in contact with a wide variety of men. Slightly less than one-third (31 percent) of students thought such work would have a negative effect on a man's interest in marriage; 54 percent thought it would have no effect.[19]

Answers to these three questions did not vary by college, demonstrating that, at the outset at least, women who attended a women's college were just as aware of the social difficulties faced by serious, feminist women as women who attended coeducational colleges. Also, women who considered themselves to be feminists were neither more or less likely than those who did not call themselves feminists to see men's marriage interests affected by a woman having a serious career or working in fields traditionally dominated by men. Self-identified feminists were, however, less likely than non-feminists to see a woman's feminist values and attitudes as having a negative effect on men's marriage interests.[20] This latter finding may mean that in order for many young women to be willing to call themselves feminists, they have to be able to convince themselves that by so doing, they will not alienate men.

Entering Students' Gender-Role Attitudes

How entering students viewed proper roles for women and men was assessed by asking them about the extent of their agreement or disagreement with eighteen statements. I combined questions from two published scales to come up with questionnaire items to measure students' gender-role attitudes, some from a frequently used Attitudes towards Women Scale (Spence, Helmreich, and Stapp 1973) and others from a scale developed by Osmond and Martin (1975). Looked at from the perspective of the late 1990s, however, some of these questions appear quite dated. Nonetheless, most entering students did not appear to have trouble answering this part of the questionnaire. Their answers reveal the extent to which they believed women and men should fulfill similar social roles and be subject to similar behavioral expectations, what is sometimes referred to as "contemporary" or "liberal" gender-role attitudes (the opposite of what is generally known as "traditional" or "conservative" gender-role attitudes).

Table 8.2 presents the eighteen items in order, from those which elicited the greatest number of traditional responses, to those which elicited the greatest number of contemporary responses. Given the way the statements were constructed, in some cases to "agree strongly" was to express the most traditional response, whereas in other cases, to "disagree strongly" indicated conservative gender-role attitudes. For only three statements did a majority of the women students give traditional responses. More than half (56.5 percent) said that they agreed (strongly or mildly) that women with preschool children should, if at all possible, stay at home with their children rather than have paid employment.[21] Given that a majority of women with preschool children do in fact have paid jobs, at least part-time (and did as well in 1984 when these students were completing these questionnaires), it is troubling that so many young women expressed disapproval. Their answers suggest that later in life, many will either have to modify their views to conform to how they live, or live in a way of which they themselves do not approve.

More than half (55 percent) of the students agreed (strongly or mildly) that swearing and obscenity are more objectionable for women than for men. Beliefs that certain types of personal behavior are more acceptable for men than for women may be some of the most deep-rooted aspects of sexism. On the other hand, a statement in this list that might seem similar is the one about intoxication, and yet only 16 percent of the women students agreed, strongly or mildly, that it is worse for women than for

TABLE 8.2 First Year Students' Gender-Role Attitudes (Percent agreeing strongly, AS, agreeing mildly, AM, disagreeing mildly, DM, or disagreeing strongly, DS)

ITEM	AS	AM	DM	DS
1. Women with preschool children should not work—if at all possible.[a]	21.5%	35	29	14
2. Swearing and obscenity are more repulsive in the speech of a woman than a man.[a]	11%	44	22	22
3. A man's self-esteem is severely injured if his wife makes more money than he does.[a]	7%	45	30	18
4. Women earning as much as their dates should bear equally the expense when they go out together.[b]	26%	38	28	8
5. Whoever is the better wage-earner, wife or husband, should be the breadwinner, if only one can work.[b]	36%	34	17	12
6. Women with children in grammar school should, if at all possible, stay at home rather than work.[a]	7%	19	37	37
7. Intoxication among women is worse than intoxication among men.[a]	2%	14	30	54
8. I would vote for a woman for President of the United States.[b]	45%	41.5	8.5	5
9. There are many jobs in which men should be given preference over women in being hired or promoted.[a]	4%	8	20	68
10. Men should take the same amount of responsibility as women in caring for home and children.[b]	64%	26	9	1
11. The way men and women behave is more a result of their genetic make-up than of the way they were brought up.[b]	1%	7	37	54
12. Women should assume their rightful place in business and all the professions along with men.[b]	71%	22	3	4
13. Career women generally are neurotic.[a]	0%	7	23	70
14. Since men have a natural urge to dominate and lead, women who challenge this actually threaten the welfare of society.[a]	0.4%	6	22	72
15. There should be low-cost, high quality child care centers for working women.[b]	70%	24	4	2
16. In general, the father should have greater authority than the mother in bringing up of children.[b]	0.4%	3.5	25.5	71

[a]means that for these items, agree strongly (AS) indicates the most traditional answer.
[b]means that for these items, disagree strongly (DS) indicates the most traditional answer.

men to be drunk. A great deal of alcohol is drunk on campuses, by women as well as men, so at least during their young adulthood, these women do not evaluate women's drinking differently from men's. Another similar item is number 4: "Women earning as much as their dates should bear equally the expense when they go out together." This question did not receive as many traditional responses as the one about swearing, but a substantial minority, slightly more than one-third of the students (36 percent) disagreed (strongly or mildly). Thus while dating norms have changed considerably over the past thirty years (cf. Komarovsky 1985, especially Chapter 8), allowing women more scope to take the initiative and more ability to interact as equals, quite a few of these women students apparently preferred old-fashioned dating, with men paying the bill. When I interviewed a sample of these women two years later, when they were juniors, some commented to me that they wished they could have dates "like my mother did."

The third item to which a slight majority gave traditional responses is one that I find methodologically troubling: "A man's self-esteem is severely injured if his wife makes more money than he does." The problem I see with such a statement is that it does not distinguish between what people believe to be a fact and what they think is appropriate behavior. In any event, 52 percent of the entering students said that they agreed with this statement, almost the same percentage that Osmond and Martin (1975) found for women juniors and seniors at a southern university about ten years earlier, when 56 percent agreed with this statement.

For half of the eighteen items in Table 8.2 students gave overwhemingly liberal responses, with 10 percent or fewer indicating traditional views. Specifically, entering students were practically unanimous in the beliefs that: (1) women should be increasingly involved in working on social issues, (2) fathers should not have any more authority over children than mothers, (3) women should take on "intellectual leadership," (4) women leaders do not threaten society's welfare, (5) career women are not generally neurotic, (6) there should be high-quality, low-cost child care centers, (7) women should assume their "rightful place" in professions and business, (8) men and women's behavior is not genetically produced, and (9) men should be as involved as women in taking care of homes and children.

These findings fit what many other researchers have found: young women have liberal gender-role attitudes compared to other social groups, and their views are more liberal now than thirty years ago. The women's movement, as well as increasing levels of education, have had the effect of making women feel that they are as entitled as men to jobs and positions in the public world and that men should be as responsible as women are for domestic work. Thus it appears that at the attitudinal level, many of the goals of liberal or equal rights feminism have been accomplished.[22] Yet these women students may eventually have trouble living according to their beliefs in gender equality. Studies generally show that men have lower levels of acceptance of equal rights feminism than women do (cf., Rice and Coates 1995), at least on issues concerning women's responsibilities toward the home and children (Mason and Lu 1988), and that married, employed women still do most of the domestic work or have a "second shift" (Hochschild 1989). A recent study on the division of labor within the home has found that gender differences are more likely to appear at some stages of family life than others, in particular, after couples have children. The sample was one that would seem most likely to have egalitarian family lives, recent cohorts of graduates of a small, liberal arts college with a feminist tradition, but the researchers still found that full-time employed women with children were doing much more domestic work than full-time employed men with children (Perkins and DeMeis 1996).[23]

With few exceptions, women students' answers to these eighteen gender-role questions did not vary by which college they attended. For only two questions did Wells students' answers indicate significantly more liberal gender-role attititudes: Wells students were more likely to say that they disagreed that a mother of preschool children should stay at home (21 percent of Wells students disagreed strongly with this, compared to between 11 and 13.5 percent of students at the other three colleges),[24] and more Wells students said they would vote for a woman for president of the United States (56.5 percent of Wells students, compared to 47 percent of Middlebury students, 46 percent of William Smith students, and 32 percent of Hamilton students).[25] This latter item is interesting in that Schreiber (1978) reported that by the early 1970s, many more women college graduates, about 90 percent, were willing to vote for a woman for president. It appears to be during their college years that many women come to see the desirability of women in important, visible leadership positions. And in fact, by the time these young women were in the last semester of their senior year, 92 percent did say that they would vote for a woman for president.

To see if students' gender-role attitudes as a whole varied by college, and to determine if they were related to students' family backgrounds and other attitudes, I created a scale from the eighteen items. Each answer was scored from 0, representing the most traditional attitude, to 3, representing the most liberal attitude, and then all 18 scores were summed.[26] Thus the possible range of values for this gender-role attitudes scale was 0 to 54; in fact, students' scores ranged from 18 to 54 (another indication that women students have quite liberal gender-role attitudes), with a mean or average score of 41.0, a median and mode of 42, and a standard deviation of 6.2. These scale scores did not vary significantly by which college students attended, although Wells students had the highest average score (42.2) and William Smith had the lowest (39.8).

Looking at correlates of students' gender-role attitudes (the scale scores), I found that parents' education and fathers' occupation were not related to students' attitudes, nor were students' attending a girls' high school or being religious. But students whose mothers worked, particularly full-time, since having children, were more likely to have liberal gender-role attitudes. Also students who came from families where the mother played a significant role in major family decision-making and where their fathers and mothers' division of domestic tasks was not along traditional sex-linked lines were more likely to have liberal gender-role attitudes, suggesting that seeing "liberation" in practice affects daughters' attitudes.[27] It was not surprising, although it was validating, that students with liberal gender-role attitudes were more likely to support the women's movement, to call themselves feminists, and to describe their political orientation as Democrat or liberal.[28] I was also interested to find that women students with liberal gender-role attitudes were the most academically ambitious, that is, they were the most likely to say they planned on getting their Ph.D.s or higher professional degrees.[29] Again, this follows: if a young woman believes that women should be free to pursue the same opportunities as men, then she should be likely to want postgraduate education for herself in order to pursue a serious career. She will not be looking to receive her major life fulfillment from marriage and children.[30]

Summary and Conclusion

In comparison to a national sample of first-year college women who entered higher education in 1984, the young women entering these four private liberal arts colleges were socially and academically privileged.[31] Their parents were better educated than families of college women nationally, and the women at the four colleges were also more likely to have attended a private high school, less likely to be women of color, and more likely to say they had no religious preference than the average college woman student in the United States (Dey, Astin, and Korn 1991). Yet there were some differences among the women students entering these four colleges. Wells students came from less privileged backgrounds than the young women entering Hamilton, Middlebury, and William Smith, confirming the recent changes in the Wells student body described in Chapter 6. Middlebury students were somewhat the opposite: they tended to come from highly educated and professional families, consistent with the trend for Middlebury students since World War II, but very different from what Middlebury students of the nineteenth and early twentieth century were like.

Regardless of differences in families' educational and occupational profiles, entering students at all four colleges described their families' patterns of decision-making and domestic division of labor in similar ways. A majority of families, according to these daughters, fell into the traditional mold of mothers being in charge of and doing most of the daily domestic and child-care tasks. This was true even though most mothers in these families have had jobs outside the home since they had children. A majority of women entering these colleges did say, however, that their parents shared decisions about such major issues as moving or buying a car.

In terms of political attitudes, perhaps only William Smith students represented continuity with previous generations of students. Women students at Hamilton were more conservative than women at the former coordinate college, Kirkland, were; Wells students and Middlebury students were more liberal than students at these two colleges used to be.[32] Compared to the national CIRP sample of college freshwomen in 1984, first-year students at these four colleges were slightly more liberal; nationally 22.7 percent of students called themselves liberal or far left, compared to 26 percent of the first-year students at the four colleges of my study. With respect to women's issues, Wells students stood out, particularly in terms of considering themselves to be feminists. Even so, slightly less than one-half of students entering Wells were willing to give themselves this much derided label. Many more students fit the pattern of "I'm not a feminist but . . . ," meaning they had liberal gender-role attitudes and said they supported most of the aims of the women's movement but still did not want to call themselves feminists (Stimpson 1979).

The next chapter discusses how these women students changed, in attitudes and plans for their futures, while they were at college. In particular I examine whether their experiences at college fit the findings of other research, described in Chapter 7, that show that women benefit from being educated separately from men. Did Wells students, and to a lesser extent, students at the coordinate college, William Smith, experience a more favorable educational climate than the women who attended the two coeducational colleges? Did these experiences affect their attitudes, career and educational goals? These are the questions I address in Chapter 9.

Notes

1   I myself did not interview the students at Wells, since my position as a faculty member could easily have affected students' responses, especially because Wells is such a small institution. I paid a staff person, Nancy Taylor, to conduct the Wells interviews; she was recommended to me by a colleague and at the time was working in the public relations office.

2   All the return rates for this study were reasonably good. Babbie (1998, 262) considers response rates of over 80 percent, which I achieved for the first and last waves of this panel study, to be "very good." He thinks return rates that characterize the second wave of this study (55 percent) are "adequate."

3   In the analysis of the survey data that follows, in this chapter and Chapters 9 and 10, I refer to statistical significance even though the data do not come from a random sample of students and hence significance levels are, from a technical standpoint, irrelevant. Following the practices of other researchers, I use them as a guide to distinguish the strength of relationships.

4   In order to make it simpler to refer to the 260 women who answered all three questionnaires, I shall describe them this way, that is, I shall not bother to say that they are not "all" the women but rather those who stayed at the colleges and completed the three questionnaires.

5   Since only one student at any of the four colleges had attended a public single-sex high school, public school can be considered to mean public coeducational school.

6   Cross-tabular analysis of public vs. private high schools with college attended showed a significant relationship, $\chi^2 = 8.9$, df = 3, sig. = .03.

7   These figures pertain to entering students' fathers or *stepfathers,* whichever the student had lived with "most" of their childhood. In fact, however, more than 80 percent of entering students at all four of the colleges said that they lived with both parents; about 6 percent lived with their mother and stepfather.

8   These figures represent the percentages across all four colleges; Table 8.1 presents the percentages for each college. Whenever background characteristics did not vary significantly by college attended, I followed this practice, that is, in the text I give the overall percentage for all 260 students.

9   Kendall's correlation coefficient = .16, sig. = .003. It is not possible to tell from correlational data, of course, which variable came first, that is, whether good self-concept came after or before academic success in high school. Renshaw (1990) criticizes the assumption that very high self-esteem is necessary for academic success as he sees it as blaming the individual and reinforcing the view that positive thinking is the key to significant individual change and social reform. Renshaw suggests that high achievement leads to high self-esteem.

10   It may be, however, that the mothers of Wells students had worked more of their adult lives or more years after having children. I did not ask a question about the length of time mothers had worked.

11   χ^2 = 24.15, df = 6, sig. = .000. Mother's employment was also related to her relative influence on running the household and on major family decisions, but the differences were not quite statistically significant. Thus while 65 percent of the mothers who were not employed had the most say on household decisions, only 51 percent of the mothers employed full-time had the most say (c^2 = 11.23, df = 6, sig. = .08). The father had the most say in major family decisions in 37 percent of the families where the mother stayed at home after children, whereas this was true for 28 percent of the families in which the mother worked full-time (χ^2 = 11.86, df = 6, sig. = .07).

12   Similarly but not as dramatically, a higher percentage of students (38 percent) said that their mothers had had a "great deal of influence" on their choice of college than said their fathers had had such influence (31 percent). Employed mothers were not more likely than mothers who had not been employed to have a great deal of influence on college choice, however, but a somewhat greater percentage (41 percent) of students who said they were closer to their mothers than those who were closer to their fathers (22 percent) said that their mother had had a "great deal of influence" on their college choice (χ^2 = 9.79, df = 4, sig = .04).

13   But see Chapter 7 for a discussion of difficulties with the concept of role models.

14   χ^2 = 11.17, df = 4, sig = .01 for having career plans by college attended.

15   On the other hand, of the students at Wells (or at any of the other three colleges) it was not those whose parents had the least education or the lowest-status occupations who were the most likely to have definite career plans or the highest academic goals. Wells students as a group, in comparison to students at the other colleges, had high academic expectations and more definite career goals, despite coming from less privileged backgrounds.

16   Writing about this question thirteen years after I included it in a questionnaire, I am embarrassed by its heterosexism. I would no longer ask a question in this format, which implicitly excludes homosexual students by assuming that marriage would be equally relevant to everyone.

17   χ^2 = 7.93, df = 3, sig. = .05 between college attended and first-year students' calling themselves feminists.

18   Calling oneself a feminist is highly correlated with support of the women's movement: 32 percent of students who called themselves feminists said they supported all (or virtually all) the aims of the women's movement, whereas only 3.5 percent of the women who did not consider themselves feminists supported all the aims (χ^2 = 42.37, df = 3, sig. = .000). It is interesting, however, that more than two-thirds of students who considered themselves feminists did not support all the aims of the women's movement, perhaps lending support to the idea that the

women's movement is out of step with young women's needs and views. Of course, without knowing what these young women thought were the aims of the women's movement, it is not possible to know why they did not support all of these aims. Support of the women's movement and considering oneself a feminist were, in turn, related to students' general politics, that is, liberals and Democrats were much more likely than Republicans and conservatives to consider themselves to be feminists (42 percent of liberals and 40 percent of Democrats, compared to 19 percent of both Republicans and conservatives) ($\chi^2 = 13.84$, df = 3, sig. = .003) and to support all the aims of the women's movement (28 percent of liberals, 14 percent of Democrats, compared to 3 percent of Republicans and 2 percent of conservatives) ($\chi^2 = 38.55$, df = 9, sig = .000).

19 More students than usual, about 22 for each of these three questions, felt they could not answer them since they believed that how a man's interest in marriage would be affected depended on the man himself. This is undoubtedly true and shows the difficulties social scientists face when trying to assess complex views in a relatively efficient manner.

20 $\chi^2 = 17.10$, df=2, sig. = .000.

21 The statement did not read exactly this way, unfortunately, as Table 8.2 shows. It actually equated staying at home with preschool children to non-work, an amazing statement to all of us who have taken care of young children! Another shortcoming of this statement is that it does not acknowledge that a father might be the parent who stays at home with young children.

22 For brief definitions of types of feminism, including liberal, socialist, and radical feminism, see Landry and MacLean (1993, 2–3).

23 Given that both of these authors are affiliated with Hobart and William Smith Colleges, it is most likely that this study was done on its alumni and alumnae and so is particularly relevant to my own research. Respondents were from the college classes of 1979, 1982, 1985 and 1989, which means that the youngest ones were actually one year younger than the women of my sample. Perkins and DeMeis (1996) do not, however, analyze their data by college class.

24 $\chi^2 = 19.61$, df = 9, sig. = .02.

25 $\chi^2 = 17.48$, df = 9, sig. = .04.

26 The Cronbach's Alpha measure of reliability for the scale was .74; dropping the most suspect item, number 3 (how a man's self-esteem is injured if his wife makes more money) did not improve the reliability and so I retained it.

27 Kendall correlation coefficients for these variables with the gender-role attitudes scale scores were as follows: .13 (sig. = .004) for mother's employment, .15 (sig. = .004) for non-traditional division of labor in the family, and .11 (sig. = .02) for mother's playing an important role in major family decisions.

28 Kendall correlation coefficients for these variables with the gender-role attitudes scale scores were as follows: .28 for support of the women's movement, .30 for

considering themselves feminists, and .30 with political views, all significant at .000.

29   Kendall's correlation coefficient between gender-role attitudes and academic goals was .13, sig. = .004.

30   And in fact, women students who reported that in ten years they planned on having children, rather than a career or some combination of both, tended to have the most traditional gender-role attitudes (Kendall's correlation = −.19, sig. = .000).

31   The data for the national sample came from a "nationally representative sample of about 600 two- and four-year colleges and universities across the United States," and were collected by CIRP, the Cooperative Institutional Research Program (Dey, Astin, and Korn 1991, 1).

32   The change in political views of Wells students is relatively easy to explain, given the correlation between the working class and Democratic Party allegiance. The change in Middlebury students' views is more difficult to explain but does fit with former Dean of Students Ericka Wonnacott's saying that the college had gotten the reputation of being "super liberal" (see Chapter 6).

Chapter 9

College Experiences and Changes in Attitudes and Aspirations of the Class of '88

The last chapter described the young women who entered Wells, William Smith, Hamilton, and Middlebury in 1984. Before I discuss the experiences of these students while they were in college and changes in their goals and attitudes, I will describe some of the major themes and events at these colleges in the years they attended, between 1984 and 1988.

Wells College's enrollment continued to decline, alarming the college's constituencies by falling to 384 students in the fall of 1986 and even further, to 370 students in the fall of 1987. The Board of Trustees responded by forming internal planning bodies, the first in 1986–87, the last year of Dr. Patti Peterson's presidency. A second planning group was established in 1987–88, when the college had an acting president, Dr. Roald Bergethon, who had been president of Lafayette College from 1958 to 1978, during which time this formerly all-male college admitted women. Both planning committees seriously considered coeducation as one way of overcoming Wells's enrollment and financial problems (Executive Summary of the Committee for the Twenty-first Century, May 1987; Memo from J. Fitzgibbon, Chair, All-College Committee on Mission and Forward Planning, November 18, 1987, WCA). Interim President Bergethon clearly favored the coeducation option but alienated many college constituencies by his insensitivity to women's issues. The trustees' commitment to remaining single-sex became evident when the next college president was announced: Dr. Irene Hecht, a graduate of Radcliffe College and a firm advocate of women's colleges. Dr. Hecht assumed the presidency in the middle of the 1987–88 academic year.

Thus although the Wells College class of 1988 experienced intense discussions of coeducation during their senior year when Dr. Bergethon was still president, by the time of their graduation they knew that the trustees had renewed their commitment to Wells's remaining single-sex. And regardless of internal debates about single-sex versus coeducation, programs for women remained strong, with continuing emphasis on internships, connections with alumnae, a women's studies program (although it was not a major field), and a Women's Resource Center.

Fraternities continued to be a major issue for Middlebury College. They received a boost in 1986 when Vermont passed a law that raised the legal drinking age, in steps, to 21, as fraternities then became the place where underage students drank alcohol. Faculty and administrators generally favored abolishing the fraternities, due to repeated instances of vulgarity and health-compromising drunkenness, but most students and trustees supported them, arguing that they were important for social life in such a rural setting (Stameshkin 1996, 237–239). In early May 1988, one of the fraternities, Delta Upsilon, hung a mutilated female mannequin outside its house during a weekend party. This event was the proverbial "last straw." The outrage over this misogynist incident ultimately led to changes that benefited women students at Middlebury. The women students in my survey answered the senior questionnaire just before this incident; they were not around to benefit from the later changes. In fact, during the years they attended Middlebury, the college had neither a women's studies program nor a women's center. Women's needs were presumed to be taken care of by coeducation, despite the dominance of fraternities.

Coordination continued to be discussed at Hobart and William Smith during the 1980s. Rather than questioning whether the colleges should become coeducational, as students had earlier, however, the benefits of coordination, particularly for women, tended to be assumed. Students voiced concerns when they believed the coordinate structure was not being fully utilized or when polls revealed that 15 percent of first-year students did not understand its meaning (*Herald*, April 15, 1988, HWSCA). Rebecca MacMillan Fox, the dean of William Smith during these years, was a graduate and former assistant dean of Bryn Mawr College. She actively promoted the benefits of the coordinate structure and worked to establish equity for women students in such areas as sports funding (Personal interview, October 1, 1993). Issues of particular relevance to women students—eating disorders and sexual harassment, for example—received programmatic attention through outside speakers and campus task forces. In early spring 1988 students established a Women's Resource Center, providing women with a "safe place" to discuss sensitive issues and sponsor films and talks (*Herald*, February 4,1988, HWSCA). At the same time, fraternities at Hobart continued to be a focus of concern and the source of problems linked to alcohol and drug abuse. A few fraternities were suspended, and all were subject to increasing college controls as part of a compact to which the fraternities agreed as a means of obtaining funds for renovation of their houses (*Herald*, September 6, 1985, HWSCA). Hobart and William Smith students were split in their views of fraternities. Many believed they were important for social life (*Herald*, May 6, 1988, HWSCA), but others argued that they were "male-run, male-initiated and male-dominated institutions" (*Herald*, April 29, 1988, HWSCA).

During the mid-1980s Hamilton College faculty were concerned about how women students were faring at the newly coeducational Hamilton, and they undertook several surveys of classroom climate, differences in men and women students' selection of majors, and students' social life (A Report of the Curriculum Committee of Hamilton 1984, HCA). In 1987 a faculty committee recommended a workshop for faculty on conscious and unconscious biases in the classroom and in advising women students (Dean Tobin to Faculty, October 6, 1989, HCA). Women students also expressed their concerns; a class in Women and Technology in winter 1984 produced a video, "Women's Fears at Hamilton," that discussed some incidents that had frightened women students, including sexual harassment by men students and by someone in a "relatively exalted position" (Video, "Women's Fears at Hamilton," 1984, HCA). During the time the class of 1988 was in college, the women's studies program became a major field, another indication that the college was addressing its women students' concerns. Fraternities continued to dominate the campus, however; the two sororities established in the post-Kirkland years were not rivals to fraternities' social dominance. Diversity, relatively overlooked during the early years of coeducation (see Chapter 6), began to receive attention once again. A task force established in 1987 studied ways in which Hamilton might improve the recruitment and retention of people of color (Self-Study Report Prepared for the Middle States Association of Colleges 1990, HCA).

Survey of the Class of 1988 in Their Sophomore and Senior Years

Because I was interested in assessing whether college had an impact on students' attitudes and aspirations, I compared students' views when they entered college—described in the previous chapter—to their views in their second and fourth years of college. While this strategy probably works well overall, it is possible that in some cases students experience anticipatory socialization from the time of their application or visits to colleges. In effect I have argued that this may have occurred for those young women who decided to attend Wells, one of the few remaining women's colleges in the country. Young women who made this statistically deviant choice might have found it necessary to defend their decision, leading them to become aware of the advantages claimed for single-sex education for women and thereby more self-consciously feminist.[1]

Not only is the decision to use college entry a somewhat arbitrary baseline for assessing the impact of college, but more troubling is how to distinguish between characteristics of students who *select* a particular college from the subsequent effects of college attendance. Failure to distinguish selection from impact has been one of the main criticisms of Tidball's research, for example (Oates and Williamson 1978). Researchers who use longitudinal data of the kind I shall be presenting in this chapter usually control for characteristics of students, in particular, their socioeconomic background, so that they do not attribute such outcomes as students' success to their college experiences when the outcomes more accurately should be attributed to students' preexisting privileges. Using statistical controls creates methodological problems, however. Sophisticated statistics assume that the data have certain characteristics that they might not have, and researchers can criticize each other for failure to include the right controls or, on the other hand, for introducing too many controls (Cohen and Cohen 1983, 413).

Partly for reasons of simplicity of presentation, I have decided not to use a highly statistical approach in analyzing my data on students' experiences, attitudes, and aspirations during their college years.[2] While I will take into account some of the information presented in the last chapter, in particular, students' attitudes and goals when they entered college, I generally will not be controlling for their family or educational backgrounds. This decision has the effect of making the material easier to understand. Moreover, I believe it is justified since the analysis is predicated on the assumption that overall, women who attend women's colleges "do better." As the information presented in the previous chapter showed, the women who entered Wells in 1984 were not beginning with advantages, in contrast to earlier cohorts of women who attended women's colleges. In fact, the women who attended Wells differed from the women at the other colleges in being more *disadvantaged* in terms of their socioeconomic backgrounds, including their parents' educational levels. Thus by not introducing statistical controls for students' backgrounds, I should not be biasing the results in the direction of attributing positive changes to single-sex education that are really due to characteristics of the women students' families or secondary schools.

Women Faculty as Role Models

Since the most common explanation of the success of the graduates of women's colleges is that they have more women faculty as role models (cf. Tidball 1973), I asked the women students at the four colleges about whom among the faculty they admired. In other words, I did not assume, as much previous research has done, that just because there were more women on the faculty of Wells and William Smith Colleges, women students at these colleges would have more women faculty as role models than students at Hamilton and Middlebury. I also permitted them to name more than one faculty member, which means, of course, that many students named both women and men faculty.

In students' sophomore year, the precise question I used was, "Are there any faculty members at your college whom you particularly admire or would like to model yourself after?" Students who answered yes were then asked how many faculty they admired in this way, and were also asked to list them by their approximate age and sex. Slightly more than two-fifths (44 percent) said they did not admire any faculty, 16.5 percent listed all men faculty, 28 percent listed both women and men, and the smallest number, 11 percent, said that they admired only women faculty. These percentages did vary significantly by which college the women students attended. In particular, women students at both Wells and William Smith were much less likely to name only men faculty than women students at Hamilton and Middlebury. Wells students were also more likely to name only women faculty, but interestingly, this was not true of William Smith students (see Table 9.1).

In students' senior year, I again asked about their relations with faculty. This time the question I used was, "While at college, have you become particularly close to any faculty members?" For those who answered yes, I asked them to indicate how many faculty members they had become close to and, of them, how many were men or women. While it might be questioned whether being "close to" a faculty member means that the faculty member was a role model, I was trying to pick up cases where a student might not think of the faculty member as influencing her but where, due to the nature of their relationship, the faculty member probably was.

TABLE 9.1 College Experiences by College Attended

	Wells (n = 47)	Middlebury (n = 79)	Wm Smith (n = 57)	Hamilton (n = 77)
A. Faculty Role Models				
(1) Sophomores				
% admire only men faculty	6%	27%	6%	20%
% admire only women faculty	20%	5%	6%	15%
% admire mixture of men and women faculty	35%	28%	36%	19%
% not admiring any faculty	39%	39%	53%	47%**
(2) Seniors				
% close to only men faculty	8.5%	18%	11%	23%
% close to only women faculty	8.5%	6%	12.5%	8%
% close to mixture of men and women faculty	53%	40%	48%	36%
% not close to any faculty	30%	36%	29%	33%
B. Activities and Leadership Roles				
(1) Average score on activities index (0–18)	7.3	5.8	5.5	5.2**
(2) % students reporting active participation in classes	38%	34%	28%	24%
C. Supportiveness of College Environments				
(1) % of following groups seen as "very concerned" about women students				
(a) other students	60%	13%	31%	18%***
(b) men faculty	32%	3%	11%	13%***
(c) women faculty	74.5%	29%	71%	60%***
(d) female administrators	53%	35%	84%	49%***
(e) male administrators	11%	11.5%	7%	7%
(2) Academic encouragement —% reporting that one or more faculty had told them that				
(a) they were one of the best students in faculty member's field	50%	63%	40%	67%*
(b) they were good candidates for graduate school	53%	56%	38%	49%*
(3) Courses taken on women's issues—% who took 3 or more such courses	13%	5%	21%	16%**

*   probability = .06
** probability < .01
***probability < .001

As would be expected, in comparison to sophomores, somewhat fewer seniors (32 percent) indicated that they did not have close relations with any faculty. The same percentage of seniors as sophomores reported being close to only men faculty (16 percent); the largest percentage of seniors, 43 percent, reported being close to both women and men faculty; and the smallest percentage, even smaller than for sophomores, said they were close to all women faculty (8.5 percent). Thus almost twice as many seniors said they were close to all men faculty as said they were close to all women faculty. Although there were fewer women faculty than men faculty for students to get close to, these percentage differences probably also reflect women students' response to the prestige of men faculty. Not only do men faculty gain from the greater status accorded to men in society at large, but also men faculty were overrepresented among the full professors at these four colleges. For this senior year question, the differences among students at the four colleges were not statistically significant, as they had been when these students were sophomores. Wells and William Smith students were still less likely than Middlebury and Hamilton students to say they were close only to men faculty, but the differences were too small to be significant (see Table 9.1).

One way that women faculty came to be seen as role models by these women students was through the students' taking many courses with them. This was true for both sophomores and seniors, but it was particularly striking by the time the students were about to graduate. Thus while no student who had taken only one or two courses with women faculty said they were close to all women faculty, 15 percent of those who had taken nine or more courses from women faculty said that all the faculty they were close to were women.[3]

During interviews with a sample of women students at the four colleges in their junior year, I did not ask them about whether they had any role models among the faculty, but I did ask them two questions that have some bearing on the question of faculty role models. First, I asked them what qualities they most admired in faculty. The most common response at all four colleges was that they admired faculty who established personal relationships with them, who were accessible, who were interested in and encouraging to students and not condescending. This response is similar to the findings of another study on "significant adults" for men and women college students. Galbo and Demetrulias (1996) found that women students said they spent time with "significant adults" to obtain advice about problems or because these adults accepted them as they were. Men students, in contrast, wanted to share interests and do things with their chosen "significant adults." Many of the women students in my study specifically mentioned appreciating faculty who were willing to talk to them about subjects not directly related to their courses, for example, students' future plans or problems that they might be experiencing. As one young woman said, "Someone who's there when you need them, on a one-to-one basis." Another student said, "Treating a student like a person, taking time to talk about future plans, internships, being interested." And yet another: "A model but also a friend." Other commonly mentioned qualities that students admired were faculty members' knowledge, enthusiasm for their subjects, and ability to teach well and make classes interesting.

The second question I asked during these interviews that is relevant to the issue of women faculty as role models was whether they perceived any differences between women and men faculty. Three common answers were that there were no differences, that women faculty were easier to talk to, and that women faculty were feminist. Some students at all colleges said that they could see no differences between women and men faculty. At Wells this response was often accompanied by the statement that this was because Wells is a women's college. One Wells student noted that at coeducational colleges men faculty might "cater" to men students, but at Wells both men and women professors were equally "dedicated" to women's education. Another Wells student said that on "other campuses," men professors talk more to men students.

Some students at all colleges said that they found it easier to talk to women faculty or that women professors tended to be more interested in students. One student at Wells contrasted a woman psychology professor who used examples from her own child with a man psychology professor who, when he talked about the same topics, did so theoretically. This student's preference for the woman professor's approach was clear; she found the discussion of the professor's family life "exciting" and said that it "involved" her in the subject matter. One William Smith student noted that she could relate better to women faculty because they were not intimidating like some men professors; another said that women professors were "more willing to bring up personal experiences to illustrate."

Students who talked about women faculty's feminism were generally criticizing them. A William Smith student said that a lot of women professors "tend to be pretty feminist and bring that into their way of teaching more in a way than a male professor would, but I don't think their methods of teaching or the way they test or whatever are really very different . . . [but] they like to bring in the fact that they're feminist. . . . It's interesting." A Hamilton student said that "a lot of the women . . . were very feminist . . . they drove me crazy. . . . Women have always been treated like dirt and it's . . . men's fault but it's also society's fault and women's fault for letting them do that." One student at William Smith did say something positive about women faculty's feminism: they were not as sexist as men faculty, who made many sexist remarks without even being aware of what they were doing.

Middlebury students' responses to the question about differences between men and women faculty were somewhat unique. They were the only students who talked about the difficulties women faculty faced in fitting into departments that were composed mostly of men and how such difficulties may have made them more insecure. One student noted that women professors tried to be strict "so as not to fall into [the] stereotypical role," especially when the professor was the only woman in the department. A couple of Middlebury students also noted that women professors tended to be made nervous by men students; one woman interviewed saw this as a sign of "weakness."

In summary, most women students in this study appeared to admire both women and men faculty. Even at Wells most students did not choose only women professors as role models, despite Wells students' having had the greatest number of courses with women faculty (not surprisingly since the percentage of women on the faculty was higher than at the other three colleges).[4] Professors' accessibility and willingness to talk with students about a wide variety of subjects were traits that many students said they admired. Clearly both women and men faculty have such traits, although some women students did say that they believed women faculty were more likely to be interested in students.

How do these findings fit with those of researchers who attribute the success of graduates of women's colleges to the presence of many women faculty (role models)? While they do not show conclusively that young women need women on the faculty to encourage them to achieve in later life, these findings do indicate that given a choice, most young women students will identify with at least some women professors. As one William Smith student said, it was "neat to have a woman in science you can really relate to," and yet she went on to talk about a man professor who was "caring" and would talk about math even out of class—"a nice mixture." When there are many women on the faculty, as there are at Wells College, women students are less likely to choose only men professors as role models and better able to find particular women and men whom they admire.

Students' Activities and Leadership Roles at College

As I discussed in Chapter 7, the experience students gain from leading college organizations and being actively involved in all arenas of college life has been one explanation given for why they are more successful in later life than alumnae of coeducational colleges. In this section I present data from my own four-college study to determine if students at Wells, class of 1988, were more actively involved in college life than students at the other three colleges.

Both the sophomore and senior year questionnaires asked students many questions about their activities at college: how many clubs they belonged to and whether they were officers of any; whether they were involved in student government and if so, were they elected to any office; did they work for any student publications (newspaper, yearbook, literary magazine) and if so, did they have a formal position; had they organized any college events and if they had, the nature of their involvement; whether they held a position in residential life; and whether they participated in sports and sports teams and if so, were they were a (co-)captain of any teams. In addition, students assessed how frequently they saw faculty, and rated their own perceptions of how frequently they participated in class discussions. During interviews in their junior year with a small sample of students at each college, I asked them about the image of athletic women and about their perceptions of men and women students' behavior in class.

Based on all these questions, it is clear that students at Wells were much more actively involved in college life than students at the other colleges. When particular activities are examined, Wells students did not always turn out to be the most involved, however. For example, a greater percent of Middlebury students than students at any of the other three colleges were active in student publications, and they were also most likely to have key positions, such as editor-in-chief (in great contrast to their status in earlier years, as I discussed in Chapter 3). Nor were Wells students the most likely to be involved in sports: Middlebury and Hamilton students had the greatest sports participation, probably due to Title IX, which put pressure on coeducational colleges to devote equal resources to women's and men's athletics. But Wells students were more likely to belong to and be officers of clubs, to be involved in and hold elected positions in student government, to have positions in residential life, and to have played key roles in organizing college events. In order to get an overall view of students' activities at college, I added together the values of the separate measures of students' involvement in clubs, student government, publications, residential life, organizing college events, and participation in sports. On this additive index, where student scores ranged from 0 to 18, Wells students on average scored significantly higher than the students at the other three colleges (see Table 9.1).

Wells students were not significantly more likely than students at the other three colleges to say that they participated in classes frequently by asking questions and making comments (see Table 9.1). This result was surprising since many, although not all, researchers have found that in coeducational colleges, men students dominate in class discussions, as I described in Chapter 7. But in my study I did not have a direct measure of students' participation, only their *perceptions* of their own participation. It may be that at Wells, many women students are active, so that any particular student would measure her participation relative to this rather inflated standard. Across the four colleges, students who reported being the most active in classroom discussions tended to be the most active in the other aspects of college, as measured by the index of activities discussed above.[5]

During the interviews with a small sample of juniors, I asked students at Middlebury, Hamilton, and William Smith about their perceptions of men and women students' behavior in classes. Many had clearly not thought about this issue before, but upon reflection, most thought that men students did talk out more than women students, even if the men did not know more about the issue being discussed. One Hamilton student said that more "guys" were "pseudo-intellectuals" who feel they have to say something in classes. Most of the women qualified their answers, however, by noting that who spoke out the most depended on such factors as the size of the class or more precisely, the gender ratio or the number of men students compared to women students; the sex of the professor; and the discipline. A couple of students at Hamilton College mentioned that some professors were sensitive to the effects of students' gender on classroom dynamics. One gave the example of a professor who noted that women students weren't talking as much as the men and said, "Come on, you girls. Let me hear from you. I'm not hearing from you as much as I should."[6]

Another question that I asked during these interviews was about the image of women athletes on campus and how their image compared to the image of men athletes. Most students interviewed said that women athletes could be popular; in fact, some said that being athletic added to women's social life because they were seen as "fun" people. Many qualified this answer, however, by saying that popularity depended on the sport, with individual sports like swimming or tennis being seen as more acceptable than team sports like hockey, or that popularity required a woman athlete to be thin or not too muscular (if she's not a "brute," one student commented). A few women said that men tended to think of women athletes as "unfeminine," feminists, and perhaps even lesbians. Women at the coeducational colleges (including the coordinate, William Smith) commented on how men's sports were taken more seriously; some young women, especially at William Smith, were clear about how much they resented this. Many interviewees, including those at Wells, contrasted women students who did athletics as *one* of their activities with more single-minded men students who often lived up to the stereotype of a "dumb jock," especially if they played football or belonged to particular fraternities. Wells students were apt to contrast their experiences at a women's college, where they believed everyone felt free to be involved in sports, with the more constricting atmosphere of coeducational colleges.

I also asked juniors during these interviews to describe "the most popular woman student" they knew. Interviewees at each of the four colleges associated popularity with a woman who was friendly or outgoing, kind to everyone, and fun to be with. Not surprisingly, given the stress on women's personal appearance in our culture, popular women were also often described as "cute" or "pretty." Some of the juniors were anxious that prettiness not be equated with beauty; they seemed to be trying to make the point that beauty was too serious, whereas for a woman to be popular, she had to be appealing but not threatening. One of the characteristics also associated with popularity at each of the colleges was being active in college affairs, sometimes described as being a leader. As one student at William Smith said, the two most popular women she knew were "active in campus activities—not just a member but the organizer or head." Another common trait of popular women students was intelligence, although frequently interviewees added that to be popular a woman should seem intelligent "without too much effort," or she should be a "fairly good student." A few students said that popular women played down their intelligence, or didn't talk about intellectual things, at least around men.

These results support the idea that at women's colleges, women are able to develop many skills that at coeducational colleges they have less opportunity to develop or for which they face the risk of social disapproval from men students. Although Wells students were aware of popular images of women in various sports, they knew that in the single-sex environment, such views were not pertinent. One of the striking implications of what junior women students said was the balancing act required of young women. If they wanted to be popular, they needed to be outgoing and active in college affairs, and yet at the coeducational colleges, they had less opportunity to take positions in college clubs. Women knew they could play sports and still be popular, but they also were aware that they should not become too muscular or play the "wrong" type of sports. Women students generally admired women who were intelligent and good at their academic work, and yet they said that it was men students who took a more active role in many classes. These conflicting pressures on women students at coeducational institutions may be one reason why many young women at women's colleges value their experiences so highly: they can engage in the kinds of activities they enjoy without worrying about the implications for their relations with men students.[7]

The Supportiveness of the College Environments

Role models and college activities are fairly straightforward concepts, but the other explanation of why women benefit from single-sex educational environments—being in a supportive environment, a "room of their own"—has a variety of possible meanings. I asked women students several questions on the sophomore and senior questionnaires designed to determine if students at Wells (and, to a lesser extent, William Smith) found their colleges to be supportive of their academic and personal goals.

In their sophomore year, I asked students a direct question about the supportiveness of their college environments: how concerned male faculty members, female faculty members, male college administrators, female college administrators, and students were with the "special needs or problems of women." A greater percentage of Wells students than students at the other three colleges said that male faculty, female faculty, and students were "very concerned" about their needs, with their responses differing most strikingly for other students and men faculty members (see Table 9.1). William Smith students were the most likely to say that women administrators were very concerned about them. At the time of this survey, the dean of William Smith, Rebecca Fox, was actively promoting the benefits of the coordinate structure for women students. William Smith students appear to have found her stance and actions on their behalf supportive.

Middlebury stands out among the four colleges in terms of being the least supportive environment for women students. A lower percentage of

Middlebury students than students at the other three colleges saw men faculty, women faculty, women administrators, and students as "very concerned" with their needs (and there were not significant differences among the colleges in students' perceptions of male administrators' concerns). In no case did a majority of Middlebury students see any one of these five campus groups as very sensitive to their needs; at all the other colleges, a majority of students saw at least one campus group as very concerned about them. Men faculty, in particular, were seen as unsupportive at Middlebury; only 3 percent of the Middlebury students saw them as "very concerned" with their needs. That women students at Middlebury do not receive much support fits the historical record, discussed in Part One of this book. Women students were reluctantly admitted to Middlebury, and for many years, the college remained, in essence, a men's college with women students present.

Students' responses to four questions on the sophomore questionnaires about support (or discouragement) for academic work produced quite a different pattern, however. I asked sophomores whether any faculty had given them the impression that: (1) they were not well-suited for their major field, (2) they were not serious students, (3) they were one of the best students in his or her classes or field, or (4) they were good candidates for further education, such as graduate or professional school. In general, few students (less than 20 percent at all colleges) reported that any faculty members had explicitly discouraged them by saying that they were not suited for their major field or that they were not serious students. Those students who did report having been told either of these things tended to have low grade point averages. Students at the coeducational colleges were neither more nor less likely than students at Wells or William Smith to say that faculty had discouraged them in these ways.

In contrast to what I had expected, more students at Middlebury and Hamilton had received academic encouragement than students at either Wells or William Smith, in terms of having been told that they were one of the best students in a faculty member's field, as I show in Table 9.1. Not surprisingly, students with higher grade point averages were more likely to have been told this. Students who were encouraged in this way also tended to see faculty members frequently outside of class, to say that they admired faculty, and to have high academic goals.[8]

Why did students at the women's college not conform to the expectation that they would be the ones receiving the most academic encouragement? At all colleges except Wells, 70 percent or more of the students reported GPAs in a middle range. Wells was more bipolar; along with

Middlebury, it had the highest percentage of students with high GPAs, but Wells also had a higher percentage of students with low GPAs than any of the other three colleges. This, in turn, means that although students at Wells who had high grade point averages *were* being encouraged, more Wells students did not have good grades and so, appropriately, were not being told they were very good students. When I looked at the relationship between students' grade point averages and being told they were one of a faculty member's "best" students for each college separately, the percentage of Wells students with high GPAs who were being encouraged in this way (73 percent) was not very different from those at Hamilton (78 percent) and Middlebury (84 percent). William Smith students with high GPAs fared the least well: only 57 percent of them were praised as one of a faculty member's "best" students.

Another way a college can support its women students is by having courses on women's issues, such as women and the arts, or the sociology of women. According to this measure, William Smith students had the most supportive environment, while Middlebury students had the least supportive one. Slightly more than one-fifth (21 percent) of students at William Smith had taken three or more such courses, compared to 16 percent or fewer of students at the other three colleges (see Table 9.1).

In order to learn if women students at these four colleges felt that doing well academically was supported on their campuses, I asked those I interviewed during their junior years what the image of intelligent or "brainy" women students was (and whether it differed from the image of intelligent men). Their answers were similar to what they said about the image of athletic women in that most claimed that it was not a social disadvantage for a woman to be intelligent (some even maintained that it was an advantage), as long as the woman was seen as well-rounded. In other words, a woman could be intelligent and popular, as long as she was also outgoing, fun-loving, "played hard," and was "not really aggressive." A few women at each campus gave more traditional answers. One woman at Middlebury, for instance, said that it was attractive to "guys" if women students were "not dumb but . . . a little bit naive." At William Smith one of the interviewees said that intelligent women students tended to be seen as feminists and other students don't "go for strong feminist kind of stuff." Wells students were inclined to believe that they were protected from the situation at coeducational colleges, where it would be a social liability to be intelligent, but they did mention pressures at Wells for intelligent women to be involved in many activities and not to be perceived as "really aggressive."

More surprising to me than these views of intelligent women students were what the women at the coeducational colleges said about the images of intelligent men—they were much more negative. They reported that academically successful men were stereotyped as "nerds," "geeks," "dweebs," and as living in "squid houses" (fraternities whose members had high grade point averages). Many of the women students I interviewed admitted that they could not understand why, but thinking of men students studying hard did not "seem right." Men students were expected to "blow things off," and to laugh when they received bad grades. One student at William Smith suggested that negative images of "brainy" men students might be a result of fraternities since intelligent men were not invited to join, making the social cost of doing well too high. And it is true that fraternities existed at all three coeducational colleges in 1986–87 when I conducted these interviews.

In summary, the environment of the women's college, Wells, appeared to be more supportive of women students than the environments of the other three colleges in general, nonspecific ways. Wells students were the most likely to perceive women and men faculty and other students as supportive of their concerns. Students at William Smith also saw their environments as quite supportive; in particular, they were likely to say that women administrators and women faculty were concerned with their needs, and they reported having taken the most courses on women's issues. But students at Wells and William Smith were not more likely to say they had been encouraged in their academic work by faculty. In fact, Middlebury and Hamilton students were most likely to report being praised by faculty as one of the "best" students in the faculty member's field. This difference in academic encouragement is partly explained by differences across the colleges in students' GPAs. It may also be a result of faculty members at these two coeducational colleges finding that most men students, in an attempt to get into one of the "cool," not nerdy, fraternity houses, do not take their academic work seriously, making women the most promising or rewarding students.[9]

Relation Between College Experiences and Changes in Students' Self-Esteem, Goals, and Attitudes

Not only did I want to learn if students at these four colleges had different college experiences in ways predicted by the literature on the advantages of single-sex education for women, but I also wanted to determine if differences in experiences were related to changes during the college years, what some other researchers call educational "outcomes."[10] Specifically, I was interested in students' changes in self-esteem, educational goals, and attitudes toward the women's movement, gender roles, and feminism. In other words, I wanted to determine if some usual explanations of why women fare better in single-sex educational institutions were found to be true for my four-college study. What follows is a discussion of the degree to which changes in women students' goals and attitudes were correlated with each of the three types of college experiences discussed above (women faculty as role models, leadership in college activities, and supportiveness of the college environment).

Changes in Students' Self-Esteem

The questionnaires for both the first year and sophomore year contained the following question: Do you agree or disagree with the following statement: "On the whole, I am satisfied with myself." Among entering students, Wells students were actually slightly less likely than students entering the other three colleges to say that they "agreed strongly" with this global measure of self-esteem (see Graph 9.1). Only 30 percent of Wells students said this, compared to 32 percent at William Smith, 38 percent at Middlebury, and 50 percent at Hamilton. But by the end of their sophomore year, Wells was the only one of the four colleges in which the percentage of students who "agreed strongly" increased (by 17 percent, from 30 to 47 percent); at William Smith the percentage stayed the same, and at Middlebury and Hamilton the percentage decreased (from 38 to 32 percent among the Middlebury sample and from 50 to 41 percent for the Hamilton sample).[11] This finding does provide some support for the idea that women's colleges like Wells provide young women with an environment in which they can become more self-confident.[12]

I did not ask the seniors the same question, but instead I asked them about their *perceptions* of how their self-confidence had changed during their college years. In general, seniors reported that their self-confidence had increased during the college years. Almost two-thirds of all seniors, 64 percent, said they had become "much more" self-confident compared to when they entered college, and only thirteen students (5 percent) said they had become "a lot" or "a little" less self-confident" during these four years. These perceptions varied slightly, but not quite significantly, by which college students attended, with 77 percent of Wells seniors, 67 percent of Hamilton seniors, 60 percent of William Smith seniors and 58 percent of Middlebury seniors reporting that they had increased a great deal in self-confidence (see Graph 9.1).[13] And so students' subjective

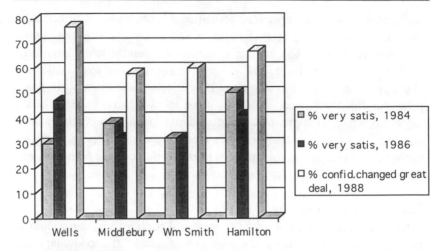

Graph 9.1 Self-Esteem by Year and College

assessment of their changes in self-confidence also somewhat supports the contention that self-confidence is more likely to increase in an all-women's college.

To understand which specific aspects of a women's college might lead young women to become more satisfied with themselves, I correlated measures of students' college experiences with their levels of self-esteem. In other words, I investigated whether the three aspects of their experiences discussed above—having women faculty as role models, participation in and leadership of college activities, and finding their college environments supportive—made a difference to their levels of self-esteem. For role models, I found that women students who in their senior year said that they were close to a mixture of men and women faculty were slightly more likely than those women students who were not close to any faculty, men or women, to say that their confidence had increased a great deal during college.[14] Having at least some faculty role models was more important than the gender of those models, at least for changes in students' self-confidence.

I had expected that women students who participated in and led many activities at college would be the ones most likely to increase in self-esteem. The findings were not so straightforward, however. On the one hand, those students who *began* college with positive feelings about themselves were slightly more likely than others to get involved in college activities.[15] But it was not the most active students who as seniors said that their self-confidence had increased the most during their college years;

instead, students who scored in the mid-range of the college activities index were slightly more likely than the most active students to report that their confidence had greatly improved (but those least active were the least likely to report an increase in confidence).[16] It is difficult to know how to interpret this finding. It could be that for the development of self-esteem, there is an optimal level of involvement in and leadership of college activities. While students who did not participate much at all did not develop skills that could have improved their self-esteem, those who participated in and led (too) many activities may have been "spread too thin," meaning that they were not able to become proficient at any of them, and so did not develop self-confidence.

Another way in which being active in college helped students develop self-confidence was through active participation in classes, although the effect was slight. Whereas just over half (51 percent) of students who said that they often talked in class reported high satisfaction with themselves as sophomores, only 28 percent of those who seldom participated in classes reported such high self-satisfaction.[17] The results I discussed above did not indicate that Wells students participated more actively in class than students at the other three colleges. However, given that this information comes from students' own assessments of their in-class behavior, and given that many other, observational studies of men and women in classes have found that men students tend to dominate class discussions, it seems possible that one mechanism leading graduates of women's colleges to succeed in later life is through their positive feelings about themselves, encouraged by expressing themselves in an all-women environment.

Students who perceived their colleges as supportive of women did not, in general, have higher levels of self-esteem. One exception to this was that sophomores who believed that men faculty were very concerned with their needs as women students were more likely to have higher self-esteem than sophomores who did not believe men faculty were concerned.[18] Perhaps because women faculty tend to be seen as "naturally" more concerned with women's issues, their support was not as critical for validating young women's sense of self-worth.[19] Faculty members' reactions to students' academic work—more precisely, their criticism of students—was also somewhat important in a negative way. Students who said that faculty members had told them they were not serious about their studies were slightly more likely than students who had not received such negative comments from faculty, to report lower levels of self-esteem in their sophomore year.[20] This finding takes on more significance because I found that students' doing poorly or well academically was not related to their self-esteem. It is also somewhat surprising that faculty members' active encouragement of students' academic work did not affect their confidence levels in a positive way.

Given the importance of social life to college students, I investigated its impact on their self-esteem. On the sophomore questionnaires, I asked students if they had an active social life and whether they were dating a man at present (or more than one man, or if they did not want to date men). Having an active social life in students' second year of college was related both to their self-esteem when they entered college and to their self-esteem in their sophomore year. Forty-two percent of the (179) students who said their social life was active, compared to 28 percent of the (75) students who said they did not have an active social life, reported high self-esteem in their sophomore year.[21] It would appear, then, that more confident women are better able to establish active social lives and that this in turn contributes to their maintaining a positive image of themselves. Even though students who were dating were more likely to say they had an active social life, dating by itself was not related to self-esteem for either entering students or sophomores.

Wells sophomores were much *less* likely than sophomores at the other colleges to say their social lives were active: only 45 percent of Wells students said their social lives were active, compared to between 72 and 82 percent of students at the other three colleges.[22] Given that students who had active social lives were more likely to report high self-esteem, this makes the increase of self-esteem for Wells students between their first and second years of college even more remarkable.

During interviews with a sample of juniors at each college I asked them what they believed was necessary for a good social life. Their answers made it clear that dating men was not critical to their definition of social life. Going out in groups, some of which were mixed-sex, to engage in activities that they thought were fun, was much more central. Activities that they mentioned included going to concerts or films, attending parties, playing pool, or even participating in a student jazz band. With this broad definition of social life, it is possible to see how self-confident young women would be in a better position to negotiate an active social life, which in turn could help them maintain an image of themselves as someone who knows how to cope well with a variety of demands and circumstances.

In summary, the results of the surveys show only limited relationships between young women's college experiences, as measured in this study, and their self-esteem. Having at least some faculty as role models, being moderately involved in college activities and active in class discussions, seeing men faculty as supportive, and not being criticized by faculty for academic work, were the only predicted ways students' experiences at college had an impact on their self-esteem. Not hypothesized but nonetheless important, at least for the first couple of years at college, were students' social lives. Informal activities, even more than participation in college-sponsored ones, appear to reinforce young women's positive feelings about themselves.

Academic Goals

Each time I surveyed women students at the four colleges, I asked them how far they intended to go in their education: did they intend to stop with a bachelor's degree, receive a master's, or continue on for a Ph.D., M.D., or law degree? The percentage of students who planned on continuing to the highest degrees stayed almost constant (27 percent of first-year students, 29 percent of sophomores, and 28 percent of seniors planned on pursuing their Ph.D.s). But by their senior year, a somewhat greater number of these women students planned on obtaining a master's degree (56 percent of first-year students, 51 percent of sophomores, and 61 percent of seniors), and a smaller number planned on stopping their education when they had finished their bachelor's degrees (17 percent of freshwomen, 20 percent of sophomores, and 11 percent of seniors).

Given the research that shows that graduates of women's colleges are proportionately more likely than graduates of coeducational colleges to become leaders in their fields, I predicted that Wells students would have the highest academic goals. This was true for first-year students, as I discussed in the last chapter, in that those beginning at Wells tied with those entering Hamilton College in having the highest percentages (35 percent) of students planning on receiving the highest educational degrees. But when this question was asked of sophomores, the percentage of students aiming for Ph.D.s had increased at all colleges *except* Wells, where it had decreased by 10 percent. An even lower percentage of Wells seniors than sophomores said that they planned on getting their Ph.D.s or professional degrees, whereas the percentage stayed the same at Hamilton and Middlebury and increased slightly at William Smith (see Graph 9.2a). So by the time students were seniors, a greater percentage of Hamilton students (39.5 percent) planned on continuing their education to the highest level than the percentages of seniors at the other three colleges (where the percents were 27, 24, and 20 for William Smith, Middlebury, and Wells, respectively).[23]

Why did more Wells students than students at the other three colleges decrease their academic goals from the highest levels? One possibility is

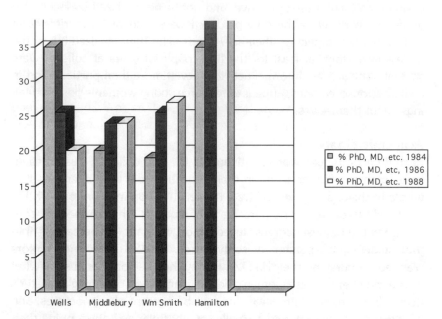

Graph 9.2a % Ph.D. and Higher Professional Degree Goals by College and Year

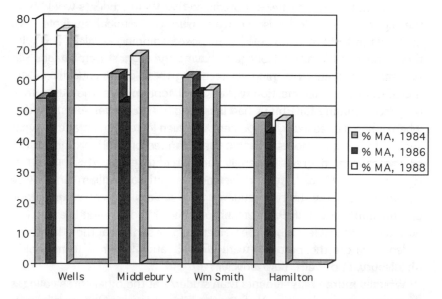

Graph 9.2b % MA Goals by College and Year

that students entering Wells had unrealistic ideas of what obtaining a Ph.D. or higher professional degree involved; after all, their parents were much less likely to have graduated from college than the parents of the women students at the other three colleges.[24] It is also important to realize that although by the time they were seniors, Wells students were the least likely to plan on getting their Ph.D.s, they were actually the most likely to plan on getting a master's degree (see Graph 9.2b). So in fact, fewer seniors at Wells than at the other three colleges intended to end their education with a bachelor's degree.

Which college experiences contributed to these students' developing high academic goals? Women faculty as role models did have a slight effect: 43 percent of those seniors who said that they were close to women faculty planned on obtaining the highest academic degrees, compared to 31 percent of those close to both women and men faculty, 29 percent of those close to only men faculty, and 22 percent of those seniors who were not close to any faculty.[25] Students who were generally more active in and leaders of college organizations did not have the highest academic goals, although those students who saw faculty members frequently, both in and outside of class, were somewhat more likely to have the highest academic goals in both their sophomore and senior years.[26] This suggests that being active in a way that furthers intellectual interests—conversations with faculty members—supports academic ambitions, but being active in college affairs more generally does not. Similarly, I found that students who perceived their colleges as being supportive of women's interests and needs did not have the highest academic goals. However, those women students who reported that faculty had praised them for their academic work, by telling them that they were one of the best students in the faculty member's field or even more strikingly, by telling them that they were good candidates for graduate school, were much more likely to have high academic goals than students who were not so praised.[27] The effect of praise was not just due to the best students' receiving praise, either, as controlling for students' grade point averages reduced the correlation only slightly. Thus generally supportive environments for women students did not affect their academic goals, but environments that were supportive of their *specific academic* interests did help them develop and maintain high academic goals.

Women Students' Feminism, Gender-Role Attitudes, and Support of the Women's Movement

When they entered college in 1984, less than one-third (30 percent) of the women students in this sample considered themselves to be feminists, as I noted in the previous chapter. Between their first and second years in college, many students' identification with feminism changed; those who had initially considered themselves to be feminists were particularly likely to change to become non-feminists. Specifically, 42 percent of those who originally called themselves feminists in their first year no longer did so by the end of their sophomore year (30 of 71 students). A smaller percentage (23 percent) of those who had not considered themselves feminists when they entered college did define themselves as feminists by their second year (38 of 163). In absolute terms, given the larger number of first-year students who did not consider themselves feminists, this means there were 8 more self-defined feminists at the end of the second year of college than there were when these women students entered college.

The pattern was very different, however, between the second and last years of college. The overwhelming majority of sophomores who defined themselves as feminists continued to do so in their senior year (91 percent or 72 of 79). Moreover, a sizeable minority of those who did not consider themselves to be feminists in their sophomore year came to define themselves as feminists in their last year of college (40 percent or 62 of 155). Thus by the end of college, a majority of these women students, 58 percent (144 of the 249 students who answered this question), were self-proclaimed feminists, even though only 38 had considered themselves to be feminists at all three points in time, compared to 79 who had steadfastly defined themselves as non-feminists.

These patterns show that there was a great deal of instability during college in students' definition of themselves as feminists or not, but after the second year, almost all the change went in the direction of non-feminists coming to consider themselves feminists. Overall, there was slightly more than a 25 percent increase in the number of women students who considered themselves to be feminists between the time of their entry to their last semester in college.

Women students' willingness to call themselves feminists varied by which college they attended. As I noted in the last chapter, students entering Wells were much more likely than students at the other three colleges to call themselves feminists. While the percentage of students who called themselves feminists increased at all four colleges over the four years, the percentage increased the most at William Smith College, particularly between the sophomore and senior years. By the end of college about the same percentage of William Smith and Wells seniors labeled themselves feminist, 74 percent at Wells and 72 percent at William Smith. In contrast, slightly less than 50 percent of women students at the other two colleges, 49 percent of Hamilton students and 46 percent of Middlebury students, considered themselves feminists (see Graph 9.3).[28] The strong, visible role of key administrators at William Smith during this time period may have been a reason why so many William Smith students came to call themselves feminists. The dean of William Smith, Rebecca Fox, and her staff, emphasized the benefits of the college's separation from Hobart, arguing that the coordinate college gave women a sense of identity and their own space in the way that women's colleges do. Students' awareness and acceptance of such arguments could have led them to see themselves as feminists. Also, more William Smith students took courses on women's issues than students on the other campuses, and this in turn was correlated with students' defining themselves as feminist (see Graph 9.3).

Students' support for the women's movement increased over their years at college, but not as dramatically as their self-identification as feminists did. As I noted in the last chapter, only 12 percent of the entering women students said that they supported all or virtually all of the aims of the women's movement. By the sophomore year, this percent had increased to 16, and in the senior year, just over one-quarter (26 percent) of the students said that they supported all the aims of the women's movement. Wells students were the most likely to say they supported all the aims of the women's movement in both the first and sophomore years (although this difference was statistically significant only in the sophomore year), but by the time they were seniors, about one-third of both Wells and Hamilton

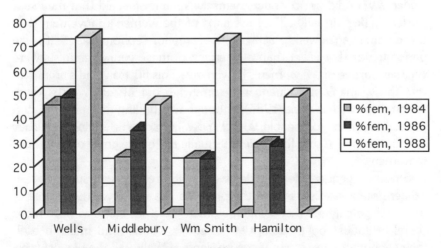

Graph 9.3 % Feminist by College and Year

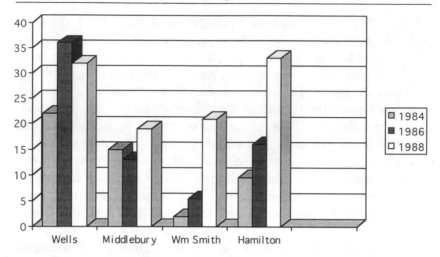

Graph 9.4 % Who Support All Aims of Women's Movement by Year and College

students (32 and 33 percent, respectively) said they supported all the aims of the women's movement, compared to about one-fifth of William Smith and Middlebury students (21 and 19 percent, respectively) (see Graph 9.4).[29]

Not surprisingly, students who described themselves as feminists were also the ones most likely to say they supported all the aims of the women's movement. For example, in their senior year, 41 percent of those students who called themselves feminists, compared to 7 percent of those students who did not consider themselves feminists, said that they supported "all or virtually all" of the aims of the women's movement (and these percentages were practically the same for sophomores).[30] It is sobering to see that fewer than 50 percent of these young feminists were very supportive of the women's movement. This fits Rowland's argument that the women's movement was somewhat out of touch with young women's views (Rowland 1984), although this finding may also reflect a general tendency for people to feel more comfortable saying that they support "some" rather than "all or virtually all" of the goals of *any* social movement.[31]

Students' gender-role attitudes were measured in each survey by an 18-item scale, as discussed in the previous chapter. Over the course of their college careers, these young women generally came to have more liberal attitudes about appropriate roles for women and men. In both their sophomore and senior years, students at Wells had the highest average scale scores, that is, the most liberal views, although by the senior year, the scores at all four colleges were not significantly different (the average scores on the scale, whose highest possible value was 54, were 45.9 for Wells seniors, 45.2 for Hamilton seniors, 44.2 for William Smith seniors, and 43.8 for Middlebury seniors). Not surprisingly, self-identified feminists had significantly more liberal gender-role attitudes than non-feminists, especially in the senior year.[32] Similarly, those students who said they supported "all or virtually all" of the aims of the women's movement had the most liberal gender-role attitudes, and again, this correlation was stronger for seniors than for sophomores.[33]

In summary, I found consistent patterns in how these women students' attitudes toward women's issues changed during their college years. Whether I looked at their self-identification as feminists, support of the women's movement, or their gender-role attitudes, I found that by the time they were seniors, their attitudes were more sympathetic to women's issues. Students at Wells generally had the most liberal or feminist views, although about the same percentage of Hamilton as Wells seniors said they supported all the aims of the women's movement, and seniors at William Smith were about as likely to call themselves feminists as were Wells seniors.

Which college experiences were conducive to these women students being concerned about women's issues? Having women faculty as role models (or, more precisely, not having just men faculty as role models) was associated with students' defining themselves as feminists and to a lesser degree, with their supporting the women's movement and having liberal gender-role attitudes.[34] Being active in and a leader of college activities, including seeing faculty often and participating actively in classes, did not generally affect women students' willingness to call themselves feminists, although students who were active participants in their classes were somewhat more likely to define themselves as feminists in their sophomore (but not senior) year.[35] Being active in college was a more consistent predictor of students' support of the women's movement and liberal gender-role attitudes; those students who participated actively in their classes were, in particular, most likely to support the women's movement in both their sophomore and senior years and to have liberal gender-role attitudes in their sophomore year.[36]

The relationship between colleges' being supportive of women students' concerns and students' feminism depended on the type of support being considered. Students who said that men faculty were very concerned with their needs were slightly more likely to define themselves as feminists and to support all the aims of the women's movement (although this result was partly due to Wells students' saying that men faculty were the most concerned about their needs and Wells students also being the most feminist).[37] On the other hand, students who said that male administrators were very concerned with their needs were slightly *less* likely to support all the aims of the women's movement, and they were also significantly more likely to have *traditional* gender-role attitudes.[38] It is intriguing that the support of male faculty and male administrators appear to have opposite effects. I suspect that men faculty who are concerned about women's issues are more knowledgeable about feminist scholarship and so encourage students to support feminism and the women's movement, while men administrators' concern may be based more on a protective, traditional attitude toward women.[39]

Students who reported academic encouragement from faculty tended to have liberal gender-role attitudes.[40] Most striking of all, students who had taken several courses on women's issues, for example, women and music or the psychology of women, were much more likely to define themselves as feminists, both in their sophomore and senior years. In their senior year, for example, while 42 percent of students who had taken no courses on women's issues defined themselves as feminists, 97 percent of those who had taken three or more such courses considered themselves to be feminists.[41] Taking courses on women's issues was also related to students' support of the women's movement and liberal gender-role attitudes, but only in the senior year.[42] This accounts for the big change in William Smith students' identification with feminism since they had taken more courses on women's issues than students at any of the other colleges had.

The reason for these findings was *not* just that students who defined themselves as feminists took courses on women's issues. Students who defined themselves as feminists when they entered college were neither more nor less likely than students who did not consider themselves to be feminists to take such courses. Faculty who teach courses on women's issues should therefore not feel that they are only "teaching to the converted." An unsolicited comment a student wrote on a questionnaire demonstrates the impact these courses can have:

> My senior year was the year of the most change in my attitudes towards expectations of men and women. I believe this change was caused in part by an enlightening and subversive course called "Feminist Literary Criticism" that I took in my last year. The course uncovered some ideas I had about society that hadn't been really acknowledged by myself until then. It helped to change most of my value systems.

Summary and Conclusions

During a period when women's colleges declined markedly in popularity, as discussed in Chapter 6, students who attended Wells College still benefited from their single-sex educational experience. The benefits did not depend on their having come from advantaged family backgrounds since, as I noted in Chapter 8, the fathers of Wells students in the class of 1988 had less education than the fathers of women students at Middlebury, William Smith, or Hamilton College, and Wells students were less likely than the students of the other three colleges to have attended private secondary schools. Some commentators have lamented the decline in the academic qualifications of women who attend women's colleges (Gose 1995), but there are advantages to having the link between privilege and single-sex education broken so that the benefits of single-sex education can be experienced by a broader sector of the population.

My study of the educational environments of students at a women's college, a coordinate college, a long-time coeducational college, and a college that has only recently become coeducational has found support for my general hypothesis that single-sex environments are favorable to women students. I found that at Wells, and to a lesser extent, at William Smith, women students were more able than women students at the two comparable coeducational colleges, Middlebury and Hamilton, to find faculty role models of both genders; to assume leadership roles in college activities; and to experience their college as generally supportive. Not all of my specific hypotheses were supported, however. It was women students at the two coeducational colleges, Hamilton and Middlebury, who reported the greatest academic encouragement from faculty. I believe this results from these women students' stronger academic backgrounds (in comparison to those of Wells and William Smith students) and also to women students' seeming more academically serious in comparison to men students at many coeducational institutions, although I am not certain why this pattern did not apply to Hobart and William Smith as well.

The outcomes I looked at were limited to changes among the students while they were in college. The results were mixed, that is, they did not completely favor students at Wells or William Smith. On the one hand, Wells students did seem to gain in confidence during college more than students at the other three colleges did, but on the other hand, their academic goals tended to drop during college, whereas the goals of students at the other colleges tended to rise. Wells students expressed more solidarity with women in terms of their willingness to call themselves feminists (although William Smith students matched them by the end of college). In other manifestations of gender solidarity, the women students at all four colleges converged somewhat by their senior year, for instance, in their support of the women's movement and in their views on appropriate gender roles.

College experiences did relate to these educational outcomes but mostly in rather specific ways. Experiencing college as generally supportive of women, for instance, did not have any bearing on students' academic goals, but receiving encouragement for academic work did relate positively to students' aspirations. Some of the more intriguing relationships that I found were that students who had some role models among faculty were more likely to have high self-esteem than students who had no role models among faculty; self-esteem was slightly higher among students who participated actively in classes; and students who felt that men faculty were concerned with their needs also had higher self-esteem. Feminism and support for the women's movement were greater among students who had at least some women faculty role models, who participated actively in classes, who perceived men faculty as being concerned with them, and especially among those who had taken courses on women's issues. While only a few of these relationships were strong, they do show that the supportive yet challenging environments for which women's colleges are renowned do make some demonstrable differences. Even if they did not, however, I would argue that women students of all races, social classes, and sexual orientations, deserve an educational environment in which they are comfortable and supported. Wells and other women's colleges do not meet those needs perfectly, but they do seem to be doing a better job than many coeducational colleges.

In the next chapter I look at some of these same students six years later to see if their attitudes and experiences were related to which college they attended. While six years after college is not a sufficient length of time to determine if the graduates of the women's college (and the coordinate college, to a somewhat lesser extent) are more likely to become leaders in their fields, as Tidball's studies suggest, it is enough time to determine whether attitudinal differences remain and whether the women's retrospective views of their college experiences conform to the views they had when they were still students.

Notes

1   As I discussed in Chapter 8, I do not believe that this is the only reason women who entered Wells in 1984 were more likely than the women who entered the other three colleges to call themselves feminist. Undoubtedly women's colleges appeal more to women who already have some concerns about or interests in women's issues.

2   Readers who want to see some of the data discussed in this chapter analyzed using hierarchical regression can refer to my article (Miller-Bernal 1993).

3   χ^2 = 39.92, df = 9, p = .000. It is, of course, possible that women who admired women faculty members or who felt close to them took courses with them for that reason. In other words, it is not possible to tell which is the cause and which the effect. But it seems likely that taking courses with women faculty helped students develop a relationship with them. I also investigated whether this result was due to the fact that many more Wells students had taken a large proportion of their courses with women faculty and Wells seniors were somewhat more likely than students at Hamilton and Middlebury to say they were close to all women faculty. I looked at each college separately and found that at each college, seniors who said that they had taken the most courses from women faculty were the most likely to say they were close to all women faculty. Actually this result held up least well at Wells, but this is partly because there was little variability among the students in the number of courses they had taken from women faculty: 96 percent of Wells students had taken at least 6 courses from women professors.

4   See Table 5.1 in Chapter 5. The percentage of women faculty at Wells was 44 percent when these students entered college in 1984, compared to about 25 percent at the other three colleges.

5   The cross-tabular analysis of class participation (three categories) and the index of college activities divided into a low, medium, and high category yielded a χ^2 = 14.67, df = 4, p = .005.

6   The sex of this professor, who apparently referred to the women students as "girls," was not identified.

7   While this statement may seem applicable only to heterosexual women students, I am not so sure. Even if one is not sexually interested in men, their opinions probably matter, especially since they tend to dominate classes and extracurricular activities.

8   The chi-squares for these relationships are as follows: with cumulative GPA, χ^2 = 38.77, df = 4, p = .000; with seeing faculty frequently χ^2 = 35.50, df = 4, p = .000; for admiring faculty, χ^2 = 11.38, df = 2, p = .003; and for academic goals as sophomores, χ^2 = 20.24, df = 4, p = .000.

9   The relative lack of academic encouragement of William Smith students, even those who had high GPAs, is difficult to explain but may be due to the party school image of Hobart and William Smith Colleges (see Chapter 10).

10   More specifically, Pascarella and Terenzini (1991, 5–7) classify these outcomes as "affective" and note that such outcome measures focus on the question of whether different experiences within the same institution have different effects. My study, however, complicates this question by seeking to determine if the experiences and their effects vary depending on whether the college is single-sex or coeducational.

11   In neither the first nor second year did the relation between students' satisfaction with themselves and college attended achieve statistical significance, but the differences came quite close to being statistically significant in the sophomore year (χ^2 = 14.1, df = 9, sig. = .12).

12   The data I present here are measures of *net* change rather than *individual* change. For an excellent discussion of this distinction, as well as "floor" and "ceiling" effects and other difficulties in measuring changes in students attributable to college attendance, see Feldman (1972).

13   χ^2 = 15.05, df = 9, p = .09.

14   χ^2 = 18.87, df = 9, p = .03.

15   χ^2 = 13.63, df = 6, p = .03.

16   χ^2 = 14.97, df = 6, p = .02.

17   χ^2 = 11.21, df = 6, p = .08. It should also be noted that students who came to college with the highest measured levels of self-confidence did not tend to report participating in classes a lot. This suggests that self-confidence was the *result*, not the cause, of higher class participation.

18   χ^2 = 20.88, df = 6, p = .002.

19   This finding is not just a "Wells effect," either; that is, it is not merely that Wells students are most likely to report that men faculty are very concerned with their needs and also to have the highest self-esteem. Removing Wells students hardly changes the value of the coefficient.

20   χ^2 = 23.48, df = 6, p = .001.

21   χ^2 = 9.24, df = 3, p = .03.

22   χ^2 = 19.81, df = 3, p = .000. Wells students did not differ from students at the other three colleges in terms of the percentage who were dating men, however.

23   The differences in percentages by college achieved significance only in the senior year (χ^2 = 14.44, df = 6, sig = .03).

24   Some support for this argument comes from the finding that although at all three points in time students' grade point averages were correlated with their academic goals, the correlation was stronger in their senior years than in either their first or sophomore years. This suggests that during their college years, students became more knowledgeable about what it takes to go on to receive a top professional degree.

25   Chi-square = 11.1, df = 6, sig = .08.

26   In almost all of these correlations, it could be argued that the causal flow was actually the other way around; for example, in this instance, it could be that women students with the highest academic goals sought out faculty frequently. But I asked *sophomores* about how frequently they saw faculty and this correlated with their academic goals two years later. It is true, however, that between their sophomore and senior years, two-thirds of these students did *not* change their academic goals. Perhaps some of these students would have decreased their goals had they not had frequent contact with faculty. In other words, while we cannot be certain that contact with faculty was the deciding factor, talking with faculty probably at least reinforced the aims of students whose academic goals were already high.

27   χ^2 = 44.93, df = 4, sig = .000 for sophomores' being told they were good candidates for graduate school and seniors' academic goals. Interestingly, students who were told negative things about their academic work were not less likely (or more likely) than students not so criticized to have high academic goals. This supports the general psychological principle that negative reinforcement is less effective than positive reinforcement in changing people's behavior.

28   The differences in percentages of students who considered themselves feminists at each college achieved significance in all three years, but it was most significant in the senior year (χ^2 = 15.95, df = 3, sig. = .001).

29   The differences by college achieved significance only in the sophomore year (χ^2 = 27.43, df = 9, sig. = .001), but they were quite close to significance in the other two years.

30   χ^2 = 47.98, df = 3, sig. = .000 for seniors.

31   Comparing the percentages of Graphs 9.3 and 9.4, William Smith stands out in terms of having a very high percentage of seniors who considered themselves feminists but not a very high percentage of seniors who supported all aims of the women's movement. In contrast, Hamilton seniors were not particularly likely to consider themselves feminists, but they were the most likely of all to say they supported all aims of the women's movement. A comparison of senior year "feminists" at each college shows that those at Hamilton were the most likely to say they supported all the aims of the women's movement, while those at William Smith were the least likely. Specifically, only 28 percent of William Smith feminists said they supported all aims of the women's movement, compared to 41 percent of Wells feminists, 39 percent of Middlebury feminists, and 63 percent of Hamilton feminists. The explanation of these patterns remains unclear.

32   In the sophomore year the mean gender-role attitudes score for non-feminists was 41.4, while for feminists it was 45.1; in the senior year, the mean gender-role attitudes score was 41.6 for non-feminists and 47.1 for feminists. Both of these relationships were significant at the .000 level.

33   While the relationship was highly significant for both years, at the .000 level of significance, the F value for the oneway analysis of variance was higher for the

senior year than it was for the sophomore year: $F_{(3,251)} = 20.03$ for sophomore year, $F_{(3,252)} = 35.27$, sig. = .000 for senior year.

34    $\chi^2 = 17.75$, df = 3, sig. = .001 for seniors' self-identification as feminists cross-tabulated with their closeness to no faculty, men faculty, both men and women, or just women faculty; the other relationships did not quite achieve statistical significance but in all cases, students who were close to or admired only men faculty were less likely than the other students to support the aims of the women's movement or to have liberal gender-role attitudes.

35    $\chi^2 = 13.01$, df = 2, sig. = .001.

36    $\chi^2 = 20.25$, df = 6, sig. = .0025 for class participation and sophomores' support of the women's movement; $\chi^2 = 16.95$, df = 6, sig. = .009 for class participation and seniors' support of the women's movement; $F_{(2,252)} = 5.43$, sig. = .005 for class participation and sophomores' gender-role attitudes. Again, it is difficult to know which came first, i.e., it may be that students who supported the women's movement and who had liberal gender-role attitudes were most concerned to overcome women's traditional passivity by being active in their classes.

37    $\chi^2 = 6.52$, df = 2, sig. = .04 for concern of male faculty and feminism in the senior year; $\chi^2 = 10.79$, df = 6, sig = .10 for concern of male faculty and support of the women's movement in the senior year.

38    $\chi^2 = 21.49$, df = 6, sig. = .0015 for concern of male administrators and (non) support of the women's movement in the senior year; $F_{(2,243)} = 5.70$, sig. = .004 for concern of male administrators and traditional gender-role attitudes in the senior year.

39   Tidball (1976) found that more men faculty at women's colleges than men faculty at coeducational colleges had attitudes that were more supportive of women students. Her finding fits the results that I present here since Wells students were the most likely to report men faculty being concerned with their needs, and such concern helped students develop feminist attitudes.

40    $F_{(2,249)} = 4.93$, sig. = .008 between sophomores' being told by faculty that they were good candidates for graduate school and seniors' gender-role attitudes.

41    $\chi^2 = 32.57$, df = 2, sig. = .000 for senior year; $\chi^2 = 13.91$, df = 2, sig. = .001 for sophomore year.

42    $\chi^2 = 31.13$, df = 6, sig. = .000 between taking courses on women's issues and support of the women's movement; $F_{(2,255)} = 11.99$, sig. = .000 for taking courses on women's issues and gender-role attitudes.

Chapter 10

Alumnae's Experiences and the Four Colleges in the 1990s

This book has focused primarily on experiences women students had while they were in college, both historically and in more recent years. In this chapter, however, I describe the lives of women in the class of 1988 after they left college. Six years is not sufficient to determine if attending Wells had the long-term benefits that some other research indicates single-sex education confers. Yet this study of alumnae's experiences in 1994 does provide some insights into the different ways these women began to establish themselves in careers and graduate education. Besides discussing what these women were doing after college, this chapter also examines their views of their years in college. Such retrospective accounts are less valuable as descriptions of what occurred during college than as indications of how these women came to judge their time in college in light of their experiences after college. This chapter also reports on alumnae's attitudes toward such issues as feminism and the women's movement to determine if their views had changed since they left college.

Not only have the women who attended these four colleges changed, but the colleges, too, are not the same as they were when these women were undergraduates. Therefore, the second part of this chapter describes key events at the four colleges during the past decade. I focus particularly on how the colleges have responded to what I described in Chapter 6 as major issues at Wells, Middlebury, Hobart and William Smith, and Hamilton.

The Alumnae Survey

In 1994 I surveyed some of the same 260 women who had responded to my three earlier questionnaires during their college years. I attempted to reach all of them, but some did not want to respond and others could not be located.[1] Ultimately, 149 alumnae completed surveys, which represents 57 percent of the original 260 students of my study: 33 alumnae of Wells, 45 of Middlebury, 35 of William Smith, and 36 of Hamilton. A comparison of those seniors who answered the alumnae questionnaire to those who did not found no significant differences in their attitudes as seniors toward a wide variety of issues or their educational or career goals. Thus it seems that the alumnae represent a fair sample of the women I surveyed in 1984, 1986, and 1988.

Alumnae's Living Arrangements, Work, and Education

In 1994 slightly more than two-fifths (42 percent) of the alumnae were living with a spouse (only one had been divorced), and 17 percent were living with a man or woman partner (see Table 10.1). Almost one-quarter (23 percent) of the alumnae lived alone, 4 percent were living with their parents, and 13 percent lived with groups of friends, other relatives, or arrangements such as dormitories. Very few of the alumnae, 13 percent, had had children, and only four (3 percent) were pregnant. Virtually all of the alumnae who were pregnant or who had children were married, but one alumna wrote that she had had artificial insemination in order to have children with her woman partner, and one alumna was divorced and lived with her child. All the pregnant alumnae were working full-time, and a majority of those with children were working, too—9 of the 19 alumnae with children had full-time jobs, and 5 had part-time jobs.

Table 10.1 also shows that two-thirds (66 percent) of the alumnae were working in full-time jobs in 1994; most of the rest were working in part-time jobs (14 percent) or were students (13 percent). Only four of the alumnae were involuntarily unemployed at the time of the survey (although a much larger number, 46 or almost one-third of the sample, had been unemployed for at least a month since graduation), three described themselves as volunteers, and three were homemakers.

Considering only those 98 alumnae who were working full-time, about the same number were businesswomen as were professionals, and in both cases, more had jobs in the lower than in the higher echelons. In the professional field, for example, 20 alumnae had positions in minor professions, such as primary school teacher or legal assistant; 14 were working as secondary or special education teachers or trained social workers; and 12 were full-fledged professionals, i.e., lawyers, doctors, or college professors.

TABLE 10.1 Overview of Alumnae's Lives Six Years After Graduation

Living arrangements	Frequencies	Percentages
Living with parents	6	4%
Living alone	34	23%
Living with partner (woman or man)	26	17%
Living with spouse	63	42%
Living with friends, relatives, or other arrangements	20	13%
Have children?		
No	126	85%
Pregnant	4	3%
Yes	19	13%
Employment		
full-time paid job	98	66%
part-time job	21	14%
student (TA or RA)	20 (8)	13% (5%)
involuntarily unemployed	4	3%
homemaker or volunteer	6	4%
Of those in full time employment:		
clerical or technical jobs	11	11%
lower-level business job	23	23%
minor professional	20	20%
secondary school teacher, trained social worker	14	14%
high-powered business job	18	18%
professional (doctor, lawyer, college professor)	12	12%
Pre-tax earnings (of 119 alumnae who reported them)		
Less than $15,000	17	14%
$15,001-$25,000	21	18%
$25,001-$35,000	35	29%
$35,001-$45,000	26	22%
$45,001-$55,000	10	8%
$55,001-$65,000	6	5%
Over $65,000	4	3%
Education		
Degrees already received:		
Master's level (M.A., M.S., M.B.A., M.S.W., etc.)	49	34%
M.D., J.D., or Ph.D.	13	9%
Currently (1994) a student:		
in full-time study	24	16%
part-time study	24	16%

TABLE 10.1 Continued

Living arrangements	Frequencies	Percentages
Degree being pursued (if any):		
Another bachelor's	2	1%[1] (5%)[2]
Master's level	20	13% (47%)
JD or MD	5	3% (12%)
Ph.D.	16	11% (37%)

[1] Of all alumnae.

[2] Of those 43 alums pursuing degrees (5 alums who are students are not pursuing degrees)

In terms of earnings, Table 10.1 shows that a majority of the alumnae had annual incomes of between $25,000 and $51,000; while one-third had incomes lower than $25,000, most of these were alumnae who were working part-time (53 percent of the low earners) or were students (34 percent of these low earners).[2] Ten alumnae, almost 10 percent of those who reported their incomes, had pre-tax incomes of over $55,000; all but one of these high-earning women were in business, usually banks or the financial side of large corporations. The only alumna who was not in business but had such a high salary was an attorney who was an associate in her firm.

Many alumnae of these four colleges had already obtained graduate degrees, and many more were working toward a degree when they were surveyed in the autumn of 1994. Specifically, as Table 10.1 shows, slightly more than two-fifths had obtained a graduate degree—34 percent at the masters level, and 9 percent professional degrees or Ph.D.s. Yet almost one-third were students at the time they were surveyed, 24 as full-time students and 24 as part-time. Assuming those who were students complete the degree they were studying for, eventually almost one-quarter of this sample will have their M.D., J.D., or Ph.D. and almost one-half (47 percent) more will have a master's degree. And of course, other alumnae who were not students in 1994 may eventually pursue more formal education. When asked if they wanted a "further educational degree," only 24 alumnae said no.

Many of the alumnae had complicated lives. Of the 98 alumnae with full-time jobs, 17 were also part-time students. Of the 21 alumnae with part-time jobs, 5 were also full-time students, and another 4 were studying part-time. Moreover, most alumnae were involved in other activities, especially sports or athletics (only 19 percent said they were *not* doing any athletic activities). Just over half were involved in theater, music, or art; just under 40 percent worked as volunteers; and also just under 40 percent belonged to clubs or community organizations. Of the activities asked about, the one that the fewest number of alumnae had anything to do with was politics; only 16 percent reported any political involvement.

Factors Related to Alumnae's Further Education

Because so many alumnae (29 percent) were still working on graduate degrees when I surveyed them in 1994, for the purpose of analysis I combined those who were in the process of obtaining degrees with those who had already received them. Fifty-eight alumnae (41 percent of the 143 alumnae who answered these questions) had not received any further degrees after college, nor were they working on obtaining another degree; 51 alumnae (36 percent) had a master's level degree or were working on obtaining one (in a few cases, a second master's degree); and 34 alumnae (24 percent) were either working on or had received a Ph.D., J.D., or M.D., in many cases after already having a master's degree. Alumnae of Middlebury were the most likely of all alumnae to be involved in the highest reaches of postgraduate education; 38 percent of Middlebury alumnae had obtained or were obtaining Ph.D.s, J.D.s, or M.D.s, compared to 24 percent of Hamilton alumnae, 23 percent of Wells alumnae, and 9 percent of William Smith alumnae.[3]

It is not so surprising that alumnae of Middlebury were pursuing the highest academic degrees, as they did the best academically while undergraduates; i.e., Middlebury had the greatest percentage of seniors who graduated with honors or were elected to Phi Beta Kappa.[4] What seems in many ways more impressive is the relatively high standing of Wells alumnae given their family backgrounds: only slightly more than one-quarter (27 percent) of Wells alumnae's fathers had graduate or professional degrees, compared to about 50 percent (between 47 and 59 percent) of the fathers of other colleges' alumnae. Women who chose to attend the women's college, Wells, appear to have been highly academically motivated, as evidenced by their initially very high academic goals, discussed in Chapter 8. It is interesting to learn that having high academic goals as entering students has quite a strong positive relationship to pursuing such goals ten years later.[5] Not only did young women come to Wells planning to obtain much more education than had their parents,[6] but they experienced a college environment that encouraged, or at least did not discourage, such ambitions.[7] Wells alumnae were the most likely to report having women professors at their undergraduate college as mentors or role models (discussed below), and having such mentors has a slight positive relationship to alumnae's post-graduate education. Similarly, Wells alumnae were the most likely to say that their college encouraged their career choices, and this again is slightly related to having gotten or working on postgraduate degrees.[8]

Other variables that I found to be significantly related to alumnae's pursuit of postgraduate education were how well they did academically while at college and the encouragement and praise they received from faculty. The correlation between being on the Dean's List often and postgraduate education was stronger,[9] but faculty encouragement also had an important effect on students' decisions to continue their education.[10] Moreover, each of these variables had an independent effect on pursuit of further education, as controlling for the effect of the other variable had little effect on the strength of the relationships.

Alumnae's Mentors

Overall, 63 percent of the alumnae said that role models or mentors had affected their career choice or career path, a percentage that was not significantly affected by the undergraduate college these women had attended (see Table 10.2). I asked those alumnae who indicated that mentors had had an effect on their careers to indicate who these mentors were. I gave them fourteen category choices, all identified by gender, as well as an "other" category, from which they could choose as few or as many mentors as they believed had affected their careers (see Table 10.2). In order of frequency of choice of mentor, alumnae checked: mother, father, female college professor, other, male college professor, male partner or husband, female employer, older woman, female graduate school professor, female public figure, male graduate school professor, male employer, older man, male public figure. No alumna checked a female partner as a mentor. The list of frequencies shows the strong influence of parents on young college-educated women's careers and perhaps not surprisingly, the greater influence of women than men in virtually any given category (for example, alumnae mentioned female college professor more than male college professor, older woman more than older man).

When I examined the use of specific types of mentors for each college's alumnae, I found that the alumnae of Wells differed most from the alumnae of the three other colleges in saying that women college professors served as their mentors or role models (50 percent of Wells alumnae said

TABLE 10.2 Alumnae's Mentors

Have role models or mentors affected career choice or path?

	Frequencies	Percentages
YES	94	63%
NO	55	37%

Description of who these mentors were

	Frequencies	Percentages
Mother	33	35%[1]
Father	31	33%
Female college professor	25	27%
Male college professor	22	23%
Female partner	0	0%
Male partner/husband	20	21%
Female employer	20	21%
Male employer	11	12%
Female public figure	14	15%
Male public figure	2	2%
Female grad school professor	17	18%
Male grad school professor	11	12%
Older woman	23	24%
Older man	12	13%
Other than on list	20	21%

Gender of Mentors by College Attended

	Wells	Middlebury	Wm Smith	Hamilton
Only women	36%	15%	24%	20%
Mixed sex	60%	74%	60%	40%
Only men	5%	11%	16%	40%
	101%	100%	100%	100%
	(22)	(27)	(25)	(20)

Chi-square = 13.56, df = 6, p = .03

How Undergraduate College Affected Career Choice

	Wells	Middlebury	Wm Smith	Hamilton
Encouraged	63%	43%	56%	36%
Focused	9%	11%	6%	14%
Did not affect	25%	36%	35%	44%
Discouraged	3%	9%	3%	6%
	100%	99%	100%	100%

Chi-square NS but Spearman's (with colleges coded 1 = Wells,
2 = Wm Sm, 3 = Hamil, 4 = Midd) = −.17, sig. = .02

TABLE 10.2 Continued

Used "old girls" network to further career?

	Wells	Middlebury	Wm Smith	Hamilton
YES	24%	11%	23%	8%

Chi-square NS but Spearman's = −.16, sig. = .03, with coding as above

[1]Percentages are based on the 94 alumnae who said they did have mentors.

this, compared to 26 percent of Middlebury alumnae and about 16 percent of both William Smith and Hamilton alumnae).[11] When they were still undergraduates, Wells (and William Smith) students had not differed much from students at the other two colleges in their admiration for (just) women faculty, but they were less likely than students at Middlebury and Hamilton to say that they admired or were close to (only) men faculty. Six years later, women who had graduated from Wells and William Smith were still slightly less likely to say that male college professors had been mentors (12 percent and 14 percent said this, respectively, compared to 25 percent of Hamilton alumnae and 41 percent of Middlebury alumnae).[12]

Middlebury alumnae were significantly more likely than the alumnae of the other colleges to say that female, as well as male, graduate school professors have served as their mentors. Middlebury alumnae's use of graduate school professors is partly, but not entirely, explained by a greater percentage of them having taken courses in graduate school. While 89 percent of Middlebury alumnae had taken at least some graduate courses by the fall of 1994, compared to 73 percent of Wells alumnae, 66 percent of Hamilton alumnae, and 57 percent of William Smith alumnae, their use of graduate school professors as mentors was much greater than these percentage differences would suggest. Forty-one percent of Middlebury's alumnae said that they had female graduate school professors as mentors, compared to only 14 percent of the next highest alumnae group, Wells. Similarly but less striking, 26 percent of Middlebury alumnae, compared to 14 percent or fewer of the alumnae of the other three colleges, said that male graduate professors served as mentors for their careers.[13] Given that Middlebury is the most academically selective of these four colleges, it may be that Middlebury's alumnae are more serious about their graduate education and thus find it more important to have mentors.

To determine if women who graduated from Wells and William Smith were more likely than the graduates of the coeducational colleges,

Middlebury and Hamilton, to have women as mentors, I grouped alumnae's mentors into three categories: all women, mixed-sex, and all men (see Table 10.2). Alumnae of Wells were significantly more likely to have just women as mentors (more than one-third did), and least likely to have only men mentors. William Smith alumnae were similar, although the tendencies were less pronounced (and in fact, a lower percentage of Middlebury alumnae than William Smith alumnae had only men as mentors). A high percentage of Hamilton alumnae (40 percent) had just men as mentors, whereas almost three-quarters of Middlebury alumnae had both men and women mentors.

I asked alumnae two other questions about influences on their career paths: (1) whether their undergraduate college had encouraged, focused, not affected, or discouraged their career choice, and (2) if they had used an "old girls' network" to further their careers (see Table 10.2). Overall 49 percent (of the 146 alumnae who answered this question) said that their college had encouraged their career choice; alumnae of Wells and William Smith were the most likely to report that they had been encouraged (63 percent of Wells and 56 percent of William Smith alumnae, compared to 43 percent of Middlebury alumnae and 36 percent of Hamilton alumnae).[14] This is one indication that in comparison to coeducational college, the women's (and coordinate) colleges provide women students with more "social capital," that is, support, encouragement, and attention that they can then use in pursuit of their own goals (see Riordan 1994, 503-4, for a discussion of this concept).

Only 16 percent of all the alumnae said that they had used an "old girls' network" to further their career, but the percentage of both Wells and William Smith alumnae who had (24 and 23 percent, respectively) was somewhat higher than the percentages of Middlebury and Hamilton alumnae (11 and 8 percent, respectively).[15] When alumnae were asked who was in this "old girls' network"—was it college alumnae, the college placement office, business and professional women, graduate school classmates, or friends—the highest number of alumnae (17) checked business and professional women; only between 5 and 8 alumnae checked the other groups.

In summary, a majority of these 149 alumnae had used mentors in establishing themselves in careers. A significant proportion (over two-fifths) of their mentors were parents or undergraduate college professors. Alumnae from the women's college, Wells, and to a somewhat lesser extent, alumnae of the coordinate college, William Smith, differed from alumnae of the coeducational colleges in being more likely to turn to other women for inspiration or career advice. Middlebury alumnae were the most likely to have mentors, both male and female professors, from graduate school.

Alumnae's Retrospective Views of Their College Experiences

Six years after they graduated from college, these young women appeared to look back favorably on their time in college. Many more of the experiences they were questioned about—friendships, coursework, relations with faculty and administration, co-curricular activities, campus events, off-campus study—were rated positively than negatively.[16] In fact, alumnae gave more than twice as many positive ratings to their colleges than negative ones: 269 to 124. There were few differences by college attended; as discussed below, only coursework and relations with faculty and administration differed in positive evaluations according to which college alumnae had attended.

The aspect of college that alumnae rated most positively was friendship, said to be a positive experience by 127 alumnae or 85 percent (see Table 10.3). Alumnae of all four colleges were about equally likely to see their college friendships as positive. The enduring nature of friendships formed during college was a common theme—"friends I will have forever," as one alumna wrote. Many alumnae attributed beneficial changes in themselves during college to the influence of friends. Some said that they had learned about themselves through their friends or that they had learned to become sociable. Others believed that it was their friends who inspired them or made them motivated to study—"Having a good circle of good friends who were good students helped *me* to be motivated"—or in one interesting case, led the student to become a "strong" woman:

> I met a lot of independent "strong" women at school with whom I am still friends. I don't think I was a "strong" woman while attending college, but I have become that person over the years and now look back at college and see how that shaped me . . . [William Smith alumna]

Many alumnae mentioned that they felt more comfortable with the students they met in college than they had with peers in high school. "Fitting in" due to shared interests with other intelligent people appears to have been an important reason friendships were frequently a positive aspect of college:

> I made a lot of smart, interesting and wonderful friends who continue to be my closest friends today. [Middlebury alumna]

TABLE 10.3 Alumnae's Retrospective Views of Their College Experiences

| | Alumnae who saw this aspect as: | | | |
| | Positive | | Negative | |
A. Six Aspects of College	Number	%	Number	%
1. Friendships & social life	127	85%	42	28%
2. Courses	91	61%	23	15%
3. Relations with faculty/admin.	67	45%[1]	21	14%
4. Co-curricular activities	58	39%	12	8%
5. Off-campus study	41	28%	5	3%
6. Campus events	12	8%	21	14%

B. Would alumnae attend the same college again?

YES	100	68%
UNSURE	37	25%
NO	11	7%

C. How well did college prepare alumnae for the following kinds of post-college experiences?

| | Good Preparation | | Inadequate Preparation | | Not Relevant | |
	No.	%	No.	%	No.	%
Further education	121	82%	8	5%	18	12%
Technical requirements of jobs	94	64%	25	17%	28	19%
Dealing with sexist attitudes or sex discrimination	88	62%	32	22%	23	16%[2]

[1]Alumnae differed significantly by college: 70% of Wells alums described their relations with faculty and administration as positive, compared to 43% at William Smith, 38% at Middlebury, and 33% at Hamilton (chi-square = 11.13, df = 3, p = .01).

[2]Alumnae differed significantly by college, with the following percentages from each college saying that their preparation for dealing with sexist attitudes was good: 90% of Wells alumnae, 90% of William Smith alumnae, 77% of Hamilton alumnae, and 41% of Middlebury alumnae (chi-square = 26.67, df = 3, p = .000).

Friendships—did not fit in well in high school, felt much more comfortable with college friends. [Middlebury alumna]

Friendships had also been positive, according to alumnae, in helping them weather periods of stress, or in cases where they perceived themselves to be different from the majority of students, in enabling them to get the support they needed for their minority views:

Being a Christian was difficult at a secular college . . . Hobart & William Smith Christian Fellowship was a place I made wonderful friends. They were encouraging and there to laugh, cry, and pray with.

> Being "pres" of Jewish group helped me again be a minority in a mostly Catholic [sic] town. [Wells alumna]

Not only were friendships the aspect of college that alumnae rated the most highly; they were also the aspect of college that more alumnae rated negatively than any of the other five aspects of college they were asked about, and again, this did not vary significantly by college attended. Forty-two alumnae or 28 percent rated friendships in college negatively, although many of these alumnae also had positive things to say about friendship—only 11 alumnae (7 percent) felt that friendship had been a solely negative aspect of their college experiences. One of the most common reasons given for friendships being a negative experience, at all colleges except Wells, was the difficulty some alumnae had had in "fitting in" since most students were from wealthy families and/or had different interests.[17] In this connection, alumnae frequently mentioned their negative reactions to others' drinking or taking drugs:

> I had only 1 close friend throughout my 4 years. I didn't fit in with typical Hamilton students. I didn't party or drink. Didn't come from a wealthy or upper middle class family . . .

> *Too* much socializing, *too* clique-oriented. Large populations of wealthy students . . . dry cleaning socks, etc. so the campus had an air of non-reality. [William Smith alumna]

Related to feeling that they could not make friends because they did not "fit in" was the belief that friendships were hampered because their college was comprised of "cliques":

> Middlebury was extremely clique oriented, socially. A lot of people made friends on their freshman hall and never expanded from there . . .

A few alumnae, one at each college with men students, mentioned that they had had unpleasant experiences with men on their campus. A William Smith student, for instance, talked about the "negative" experiences she had had with some "butt-headed" men, while a Middlebury student said:

> I didn't make any male friends and had almost no boyfriends. I found most of the men at Middlebury chauvinistic and difficult to get along with.

The aspect of college that was rated most positively after friendships was coursework, seen to be positive by 91 alumnae or 61 percent. Alumnae from Middlebury were slightly more likely to rate this aspect of college positively than alumnae of the other colleges (76 percent of Middlebury alumnae vs. 61 percent of Wells, 54 percent of William Smith, and 50 percent of Hamilton alumnae).[18] Comments from alumnae of all colleges on their courses stressed how "challenging" and "interesting" they found classes, and how they were exposed to "new ideas" that they found to be "broadening" or that stimulated their "intellectual growth." Some alumnae talked about their courses as good preparation for their careers or for further study; others mentioned more general skills that they learned, such as how to think or organize their thoughts or even the self-confidence they gained from being able to do the challenging work. Quite a few alumnae mentioned the value of small classes; one alumna said that discussions had enabled her to get over her fear of giving the wrong answer and her fear of speaking in public. Most alumnae did not mention specific courses, but one noted that writing her senior thesis gave her a "sense of accomplishment."

Courses were also rated second in *negative* aspects of college by the alumnae, although many fewer alumnae, 23 or 15 percent, rated courses negatively than positively, and this did not vary by which college alumnae had attended. One negative aspect that alumnae mentioned was that the courses had little bearing on their lives after college or were too "ivory tower." Some alumnae blamed themselves for finding courses uninteresting; for example, they may have been in the wrong major or they had not studied enough. A few alumnae mentioned not having sufficient selection in courses or that they were unable to take the courses they were interested in due to scheduling problems. One alumna mentioned that courses in her first year were large lecture classes that she did not enjoy, whereas another alumna said that she found discussion courses intimidating and never felt comfortable enough to express her views. Other isolated negative comments were that courses were biased by the "socialistic leanings of professors" (said by only one alumna) and that low grades in science courses damaged one alumna's self-esteem.

The aspect of college that alumnae rated third, both in positive experiences at college as well as in negative experiences, was relations with faculty and administration. Sixty-seven alumnae (45 percent) rated their relations as positive; twenty-one (14 percent) rated them negatively. Alumnae of Wells were significantly more likely than alumnae of the other three colleges to rate their relations with faculty and administration as positive; 70 percent of Wells alumnae rated their relations positively, compared to between 33 and 43 percent at the other colleges.[19]

When these same young women were undergraduates, as I mentioned in Chapter 9, both Wells and William Smith students reported that faculty and administrators were supportive of them, but six years later, graduates of Wells stood out in terms of recalling their relations with college authorities in a positive way. Part of the reason students at Wells were so positive may have been their ability to form close relations with faculty because the college is so small. It is also possible that Wells alumnae felt positively about faculty and administrators because as students, they were not in competition with men students for attention and because there were so many women on the faculty. A factor that affected all alumnae's ratings of faculty and administrators was their academic performance as students. Alumnae who had graduated with higher final GPAs were more likely to give faculty and administration positive ratings.[20]

Alumnae who rated faculty and administrators positively did so because they found them encouraging, inspiring, caring, and helpful. Many alumnae mentioned the advantages of their college's small size and the consequent availability of faculty—"a big big plus," as one alumna wrote. Several alumnae mentioned specific ways faculty had helped them. One alumna mentioned a man professor who had encouraged her in math, which helped her later when she worked in a male-dominated field, as she was then able to remind herself how as a student she did better than many of the men students in her major. Another alumna mentioned that a supportive woman professor had showed her the benefit of making risky choices. Many alumnae remembered how some faculty made learning more interesting and enjoyable. One alumna remembered in particular the relationships she formed with professors in her last two years, which she said brought "learning back to something people do together."

Alumnae who felt that relations with faculty and administrators were a negative part of their college experiences described faculty as inaccessible, aloof, or even "condescending." One alumna recalled a particular professor who had "belittled students," making them "feel like a failure." Several alumnae said that they had not formed relations with faculty because as students they were shy or insufficiently confident. Some regretted that they had not had mentors, as they believed they would have achieved more if they had. Negative attitudes toward administrators often appeared to hinge on a particular incident. One alumna, for example, said that she did not receive support from the administration after an incident with her boyfriend but rather that the administration turned it into a "boys against the girls" issue. Negative views of faculty and administrators, unlike positive views, were not related to college attended, nor to how good students the alumnae were.

Co-curricular activities were mentioned as a postive part of college life by 58 alumnae, or 39 percent. They were seen negatively by only 12 alumnae or 8 percent (see Table 10.3). Campus clubs and sports appeared to have been valued not only because they were fun and a way of making new friends, but also because they helped develop self-confidence, discipline, leadership abilities, and organizing skills. Occasionally campus activities led students to develop specific interests with career relevance. One student who did community work while at college, for example, later went into the social work field. Another student who was involved in campus-related political organizing became committed to political work, which she believed was critical for her winning a national fellowship for study in Latin America. An alumna from Wells was positive about the college's co-curricular activities because they enabled young women to excel regardless of their social backgrounds, which she had found not to be the case in high school when she lost elections each year to some "rich kid": "At Wells economic status never mattered. Through clubs and offices I fine-tuned my speaking abilities and self-confidence."

The few alumnae who recalled co-curricular activities as a negative aspect of college life often referred to their own failures; they did not feel comfortable with the kinds of people who joined the clubs they were interested in, for example, or they did not play a particular sport well.[21] In a few cases alumnae recalled negative aspects to the competition of athletic teams, in one instance due to peer pressure to be "cool" and drink. One alumna from Wells said that activities had been too small and too experimental, not stable enough. On the other hand, another alumna from Wells said that there were too many options and it was too hard to choose.

Off-campus study was viewed as a positive aspect of their college experiences by 41 alumnae or 28 percent; only 5 alumnae had anything negative to say about off-campus study, and three of those responses were unclear. When alumnae mentioned off-campus study, they usually were referring to study in a foreign country but sometimes also described internships or study in other institutions in the United States. Alumnae wrote that they had benefited from study abroad by becoming more independent, mature, and self-confident. "Friendships and semester abroad gave me confidence and the feeling that I can survive on my own (especially with my friends behind me)." A few alumnae attributed their career interests to their experiences abroad, for instance, one spent time as a student in the Indian subcontinent, and later went into the Peace Corps and decided she wanted to become a nurse. Even those alumnae whose off-campus study had been at another college or university in the United

States found the differences with their alma mater "broadening." All the alumnae who mentioned internships as part of their off-campus study experiences said that they were useful for exploring their career interests.

The sixth and final aspect of college alumnae were asked about was campus events. Not only did the fewest number of alumnae rate this aspect of college positively, with only 12 alumnae or 8 percent doing so, but this was the only aspect of college life they were questioned about in which negative ratings exceeded the positive ones—21 alumnae or 14 percent said that campus events had been a negative aspect of college life. This category is difficult to interpret, however, as alumnae seemed to interpret "campus events" in a variety of different ways.

Most comments written in on the questionnaires were not specific about the positive aspects of campus events, with one exception in which an alumna wrote that they were "diversions" that helped to "round" her out. On the other hand, many comments on the negative aspects were specific but very varied. Hamilton alumnae tended to complain about the "frat scene" and the stress on alcohol. One Hamilton alumna also mentioned her dissatisfaction that sports were emphasized, and not the arts, which she was more interested in. A Middlebury alumna gave a long, moving description of campus reactions to the notorious "mannequin" incident, described in Chapter 9 and later in this chapter, in which a mutilated female mannequin was hung in effigy during a fraternity party. She and some friends went to a meeting about this issue in which administrators were supposed to speak but did not show up. This alumna wrote about how upset she and her friends were with the reactions of some of the men students at the meeting, who demonstrated their "unwillingness or inability to understand a female point of view, to listen to the women who had been offended." Three Wells alumnae were quite damning about their college's small size, and two also mentioned the negative aspects of being a women's college. "Socially, Wells was disabled because men often did not attend our events and, if they did, we had to defend our choice to be at a women's college." Only a couple of William Smith alumnae commented in this section of the questionnaire; they remarked on the pressure to drink, do foolish things, and to have a boyfriend.

Overall, however, alumnae's generally positive views of their college experiences were evident from their response to a question about whether they would attend the same college again. Slightly more than two-thirds (68 percent) said yes without any qualifications, one-quarter were not sure, and only 7 percent said no (see Table 10.3), and these percentages did not vary significantly by college. A few alumnae wrote in comments about why they were unsure or would not attend the same college again. Many thought they might have been happier in a large college with more diverse students. Wells alumnae were the most likely to use the term "isolated" and to express dissatisfaction with this aspect of their college. "I question the social value of ISOLATED single-sex schools," was the way one Wells alumna expressed it. Several alumnae from Hamilton and Middlebury said that they might have done better at a women's college, one basing her comment on the very positive experiences she had had as a graduate student at Smith College. Interestingly, one alumna from Hamilton said that she thought she might have "taken more chances" at a women's college, suggesting that the coeducational environment had circumscribed her behavior or perhaps her course and extracurricular selections. One Middlebury alumna said that if she did attend again, she would be "more challenging and vociferous against the status quo and old-boy atmosphere . . . I was extremely naive."

The surveys also asked alumnae whether they thought that their college had prepared them for three kinds of possible postcollege experiences: further education, technical requirements of jobs, and dealing with sexist attitudes or discrimination that they had faced as women (see Table 10.3). More than four-fifths of the alumnae felt that college had prepared them well for further education. While a majority, almost two-thirds, also believed that they had been well-prepared for the technical requirements of jobs, some felt that they had had insufficient training in computers, and others were unsure whether a liberal arts education was capable of giving students good technical training.

A majority of the alumnae, 62 percent, believed that their college had prepared them well for dealing with the sexism they have since encountered, but this varied significantly by college attended, with Middlebury alumnae being the least likely by far to say that they had been well-prepared (only 41 percent of Middlebury alumnae felt their preparation in this area had been good, compared to 90 percent of both Wells and William Smith alumnae, and 77 percent of Hamilton alumnae).[22] While many alumnae expressed doubts about whether workshops, seminars, or even speakers on the topic of sexism could help much, they still tended to feel that their colleges, especially Middlebury, could have done more to address this issue. As one Hamilton alumna said, "Being given tools to handle sexism would have helped." A William Smith alumna made an unusual comment: she said that her college "provoked strong female consciousness," which she judged to be good, yet she felt that having professors who were "highly sensitive" to women's issues did not prepare her for the "real world," where the majority of people have "never been exposed to Women's Studies." Several Middlebury alumnae remarked that at college they were treated equally to the men students, which is why, combined with a lack of workshops on sex discrimination, they were not prepared for what they experienced after college. As one Middlebury alumna noted, at college the women students were at least equal, if not superior, to the men students, which is probably why "real world" discrimination was "such a slap in the face." A few alumnae from Hamilton and Middlebury said that they thought that today their college was doing more in this area, especially given recent media attention to sexual harassment.

In order to examine how positive alumnae were about their college experiences overall, I created a summary index of the six aspects of college life the questionnaire asked alumnae about (friendships, co-curricular activities, courses, relations with faculty and administrators, campus events, and off-campus study). Possible scores ranged from 0 for those alumnae who did not find any aspects of their college experiences to be positive (no alumnae were so negative, however) to 6 for those who found all aspects positive (one alumna). Scores of 3 and 4 were most frequent (46 alumnae each). The alumnae did not differ significantly on this index according to which college they had attended, but Middlebury and Wells alumnae were slightly more positive (with average scores of 2.87 and 2.79, respectively) than William Smith and Hamilton alumnae (2.60 and 2.33 averages, respectively). Alumnae who had done well academically when they were students, in terms of having been on the Dean's List often, were most positive about their college experiences. Those who as seniors said they had close relations with many faculty, and those women who had played active, leadership roles in campus organizations, were also slightly more likely to be positive.[23]

In summary, alumnae's retrospective evaluations of their time in college fit with other research showing that students from small colleges are generally satisfied with their relations with faculty and with their instruction (Astin, 1977, 230) and that the more involved students are in campus life, the more satisfied they are (Pascarella and Terenzini 1991, 379). There were only a few statistically significant differences in alumnae's evaluations according to which college they attended, with Middlebury's alumnae being slightly more positive about their coursework but more negative about their perceived lack of preparation for handling sexism in the world at large, and Wells's alumnae being more positive about their relations with faculty and administrators.

Alumnae's Self-Esteem, Attitudes Toward Feminism, and Gender-Role Attitudes

Self-Esteem

The alumnae of these four colleges had, on the whole, high self-esteem. I measured their self-esteem by presenting them with several statements to which they could agree strongly, agree, disagree, or disagree strongly. More than a majority agreed strongly with the statements, "I have much to be proud of about myself" (57 percent) and "I have many good qualities" (61 percent). Slightly less than a majority of alumnae (46 percent) agreed strongly with the statement, "On the whole, I am satisfied with myself" (see Table 10.4).

TABLE 10.4 Attitudes of Alumnae Toward Self, Feminism, Women's Movement, and Gender Roles

A. Self-Esteem	Agree Strongly	Agree	Disagree	Disagree Strongly
I have much to be proud of about myself.	57%	37%	5%	1%
I have many good qualities.	61%	39%	0%	0%
On the whole, I am satisfied with myself.	45%	48%	5%	2%

B. Feminist Views by College Attended	Wells	Middlebury	Wm Smith	Hamilton
1. Percent of alumnae con- sidering themselves feminists	73%	70.5%	70%	56%
2. Alumnae's support of the women's movement				
Does not support—women & men inherently different	0%	4.5%	6%	0%
Does not support—unnecessary today	9%	2%	0%	3%
Supports parts	50%	48%	67%	63%
Supports all or virtually all aims	41%	45.5%	27%	34%
3. Gender-role attitudes, truncated index, for same students as first-year students, sophomores, seniors, and alumnae, by college[1]				
When alumnae were first-year college students	6.9	7.4	7.1	7.0
When alumnae were sophomores	8.1	7.3	7.9	7.1
When alumnae were seniors	9.1	8.1	8.3	8.3
As alumnae	13.1	13.6	12.4	12.9[2]

[1]Mean score on an index of 4–16, with higher numbers indicating more liberal gender-role attitudes

[2]$F_{(3.138)}$ = 2.98, significance=.03.

Although as undergraduates, women students at Wells were the most likely to increase in self-esteem during their college years, as alumnae's views of themselves did not vary by college attended. A few of the experiences these alumnae had had at college were related to their self-esteem six years later, however. Moreover, some of the same factors that were important for self-esteem when these women were undergraduates were still significant six years later.[24] In particular, women who had been more active in college activities while undergraduates, those who as seniors had become close to some faculty members, and those who felt that some members of the college community, particularly women administrators or men faculty, had been concerned with their needs as women students, were somewhat more likely to have higher self-esteem as alumnae.[25]

I had expected that those alumnae who were earning the most money or who had achieved advanced degrees to have the highest self-esteem, but this was not the case. Use of an "old girls' network" was slightly related to the alumnae's self-confidence (and Wells and William Smith alumnae were the most likely to have used such contacts). This relation between network use and self-esteem is related to the apparent importance of friendship for self-esteem. Alumnae who said that friendship was very important in their lives at the present time and who said that they saw college friends at least once a year tended to be alumnae with the highest self-esteem.[26] It is impossible to know from these data whether women who had high self-esteem were more confident about making and sustaining friendships, or whether women who valued and maintained friendships became more confident through these relationships. It seems likely that it works both ways, with friendships both a cause and an effect of self-esteem.

Views about Women's Issues

In Chapters 8 and 9 I discussed how as entering students, a greater percentage of young women who attended Wells considered themselves feminists than the women who attended the other three colleges. By the last semester of their senior year, William Smith students had "caught up" with Wells students, by which time the percentages who called themselves feminists at each college were as follows: 79 percent of Wells seniors and 76 percent of William Smith seniors, compared to 50 percent of Hamilton seniors and 45.5 percent of Middlebury seniors.

When they were surveyed six years after graduation, however, the situation had changed (see Table 10.4). Now alumnae of Middlebury were just about as likely as those of Wells and William Smith to call themselves feminists (73 percent of Wells, 70.5 percent of Middlebury, 70 percent of William Smith, and 56 percent of Hamilton alumnae considered themselves to be feminists). The increase of Middlebury graduates who considered themselves feminists was not due simply to more feminists from the senior year having answered the alumnae questionnaire. The number of graduates who had changed from being non-feminist in their senior year to feminist six years later was greater for Middlebury graduates (12) than for students at the other three colleges (4 from Wells, 3 from William Smith, and 5 from Hamilton).

In terms of their support for the women's movement, over 90 percent of alumnae said they supported its aims, at least in part. Although the differences in support by college attended were not significant, a slightly higher percentage of Middlebury alumnae than alumnae of the other colleges said they supported all of the aims of the women's movement (see Table 10.4). Similar to the finding about self-identification as a feminist, the attitudes of Middlebury women changed most after they left college, since when they were seniors, a lower percentage of Middlebury women than women at the other three colleges supported all the aims of the women's movement (see Graph 9.4 in Chapter 9).

I measured the gender-role attitudes of alumnae in a more truncated manner than I had when these women were undergraduates, using only four of the original eighteen Likert-type statements: (1) Swearing and obscenity are more repulsive in the speech of a woman than a man (reverse coding); (2) Among heterosexual couples, men should take the same amount of responsibility as women in caring for home and children;[27] (3) Women with preschool children should not work—if at all possible (reverse coding); and (4) Women earning as much as their men dates should bear equally the expense when they go out.[28] By summing the answers to each of these statements, I created indices of gender-role attitudes, for the college years as well as for alumnae, with higher numbers indicating more liberal or contemporary attitudes.[29]

Comparing the average scores on the gender-role index for the same women when they were first-year students, sophomores, seniors, and then alumnae, I found a linear positive change, with the average score of first-year students being 7.11 (out of a possible 16); that of sophomores, 7.55; seniors, 8.4; and alumnae, a very high 13.0. When the young women were undergraduates, there were no significant differences in average scores by college attended, although for the sophomore year and senior year scores, alumnae who had attended Wells had somewhat higher averages (see Table 10.4). But among the alumnae, average scores did differ significantly according to which college the women had attended, and the women who had attended Middlebury had the most liberal scores.[30] Thus gender-role attitudes follow a pattern similar to that of self-identification as a feminist and support of the women's movement—six years after graduation alumnae of Middlebury had changed the most, which in the case of gender-role attitudes, led them to surpass those of Wells. The similarity among these patterns is not surprising, since alumnae who considered themselves feminists had the most liberal gender-role attitudes, an average gender-role attitudes index score of 13.44, compared to 12.15 for the non-feminists,[31] and self-identification as a feminist is also strongly related to support of the women's movement.[32]

Alumnae's gender-role attitudes were not related to their family backgrounds (parents' education or occupation), but they were weakly related both to where alumnae themselves had been heading as seniors in terms of their educational goals and the amount of postgraduate education they had had when surveyed as alumnae.[33] Alumnae's gender-role attitudes were strongly related to their general political views, with liberal alumnae being much more likely than conservative alumnae to have contemporary gender-role attitudes.[34] In contrast, those alumnae who said religion was very important to them were more likely to have conservative gender-role attitudes, as I expected since religious teachings reinforce the view that men are superior to or at least have different roles to play than do women. Alumnae's gender-role attitudes were also slightly related to two experiences from their undergraduate years: their involvement in and leadership of campus organizations and their having taken courses that dealt with issues pertaining to women.[35] The correlations with alumnae's educational goals and achievement, and more weakly, with their activities at college, suggest that education, broadly conceived, has affected alumnae's attitudes toward men's and women's roles—not only formal educational attainment, but also the kind of learning that comes from participating in and leading organizations. More educated and active alumnae tend to have gender-role attitudes that "match" their styles of life.

Alumnae's Future Plans

In some ways, the alumnae of these four colleges seem quite traditional in their desired lifestyles. In addition to the 64 alumnae who were married when I surveyed them in 1994, another 65 hoped to get married; in fact, only 4 said they would not like to get married, and 16 were unsure (see

Table 10.5). Also, more than two-thirds of the 126 alumnae who were not pregnant or did not already have children said they wanted to have children. Only a minority (11) were clear that they did not want children, and 27 were unsure.

On the other hand, of the 93 alumnae who answered a question about how they planned to combine employment with children, only a few (4) alumnae said they intended to stay at home indefinitely with their children, and not many more (8) said they would like to stay at home until their children reached school age. The largest number (32) said they planned

TABLE 10.5 Alumnae's Future Plans

A. Toward marriage, children, and employment
1. Of those 86 alumnae not married in 1994[1]
   - 65 hoped to marry
   - 16 were unsure
   - 4 did not want to marry

2. Of those 126 alumnae without children in 1994
   - 88 wanted to have children sometime
   - 27 were unsure
   - 11 did not want to have children

3. How alumnae planned to combine children and employment[2]
   - 32 planned to work full-time after a short period off
   - 16 planned to work part-time after a short period off
   - 8 planned to work full-time after a year or so off
   - 14 planned to work part-time after a year or so off
   - 8 planned to stay at home until children reached school age
   - 4 planned to stay at home indefinitely
   - 11 had other ideas

B. Work-Related Goals
The importance to alumnae, on a scale of 1 to 6, with 6 being most important, of:

	Mean score
1. Having work that is important and interesting	5.6
2. Having the freedom to make their own decisions	5.6
3. Being successful in their line of work	5.3
4. Having lots of money	3.8
5. Job security and permanence	4.6

[1]There was one missing answer to this question.
[2]These frequencies are based on 93 alumnae. Those 11 alumnae who said they did not want children were not expected to answer this question. Some of those who were unsure if they wanted children chose not to answer. On the other hand, some alumnae who already had children did answer this question.

to return to full-time employment after only a short time off after the birth of their children, with the next largest number (16) saying they intended to return to part-time work shortly after their children were born. Twenty-two planned to return to work either full-time or part-time after a year or so off. Eleven alumnae could not put their ideas into one of these categories, many because they felt that what they would do depended on their financial situation. Some had more specific ideas. One Middlebury alumna said, for example, that as an academic she hoped to plan childbirth to have a summer and semester off, then get part-time day care and work at home whenever possible. She also thought research fellowships might enable her to work at home. A William Smith alumna mentioned wanting to stay at home and start her own business when she had her "next child." Admittedly, these women who had definite ideas may not do exactly what they think they will after having children (*if* they have them), since it is always difficult to predict later life circumstances. Yet the reality of both parents' needing to work, as evidenced by today's statistics, appears to have been recognized by these women as they think about their lives in the future.

I asked alumnae to indicate how important the following five work-related goals were to them: having work that is important and interesting, having the freedom to make their own decisions, being successful in their line of work, having lots of money, and having job security and permanence. The alumnae rated each goal on a scale of one to six, with one being unimportant and six being very important (see Table 10.5). Two of these goals were equally very important to these women—having the freedom to make their own decisions (with a mean score of 5.6) and having important and interesting work (also mean of 5.6). Being successful in their work ranked third, with a mean of 5.3. The other two goals received much lower mean ratings: having job security (mean = 4.6) and last of all, having "lots of money" (mean = 3.8).

For three of these five work-related goals, the alumnae gave statistically significant different answers depending on the college they had attended. Specifically, women who attended Middlebury rated having lots of money and job security as less important goals than did the alumnae of the other three colleges.[36] On the other hand, the alumnae of Hamilton gave interesting work a lower rating than did the alumnae at the other three colleges.[37] While it is difficult to understand the last finding, the other two appear to be related to Middlebury students' academic achievements, that is, students who as undergraduates had done well academically tended not to consider being financially successful or having a secure, permanent job as very important.[38] Rating job security as important was also weakly related to alumnae's having less advantaged backgrounds, which is understandable—if someone's background has been financially difficult, she may well care about making her future secure.[39] The other three goals seem to characterize alumnae who were ambitious as undergraduates: caring about having interesting work, being free to make their own decisions, and being successful were all positively correlated with these women's academic goals when they were seniors.[40]

Thus it appears that a majority of the alumnae of these four colleges see their future lives as involving careers, mostly in combination with having children. They would like to work at interesting jobs in which they have autonomy, and they would like to be successful at their work, but they are less concerned about their jobs being secure or having high salaries. Of course, when these women were surveyed, they were still quite young, generally under thirty; their priorities may change as their family responsibilities increase.

Summary: Alumnae Survey

College seems to have had a generally leveling effect on the women who graduated from these four colleges. Rather than finding correlations between alumnae's family backgrounds and what they were doing six years after graduation, I found that how well these young women did in college and the kind of encouragement they received from faculty mattered the most in terms of their pursuit of advanced degrees. Women who attended Wells had family backgrounds distinctly different from those of students at the other three colleges, in that their parents were much less likely to have graduated from college or to have professional or high-status occupations. Yet graduates of Wells were involved in advanced education at a level equal to graduates of Hamilton and only slightly behind women graduates of Middlebury, the most academically selective of the four colleges.

The alumnae surveys did not show many differences in alumnae's lives, attitudes, or goals according to which college they had attended. This would seem to indicate that the benefits of attending a women's college are mostly limited to the time when women are actually in college. And yet I would agree with Stoecker and Pascarella (1991a)—who, like me, studied alumnae who had been out of college for only six years—that differences may appear later. The alumnae of my study had not yet established themselves in careers, so it is probably too soon to determine if there are long-term benefits to single-sex education as Tidball and others have argued (see Chapter 7). Two of the few differences that did emerge showed that women who had attended Wells and William Smith were slightly more likely to say that they had used an "old girls' network" to further their careers and that their colleges had prepared them well for dealing with sexism. But the alumnae of Middlebury were perhaps the most surprising in the degree to which they changed their attitudes toward women's issues. Despite their lack of preparation for dealing with sexism, and despite the few courses in women's issues they had taken as undergraduates (see Chapter 9), a large majority of Middlebury alumnae defined themselves as feminists and had liberal gender-role attitudes. One reason for this surprising finding is that Middlebury alumnae were the most involved in postgraduate education, which seems to make women supportive of women's issues.

The Four Colleges in the '90s: Better Places for Women?

In this part of the chapter, I discuss major developments at each of the colleges in the decade since these alumnae graduated. Specifically, I am concerned with the issues that I identified in Chapter 6 as being problematic in the mid-1980s for each college, namely enrollment and financial difficulties at Wells, and the dominance of men students and fraternities at the other three colleges. I also consider whether alumnae's concerns about their college experiences have been addressed in any way.

Wells College

Wells College in the 1990s has continued to struggle for survival. As Table 10.6 on page shows, enrollment declined a further 25 percent between 1990 and 1998. Too few students has created other problems, not only financial difficulties, with almost every admitted student receiving financial aid, but also other, more indirect problems. The turnover in top administrators has been high, for example, probably related to the difficulties of governing in times of crisis, and the tendency to seek a scapegoat when programs are cut or unpopular initiatives taken.

The class of 1988 at Wells graduated just after a new president, Dr. Irene Hecht, had taken office. About two years later, Dr. Hecht was forced to resign as a result of overwhelming votes of no confidence by faculty, staff, and students. Dr. Hecht's short tenure was not characterized by gross malfeasance but rather a management style that was seen as inept—inability to delegate, interference in others' jobs, frenetic but unfocused activities, and no overall plan for turning the college around (Dieckmann 1995, 229–230). The next president, Dr. Robert Plane, was an experienced administrator, having been a provost of Cornell University and the president of Clarkson University. Including the time he served as interim president, he lasted at Wells for about four years, until spring 1995. He stepped down at a time of major student and faculty protests at his insistence that $250,000, translated into five full-time-equivalent faculty positions, be cut from the academic program (*The Onyx*, February 3, 1995, WCA). The trustees appointed the next president, Lisa Marsh Ryerson, without a national search. She was promoted from the position of dean of students at Wells, to which the title of vice-president had been added. President Ryerson has a couple of unusual characteristics: she is the first alumna president, and she does not have the usual academic qualification of a college president, the Ph.D. (her highest degree is an M.A. in reading education). Thus by 1995, seven years after the class of 1988 graduated, Wells College had had three presidents.

Alumnae are playing a prominent role in the college: approximately two-thirds of the trustees of 1997–98 were alumnae; all chairs of the board have been alumnae since 1989, when Janet Taylor Reiche '52 was appointed; between 1994 and 1998, all commencement speakers were alumnae; and as I mentioned above, Wells has its first alumna president. The positive interpretation of such alumnae involvement is that students see the leadership potential of their education, providing them with concrete evidence of the benefits of attending a women's college. Students did protest, however, when President Plane limited their choice of commencement speakers (*The Courier*, October 12, 1994, WCA).[41] Alumnae's loyalty to their alma mater is great, as it is at many women's colleges, and their financial support is important. Wells has been ranked highest in alumnae support per student by *U.S. News and World Report* (*The Onyx*, October 1, 1997, WCA). On the other hand, having alumnae as administrators contributes to some faculty's sense that the college, in a mistaken attempt to be financially prudent, is not always obtaining the best qualified persons. Many key posts, not only the president but also the dean of students and the director of admissions, have been staffed by alumnae or people already at the college. A major exception to this pattern is Dean of Faculty and Vice-President for Academic Affairs, Ellen Hall, who was appointed from a national search after Lisa Ryerson became president. Dean Hall has a Ph.D. in French literature from Bryn Mawr and has not only been a dean at other institutions, but a president of another women's college, Converse College in South Carolina.

Wells College has conducted many studies on ways to increase its revenues and enrollments, some using consultants, others simply in-house. As a result of the report of consultants appointed by President Plane, the number of major fields was reduced from thirty-one to sixteen by combining related areas and making them have an interdisciplinary focus. Wells also established a Women's Leadership Institute, a relatively expensive venture which never had a clear focus. After two years the Women's Leadership Institute was greatly pared down, becoming primarily a summer conference program.

President Ryerson's approach to reviving the college began with a couple of internal committees, but in the fall of 1997, she obtained the backing of the Board of Trustees to spend money to do a much more thorough study of possible options. She appointed a large committee, the Critical Issues and Action Committee (CIAC), comprised of top administrators, staff, trustees, faculty, an alumna, and a student; she hired three different consultant groups; and she gave three faculty members stipends to conduct research requested by the committee. Officially the committee was meant to consider all options, but given that a major Capital Campaign was underway at the same time, and some money had been received with the proviso that the college remain single-sex, it is unlikely that coeducation was ever a real possibility. In fact, a few years earlier, the chair of the board, Shirley Schou Bacot '58, explained to students that coeducation had been rejected because it would not increase revenues, partly because gifts were tied up with the College's remaining single-sex (*The Onyx*, May 17, 1995, WCA). In any event, the major decision reached by CIAC was recommended by one of its consulting groups: "slash" tuition by 30 percent beginning in the fall of 1999. Given that Wells College has subsidized students so heavily, it will not take much increase in enrollment to make up this loss of revenue. Other recommendations of CIAC included more advertising so that Wells will become better known, especially when it reduces its tuition; spending money on academic programs, particularly the well-enrolled education program; and increasing ties with nearby educational institutions, particularly Cornell University.

Students have not been passive actors during this period of uncertainty about the college's future. They protested cuts in academic programs vigorously, pointing to the decline in the "quality" of their education (*The Onyx*, January 17, 1995, WCA). In fact, probably due to student and faculty protests, President Ryerson convinced the board to accept fewer cuts to the academic program than the previous president, Dr. Plane, had intended. On occasion students have formed their own organization to do "their part" in saving the college: raising money, contacting prospective students, even planning to write grant proposals (*The Onyx*, February 3, 1995, WCA). The awareness of Wells's fragile state permeates all parts of the small college. Arguments for developing a softball team, for example, were made on the ground that it would improve both admissions and retention at a time that the college is "desperately seeking ways to attract potential students" (*The Onyx*, November 26, 1996, WCA). Most Wells students seem adamantly opposed to admitting men students as a way of surviving. When the trustees of Mills College in California voted in 1990 to become coeducational, and the women students there erupted in protest (so much so that the trustees rescinded their original decision), Wells students demonstrated in support of their "sisters" and sent them a large signed poster/letter of solidarity. Occasionally, though, at least in the past, letters in the student newspaper have expressed the sentiment that it would be better to admit men than to see the demise of Wells (cf. letters to the editor by Annie Coburn, December 5, 1986 or Lynne Dewhurt's letter, Fall 1987, *The Courier*, WCA).

Women's issues receive a great deal of attention at Wells College. Students have organized their own conference on women's colleges, inviting people from other women's colleges as well as the executive director of the Women's Colleges Coalition, Jadwiga Sebrechts (*The Onyx*, April 3, 1998, WCA). The student newspaper has published a special women's insert that contains articles written by students who have firsthand experience with rape or sexual abuse. The lesbian and bisexual student organization has been strong and visible, sometimes encountering a backlash from other students which, while unfortunate, has provoked lively debate (cf. *The Onyx*, December 7, 1994, WCA). An organization for minority women, using various names, has been active for about thirty years. Like the lesbian and bisexual association, the minority women's organization occasionally encounters criticism for being separatist (*The Onyx*, November 6, 1996, WCA). African-American women have held leadership positions in the student government, but clearly being a student leader in an overwhelmingly white environment can be a strain (*The Onyx*, November 16, 1994, WCA).

Wells students experience their college as supportive of their concerns and interests, as my survey data also indicate. Moreover, many feel they have particularly close ties with their fellow students. Henry Wells's vision for the institution he founded—that it should function as a Christian family—has been updated to fit the late twentieth-century society. One student, Heather Campbell, argued that the college should not be referred to as a "family," because "the family model, especially at the institutional level, is a hierarchical, and inherently patriarchal framework, that is detrimental to women." She advocated instead referring to Wells as a "community" (*The Onyx*, December 7, 1994, WCA). And in fact, terms such as "sisterhood" and "community" appear frequently in the student newspaper. But limited resources affect how well students' interests can be supported, for instance, in the women's studies major. Due to recent faculty cuts, some of the courses required for the major have had to be staffed by adjunct professors.

Governance issues and charges of administrative interference have preoccupied many members of the Wells College community in recent years. Students have raised the issue with respect to what they can publish in their student newspaper. An editor of the student newspaper, Terri Snell, wrote that she was "morally opposed to" administrative involvement in student affairs and that the paper would never portray what the Public Affairs office wanted: the image that Wells is a "flowery package of perfection" (*The Onyx*, April 5, 1995, WCA). Students also protested when the Board of Trustees forced an alumna and a student trustee to resign on the grounds that they had violated trustee responsibilities by their e-mail communication with students (*The Onyx*, October 1, 1997, WCA). Faculty have been concerned by the administration and board's overturning personnel decisions made by faculty committees. A faculty member denied tenure took her case to court, and the court ruled that the College had failed to follow its own rules (*The Onyx*, September 27, 1995, WCA). Although difficult to prove, it does seem possible that the Board and administration have behaved more autocratically given the general sense of crisis.

Whether Wells College can survive in its present form remains uncertain. Many women's colleges have adapted to young women's lack of interest in single-sex education by developing evening and part-time programs. This option is not available to Wells due to its rural, lakeside location and the northeastern climate, which makes travel difficult for about six months of the year. The Board of Trustees hopes that a successful capital campaign, more publicity of the benefits of single-sex education, coupled with strengthening the academic program and making the college more financially attractive by the major reduction in tuition, will end the current fiscal and enrollment crisis.[42]

Middlebury College
As I briefly mentioned at the beginning of Chapter 9, in May 1988, just before women in my sample were about to graduate, but after they had

responded to my last questionnaire, a mutilated female mannequin was hung outside a fraternity house during a party weekend at Middlebury. The fraternity was suspended for two years and ordered to participate in and help organize educational events on sexism and violence against women. But students' reactions swung from outrage immediately after the incident to a majority feeling, a semester later, that the fraternity had been punished too harshly (*Middlebury Magazine*, Winter 1989, MCA). Faculty and administration at Middlebury were less ambivalent, however. The incident inspired them to examine once again the role of fraternities and ultimately to implement programs to address gender inequality.

In the aftermath of the mannequin incident, President Olin Robison appointed a committee to examine "attitudes toward gender." The committee issued a comprehensive and disturbing report that revealed pervasive, but heretofore mostly unacknowledged, gender inequality on campus. While women students generally reported that they felt treated equally to men students in the classroom, their social experiences were dramatically different. Comments on the questionnaire indicated that many women students felt pressured to be thin and beautiful, to accept sexist comments as "jokes," and not to protest at the treatment they received. Seventeen percent of the (228) women student respondents reported having been forced to engage in sexual activity against their will while on a date (compared to only one man student), and even more, 22 percent, said they had been sexually harassed (compared to 8 percent of the 118 men student respondents) (Final Report of the Special Committee on Attitudes Toward Gender, 1990, MCA).

Another major report, released at approximately the same time as the "Gender Report" described above, focused specifically on fraternities at Middlebury, although officially it was a report of the task force on "student social life." After the mannequin incident the faculty voted overwhelmingly to recommend the abolition of fraternities. In comparison, a poll of students taken by the task force working on students' social life indicated that almost half favored maintaining fraternities as they were, and slightly more than one-third wanted them kept but reformed. The task force's report noted that the law raising the drinking age had made fraternities more desirable as a place for parties. Drunkenness and "unacceptable group behavior" in fraternities in turn encouraged sexual harassment and abuse. A majority of this task force, composed of students, faculty, alumni, trustees, and administrators, recommended abolishing fraternities by May 30, 1990, because they "are rooted in a tradition of male dominance" and because rather than working toward appreciation of cultural diversity, they are "exclusive, not inclusive." A minority of the task force argued for reforming fraternities until they became "fully co-educational social/residential groups." The majority argued directly against this notion of evolutionary change, however, pointing out that previous reforming attempts had failed and predicting more "resistance and un-rest" if piecemeal change were attempted. All task force members agreed that Middlebury needed coeducational residential/social clubs ("The Task Force Report on Student Social Life," 1990, MCA).

The end result was that in 1990 all-male fraternities were abolished at Middlebury, at least theoretically. The former fraternity houses are now "social houses," which are not allowed to be more than two-thirds men (or two-thirds women). Yet the dean of students, Ann Hanson, noted that a couple of fraternities refused to become coeducational, and one is "supposedly" an alumni house. Even the coeducational social houses seem to encourage "fraternity-like" behavior, she said, and they remain the hub for the campus's social life. About 15 percent of the student body resides in these houses rather than in the dormitories, which have been orga-nized into a commons system, with a governance structure, social activi-ties, and affiliated faculty (Personal interview with Ann Hanson, July 20, 1998). The administration plans to enlarge the commons system as the size of the student body is increased, but students are protesting these changes, saying they are destroying social life and the advantages of a small liberal arts college (cf. *The Campus*, April 3, 1998, MCA). Some students also argue that social houses do better in deterring binge drink-ing because students drink out in the open, unlike the drinking that goes on behind doors in the dorms (*The Campus*, January 28, 1998, MCA).

Another result of the mannequin incident was the establishment of a separate house for women's groups. Chellis House, named after the first woman graduate of Middlebury, is an attractively renovated frame house, with its own kitchen and library as well as meeting rooms and a few faculty offices. It is used by several groups on campus, including an orga-nization of women of color, and the lesbian, gay, and bisexual student organization. The history of how it was established is interesting. The part-time administrator of the facility, Mary Duffy, explained to me that an alumna who has become a member of the college's Board of Trustees, Drucilla Cortell Gensler '57, was outraged by the mannequin incident and decided to use some of her wealth to establish a women's center on campus (Personal interview with Mary Duffy, July 22, 1998). The reac-tion of this alumna is one reason why it is important to have a diverse group of trustees—not only for serving as role models but also for acting as advocates. Such a center was also recommended by the Committee on

Attitudes Toward Gender (discussed above), but for implementation, it helped that someone with money had the same goal.

Key people at Middlebury who are concerned with gender equality believe that the climate for women in the late 1990s is "dramatically better" than it was in 1988 (Personal interview with Mary Duffy, July 22, 1998; Report of the Task Force on the Status of Women at Middlebury College, 1997, 3, MCA). In addition to Chellis House and the elimination of fraternities, they cite such progress as establishing a women's studies major; workshops on issues concerning women, such as sexual harassment and eating disorders; a woman chair of the Board of Trustees, Claire Gargalli; greater equality in the treatment of women and men athletes; and formal mechanisms for equalizing the pay of men and women in comparable positions.

Yet problems persist. The women's studies program feels marginal, according to Robert Schine, dean of the faculty (Personal interview, July 22, 1998), and it has no full-time faculty, not even joint appointments (Report of the Task Force on the Status of Women at Middlebury College, 1997). Women faculty do not progress up the ranks at the same rate as men faculty, which is a major reason why there are so few women top administrators, given the college's practice of selecting senior faculty for such positions (Personal interview with Robert Schine, July 22, 1998). Occasionally articles in the student newspaper comment on the lack of women "role models" in the faculty and administration (*The Campus*, April 10, 1997, MCA) and the insufficient number of women and people of color on the Board of Trustees (*The Campus*, October 30, 1997, MCA). Women students feel unsafe and are pressuring the college to install more call boxes and blue lights; they also do not believe the college has a clear or effective sexual assault policy (Personal interview with Mary Duffy, July 22, 1998). Binge drinking, the cause of many sexual assaults, continues to be a problem, and feminism still has a "bad name," making some women students unwilling to attend events at Chellis House, according to the dean of students, Ann Hanson (Personal interview, July 20, 1998; see also the article on feminism in the student newspaper, *The Campus*, November 19, 1997, MCA). Women of color, as well as lesbians, bisexuals, and gay men, need additional support to feel comfortable in this largely white, rich, and small academic community (Report of the Task Force on the Status of Women at Middlebury College, 1997, MCA). A complaint of the alumnae of 1988 whom I surveyed, that women students are not well prepared for handling sex discrimination in the "real world," is still a problem, according to staff of the college's career services

(Report of the Task Force on the Status of Women at Middlebury College, 1997, 18).

Issues that concern underrepresented groups at Middlebury have the potential of creating coalitions. This happened in the spring of 1998 as a result of an April Fool's issue of the campus newspaper in which a racist "joke" advertisement appeared, featuring a photo of three black men who were said to be adding "life" to the "sleepy Vermont town," as "drug dealers, gang members, rapists, arsonists." The protests that ensued did not focus only on concerns of minorities, but also included issues of campus homophobia and violence toward women. A slogan used during the protests encompassed all these groups' concerns that they were not being heard: "Silence equals violence" (The Campus, April 16, 1998, MCA).

Other issues that might affect the quality of life for women at Middlebury seem not to be given any attention at all. For example, there are no faculty workshops on "chilly climate" issues, Dean Schine told me, because faculty are "assumed" to know the research (although he did admit that they might not know what to do about male dominance in the classroom and that this could be a useful topic for new faculty orientations) (Personal interview with Robert Schine, July 22, 1998). When I asked Dean of Students Ann Hanson whether any group is monitoring leadership of campus organizations to see whether women students were fairly represented, she said that this was "not an issue in the student culture" (Personal interview, July 20, 1998).

The fact that in the past eight years, three major reports on issues directly related to women have been written and released to the Middlebury College community is evidence of greater attention to women's issues in the late 1990s than in the late 1980s. Progress may occur mostly in reaction to horrible incidents like the mannequin hanging, or in an attempt to improve the college's national ranking. But motivations matter less than actions. Women of different statuses and backgrounds are today more visible and better able to pressure Middlebury to move in the direction of making them feel as much a part of the academic community as (white, heterosexual, economically privileged) men.

William Smith

The identity of William Smith College as a coordinate institution has remained strong, despite some administrative reorganization to achieve greater efficiency. New students' orientation is focused on explaining the coordinate system and maintaining links with the past. William Smith first-year students, for example, are given plants, because their college's founder, Mr. William Smith, was a nurseryman (Personal interview with Dean DeMeis, August 12, 1998). The student newspaper frequently has editorials or letters about what the coordinate system means to students or how students are not "living up to" its ideals (see, for example, *The Herald*, September 26, 1997, or September 3, 1989, HWSCA).

Awareness of the distinction between coordination and coeducation remains stronger among William Smith than Hobart students. One perceptive first-year William Smith student argued that the coordinate system was bound to mean more to women since it is "more important for women to have a sense of independence because men already have it thrust upon them from the day they were born" (*The Herald*, January 16, 1998, HWSCA). And yet the dean of William Smith, Debra DeMeis, argued that the coordinate system strengthens not only women's ties with each other, but also men-men ties. The coordinate structure was, in fact, important to the development of an unusual program—men's studies—according to one of its founders, sociologist Jack Harris (*The Herald*, September 7, 1997, HWSCA). It may also be why single-sex residence arrangements are much more popular at Hobart and William Smith than they are at either Middlebury or Hamilton College.

The distinction between a coeducational college and a coordinate college like William Smith, which does not have its own faculty, Board of Trustees, or facilities, does not seem obvious to many outsiders. Yet insiders like Dean DeMeis of William Smith argue that it is distinctly different, in that it gives women (and men) an institutional voice. Women's input in any decision is automatically obtained, whereas in coeducational colleges, it would first have to be decided if women had a legitimate interest in a particular issue, and then who should represent them. Dean DeMeis used the example of blue (safety) lights. Student representatives of both Hobart and William Smith would have to be asked about the need for them, guaranteeing that questions of safety for women, which are different from those for men, would be considered (Personal interview, August 12, 1998).

One issue that formerly concerned women at Hobart and William Smith was parity in numbers of men and women students. By the mid-1980s this was no longer much of a concern since women were about 45 percent of the student body (Self-Study Report to the Middle States Association of Colleges and Schools, 1994, HWSCA). In the 1990s, this percentage has increased even further, and in fact, in 1997–98 women students outnumbered men students for the first time (see Table 10.6). While it can no longer be claimed that the greater number of men students carries an implicit message that they are more important than women students, parity has created unanticipated problems. Women students are too numerous for all to be housed together in one part of the campus, which in turn reduces their feelings of belonging to the "same college." Previously William Smith students' identity was forged from feeling that they were the "smaller, beleaguered, but superior sister." Not only is that no longer true, but Dean DeMeis of William Smith believes that men feel their loss of privilege, and women students have to deal with men's insecurity (Personal interview with Dean DeMeis, August 12, 1998). Moreover, the declining numbers and prestige of women's colleges nationally contribute to some students at Hobart and William Smith questioning the need for coordination.

Hobart College still has fraternities, although fewer than it used to have, and only about 20 percent of Hobart students belong to one of them (*The Herald*, October 17, 1997, HWSCA). In response to incidents involving drinking and sexual abuse, the college has established a strict accreditation process. Fraternities are reviewed every two years; to be reaccredited, they must demonstrate that they perform community service, deal with gender issues, are multicultural, and support intellectual life (Personal interview with Dean DeMeis, August 12, 1998). Fraternity members rightly perceive that the administration and faculty would, in general, prefer it if Hobart had no fraternities. Their response has been to engage in rather defensive publicity. In October 1997, for instance, they advertised "little known facts about fraternities" in the student newspaper, noting that 76 percent of senators and congressmen are fraternity men, and all but three U.S. presidents in the last century were fraternity men (*The Herald*, October 17, 1997, HWSCA). In the same article fraternity brothers pointed out the positive things they had done, for instance, holding a party in support of National Coming Out Day. It does seem that fraternities at Hobart do not have the same preeminent social status that fraternities did at Middlebury (and may still do in their current form of social houses) and continue to have at Hamilton. In fact, one Hobart student, Scott Negron, writing an opinion piece on the futility of trying to stop all underage drinking on campus, recommended *making the fraternities "the center of social activity on campus"* (*The Herald*, October 24, 1997, HWSCA, my emphasis).

Hobart and William Smith Colleges have demonstrated their concerns about gender equity in several ways. They celebrate events important in the history of both colleges, such as Founder's Day at William Smith and Charter's Day at Hobart; they monitor issues of concern through special task forces, for example, a task force on gay, lesbian, and bisexual issues; they give curricular attention to gender issues through women's studies, men's studies, and a cluster of courses called "Lesbian, Gay and Bisexual Studies"; and they conduct workshops for students in the residence halls on such sensitive issues as date rape. In fall 1998 a new institute, the Fisher Center for the Study of Men and Women, was inaugurated. Some students have complained that gender issues are given too much attention, while diversity issues receive insufficient attention (*The Herald*, November 4, 1994, HWSCA), and yet the intersections between race and gender are unfortunately apparent. Several incidents on campus have involved women of color as targets of threatening phone calls and racist graffiti (*The Herald*, October 21, 1994, HWSCA).

In some ways it seems that William Smith students are beginning to dominate the colleges: they are a slight majority of students, they are more likely than Hobart students to be involved in the honors program, and their sports teams have done very well since the mid-1980s, whereas Hobart sports teams have not been as successful. It is telling, though, that even in the years that William Smith sports teams have done exceptionally well, stories and photos of their successes do not dominate the student newspaper. In 1997–98 of eighteen issues of the student newspaper that had sports photos, exactly half of these (40) photos were of women's teams (see Table 10.6). On the other hand, William Smith recently established a hall of honor for its women athletes and coaches (*The Herald*, October 3, 1997, HWSCA).

And yet despite the apparent dominance of women students at the colleges, it would be naive to ignore the ways men students continue to have the upper hand. In an op-ed piece for the student newspaper, Kerry Greaves claimed that power for women on campus was "generated by how they are regarded by the men." Women students are preoccupied with their appearance, she continued, because sex and dating is a "hugely significant and constant issue" (*The Herald*, September 26, 1997, HWSCA). Students writing in an alternative, "woman's paper," *Waves*, argued in 1992 that two of the "most sensitive" issues on campus, fraternities and gender issues, needed more discussion. They claimed that instances of rape, assault, and harassment were "down-played" (*Waves*, Vol I, 1992, HWSCA). But while such incidents continue to occur, educational programs exist that attempt to make them less frequent, and students and the administration are better prepared to respond quickly when they do occur. The Women's Resource Center, staffed by students, many of whom are "survivors" of rape or sexual abuse (*Waves*, September 5,

1992), and who are trained in peer counseling, offer women in crisis a "safe space" where they can get advice, discuss incidents, and explore their feelings (*The Herald*, October 10, 1997, HWSCA).

The emphasis on the coordinate structure of Hobart and William Smith has varied over time. In the past thirty-five years, for example, it has changed from being seen as basically a hindrance to full coeducation, to being revived so as to provide women students with some of the benefits of single-sex education, namely leadership opportunities and a support- ive environment. It may be going through yet a third stage. The new Dean of Hobart, Clarence Butler, who has been associated with the col- leges for almost twenty years, hopes to make the coordinate system as successful for the men students as it appears to have been for the women. To this end he is initiating a program aimed at first-year Hobart students that will explore issues related to the transition from being high school "boys" to college "men" (Personal interview with Dean Butler, August 21, 1998). Whether coordination can survive this permutation without replicating the male dominance typically found in mixed-sex settings re- mains to be seen.

Hamilton

Probably the key event for gender relations at Hamilton College during the 1990s was the residential life decision of 1995. The decision repre- sented Hamilton's attempts to deal with problems associated with frater- nities—heavy drinking, sexual abuse, and gender discrimination since men students have more residential and dining options than women students have. Fraternities were not abolished, but all students were required to live and eat on campus, and the college set about buying the fraternity houses (The Report of the Committee on Residential Life, March 1995, HCA). Thus fraternities (and sororities, which never had their own houses) con- tinue to exist at Hamilton; there are "rushes" for members, and they have meetings and give parties. According to the dean of faculty, Bobby Fong, one effect of this policy is that "fraternity-like" behavior has entered the dormitories, facilitated by block housing, which means that up to eight students can ask to live near each other in the dorms (Personal interview, July 29, 1998).[43]

Hamilton has dealt with fraternity problems in a more piecemeal way than Middlebury. Its approach has generated the kind of opposition that was predicted at Middlebury had it tried to reform rather than abolish its fraternities. Four Hamilton fraternities are suing the college on antitrust

grounds, arguing that their options for living and dining have been curtailed (*The Observer-Dispatch*, July 14, 1995; *The Spectator,* October
17, 1997, HCA).[44] The fraternities' opposition to the residential policy
has been so intense that according to Dean Fong, some alumni members
of the Board of Trustees have changed their views, from pro to anti-
fraternity (Personal interview with Dean Fong, July 29, 1998).

Thus despite the 1995 residential life decision, fraternity life, and arguments about its problems and benefits, continue at Hamilton. The passions on both sides were evident in the autumn of 1997 in reactions to an
incident involving one of the fraternities. Two women strippers were hired
for the entertainment of members; completely nude, they simulated sex
with each other. President Tobin suspended the fraternity for two years,
citing lewd behavior, violation of an agreement between the college and
private societies, and improper use of the college's social space (*The
Spectator*, September 26, 1997, HCA). Many students were outraged at
this administrative decision; about one-quarter of the student body signed
a petition calling for the reinstatement of the fraternity (*The Spectator*,
October 10, 1997, HCA). Students argued that the administration had
behaved autocratically by not using student groups to decide the appropriate response to the fraternity's entertainment, and some students worried
what other actions might be defined as "lewd." On the other side were
students and many faculty who, in forums held to discuss the incident,
argued that this entertainment degraded women and was inappropriate
in an institution of higher learning.

At the same time that fraternities continue to cause problems at
Hamilton, the pro-woman heritage of Kirkland is evident. One manifesta-
tion of this heritage is the willingness to investigate issues of gender
equity. Just after the class of 1988 had graduated, a visiting instructor of
sociology conducted a survey of students and faculty on the college's
classroom climate, finding, not surprisingly, that women were seen as less
involved than men students in classroom interactions ("A Study of Classroom Climate at Hamilton College," Margo MacLeod, April 1989, HCA).
The study's findings were distributed to the faculty, accompanied by a
letter from the president. The women's studies program has also grown;
unlike the situation at the other three colleges, the faculty who teach in it
do not all have appointments in other traditional departments. In 1997–
98, one professor, Chandra Talpade Mohanty, had an appointment just
in women's studies, and another professor, Margaret Gentry, had a joint
appointment in psychology and women's studies. In addition, the college

had a visiting professor of women's studies who taught part-time (1997–98 Hamilton Catalogue, HCA). Four local sororities are also strong, according to the dean of students, Janis Coates (Personal interview, November 16, 1998).

Other organized groups at Hamilton College representing women's interests include a caucus of women faculty; the Kirkland Endowment, which provides about $60,000 a year for sponsoring speakers and conferences; and recently the Kirkland Project for the Study of Gender, Society, and Culture. The purpose of the Kirkland Project, according to its key organizer, Professor Nancy Rabinowitz, who started at Hamilton as a Kirkland faculty member, is to focus on the intersections of gender, race, class, and sexual orientation and to try to "change the climate of the world by changing the climate here" (*The Spectator*, September 12, 1997, HCA). More specifically, the Kirkland Project has established a student seminar for students who work with mentors to do research on some aspects of the intersections of race, gender, class, and sexuality; it has organized speakers series; and it is trying to obtain funding for such activities as supporting visiting scholars and student interns (Personal interview with Nancy Rabinowitz, November 16, 1998).

Recently Hamilton College has begun to acknowledge the contributions Kirkland College made to the current academic community. Kirkland alumnae used to not feel part of the alumni association and did not feel comfortable returning to the college. Two reunions have helped rectify this situation, especially one in June 1997, which celebrated the 25th anniversary of Kirkland's charter class's graduation. Not only did former Kirkland President, Sam Babbitt, and his wife Natalie, return to campus, but for the first time a president of Hamilton, Eugene Tobin, participated.

Hamilton College in the 1990s still appears split between a progressive aspect, primarily inherited from Kirkland, and a traditional aspect, dating from the long period—more than 150 years—in which Hamilton was a conservative men's college. Students are aware of the stereotypes associated with each side of the campus, now referred to as the "dark" side (ironically, the modern Kirkland part) and the "light" side (the older Hamilton part), with students on the former side being seen as "artsy-fartsy intellectual snobs" who "sit under trees and write poetry," and students on the Hamilton side being viewed as "forever adorned in J. Crew apparel . . . in a perpetual drunken bliss" (*The Spectator*, September 12, 1997, HCA). The split is also apparent in another way. A strong women's studies program, and organized groups and projects representing women's concerns, coexist with fraternities that dominate the social scene, engage in at least occasional misogynist incidents, and yet receive a great deal of student support.

It is instructive to compare Hamilton, a formerly coordinate college, with Hobart and William Smith. While the latter is able to celebrate its history of women and to keep separate traditions alive, Hamilton has difficulty resuscitating an even-handed image of its past women's college or preventing negative stereotypes from being associated with its vestiges. One factor accounting for this difference may be how much time has elapsed since the founding of each institution. Unlike William Smith, which is about 90 years old and hence seems to current college constituencies almost as old as Hobart, Kirkland was a much more recent "experiment." Moreover, its hostile takeover prevented evolution of its coordinate structure in a way that may have benefited women students. In fact, there seemed to be a desire for institutional amnesia, to act as if coeducation had been intended all along. Yet there also seems to be guilt at what happened and a desire to compensate faculty and women students for their losses. The Kirkland Endowment has been one institutional mechanism for programmatic initiatives directed at women students. The recent moves toward recognizing the contributions of Kirkland, and toward weakening the fraternities, would also seem to augur well for making Hamilton College more unified and a better place for women.

Conclusions: Alumnae and Their Colleges

While alumnae at all four colleges were positive about their undergraduate experiences, two caveats are in order. First, these were the views only of women who stayed to graduate. Secondly, satisfaction does not necessarily mean that the colleges provided the best experiences for their women students, if by "best" we mean an environment in which they developed all their abilities to the greatest extent possible. Interestingly, while Middlebury alumnae were the angriest about their lack of preparation for sexism they encountered in life beyond college, they have gone the furthest in postgraduate education and have changed the most in attitudes toward feminism, now matching Wells graduates. Wells and William Smith alumnae were more likely than the alumnae of Middlebury or Hamilton to use female networks to further their careers.

It is surprising that William Smith students, traditionally academically stronger than Hobart men, and with a sense of their own institutional identity, have not gone on to graduate school in greater numbers. It may be that a concern of administrators and faculty that William Smith has a reputation as a "party school" is well-founded. Also, given that William

Smith students on average are weaker academically than Middlebury and Hamilton women students, but about the same as Wells students, perhaps it would take a completely separate, supportive environment for William Smith alumnae to pursue academics more than social life. In addition, there are undoubtedly differences in the type of student who applies to William Smith rather than Wells. Young women who go to women's colleges tend to be more serious about their career goals, as Lentz (1980) reported and which fits with my finding that students entering Wells were the most likely to say they had "definite" career goals.

Table 10.6 presents some comparative data on the colleges from the late 1980s to the late 1990s. Wells is the one college whose enrollment has declined substantially since the class of 1988 graduated. Although Hobart and William Smith's enrollment has declined by about 10 percent, this was by design, and the number of *women* students has actually increased since 1989. Both Middlebury and Hamilton have increased in size; Middlebury plans to grow even more, a decision that displeases some students.

Wells College stands out in terms of the number of women on its faculty, as top administrators, and on its Board of Trustees. More striking than the high percentage of Wells faculty in 1997–98 who were women— 55 percent, compared to between 32 and 41 percent at the other colleges—was the percentage of full professors who were women—almost half at Wells, compared to less than 20 percent at the other three colleges. It is also notable that at Middlebury, the percentage of women on the faculty stayed virtually constant during the 1990s at just under one-third; at Hobart and William Smith and Hamilton, the percentage of women on the faculty increased somewhat during the '90s decade, to 41 percent at Hobart and William Smith, and to 36 percent at Hamilton. The percentage of full professors who were women likewise increased at all three coeducational (and coordinate) colleges, but by no more than 8 percentage points, and was still only between 14 and 18 percent.

The top administration at Wells became increasingly dominated by women during the 1990s so that by 1997–98, it was entirely women. At Middlebury and Hamilton, by contrast, the top administration is male-dominated, a fact that both colleges recognize and give lip-service, at least, to trying to change. Hobart and William Smith has a minority of women in top administrative positions, but a more substantial minority, close to two-fifths.

At all four colleges, the percentage of women on the Board of Trustees increased during the 1990s, but only at Wells did they become a majority. In contrast to the representation of women in the other parts of

TABLE 10.6 Comparisons of the Four Colleges in the 1990s

	Wells	Middlebury	Hobart & Wm Smith	Hamilton
Number of students, by gender				
1989–90	408	2,031: 1,045 men, 986 women (49%)	1,933: 1071 men, 862 women (45%)	1,663: 895 men, 768 women (46%)
1994–95	358	2,007: 1,027 men, 980 women (49%)	1,737: 874 men, 863 women (50%)	1,733: 935 men, 798 women (46%)
1997–98	301	2,131: 1,055 men, 1,076 women (50.5%)	1,764: 831 men, 933 women (53%)	1,780: 947 men, 833 women (47%)
Faculty				
a) % women				
b) % women of full professors				
1989–90	a) 43% b) 32%	a) 32% b) 9%	a) 29% b) 15%	a) 32% b) 9%
1994–95	a) 54% b) 33%	a) 33% b) 12.5%	a) 37% b) 12%	a) 37% b) 15%
1997–98	a) 55% b) 48%	a) 32% b) 17%	a) 41% b) 18%	a) 36% b) 14%
Top administrators—Pres, V-Ps, Deans: % women				
1989–90	5 of 6 = 83%	1 of 9 = 11%	2 of 5 = 40%	1 of 6 = 17%
1994–95	4 of 6 = 67%	2 of 9 = 22%	3 of 8 = 37.5%	1 of 6 = 17%
1997–98	4 of 4 = 100%	1 of 9 = 11%	3 of 8 = 37.5%	1 of 6 = 17%
Board of Trustees: % women				
1989–90	61%	32%	28%	14%
1994–95	65%	36%	30%	28%
1997–98	68%	42%	33%	24%
Student organizations—Gender of leaders				
a) Editor-in-chief of student newspaper				
b) Head of student government				
1989–90	a) woman b) woman	a) man b) man	a) man b) woman (& man)	a) man b) woman
1994–95	a) woman b) woman	a) man b) man	a) man b) woman (& man)	a) man (Spring) b) man
1997–98	a) woman b) woman	a) woman b) man	a) woman b) woman (& man)	a) woman (Spring) b) woman

TABLE 10.6 Continued

	Wells	Middlebury	Hobart & Wm Smith	Hamilton
Sports photos in college newspaper: % of sports photos of women students, 1997–98				
	6 of 6 sports photos in 8 issues of paper: 100%	51 of 120 sports photos in 22 issues 42.5%	20 of 40 sports photos in 21 issues: 50%	27 of 75 sports photos in 22 issues: 36%

Information obtained from college catalogues, student directories, and student newspapers. See note at end of Table 3.1 about determination of gender of trustees and faculty.

the college, Middlebury had more women (43 percent) on its Board of Trustees than Hobart and William Smith (33 percent) or Hamilton (24 percent). Yet articles in the Middlebury student newspaper have commented on the overrepresentation of white men on the Board of Trustees and the lack of women on the faculty, saying that this belied Middlebury's rhetoric about preparing women students to assume "leadership" in the world at large (*The Campus,* April 10 and October 30, 1997, MCA).

In terms of student leadership positions, it is inevitable that all are held by women at Wells. Hobart and William Smith and Hamilton did quite well during the 1990s in terms of the gender mix of students in the two top positions of head of student government and editor-in-chief of the newspaper. At Middlebury these top positions still tended to go mostly to the men students, an unfortunate legacy of the past when it was institutionalized that the men be given the top post, women students the second-in-command positions.[45] In terms of the visual representation of women students in sports photos, for the 1997–98 academic year, exactly half of the sports photos in the Hobart and William Smith's student newspaper were of women; at Middlebury, women were in over two-fifths of the photos (not including those photos that had both women and men in them), and at Hamilton, slightly over one-third of the sports photos were of women. While all the photos of sports teams at Wells were of women, it is striking how few photos there were and how few issues of the student newspaper appeared during the academic year—only eight issues, compared to 21 or 22 at the other three colleges.

In some ways the sports photos epitomize the general situation for women at these four colleges. At Wells women students are the sole focus, but given enrollment and financial problems, they are not receiving the same amount of resources, in an absolute sense, that women students at the other three, larger and richer colleges, are. This difference between Wells and the other colleges began manifesting itself in the mid-1970s, but by the late 1990s, it had increased. In the concluding chapter I move beyond these four colleges to consider current trends in single-sex and coeducation. How can lessons of the past improve the future of higher education for women, now the majority of undergraduates in the United States?

Notes

1   Not all of the seniors gave me permission in 1988 to contact them again, although a large majority (75 percent) did so. Most of those who did not give me permission did not refuse me but rather, never returned a postcard to me indicating their willingness to be surveyed again. When questionnaires were sent out in the fall of 1994 to those from whom I had received permission, some were returned, marked as addressee unknown, and I was unable to obtain more recent addresses from the colleges' alumnae offices. I wrote only to the alumnae of three of the schools since as a faculty member at Wells I did not need permission to contact Wells alumnae. Thus the postcard return rate of 75 percent is based on alumnae of three, not four, colleges.

2   These are not mutually exclusive categories, i.e., some of the part-time workers were also students, as noted below.

3   This relationship is not statistically significant using chi-square (χ^2 = 9.71, df = 6, sig = .14), but it is significant using nonparametric correlation coefficients that measure linear relationships, with Wells coded as 1, William Smith coded as 2, Hamilton coded as 3, and Middlebury coded as 4 (Spearman's correlation = .18, sig. = .02).

4   And receiving such honors as graduating seniors is quite strongly related to pursuing graduate degrees: χ^2 = 6.5, df = 2, sig. = .04 for graduating with a prize; χ^2 = 17.54, df = 2, sig. = .000 for Phi Beta Kappa.

5   Spearman's correlation = .29, sig. = .000. The correlations between educational accomplishments as alumnae and students' academic goals as sophomores and seniors are also significant, and in fact, slightly stronger: for sophomores, Spearman's correlation coefficient = .42, sig. = .000; for seniors, Spearman's = .35, sig. = .000. This pattern of relationships between students' academic goals and their educational achievements six years later holds up for each college considered separately, except for alumnae of William Smith, for whom the only significant correlation is between their academic goals as sophomores and their educational achievements six years later.

6   It is also interesting in this regard that only for the alumnae of Wells was there a negative relationship between their fathers occupation (and education) and alumnae's pursuit of higher education, suggesting that Wells is a particularly supportive environment for young women of less privileged backgrounds. In part this is explained by characteristics of incoming students at Wells, i.e., those with the highest high school grade point averages tended to come from families where the parents, particularly the mothers, had the least education and held the least prestigious jobs, suggesting that richer but weaker students were admitted as well as poorer but stronger students. On the other hand, for incoming students at Hamilton, those with the highest grade point averages also tended to have parents who had the least education, but alumnae of Hamilton whose family backgrounds were less privileged were not more likely to go on to higher education.

7   And yet, as discussed in Chapter 9, the academic goals of Wells students tended to decline during their college years, unlike the goals of students at the other colleges. It seems that Wells students had unrealistically high goals at first and so their decline may have been inevitable.

8   Spearman's correlations are .22, sig. = .02 for women professors as mentors and alumnae's pursuit of graduate education, and .20, sig. = .01 for the relationship between undergraduate college encouraging career choice and alumnae's pursuit of graduate education (on a larger number of alumnae since not all alumnae reported having mentors).

9   χ^2 = 14.23, df = 4, sig. = .007 between being on the Dean's List and post-graduate education.

10   χ^2 = 11.09, df = 4, sig. = .03 for being told they were good candidates for graduate school and their pursuit of further education.

11   χ^2 = 8.99, df = 3, sig. = .03 for female college professors as mentors of alumnae by alumnae's undergraduate college.

12   The relationship between having male college professors as mentors and alumnae's undergraduate college does not quite achieve statistical significance—χ^2 = 7.54, df = 3, sig. = .06.

13   χ^2 = 13.88 df = 3, sig. = .003 for female graduate school professors as mentors by alumnae's undergraduate college; χ^2 = 9.55 df = 3, sig. = .023 for male graduate school professors as mentors by undergraduate college.

14   This relationship is not significant by chi-square, but Spearman's correlation coefficient = −.17, sig. = .02 with colleges coded, as indicated above in footnote 3, Wells = 1, William Smith = 2, Hamilton = 3, Middlebury = 4.

15   Again this relationship was significant only for Spearman's, with colleges coded as above. Spearman's coefficient = −.16, sig. = .03.

16   The question I asked alumnae was: "Looking back on your years in college, what would you say were the most *positive* aspects for you? Please check the general category(ies) and then explain why these were so positive for you." This question was then repeated, except asking for "the most *negative* aspects."

17   One Wells alumna did mention the "snobbery of some people," and an alumna who is a woman of color talked about the "prejudice and racism" she experienced but did not recognize until she "got older." But perhaps because so few Wells students were from wealthy families, cliques did not appear to have formed around social class background. They did earlier in Wells's history, as I discussed in Chapter 5.

18   The relationship beween college attended and saying that coursework was positive does not quite reach statistical significance by either chi-square or Spearman's (χ^2 = 6.51 df = 3, sig. = .09; Spearman's = .12, sig. = .07).

19   χ^2 = 11.13, df = 3, sig. = .01.

20   Spearman's coefficient = .20, sig. = .009.

21   In one case, however, an alumna angrily recalled sitting on the bench, convinced
      that had she been allowed to play a sport more often, she would have become
      better at it.

22    $\chi^2 = 26.67$ df = 3, sig. = .000.

23   Spearman's correlation coefficients for these relationships with alumnae's posi-
      tive scoring of their college experiences were: (1) with being on the Dean's List,
      .24, sig. = .001; (2) with seniors' closeness to some faculty, .16, sig. = .03, and
      (3) with activities as undergraduates, .13, sig. = .06.

24   This finding is not so surprising when it is recognized that all measures of alumnae's
      self-esteem were significantly correlated with their level of self-esteem when they
      were undergraduates. The (Spearman's) correlations were not exceptionally high,
      however, ranging from .22 to .37, which probably indicates that although these
      women's self-esteem may have been fairly stable, their self-regard was also af-
      fected by their life events, including their college experiences. Measures of self-
      esteem may not have high reliability, which would be another reason why the
      correlations among the measures were not greater.

25   All of these correlations were statistically significant at p < .05, but none was
      significant with all three measures of alumnae's self-esteem (feeling proud of them-
      selves, believing they had many good qualities, or being satisfied with themselves
      in general).

26   An index of self-esteem, created by adding together the three values of the (highly
      correlated) measures, was correlated with these variables as follows: with use of
      an "old girls" network, Spearman's coefficient = .15, sig. = .03; with the impor-
      tance of friendship, Spearman's coefficient = .26, sig. = .001; and with seeing
      college friends once a year, Spearman's coefficient = .14, sig. = .05.

27   The original questionnaires, distributed in 1984, 1986, and 1988, did not have
      the preliminary part of this statement, i.e., they did not indicate that this per-
      tained to heterosexual couples.

28   The original questionnaires did not specify "men" dates.

29   The coefficients of reliability, Cronbach's alpha, were .49 for the index of alumnae's
      answers, .52 for the index of seniors' answers, .49 for the index of sophomores'
      answers, and .49 for the index of first-year students' answers.

30    $F(3,138) = 2.98$, sig. = .03

31    $F(1,138) = 18.03$, sig. = .000

32    $\chi^2 = 38.70$, df = 3, sig. = .000.

33   r = .17, p = .02 for the correlation between seniors' educational goals and alumnae's
      gender-role attitudes; r = .16, p = .03 for the correlation beween alumnae's graduate
      education and their gender-role attitudes.

34   r = .56, p = .000 for the correlation between general politics and gender-role attitudes; r = −.26, p = .001 for the correlation between religious feeling and gender-role attitudes.

35   r = .13, p = .07 for the correlation between alumnae's gender-role attitudes and their leadership of campus organizations as undergraduates; r = .12, p = .08 for the correlation between alumnae's gender-role attitudes and their having taken courses on women's issues.

36   F(3,146) = 3.13, sig. = .03 for the differences in means among the four colleges for the "lots of money" goal, and F(3,146) = 3.8, sig. = .01 for the differences in means among the four colleges for the "job security" goal.

37   F(3,146) = 3.4, sig. = .02 for the differences in means among the four colleges for the interesting work goal.

38   Spearman's correlations were −.28, sig. = .000 for being on the Dean's List and rating "lots of money" as important, −.24, sig. = .002 for being on the Dean's List and rating job security as important.

39   Spearman's correlations with rating job security as important were −.16, sig. = .03 for alumnae's father's occupational status, −.19, sig. = .01 for alumnae's father's education, and −.16, sig. = .03 for mother's education.

40   Only for the goal of interesting work was there a linear relationship with academic goals as seniors: Spearman's correlation = .14, sig. = .045. For decision-making freedom and being successful, it was seniors who intended to get a master's degree (rather than a Ph.D. or law or medical degree) who ranked these goals the highest. Chi-square for academic goals as seniors and valuing decision-making freedom = 18.33, 6 d.f., sig. = .005; for seniors' academic goals and success goal, chi-square = 24.32, 8 d.f., sig. = .002.

41   More recently Wells students reported that they had been told that commencement speakers had to "understand and respect the women's college environment" (*The Onyx*, October 1, 1997, WCA). The 1999 commencement speaker, lawyer Sarah Weddington of Roe v. Wade fame, was not an alumna of Wells.

42   These tactics appear to be working, at least in terms of increasing enrollment for the fall of 1999. The incoming class of 2003 is projected to be about 50 percent larger than the class of 2002.

43   According to Hamilton's dean of students, Janis Coates, now students can live in blocks of only 6 or 4 students (Personal interview, November 16, 1998).

44   These fraternities were presumably heartened by an October 1998 non-binding resolution of the U.S. Congress. This "sense of Congress" resolution, part of the Higher Education Act, was sponsored by then-Rep. Bob Livingston, a former Delta Kappa Epsilon member at Tulane University. It "expresse[d] lawmakers' belief that colleges should not act to prevent students from exercising their freedom of association" (Gose 1998). National heads of several fraternities have written to colleges like Middlebury that have abolished fraternities, citing this resolution and asking the colleges not to interrupt rushing on their campuses. But so

far, at least, the colleges do not appear to be intimidated, noting that their decisions have been upheld in the courts.

45 And yet see Chapter 8 where I note that in the mid-1980s a greater percentage of Middlebury women had top positions in college publications than women at the other three colleges.

Chapter 11

Conclusion:
The Future of Separatism

The philosophers have only *interpreted* the world . . . the point, however, is to *change* it. (Karl Marx, *Theses on Feuerbach*)

While women's colleges are by no means a panacea for gender inequity, they have made important contributions to enhancing women's lives. In the nineteenth century, they were critical for ensuring that women received higher education, since separate spheres were more acceptable than mixed-sex institutions. Nineteenth-century women's colleges often were as concerned with the cultivation of social graces as they were with academic training. They did, however, respond to changing interests and needs of their students (as well as to the standardization of higher education, in general) by improving their academic programs and, in some cases, by offering a few vocationally relevant programs. In the first two-thirds of the twentieth century, women's colleges served mostly privileged women, but they served them ably, both in extracurricular opportunities for leadership as well as intellectually demanding academic programs. More recently, women's colleges have offered extensive financial aid and educated a student body that is much more diverse—racially, ethnically, and in terms of social class background.

Coeducational colleges have also been important in giving women access to higher education, but in many cases, it took persistent efforts by women and their men allies for women to gain entrance to formerly men's colleges. Once women gained admission, they found they were marginalized. Despite women students' fine academic records, their presence was often not welcomed, to the degree that some coeducational colleges, like Middlebury, considered trying to get rid of them. Men students dominated purportedly coeducational colleges—in campus leadership positions, in classroom interactions, in athletics, and in the attention faculty and administrators paid to them. Thus women's subordinate status in society was reinforced by their educational experiences.

For about the past twenty-five years, many women's colleges have had severe financial and enrollment problems. The thrust of the 1960s toward equality and integration, which in the educational field resulted in most remaining men's colleges admitting women, has meant that women's colleges now seem unnecessary to many people. Despite the publicity the Women's Colleges Coalition has given to the research showing the long-term benefits of single-sex education for women, the overwhelming majority of young women consider only coeducational colleges. One simple indicator of the difficulty women's colleges have in attracting students is that between 1976 and 1993, enrollments of full-time women students increased by 40.6 percent at all institutions of higher education, whereas at 76 women's colleges they increased by only 5.4 percent (U.S. Department of Education 1997, 64).[1]

Women's colleges have used many strategies to survive declining enrollments and financial difficulties, so that at the edge of the twenty-first century, they look very different from women's colleges of thirty-five or forty years ago. With the exception of a few women's colleges with very high endowments (Wellesley, Smith, Agnes Scott, and Mount Holyoke) and several women's colleges in the southern states, which have a regional enrollment base, most women's colleges have adopted one of two survival strategies: establishing close relationships with a coeducational or men's college, or developing part-time and evening programs that enroll older students and often include men students.[2] The first strategy has meant that some women's colleges approximate a coordinate structure even if they do not call themselves a coordinate institution. Bryn Mawr's relationship with Haverford is one well-known example; Saint Mary's, which has a close relationship with the University of Notre Dame, is another. The second major approach to survival, developing part-time and evening programs, has resulted in a form of women's colleges in which full-time, residential women students may be a minority of all students. Wilson College in Pennsylvania, for example, whose enrollment and financial problems in 1979 were so severe that its Board of Trustees ordered it closed, had 875 students in 1993. Only 182, or 21 percent, were full-time women students, however; 519 were part-time women, and the remaining 174 were part-time or full-time men (U.S. Department of Education 1997, 112).

In addition to these major changes, women's colleges, like many other small, private colleges, have experimented with some of the following means to attract more students: extensive financial aid, which has resulted in many more students from working and lower middle classes enrolling; developing strengths in particular or unusual academic programs, such as medical technology, health sciences, or pre-professional programs in law and medicine; innovative approaches to education, sometimes off-campus (for example, Chatham College's international programs in one of four locations during students' January term); and relations with other colleges not in their immediate vicinity (for example, Chestnut Hill College in Philadelphia, which advertises the ease with which students can study for a year at any of twelve colleges around the country that are in a consortium of Catholic colleges) (Adler 1994; Reeves 1994).

Despite these attempts to improve enrollments, many women's colleges have found that the easiest and probably surest way is to admit men. Some women's colleges, notably Vassar, Connecticut, Skidmore, and Elmira, became coeducational in the late 1960s or early 1970s, at approximately the same time that many men's colleges did. In the late 1980s two more well-known women's colleges, Wheaton and Goucher, admitted men, over the furious protests of students and faculty. The protests were particularly intense at Wheaton, which had just finished a capital campaign and had achieved fame for its gender-inclusive curricular innovations (Sadovnik and Semel 1996). Other women's colleges, such as Russell Sage (which actually is part of a larger university, most of which is coeducational) and Wells, considered the coeducational option but rejected it. Mills College announced that it was admitting men in 1990 but rescinded this decision fairly quickly due to the intensity of student, alumnae, and faculty protests.

One breakdown of the earlier changes in women's colleges showed that between 1960 and 1980, 55 women's colleges became coeducational, 5 merged with another college, and 81 had fates unknown but presumably had ceased operation (Chamberlain 1988, 121).[3] These trends have continued; in the late 1990s, a few more women's colleges announced that they would be admitting men and one, Mount Vernon, was absorbed by a university. In 1998 there were only 79 women's colleges; excluding the two-year institutions, there were 72.[4] This contrasts with 233 women's colleges in 1960 and 90 in 1986 (U.S. Department of Education 1997, 28).

The overwhelming trend toward coeducation does not mean that it is the best institutional structure for meeting the needs of all women students. As the great late-nineteenth-century sociologist and historian, Max Weber, said about another inexorable trend, that toward bureaucratization, we do not have to embrace the future just because it is inevitable.

I wish to argue further that we should look closely at the benefits of separatism for social groups that do not yet share equally in society's resources. The political dangers of separatism are real—the 1954 Supreme Court ruling in Brown v. Board of Education that separate but equal is always unequal must not be forgotten. But separatism is different when it is chosen, not coerced. It is also important to distinguish separate institutions for superordinate versus subordinate groups. As anthropologist and president of Barnard College Judith Shapiro has noted, "In a society that favors men over women, men's institutions preserve privilege; women's institutions challenge privilege" (Shapiro 1994). Thus separatism can be conceived of as a strategy that may be useful for furthering gender equality.

Separate education for girls and women is no longer easy to find, however. Even if a few women's colleges (and all-girls' secondary schools) persist, it is undoubtedly true that very few women will have any single-sex experiences. It is therefore imperative that those of us who wish to improve education for women understand and try to apply the successful aspects of single-sex institutions to coeducational colleges. In some essential ways, the single-sex experience, given its multifaceted nature (referred to as a "total immersion" experience by one of my colleagues at Wells), cannot be replicated in a mixed-sex environment. Yet I believe we should recognize that coeducational colleges vary in how supportive of women they are and that coeducation can be improved upon, using key features of women's colleges as a guide.

Based on my own research and that of others, I would argue that women's colleges appear to benefit women in the support they give to women in a general way, that is, in making the women students feel as if they and their concerns are important. This support, particularly from men faculty, appears to contribute to higher self-esteem of women, at least while they are students. A second advantage to women's colleges is having faculty role models that women can identify with—women and supportive men. These faculty role models help women develop in many ways, including raising or at least sustaining their academic goals. Another strength of women's colleges is the opportunity they provide for women to develop leadership skills in a wide variety of activities. My study was not able to address the long-term benefits of such leadership activities, but it is reasonable to assume that they enable women to function more successfully in many parts of their later lives, not just their careers, but also community and political affairs. Moreover, opportunities for leadership undoubtedly contribute to the enjoyment of women (and men) students while they are in college, a not unimportant consideration.

Thus to improve coeducational colleges for their women students, I recommend the following:

— Women's centers. They must not merely exist, as if an afterthought, but must be integral to the college environment. This means they must be attractive, well-funded spaces where women can meet to talk about issues that concern them—birth control, abortion, racism, sexual harassment, sexual orientation, campus life, courses, safety, eating problems, etc. Women's centers should be arenas where women students take on leadership roles for planning conferences, choosing films, and inviting outside speakers.

— Institutional commitment to monitor and rectify inequalities. Task forces and institutional researchers should examine such common sources of male dominance in colleges as sports teams and facilities, classroom dynamics, leadership in campus clubs and student government, and scholarships and grants. Fraternities are inherently discriminatory and should be abolished or at the very least, their influence should be curtailed. Once sources of gender inequality are identified and recommendations made, they need to be discussed in the wider community and implemented. Backlash should be expected and planned for, not used as an excuse for non-implementation of changes.

— Representation of women in faculty, administration, and Board of Trustees. Continued pressure is necessary to improve the representation of women—of all races and sexual orientations—within all ranks of faculty and administration, but particularly in the highest ranks where they tend to be underrepresented, and in key faculty and trustee committees. Women in these positions can not only serve as role models for students, but can also act as advocates for necessary changes on behalf of women students, staff, and faculty.

— Symbolic representation of women. One of the ways women's colleges have supported women is by the creation of an environment where women's achievements are celebrated, by paintings, statues, speakers, and traditions focused on women. Coeducational colleges, especially those that in the past were all-men colleges, usually have a deficit of symbols indicating that the college belongs to women as well as men. Ways to increase the symbolic representation of women include rewriting college catalogues so that women's history at the college is given due emphasis, bringing famous women speakers to campus, naming new buildings after women who have played a role at the college, and developing new traditions focused on women students.

— Training for faculty and staff. Workshops that discuss concepts like the "chilly climate" for women students, faculty, and staff, and suggest ways for improving the situation, should be implemented. Such training should not be thought of as a one-time-only phenomenon, but rather as something that will be needed on a continuing basis at several points in people's careers.

Notably missing from the above list is the academic field of women's studies. Women's colleges have not led in the development of this new, multidisciplinary field of study, probably because it has seemed less necessary in institutions whose *raison d'être* is women. In coeducational colleges, on the other hand, women's studies has been valuable as an academic home for those faculty with research interests in women's issues. It also provides students with courses where women's lives are the central focus. Women's studies remains important in coeducational colleges for these reasons.[5]

Writing this book has been an intellectual journey for me: my ending place is somewhat different from my starting place. I have experienced firsthand the joys for faculty and students of a women's college and know the intensity of feelings about protecting the specialness of these rare, women-focused environments. Yet I now fear more than I did when I began my study that women's colleges that do not have a close association with a coeducational college may disappear, except perhaps for a few well-known and exceptionally well-endowed institutions like Wellesley. Formerly women's colleges, like Wheaton and Vassar, may be in the best position to further gender equity by establishing a model of what true coeducation can look like. After all, they do not have a history of male dominance and fraternities to counter. Of course this assumes a continuing concern with women's welfare, not just a concern with reassuring potential men students that they are now men-friendly colleges. Programs for monitoring gender equity once men are admitted need to be in place and thoughtfully developed *before* the first men students enter. Wheaton is an example of a formerly women's college that is attempting to be a coeducational college in which women's concerns receive genuinely equal consideration with men's. To mark how unusual this is, Wheaton calls itself "consciously coeducational" or "coeducational with a difference." Research is needed to determine whether Wheaton is achieving and will be able to sustain its goal of equity.[6]

Recently I had a chance meeting with a faculty member at another small, isolated, formerly women's college. He bemoaned his college's having become coeducational, although he did acknowledge that its enrollment has subsequently more than doubled. He also made an interesting comment about its being easier to promote women at his college in practice than it is in words. What he meant was that faculty such as himself, who appreciate the benefits to women of women's colleges, could still teach in ways that acknowledge women's interests and contributions, at the same time that the college's literature proclaims an ordinary coeducational environment. Without special efforts to preserve some of the characteristics of a women's college, this newly coeducational college may soon come to have a typical chilly climate. If colleges are really concerned about their women students, programs to prevent this from happening need to be institutionalized.

A major, if obvious, conclusion is that there is no easy way of achieving gender equity, even within one institutional sector such as higher education. Programs and interest groups can help, but if we want social change, we must be prepared to continue the struggle.

Notes

1 Since most women's colleges are small colleges, however, it might be better to compare their enrollments to small coeducational colleges. C. S. Tidball has developed a database of colleges whose full-time enrollments are less than 2,000 students (which excludes some of the better-known women's colleges, for instance, Smith, Barnard, and Wellesley). Small women's colleges' full-time enrollments went from 115,391 in 1963 to 46,200 in 1993, a decline of over 69,000 students or 60 percent of the 1963 enrollment. Small coeducational colleges' enrollments went from 462,241 to 515,575 during the same period, an increase of more than 53,000 students or 11.5 percent of the 1963 figures. These figures are, of course, a result of the increase in the number of small coeducational colleges (from 481 to 503) and a large decrease in the number of women's colleges (from 173 to 60). Even more dramatically, women's change colleges, those institutions that were historically for women but which have become coeducational, had a total increase in enrollment from 3,000 in 1963 to 74,992 in 1993; the number of women's change colleges went from 6 in 1963 to 86 in 1993. Thus these figures indicate the unpopularity of women's colleges, as well as showing the increasing number of students at (and the increasing number of) formerly women's colleges (Tidball et al. 1999, 25).

2 Between 1976 and 1993, part-time women students increased by 125 percent at women's colleges, in comparison to 66 percent at all institutions of higher education (U.S. Department of Education 1997, 64).

3 C. S. Tidball's small college database leads him to estimate that in the thirty years between 1963 and 1993, about thirty small women's colleges closed, a number that excludes the ones that became coeducational (which are commonly referred to as "women's change colleges"). Tidball points out that many coeducational colleges also "closed their doors," although his data do not permit him to distinguish those that closed from those, like Middlebury, that grew beyond the size limit for a small college (Tidball et al. 1999, 160).

4 These numbers are subject to some debate, as definitions of what is or is not a women's college is not easy. My number is based on the 1997 U.S. Department of Education study, "Women's Colleges in the United States," page 44, subtracting four institutions that have announced, since this study was published, that they are admitting men or being absorbed by a university.

5 It is presumably not coincidental that when Wheaton College was all-women, it did not have a major field in women's studies but instead, emphasized a "balanced curriculum" in which issues of gender were integrated across the curriculum. After a decade of being coeducational, however, Wheaton College developed a women's studies major.

6 Such research has begun. On the basis of their preliminary findings, Sadovnik and Semel (1996) believe that Wheaton College is not as "chilly" for women students as conventional coeducational colleges are.

References

NOTE: Within the chapters, complete references to archival materials have been given, using the following abbreviations:

CUA=Cornell University Archives
HCA=Hamilton College Archives
HWSCA=Hobart and William Smith Colleges Archives
MCA=Middlebury College Archives
NYPL=New York Public Library
UVMA=University of Vermont Archives
VCA=Vassar College Archives
WCA=Wells College Archives

A.A.U.P. et al. brief, posted November 27, 1995. No. 94–1941, October term, Supreme Court, U.S.A. v. Commonwealth of Virginia.

Adams, Donald R., Jr. 1978. *Finance and Enterprise in Early America: A Study of Stephen Girard's Bank, 1812–1831*. Philadelphia: University of Pennsylvania Press.

Addams, Jane. 1910/1960. *Twenty Years at Hull-House*. New York: The New American Library.

Adler, Joe anne with Jennifer Adler Friedman. 1994. *Women's Colleges: The Inside Guide*. New York: Prentice Hall.

Allmendinger, David F., Jr. 1975. *Paupers and Scholars: The Transformation of Student Life in Nineteenth-Century New England*. New York: St. Martin's Press.

————— 1979. Mount Holyoke students encounter the need for life-planning, 1837–1850. *History of Education Quarterly* 19: 27–46.

American Association of University Women Educational Foundation. 1998. *Separated by Sex*. Washington, D.C.

Anderson, Richard E. 1977. *Strategic Policy Changes at Private Colleges*. New York: Teachers College Press.

Antler, Joyce. 1982. Culture, service, and work: changing ideals of higher education for women. Pp. 15–41 in Perun, Pamela (Ed.), *The Undergraduate Woman: Issues in Educational Equity*. Lexington, Mass.: D.C. Heath.

Appel, Toby A. 1994. Physiology in American women's colleges. *Isis* 85: 26–56.

Arey, Henry. 1877. Girard College and its founder. *The American Journal of Education* 27: 593–616.

Arnot, Madeleine. 1984. How shall we educate our sons? Pp. 37–55 in R. Deem (Ed.), *Co-education Reconsidered*. Milton Keynes, England: Open University Press.

Association of Collegiate Alumnae. 1900. Report of the Annual Meeting. Series III: 82.

Astin, Alexander W. 1977. *Four Critical Years*. San Francisco: Jossey-Bass Publishers.

Astin, Alexander W., Kenneth C. Green, and William S. Korn. 1987. *The American Freshman: Twenty Year Trends, 1966–1985*. Los Angeles: Higher Education Research Institute, University of California.

Babbie, Earl. 1998. *The Practice of Social Research*. Belmont, Calif.: Wadsworth Publishing Co.

Banks, Olive. 1981. *Faces of Feminism*. New York: St. Martin's Press.

Barnard, Eunice Fuller. 1933. Our colleges for women: Co-ed or not? *New York Times Magazine* (March 26): 4–5.

Basow, Susan A. and Karen Glasser Howe. 1980. Role-model influence: Effects of sex and sex-role attitude in college students. *Psychology of Women Quarterly* 4: 558–572.

Belenky, Mary F., Blythe M. Clinchy, Nancy R. Goldberger, and Jill M. Tarule. 1986. *Women's Ways of Knowing: The Development of Self, Voice and Mind*. New York: Basic Books.

Blackwell, Elizabeth. 1895/1977. *Pioneer Work in Opening the Medical Profession to Women: Autobiographical Sketches*. New York: Schocken Books.

Blair, Karen J. 1980. *The Clubwoman as Feminist: True Womanhood Redefined, 1868–1914*. New York: Holmes and Meier Publishers.

Block, Jeanne H. 1984. *Sex Role Identity and Ego Development*. San Francisco: Jossey-Bass.

Boles, Janet K. 1991. Preface. *The Annals* 514: 8–9.

Bone, Ann. 1983. Girls and girls-only schools: A review of the evidence. Manchester, England: Equal Opportunities Commission.

Bowden, Henry Warner, ed., 1977. *Dictionary of American Religious Biography*. Westport, Conn.: Greenwood Press.

Brehony, Kevin. 1984. Co-education: Perspectives and debates in the early twentieth century. Pp. 1–30 in Rosemary Deem (Ed.), *Co-education Reconsidered*. Philadelphia: Open University Press.

Bressler, Marvin and Peter Wendell. 1980. The sex composition of selective colleges and gender differences in career aspirations. *Journal of Higher Education* 51: 650–63.

Bromley, Dorothy Dunbar, and Florence Haxton Britten. 1938. *Youth and Sex: A Study of 1300 College Students*. New York: Harper & Brothers.

Brown, Donald R. 1962. Personality, college environment, and academic productivity. Pp. 536–62 in Nevitt Sanford (Ed.), *The American College*. New York: John Wiley & Sons.

Brown, Marsha D. 1982. Career plans of college women: patterns and influences. Pp. 303–35 in Pamela J. Perun (Ed.), *The Undergraduate Woman: Issues in Educational Equity*. Lexington, Mass.: D.C. Heath.

Burt, Nathaniel. 1963. *The Perennial Philadelphians*. London: J. M. Dent & Sons.

Butcher, Patricia Smith. 1989. *Education for Equality: Women's Rights Periodicals and Women's Higher Education 1849–1920*. New York: Greenwood Press.

The Carnegie Commission on Higher Education. 1973. *Opportunities for Women in Higher Education*. New York: McGraw-Hill.

Carpenter, Peter. 1985. Single-sex schooling and girls' academic achievements. *Australian and New Zealand Journal of Sociology* 21: 456–72.

Carpenter, Peter, and Martin Hayden. 1987. Girls' academic achievements: Single-sex versus coeducational schools in Australia. *Sociology of Education* 60: 156–67.

Cashman, Sean Dennis. 1993. *America in the Gilded Age*. New York: New York University Press.

Chafe, William H. 1977. *Women and Equality*. New York: Oxford University Press.

Chamberlain, Mariam, ed. 1988. *Women in Academe*. New York: Russell Sage Foundation.

Cheit, Earl F. 1971. *The New Depression in Higher Education*. A General Report for the Carnegie Commission on Higher Education and the Ford Foundation. New York: McGraw-Hill Book Company.

Clarke, Edward H. 1873/1972. *Sex in Education; or A Fair Chance for the Girls*. Boston: James R. Osgood and Co.

Cohen, Jacob and Patricia Cohen. 1983. *Applied Multiple Regression/
Correlation Analysis for the Behavioral Sciences*. Second Edition. Hillsdale, N.J.: Lawrence Erlbaum.

Comstock, Anna Botsford. 1953. *The Comstocks of Cornell*. Ithaca,
N.Y.: Comstock Publications Associates.

Conable, Charlotte Williams. 1977. *Women at Cornell: The Myth of
Equal Education*. Ithaca, N.Y.: Cornell University Press.

Conaty, Joseph C., Nabeel Alsalam, Estelle James, and Duc-Le To. 1989.
College quality and future earnings: Where should you send your
sons and daughters to college? Paper presented at the 84th annual
meeting of the American Sociological Association, San Francisco.

Constantinople, Anne, Randolph Cornelius, and Janet Gray. 1988. The
chilly climate: Fact or artifact? *Journal of Higher Education* 59:
527–50.

Conway, Jill Kerr. 1983. The 19th century origins of education for women.
Middlebury Magazine 57: 8–14.

Cookingham, Mary E. 1984. Bluestockings, spinsters and pedagogues:
Women college graduates, 1865–1910. *Population Studies* 38:
349–64.

Coolidge, Calvin. 1921. Enemies of the republic. *Delineator* 98: 4–5,
66–67.

Crawford, Mary. 1905. *The College Girl of America*. Boston: L. C.
Page & Company.

Cross, Elaine. 1985. Swimming against the tide of male mythology. *School
Organization* 5: 69–77.

Cross, Whitney R. 1950/1965. *The Burned-Over District*. New York:
Harper & Row.

Current, Richard Nelson. 1990. *Phi Beta Kappa in American Life*. New
York: Oxford University Press.

Dale, R. R. 1969. *Mixed or Single-Sex School?* Vol. I, *A Research
Study About Pupil-Teacher Relations*. London: Routledge & Kegan
Paul.

———— 1971. *Mixed or Single-Sex School?* Vol. II, *Some Social Aspects*. London: Routledge & Kegan Paul.

———— 1974. *Mixed or Single-Sex School?* Vol. III, *Attainment, Attitude and Overview*. London: Routledge & Kegan Paul.

Davis, Katherine Bement. 1929. *Factors in the Sex Life of Twenty-Two
Hundred Women*. New York: Harper and Brothers.

D'Emilio, John and Estelle B. Freedman. 1988. *Intimate Matters*. New
York: Harper & Row.

Defoe, Daniel. 1697/1969. *An Essay Upon Projects*. Menston, England:
The Scolar Press Limited.

Dey, Eric L., Alexander W. Astin, and William S. Korn. 1991. *The American Freshman: Twenty-Five Year Trends.* Los Angeles: University of California, Higher Education Research Institute.

Dieckmann, Jane Marsh. 1995. *Wells College: A History.* Aurora, New York: Wells College Press.

Dobkin, Marjorie Housepian, ed. 1979. *The Making of a Feminist: Early Journals and Letters of M. Carey Thomas.* Kent, Ohio: Kent State University Press.

Douglas, Ann. 1977. *The Feminization of American Culture.* New York: Alfred A. Knopf.

Douvan, Elizabeth and Carol Kaye. 1962. Motivational factors in college entrance. Pp. 199–224 in Nevitt Sanford (Ed.), *The American College.* New York: John Wiley & Sons.

Dunn, Kathleen. 1990. The impact of higher education upon career and family choices: Simmons College alumnae, 1906–1926. Pp. 157–178 in Joyce Antler and Sari Knopp Biklen (Eds.), *Changing Education.* Albany: State University of New York Press.

Durbin, Nancy E. and Lori Kent. 1989. Postsecondary education of white women in 1900. *Sociology of Education* 62: 1–13.

Ehrhart, Julie Kuhn, and Bernice R. Sandler. 1987. Looking for more than a few good women in traditionally male fields. Project on the Status and Education of Women. Washington, D.C.: Association of American Colleges.

Epstein, Cynthia Fuchs. 1988. *Deceptive Distinctions.* New Haven: Yale University Press.

Faderman, Lillian. 1991. *Odd Girls and Twilight Lovers.* New York: Penguin.

Fass, Paula S. 1977. *The Damned and the Beautiful: American Youth in the 1920's.* New York: Oxford University Press.

Feldman, Kenneth A. 1972. Difficulties in measuring and interpreting change and stability during college. Pp. 127–42 in Kenneth A. Feldman (Ed.), *College & Student.* New York: Pergamon.

Finn, Jeremy D. 1980. Sex differences in educational outcomes: A cross-national study. *Sex Roles* 6: 9–26.

Finn, Jeremy D., Loretta Dulberg, and Janet Reis. 1979. Sex differences in educational attainment: A cross-national perspective. *Harvard Educational Review* 49: 477–503.

Flacks, Richard. 1971. *Youth and Social Change.* Chicago: Markham Publishing Co.

————— 1988. *Making History: the Radical Tradition in American Life.* New York: Columbia University Press.

Folwell, William Watts. 1933. *The Autobiography and Letters of a Pioneer of Culture*. Minneapolis: University of Minnesota Press.

Foon, Anne E. 1988. The relationship between school type and adolescent self-esteem, attribution styles and affiliation needs: Implications for educational outcome. *British Journal of Educational Psychology* 58: 44–54.

Fortune 1949. Higher education: The Fortune survey. Volume 39 (September): supplement, 1–13.

Fox-Genovese, Elizabeth. 1994. Save the males? *National Review*. (August 1): 49–52.

Freeman, Stephen A. 1975/1990. *The Middlebury College Foreign Language Schools*. Middlebury, Vt.: Middlebury College Press.

Frieze, Irene Hanson. 1975. Women's expectations for and causal attributions of success and failure. Pp. 158–71 in Martha T. Shuch Mednick, Sandra Schwartz Tangri, and Lois Wladis Hoffman (Eds.), *Women and Achievement*. New York: John Wiley & Sons.

Galbo, Joseph J.. and Diana Mayer Demetrulias. 1996. Recollections of nonparental significant adults during childhood and adolescence. *Youth & Society* 27: 403–20.

Gallaher, Grace Margaret. 1900. *Vassar Stories*. Boston: Richard G. Badger & Co.

Giele, Janet Zollinger. 1987. Coeducation or women's education? A comparison of alumnae from two colleges: 1934–79. Pp. 91–109 in Carol Lasser (Ed.), *Educating Men and Women Together*. Urbana: University of Illinois Press.

Gilbert, Lucia. 1985. Dimensions of same-gender student-faculty role-model relationships. *Sex Roles* 12: 111–123.

Gilbert, Lucia, June M. Gallessich, and Sherri L. Evans. 1983. Sex of faculty role model and students' self-perceptions of competency. *Sex Roles* 9: 597–607.

Gilligan, Carol. 1982. *In a Different Voice*. Cambridge, Mass.: Harvard University Press.

Ginzberg, Lori D. 1987. The "joint education of the sexes": Oberlin's original vision. Pp. 67–80 in Carol Lasser (Ed.), *Educating Men and Women Together*. Urbana: University of Illinois Press.

Goldberg, Philip. 1968. Are women prejudiced against women? Pp. 10–13 in C. Safilios-Rothschild (Ed.), *Toward a Sociology of Women*. Lexington, Mass.: Xerox College Publications.

Gordon, Lynn D. 1986. Annie Nathan Meyer and Barnard College: mission and identity in women's higher education, 1889–1950. *History of Education Quarterly* 26: 503–22.

————— 1990. *Gender and Higher Education in the Progressive Era.* New Haven: Yale University Press.

Gordon, Sarah. H. 1975. Smith College students: The first ten classes, 1879–1888. *History of Education Quarterly* XV: 147–67.

Gose, Ben. 1995. Second thoughts at women's colleges. *Chronicle of Higher Education*, February 10: A22–A24.

————— 1998. Do bans on fraternities violate the First Amendment? *The Chronicle of Higher Education*, November 27: A37.

Graham, Patricia Albjerg. 1978. Expansion and exclusion: A history of women in American higher education. *Signs* 3: 759–73.

Grant, Gerald, and David Riesman. 1978. *The Perpetual Dream.* Chicago: University of Chicago Press.

Grover, Kathryn. 1994. *Make a Way Somehow: African-American Life in a Northern Community, 1790–1965.* Syracuse, New York: Syracuse University Press.

Hall, G. Stanley. 1904. *Adolescence, Volumes I and II.* New York: D. Appleton and Company.

Hall, Roberta M., with Bernice R. Sandler. 1982. The classroom climate: A chilly one for women? Project on the Status and Education of Women. Washington, D.C.: Association of American Colleges.

Harper, Ida Husted. 1899. *The Life and Work of Susan B. Anthony.* Indianapolis: Bowen-Merrill Co.

Harris, Mary B. 1986. Coeducation and sex roles. *Australian Journal of Education* 30: 117–31.

Hedrick, Joan D. 1994. *Harriet Beecher Stowe: A Life.* New York: Oxford University Press.

Helmreich, Paul C. 1985. *Wheaton College, 1835–1912: The Seminary Years.* Norton, Mass.: Wheaton College.

Higgins, Kathy. 1982. "Making it your own world": Women's studies and Freire. *Women's Studies International Forum* 5: 87–98.

Hochschild, Arlie. 1989. *The Second Shift.* New York: Avon Books.

Hogeland, Ronald W. 1972–73. Coeducation of the sexes at Oberlin College: A study of social ideas in mid-nineteenth-century America. *Journal of Social History* 6: 160–76.

Holland, Dorothy C., and Margaret A. Eisenhart. 1990. *Educated in Romance: Women, Achievement, and College Culture.* Chicago: University of Chicago Press.

Horner, Matina S. 1972. Toward an understanding of achievement- related conflicts in women. *Journal of Social Issues* 28: 157–75.

Horowitz, Helen Lefkowitz. 1984. *Alma Mater.* Boston: Beacon Press.

————— 1987. *Campus Life.* Chicago: University of Chicago Press.

———— 1994. *The Power and Passion of M. Carey Thomas*. New York: Alfred A. Knopf.

Howe, Florence. 1984. *Myths of Coeducation*. Bloomington: Indiana University Press.

Huff, Robert A. 1984. Anne Miller and the Geneva Political Equality Club, 1897–1912. *New York History* 65: 325–48.

Inness, Sherrie A. 1993. "It is pluck but is it sense?": Athletic student culture in Progressive era girls' college fiction. *Journal of Popular Culture* 27: 99–123.

Jacobi, Mary Putnam. 1878. *The Question of Rest for Women During Menstruation*. London: Smith, Elder & Co.

Jacobs, Jerry A. 1996. Gender inequality and higher education. *Annual Review of Sociology* 22: 153–86.

James, Edward T., ed. 1971. *Notable American Women 1607–1950*. Cambridge, Mass.: The Belknap Press of Harvard University Press.

Jaschik, Scott. 1995. Divisions over VMI. *The Chronicle of Higher Education*, December 1: A37.

Jencks, Christopher, and David Riesman. 1968. *The Academic Revolution*. New York: Doubleday & Company.

Jimenez, Emmanuel, and Marlaine E. Lockheed. 1989. Enhancing girls' learning through single-sex education: Evidence and a policy conundrum. *Education Evaluation and Policy Analysis* 11: 117–42.

Jones, J. Charles, Jack Shallcrass, and Cathy Dennis. 1972. Coeducation and adolescent values. *Journal of Educational Psychology* 63: 334–41.

Jordan, David Starr. 1902. The higher education of women. *Popular Science Monthly* 62: 97–107.

Jung, John. 1986. How useful is the concept of role model? *Journal of Social Behavior and Personality* 1: 525–36.

Kaminer, Wendy. 1998. The trouble with single-sex schools. *The Atlantic Monthly*. 281: 22–36.

Kaplan, Susan Romer. 1978. Women's education: The case for the single-sex college." Pp. 53–67 in Helen S. Astin and Werner Z. Hirsch (Eds.), *The Higher Education of Women*. New York: Praeger.

Karp, David A., and William C. Yoels. 1975. The college classroom: Some observations on the meanings of student participation. *Sociology and Social Research* 60: 421–39.

Kehr, Marguerite Witmer. 1920. A comparative study of the curricula for men and women in the colleges and universities of the United States. *Journal of the Association of Collegiate Alumnae* 14: 3–26.

Kendall, Elaine. 1975. *"Peculiar Institutions": An Informal History of the Seven Sisters Colleges.* New York: G. P. Putnam's Sons.

Kenway, Jane, and Sue Willis. 1986. Feminist single-sex educational strategies: Some theoretical flaws and practical fallacies. *Discourse* 7: 1–30.

Kerber, Linda. 1976. The Republican mother: Women and the Enlightenment—an American perspective. *American Quarterly* 28: 187–205.

Kesselman, Amy. 1991. The "freedom suit": Feminism and dress reform in the United States, 1848–1875. *Gender & Society* 5: 495–510.

Komarovsky, Mirra. 1985. *Women in College.* New York: Basic Books.

Landry, Donna, and Gerald MacLean. 1993. *Materialist Feminisms.* Cambridge, Mass.: Blackwell.

Laviguer, Jill. 1980. Co-education and the tradition of separate needs. Pp. 180–190 in Dale Spender and E. Sarah (Eds.), *Learning to Lose.* London: The Women's Press.

Leach, William. 1980. *True Love and Perfect Union.* New York: Basic Books.

Lee, Valerie E., and Anthony S. Bryk. 1986. Effects of single-sex secondary schools on student achievement and attitudes. *Journal of Educational Psychology* 78: 381–95.

Lee, Valerie E., Susanna Loeb, and Helen M. Marks. 1995. Gender differences in secondary school teachers' control over classroom and school policy. *American Journal of Education* 103: 259–301.

Lee, Valerie E., Helen M. Marks, and Tina Byrd. 1994. Sexism in single-sex and coeducational independent secondary school classrooms. *Sociology of Education* 67: 92–120.

Lentz, Linda P. 1980. The college choice of career-salient women: Coed or women's? *Journal of Educational Equity and Leadership* 1: 28–35.

Leslie, W. Bruce. 1977. Localism, denominationalism, and institutional strategies in urbanizing America: Three Pennsylvania colleges, 1870–1915. *History of Education Quarterly* 17: 235–56.

Lever, Janet, and Pepper Schwartz. 1971. *Women at Yale.* New York: The Bobbs-Merrill Company, Inc.

Levine, David O. 1986. *The American College and the Culture of Aspiration, 1915–1960.* Ithaca: Cornell University Press.

Levine, Susan. 1995. *Degrees of Equality.* Philadelphia: Temple University Press.

Lindgren, J. Ralph, and Nadine Taub. 1993. *The Law of Sex Discrimination*. Minneapolis: West Publishing.

Lucas, Christopher J. 1994. *American Higher Education: A History*. New York: St. Martin's Press.

Lunneborg, Patricia. 1982. Role model influencers of nontraditional professional women. *Journal of Vocational Behavior* 20: 276–81.

Lutz, Alma. 1964. *Emma Willard, Pioneer Educator of American Women*. Boston: Beacon Press.

MacKay, Anne. 1992. *Wolf Girls at Vassar*. New York: St. Martin's Press.

Maher, Frances A., and Mary Kay Thompson Tetreault. 1994. *The Feminist Classroom*. New York: Basic Books.

Malone, Dumas, ed. 1934. *Dictionary of American Biography*. London: Oxford University Press.

Marland, Michael, ed. 1983. *Sex Differentiation and Schooling*. London: Heinemann.

Marsh, Herbert W. 1989a. Effects of attending single-sex and coeducational high schools on achievement, attitudes, behaviors, and sex differences. *Journal of Educational Psychology* 81: 70–85.

———— 1989b. Effects of single-sex and coeducational schools: A response to Lee and Bryk." *Journal of Educational Psychology* 81: 651–53.

Mason, Karen Oppenheim, and Yu-Hsia Lu. 1988. Attitudes toward women's familial roles: Changes in the United States, 1977–1985. *Gender & Society* 2: 39–57.

McKean, John Rosseel Overton. 1961. *Wells College Student Life, 1868–1936*. Thesis of Cornell University for the Degree of Doctorate of Education.

Miller-Bernal, Leslie. 1989. College experiences and sex-role attitudes: Does a women's college make a difference? *Youth and Society* 20: 363–87.

———— 1991. Single-sex education: An anachronism or a beneficial structure? Pp. 120–39 in Laura Kramer (Ed.), *The Sociology of Gender*. New York: St. Martin's Press.

———— 1993. Single-sex versus coeducational environments: A comparison of women students' experiences at four colleges. *American Journal of Education* 102: 23–54.

Mitchell, Juliet, and Ann Oakley, eds. 1986. *What Is Feminism?* New York: Pantheon.

Monroe, Paul, ed. 1912. *A Cyclopedia of Education*. New York: Macmillan.

Moore, R. Laurence. 1977. *In Search of White Crows*. New York: Oxford University Press.

Morantz, Regina Markell. 1982. Feminism, professionalism, and germs: The thought of Mary Putnam Jacobi and Elizabeth Blackwell. *American Quarterly* 34 (Winter): 459–78.

Newcomer, Mabel. 1959. *A Century of Higher Education for Women*. New York: Harper & Row.

Oates, Mary J., and Susan Williamson. 1978. Women's colleges and women achievers. *Signs* 3: 795–806.

———. 1980. Comment on Tidball's "women's colleges and women achievers revisited." *Signs* 6: 342–45.

O'Neill, William L. 1973. Divorce in the Progressive era. Pp. 251–66 in Michael Gordon (Ed.), *The American Family in Social-Historical Perspective*. New York: St. Martin's Press.

Ormerod, M. B. 1975. Subject preference and choice in co-educational and single-sex secondary schools. *British Journal of Educational Psychology* 45: 257–67.

Osmond, Marie W., and Patricia Y. Martin. 1975. Sex and sexism: A comparison of male and female sex-role attitudes. *Journal of Marriage and the Family* 37: 744–58.

Palmieri, Patricia A. 1987. From Republican Motherhood to race suicide: Arguments on the higher education of women in the United States, 1820–1920. Pp. 49–64 in Carol Lasser (Ed.), *Educating Men and Women Together*. Urbana: University of Illinois Press.

——— 1995. *In Adamless Eden: The Community of Women Faculty at Wellesley*. New Haven: Yale University Press.

Paludi, Michele A. 1998. *The Psychology of Women*. Upper Saddle River, N.J.: Prentice Hall.

Parelius, Ann P. 1975. Emerging sex-role attitudes, expectations, and strains among college women. *Journal of Marriage and the Family* 37: 146–53.

Pascarella, Ernest T., and Patrick T. Terenzini. 1991. *How College Affects Students*. San Francisco: Jossey-Bass.

Perkins, H. Wesley, and Debra K. DeMeis. 1996. Gender and family effects on the "second-shift" domestic activity of college-educated young adults. *Gender & Society* 10: 78–93.

Pilkington, Walter. 1962. *Hamilton College, 1812–1962*. Clinton, N. Y.: Hamilton College.

Pollitt, Katha. 1994. Subject to debate. *The Nation* 259: 190.

Reed, Helen Leah. 1903. *Brenda's Cousin at Radcliffe*. Boston: Little, Brown, and Company.

Reeves, Sandra, with Anne Marriott. 1994. A burst of popularity. *U.S. News & World Report* (September 26): 105–8.

Renshaw, Peter. 1990. Self-esteem research and equity programs for girls: A reassessment. Pp. 17–34 in Jane Kenway and Sue Willis (Eds.), *Hearts and Minds*. London: The Falmer Press.

Rice, Joy K., and Annette Hemmings. 1988. Women's colleges and women achievers: An update. *Signs* 13: 546–59.

Rice, Tom W., and Diane L. Coates. 1995. Gender role attitudes in the southern United States. *Gender & Society* 9: 744–56.

Riesman, David. 1991. A margin of difference: The case for single-sex education. Pp. 241–257 in Judith R. Blau and Norman Goodman (Eds.), *Social Roles and Social Institutions*. Boulder, Colo.: Westview Press.

Riordan, Cornelius. 1985. Public and Catholic schooling: The effects of gender context policy. *American Journal of Education* 93: 518–40.

———— 1990. *Girls & Boys in School: Together or Separate?* New York: Teacher's College Press.

———— 1994. The value of attending a women's college. *Journal of Higher Education* 65: 486–510.

Rosenberg, Rosalind. 1982. *Beyond Separate Spheres*. New Haven: Yale University Press.

———— 1988. The limits of access: The history of coeducation in America. Pp. 107–29 in John Mack Faragher and Florence Howe (Eds.), *Women and Higher Education in American History*. New York: W.W. Norton.

Rossi, Alice. 1987. Coeducation in a gender-stratified society. Pp. 11–34 in Carol Lasser (Ed.), *Educating Men and Women Together*. Urbana: University of Illinois Press.

Rossiter, Margaret W. 1982. *Women Scientists in America*. Baltimore: Johns Hopkins University Press.

Rowe, Kenneth J. 1988. Single-sex and mixed-sex classes: The effects of class type on student achievement, confidence and participation in mathematics. *Australian Journal of Education* 32: 180–202.

Rowland, Robyn, ed. 1984. *Women Who Do and Women Who Don't Join the Women's Movement*. London: Routledge & Kegan Paul.

Rudolph, Frederick. 1977. *Curriculum: A History of the American Undergraduate Course of Study Since 1636*. San Francisco: Jossey-Bass Publishers.

Rury, John L. 1991. *Education and Women's Work*. Albany: State University of New York Press.

Rury, John, and Glenn Harper. 1986. The trouble with coeducation: Mann and women at Antioch, 1853–1860. *History of Education Quarterly* 26: 481–502.

Russ, Anne. 1980. *Higher Education for Women: Intent, Reality, and Outcomes—Wells College, 1868–1913.* Ph.D. dissertation, Cornell University.

Ryan, Mary P. 1981. *Cradle of the Middle Class.* Cambridge: Cambridge University Press.

Sadker, Myra, and David Sadker. 1994. *Failing at Fairness.* New York: Simon & Schuster.

Sadovnik, Alan R., and Susan F. Semel. 1996. The transition to coeducation at Wheaton College. Paper presented at the Annual Meeting of the American Educational Research Association, New York.

Sandler, Bernice Resnick. 1987. The classroom climate: Still a chilly one for women. Pp. 113–123 in Carol Lasser (Ed.), *Educating Men and Women Together.* Urbana: University of Illinois Press.

Sarah, Elizabeth E., Marian Scott, and Dale Spender. 1980. The education of feminists: The case for single sex schools. Pp. 55–66 in D. Spender and E. Sarah (Eds.), *Learning to Lose: Sexism and Education.* London: The Women's Press.

Schneider, Frank W., and Larry M. Coutts. 1982. High school environment: A comparison of coeducational and single-sex schools. *Journal of Educational Psychology* 74: 898–906.

Schneir, Miriam, ed. 1972. *Feminism: The Essential Historical Writings.* New York: Vintage Books.

Schreiber, E.M. 1978. Education and change in American opinions on a woman for president. *Public Opinion Quarterly* 42: 171–82.

Shapiro, Judith R. 1994. What women can teach men. *New York Times*, November 23.

Sharp, Marcia K. 1991. Bridging the gap: Women's colleges and the women's movement. *Initiatives* 53: 3–7.

Shaw, Jenny. 1984. The politics of single-sex schools. Pp. 21–36 in R. Deem (Ed.), *Co-education Reconsidered.* Milton Keynes, England: Open University Press.

———— 1985. The interaction between sex, class and social change: Coeducation and the move from formal to informal discrimination. Pp. 137–51 in Len Barton and Stephen Walker (Eds.), *Education and Social Change.* London: Croom Helm.

Shmurak, Carole B. 1998. *Voices of Hope: Adolescent Girls at Single Sex and Coeducational Schools.* New York: Peter Lang.

Sicherman, Barbara. 1988. Colleges and careers: Historical perspectives on the lives and work patterns of women college graduates. Pp. 130–64 in John Mack Faragher and Florence Howe (Eds.), *Women and Higher Education in American History*. New York: W.W. Norton.

Single-sex education: A public policy issue. 1995. Final Report of the Workshop in Applied Public Policy and Administration, School of International and Public Affairs, Columbia University.

Smith, Daniel Scott. 1973. The dating of the American sexual revolution: Evidence and interpretation. Pp. 321–35 in Michael Gordon (Ed.), *The American Family in Social-Historical Perspective*. New York: St. Martin's Press.

Smith, Daryl G. 1990. Women's colleges and coed colleges: Is there a difference for women? *Journal of Higher Education* 61: 181–97.

Smith, Warren Hunting. 1972. *Hobart and William Smith: The History of Two Colleges*. Geneva, N.Y.: Hobart and William Smith Colleges.

Snodgrass, Sara. 1985. Women's intuition: The effect of subordinate role on interpersonal sensitivity. *Journal of Personality and Social Psychology* 49: 146–55.

Solomon, Barbara Miller. 1985. *In the Company of Educated Women*. New Haven: Yale University Press.

Speizer, Jeanne J. 1981. Role models, mentors, and sponsors: The elusive concepts. *Signs* 6: 692–712.

Spence, Janet T., Robert Helmreich, and Joy Stapp. 1973. A short version of the attitudes toward women scale (AWS). *Bulletin of the Psychonomic Society* 2: 219–20.

Stameshkin, David M. 1985. *The Town's College: Middlebury College, 1800–1915*. Middlebury, Vt.: Middlebury College Press.

——— 1996. *The Strength of the Hills. Middlebury College 1915–1990*. Hanover, N.H.: University Press of New England.

Stanton, Elizabeth Cady, Susan B. Anthony, and Matilda Joslyn Gage, eds. 1881. *History of Woman Suffrage*. New York: Fowler and Wells.

Stanton, Theodore, and Harriot Stanton Blatch, Eds. 1922. *Elizabeth Cady Stanton*. New York: Harper and Brothers.

Stern, Madeleine B., ed. 1974. *The Victoria Woodhull Reader*. Weston, Mass.: M & S Press.

Sternglanz, Sarah Hall, and Shirley Lyberger-Ficek. 1977. Sex differences in student-teacher interactions in the college classroom. *Sex Roles* 3: 345–52.

Stimpson, Catharine R. 1979. I'm not a feminist but . . . *Ms.* 8 (July): 62–4, 86.

Stoecker, Judith, and Ernest Pascarella. 1991a. Women's colleges and women's career attainments revisited. *Journal of Higher Education* 62: 394–406.

———— 1991b. Reply to comment. *Journal of Higher Education* 62: 410–11.

Studer-Ellis, Erich. 1995. Diverse institutional forces and fundamental organizational change: Women's colleges and the "coed or dead" question. Paper presented at the Annual Meeting of the American Sociological Association, Washington, D.C.

Sutherland, M. B. 1961. Co-education and school attainment. *The British Journal of Educational Psychology* 31: 158–69.

Talbot, Marion. 1910. *The Education of Women.* Chicago: University of Chicago Press.

Tavris, Carol. 1992. *The Mismeasure of Woman.* New York: Simon & Schuster.

Thomas, M. Carey. 1908. Present tendencies in women's college and university education. *Educational Review* 35: 64–85.

Tidball, M. Elizabeth. 1973. Perspective on academic women and affirmative action. *Journal of Higher Education* 54: 130–35.

———— 1976. Of men and research. *Journal of Higher Education* 47: 373–89.

———— 1980. Women's colleges and women achievers revisited. *Signs*: 504–17.

———— 1985. Baccalaureate origins of entrants into American medical schools. *Journal of Higher Education* 56: 385–402.

———— 1986. Baccalaureate origins of recent natural science doctorates. *Journal of Higher Education* 57: 606–20.

———— 1991. Comment on "Women's colleges and women's career attainments revisited." *Journal of Higher Education* 62: 406–9.

Tidball, M. Elizabeth, Daryl G. Smith, Charles S. Tidball, and Lisa E. Wolf-Wendel. 1999. *Taking Women Seriously.* Phoenix, Ariz.: The Oryx Press.

Tidball, M. Elizabeth, and Vera Kistiakowsky. 1976. Baccalaureate origins of American scientists and scholars. *Science* 193: 646–52.

Trickett, Edison J., Penelope K. Trickett, Julie J. Castro, and Paul Schaffner. 1982. The independent school experience: Aspects of the normative environments of single-sex and coeducational secondary schools. *Journal of Educational Psychology* 74: 374–81.

Tyack, David, and Elisabeth Hansot. 1990. *Learning Together*. New Haven and New York: Yale University Press and the Russell Sage Foundation.

Underhill, Lois Beachy. 1995. *The Woman Who Ran for President*. Bridgehampton, N.Y.: Bridge Works Publishing Co.

U.S. Department of Education. 1997. Women's Colleges in the United States. Irene Hawarth, Mindi Maline, and Elizabeth DeBra at the National Institute on Postsecondary Education, Libraries, and Lifelong Learning, Washington D.C.

Veysey, Laurence R. 1965. *The Emergence of the American University*. Chicago: University of Chicago Press.

Vinovskis, Maris A., ed. 1990. *Toward a Social History of the American Civil War*. New York: Cambridge University Press.

Wagner, David G., Rebecca S. Ford, and Thomas W. Ford. 1986. Can gender inequalities be reduced? *American Sociological Review* 51: 47–61.

Walford, Geoffrey. 1983. Girls in boys' public schools: A prelude to further research. *British Journal of Sociology of Education* 4: 39–54.

Walsh, Mary Roth. 1977. *"Doctors Wanted: No Women Need Apply"—Sexual Barriers in the Medical Profession, 1835–1975*. New Haven: Yale University Press.

Webster, David S. 1984. The Bureau of Education's suppressed rating of colleges, 1911–12. *History of Education Quarterly* 24: 499–511.

Wells, D. Collin. 1909. Some questions concerning the higher education of women. *American Journal of Sociology* 14: 731–39.

Welter, Barbara. 1973. The cult of true womanhood, 1820–1860. Pp. 224–50 in Michael Gordon (Ed.), *The American Family in Social-Historical Perspective*. New York: St. Martin's Press.

White, Andrew Dickson. 1905. *Autobiography*. London: Macmillan and Co., Limited.

Who Was Who in America., Vol. I, 1897–1942. 1943. Chicago: The A. N. Marquis Co.

Wilson, George. 1995. *Stephen Girard: America's First Tycoon*. Conshohocken, Pa.: Combined Books, Inc.

Winchel, Ronald, Diane Fenner, and Phillip Shaver. 1974. Impact of coeducation on "fear of success" imagery expressed by male and female high school students. *Journal of Educational Psychology* 66: 726–30.

Wing, Richard L. 1991. Requiem for a pioneer of women's higher education: The Ingham University of le Roy, New York, 1857–1892. *History of Higher Educational Annual:* 61–79.

Wolf-Wendel, Lisa E. 1998. Models of excellence: The baccalaureate origins of successful European American women, African American women, and Latinas. *Journal of Higher Education* 69: 141–87.

Wollons, Roberta. 1990. Women educating women: The Child Study Association as women's culture. Pp. 51–68 in Joyce Antler and Sari Knopp Biklen (Eds.), *Changing Education.* Albany: The State University of New York Press.

Woody, Thomas. 1929. *A History of Women's Education in the United States.* 2 volumes. New York: The Science Press.

Woolf, Virginia. 1929/1977. *A Room of One's Own.* London: Flamingo.

Zschoche, Sue. 1989. Dr. Clarke revisited: Science, true womanhood, and female collegiate education. *History of Education Quarterly* 29: 545–69.

Index

History of Schools and Schooling

THIS SERIES EXPLORES THE HISTORY OF SCHOOLS AND SCHOOLING in the United States and other countries. Books in this series examine the historical development of schools and educational processes, with special emphasis on issues of educational policy, curriculum and pedagogy, as well as issues relating to race, class, gender, and ethnicity. Special emphasis will be placed on the lessons to be learned from the past for contemporary educational reform and policy. Although the series will publish books related to education in the broadest societal and cultural context, it especially seeks books on the history of specific schools and on the lives of educational leaders and school founders.

For additional information about this series or for the submission of manuscripts, please contact the general editors:

Alan R. Sadovnik
118 Harvey Hall
School of Education
Adelphi University
Garden City, NY 11530

Susan F. Semel
Dept. of Curriculum and Teaching
243 Gallon Wing
Hofstra University
Hempstead, NY 11550

To order other books in this series, please contact our Customer Service Department:

800-770-LANG (within the U.S.)
212-647-7706 (outside the U.S.)
212-647-7707 FAX

Or browse online by series at:

www.peterlang.com